Illiberal Politics in Neoliberal Times

The rise of rightwing populism has brought into question prevailing assumptions in social science about multicultural Europe. In this compelling study of populist politics, Mabel Berezin argues that the emergence of the movement in the 1990s was a historical surprise rather than an expected event. She questions whether rightwing populism would exist in the absence of the Maastricht Treaty and the subsequent intensification of cultural and economic Europeanization. Using an innovative methodology, Berezin analyzes the French National Front in relation to the broader context of Europeanization and globalization. She unpacks the political and cultural processes that evoke the thin commitments characterizing citizen support, and shows that we cannot make sense of rightwing populism without considering the historical legacies and practices, both national and international, within which it arises. This book makes a novel argument about the relationship between democracy and political and social security.

MABEL BEREZIN is Associate Professor of Sociology at Cornell University. She is the author of *Making the Fascist Self: The Political Culture of Interwar Italy* (1997) which was awarded the J. David Greenstone Prize for Best Book of 1996–1997 in Politics and History by the American Political Science Association and named an Outstanding Academic Book of 1997 by *Choice*. She is also co-editor of *Europe Without Borders* (2003) and has written numerous articles on European politics, culture and history.

Cambridge Cultural Social Studies

Series editors: JEFFREY C. ALEXANDER, *Department of Sociology, Yale University, and* STEVEN SEIDMAN, *Department of Sociology, University at Albany, State University of New York.*

Titles in the series

(list continues at end of book)

Illiberal Politics in Neoliberal Times

Culture, Security and Populism in the New Europe

Mabel Berezin

CAMBRIDGE
UNIVERSITY PRESS

CAMBRIDGE UNIVERSITY PRESS
Cambridge, New York, Melbourne, Madrid, Cape Town, Singapore,
São Paulo, Delhi

Cambridge University Press
The Edinburgh Building, Cambridge CB2 8RU, UK

Published in the United States of America by Cambridge University Press,
New York

www.cambridge.org
Information on this title: www.cambridge.org/9780521547840

First published 2009

Printed in the United Kingdom at the University Press, Cambridge

A catalogue record for this publication is available from the British Library

Library of Congress Cataloguing in Publication data
Berezin, Mabel.
Illiberal politics in neoliberal times : culture, security and populism
in the new Europe / Mabel Berezin.
     p.   cm.
  Includes bibliographical references.
ISBN 978-0-521-83913-6
1. Europe – Politics and government – 1989–   2. Europe – Economic
integration – Political aspects.   3. Right-wing extremists – Europe.
I. Title.
JN12.B45   2008
324.2′13094–dc22

                                                        2008040777

ISBN 978-0-521-83913-6 hardback
ISBN 978-0-521-54784-0 paperback

For Richard Swedberg

Contents

Illustrations

Tables

Acknowledgements

Illiberal Politics in Neoliberal Times is a comparative political and cultural analysis of the salience of illiberal politics in France and Italy in the past twenty years. First begun with my work on Italian fascism and interwar Europe, this book continues to elucidate my professional and personal conviction that illiberal threats to democracy lie in the interstices of ostensibly democratic procedures and regimes. In short, challenges to democracy lie in the ordinary not the extraordinary – the banal not the egregious. The book also reflects my methodological conviction that political analysis without cultural analysis provides only a partial image of the collective forces that mobilize leaders and citizens. In short, the thick narrative description of public events is central to excavating the meaning of politics – new and old.

This project took longer than I would have expected to bring to fruition. In the course of its gestation, I have accumulated myriads of debts – large and small.

Since 1984, when the book narrative begins, I have lived and worked in various European venues. Spending periods from as little as a week to entire academic years when resources and time permitted, speaking two European languages, I have gained valuable ethnographic knowledge of Europe – writ large. An initial grant from the German Marshall Fund of the United States while I was completing *Making the Fascist Self* (Cornell University Press 1997), permitted me to spend a year at the European University Institute in Fiesole, Italy. Subsequent invitations to speak in various European venues provided additional opportunities for research abroad. I thank Gianfranco Poggi and Bo Stråth for invitations respectively to the Department of Political and Social Sciences and the Robert Schuman Centre at the European University Institute in Fiesole, Italy; Bernhard Giesen for inviting me to the University of Konstanz in

Germany; Richard Swedberg for inviting me to the Department of Sociology, Stockholm University and Jean-Louis Fabiani for inviting me to the École des Hautes Études Sciences Sociales, Paris, France. Funding from the Faculty Research Funds of the Cornell University Institute for European Studies at the Mario Einaudi Center for International Affairs as well as supplemental research funds from the Faculty Research funds at the Department of Sociology made it possible to make additional research trips to Europe.

As the manuscript was moving into production, the wonderful staff of the Cornell Sociology Department, Susan Meyer, Sharon Sandlan and Marty White, helped in various ways. The research assistance of Cornell undergraduates and graduate students was invaluable. Justin Weitz helped to research Chapters 2 and 7. Anna Karwowska designed the maps of protest in France, as well as created the article database. Paul Lee brought the tables, pictures and graphs to life. Alexa Yesukevich turned a critical eye to the bibliography. In the last moment, Matthew Hoffberg helped me pull it all together – redesigning tables and checking all my various computer errors. The translations from the French and Italian are for the most part my own. In those instances where an idiomatic phrase was simply beyond me, Susan Lo Bello generously came to my rescue.

I presented early iterations of this project to audiences at numerous academic conferences as well as at invited talks at the Departments of Sociology at the University of California, San Diego; University of California, Davis; University of Illinois, Cornell and the Center for European Studies at New York University. I thank Juan Díez Medrano, Fred Block, John Lie, Victor Nee and Martin Schain for these invitations as well as the attendees for their insights and helpful criticisms.

During the time that this book took final form, I benefited enormously from the lively intellectual community around European Studies and interdisciplinary scholarship at Cornell University where I have the privilege to be a faculty member. I extend deep thanks to Dean Harry E. Shaw and to Professors Leslie Adelson, Dominic Boyer and Douglas Mao for inviting me to participate in the 2005–2006 Mellon Faculty Seminar on Culture and Value. The collegial interactions among members of the group during our weekly meetings were invaluable and stimulated my thinking as I was moving into a final stretch of writing.

From 2004 to the present, I have been an External Faculty Fellow at Yale University's Center for Cultural Sociology. During that period, I have visited the Center on three occasions and presented the latest version of my arguments. I thank Jeffrey C. Alexander, the Center's Director, as well as its Co-directors, Philip Smith and Ron Eyerman, for these multiple invitations. Yale graduate students provided cogent comments in spring 2005. On a return visit in spring 2007, Dominik Bartmanski provided invaluable written comments on Chapter 7. Chapter 9 benefited from the invitation that the UCLA Department of Italian Studies extended to me in the spring of 2006 to discuss the work of Remo Bodei. Timothy Campbell of Cornell forced me to further clarify those thoughts when he invited me to present Chapter 9 at the Italian Studies Colloquium at Cornell.

When the book was in its penultimate form, Michèle Lamont invited me to the Center for European Studies at Harvard. I presented the manuscript to members of the seminar on Inclusion and Exclusion in Contemporary Europe. Jason Beckfield of Harvard and David Art of Tufts provided careful and challenging critique of the manuscript. David Art was exceedingly generous in sharing his own important forthcoming work on the European right, as well as providing detailed written commentary.

One writes books alone. Yet, they are always in some measure a collective enterprise and I have been exceedingly fortunate in this regard. Riva Kastoryano was an invaluable friend and interlocutor when I made my early trips to Paris, although I am sure that she would never go anywhere near the National Front! On a very early research trip, Michel Wieviorka and Pascal Perrineau pointed me in directions that would eventually be crucial to constructing the narrative of the book. During the French presidential elections of 2007, Michèle Van de Walle provided "local knowledge" as she emailed to me humorous web postings from her family and friends in France.

I have benefited from the intelligence and generosity of a group of remarkable friends and colleagues who commented upon and discussed this work with me over the years. Krishan Kumar deserves commendation for having an almost "perfect" attendance record at my numerous conference presentations. I am always astounded when I see him in the audience yet again and delighted with his astute comments afterwards. Juan Díez Medrano and I have discussed and debated this project from its inception. John Agnew (who introduced me to the importance of political geography) gave advice on the Italian chapters. Gail Kligman, an eyewitness to the April 2002 French election and its aftermath, brought her ethnographic eye to Chapter 6. Nicholas Van de Walle commented on Chapter 7.

Peter Katzenstein, Michael Mann and Sidney Tarrow were especially generous with their time (and cogent criticism!) as they read and provided written commentary on the entire manuscript. I have not incorporated all of their comments but I have learned enormously from them and hope to continue to do so well into the future. I am fortunate to have, and have had, such intellectually challenging and engaged scholars as past and current colleagues.

Ted Perlmutter helped me edit and fact check. He brought his own extensive knowledge of French and Italian politics (as well as language) to the manuscript – constantly chiding me when he thought a fact was off, an idea overstated. He was my fellow traveler in the book's opening vignette, who was edited out of the final version of the manuscript. We have learned that we will probably never agree as to the meaning of May Day 1984 in Turin. I am nonetheless grateful for his insights and sense of humor.

While it may seem banal to speak of life as chapters, especially at the beginning of a book of many chapters, all banalities contain more than partial truths. This book began in one chapter of my life and has ended in another. I want to express my joy and gratitude to those who have helped me turn the pages – at least metaphorically.

While they were not directly involved in the book production, Gail Kligman and Ruth Milkman were staunch and loyal colleagues as well as delightful friends who provided endless hours of sisterly discussion as this book, as well as the vicissitudes of life, took me from here to there.

I am deeply appreciative of the friendship, intelligence and generosity of Jeffrey C. Alexander who has been supportive intellectually and professionally in ways large and small since we first met at UCLA in 1996. Victor Nee has my unbounded appreciation for making it possible to begin yet another chapter of my life when he brought me to Cornell in 2002. He also made it possible for me to meet all those aforementioned wonderful Cornell colleagues and students who read and commented as I conceptualized, wrote and rewrote.

Richard Swedberg's devotion has enriched my life immeasurably. He introduced me to a new nation-state! He read the manuscript twice. He has continually shared his insights as a Swedish national and convinced European with me – although as a European he is always slightly perplexed as to why an American would find so interesting what he found routine. Now that the book is finished, I may have to make good on my promise to learn Swedish. As a hedge against that promise, I am dedicating this book to him. He is without doubt the best chapter!

Ithaca, New York

Acronyms

ATTAC	Action pour une Taxe Tobin d'Aide aux Citoyens
CAP	Common Agricultural Policy
CEVIPOF	Centre d'Étude de la Vie Politique Française
CFTC	Confédération Française des Travailleurs Chrétiens
CPE	*Contrat première embauche*
CPNT	Chasse, Pêche, Nature et Traditions
DL	Démocratie Libérale
ECB	European Central Bank
EDF	Électricité de France
EU	European Union
FN	Front National = (French) National Front
FRS	Forum des Républicains Sociaux
GATT	General Agreement on Tariffs and Trade
IMF	International Monetary Fund
LCR	Ligue Communiste Révolutionnaire
LDH	Ligue des Droits de l'Homme
LO	Lutte Ouvrière
MDC	Mouvement des Citoyens
MNR	Mouvement National Républicain
MPF	Mouvement pour la France
MSI	Movimento Sociale Italiano
OECD	Organisation for Economic Co-operation and Development
PACA	Provence-Alpes-Côte d'Azur
PACS	*Pacte civil de solidarité*
PCF	Parti Communiste Français
PRG	Parti Radical de Gauche
PS	Parti Socialiste
PT	Parti des Travailleurs
RPF	Rassemblement pour la France

RPR	Rassemblement pour la République
SOS Racisme	French group against racism
TNS-Sofres	Taylor Nelson-Société Française d'Enquêtes par Sondage
UDF	Union pour la Démocratie Française
UMP	Union pour la Majorité Présidentielle

Introduction
The rightwing populist moment as historical surprise

Prologue: Festa del Lavoro, 1984, Turin, Italy

On May 1, 1984, I boarded a city bus in a working-class neighborhood of Turin, Italy to take the twenty-minute ride to the center of the city to attend the annual May Day Parade. The first of May, then and now, is a legal holiday throughout most of Europe – a day set aside to honor the dignity of labor and a holiday that is increasingly a vestige of an "old" European social contract that "new" Europe is slowly rewriting. I was new to Italy and hardly spoke the language. I was a graduate student beginning work on a project that would eventually become a doctoral dissertation on Italian fascism. If there were such an entity as an ideal vantage point to observe the celebration of European labor, Turin in 1984 would be a propitious choice. Turin was historically among the reddest of the red cities in the industrial core of Italy. Turin, the adopted home of Antonio Gramsci who founded the Italian Communist Party there in 1921, had a long history of commitment to Italian communism in its intellectual and working-class circles. Militantly anti-fascist in the 1930s, Turin was a site of intense working-class protest and mobilization in the late 1960s and early 1970s (Bobbio 1979; Passerini 1984; Bagnasco 1986).[1]

More than simply a bastion of Italian communism, Turin was and is a place suffused with Italian and European history. Turin was the first capital of Italy. The original Italian Parliament, as well as Cavour's seat within it, remains intact. Liberalism as a political tradition had never had deep roots in Italy. The Turinese circle around Piero Gobetti in the 1920s

---

[1] It may seem odd to begin a book of political and cultural analysis with a memory. However, in so doing I follow the current trend in ethnography toward reflexivity, that is the conscious insertion of the researcher into the narrative for the purpose of increasing analytic precision. See Burawoy (2003) on the concept of a "revisit."

represented what liberal tradition Italy could lay claim to (Gobetti 2000). In 1948, Italians turned to Luigi Einaudi, a member of a prominent Turinese family, a leading exponent of liberalism and the Governor of the Bank of Italy, to serve as the first postwar President of the Italian Republic.

In May 1984, Turin, Italy and Europe were decidedly "old" Europe. The Italian Communist Party still existed and the Berlin Wall stood. Although the Iron Curtain was beginning to rust, it was still very much a meaningful metaphor for political division. May 1984 was five years away from the fall of the Berlin Wall and eight years away from the Maastricht Treaty. In spring 1984, old Europe commemorated the fortieth anniversary of D-Day, June 6, 1944, the day the Allies landed on the beaches of Normandy and beat back Nazism and fascism. On June 6, 1984, then American President Ronald Reagan went to Normandy to link the previous World War to his plans for missile bases in Europe. In 1984, the European Community consisted of only ten member states. The European Parliament had its second round of elections on June 14, 1984. "New" Europe was on the horizon. In February 1984, Altiero Spinelli, an Italian proponent of federalism, drafted a Treaty on European Union which passed with a large majority in the European Parliament (Moravcsik 1998, pp. 356–358).

On May 1, 1984, Italian party structures that had been in place since the end of World War II were virtually unchanged.[2] In May 1984, Turin was an Italian Communist Party (PCI) city and the culture of communism was thick. It was reasonable for me to assume that on May Day one could learn much about the élan and spirit of Italian communism – as well as Italian political culture. It was with these expectations that I boarded the bus on that gray spring morning. Like any immigrant to a foreign and unfamiliar culture, I was eager to take in as much as possible to help me make my way in that milieu; and like any immigrant with less than fluent language skills, I had to rely on my eyes, my emotions, my inner sense – I had to read the signs and images in the streets and on the faces of those whom I encountered.

What I observed in 1984 is salient today which is why I remember the otherwise unremarkable gray day. The neighborhood where I boarded the bus, the Piazza Fontanesi, was a working-class district par excellence.

---

[2] The historic convention wherein the Italian Communist Party (PCI) became the Democratic Party of the Left was seven years in the future. Kertzer (1996) provides the fullest account of this convention. In 1992, the Italian Communist Party abandoned its major symbol when it replaced the hammer and sickle on the party flag with a tree. In so doing, it not only changed a symbol but broke its link with its history.

Little machine shops that spewed out soot and noise throughout the neighborhood intermingled with apartment houses built in the 1930s. Shopkeepers who owned the small fruit, milk, bread and poultry shops that lined the main street and habitués of the small cafés still spoke Piemontese, the dialect of the region. The neighborhood around the Piazza Fontanesi represented working-class Turin, and working-class Italy at its peak. The bus that I boarded that day to head to the center of Turin was crowded with elderly men whom one did not see during the ordinary work week. These working-class men in their seventies and eighties who had put on their best clothes, worn but sturdy jackets and suits, clearly purchased as Sunday best in the 1950s and 1960s were striking. They had placed red carnations in their lapels and were heading to the center of town to join the parade. Their clothes as well as the camaraderie among the men highlighted the ritual significance of the event to them.

The annual May 1 commemoration was a performative event through which the Italian and European left acted out its political commitments. As May Day is an official holiday in Italy as well as most of the rest of Europe one does not have to be retired or unemployed to join or watch the parade.[3] To my surprise, when I got to the center of Turin and began to walk along the sides of the streets to follow the parade, old men with red carnations dominated the scene. In one of the most vibrant and politically engaged cities in Italy, and arguably Europe, home of worker movements and women's movements, there were no workers, no middle-aged men or women and, more importantly, no young people in the streets.[4] Not only was the activist generation, the 60s' generation, missing but there were no signs of the next generation. Where were they? Where were the people who today would be thirty-eight- to forty-eight-year-old leftists?[5]

There was a youth presence at the parade – but not the youth that I had expected. Who, I asked, were these apparently Middle Eastern students – Iranian, Palestinian women in veils, men with black-and-white checked headscarves – who were out in force on that gray day more than twenty years ago demanding justice and representation? Read from the vantage

---

[3] On the ritual significance of May Day celebration, see Boldini (1998).
[4] Tarrow (1989) is the paradigmatic work on social movements and militancy in Italy during the late 1960s and 1970s. Lumley (1990) provides a cultural analysis of the period; Hellman (1987) studies women as political actors.
[5] Popular culture in the form of Marco Tullio Giordana's 2003 epic, *La meglio gioventù*, provides one answer – activists as well as their children have retreated to private life. The trans-European popularity of the film, astonishing given its six-hour length, indicates that Giordana struck a resonant chord. Golden (1997) describes the defeat of labor politics in Italy during this period.

point of the present, those signs in the streets, signs that were not unique to Italy, were a harbinger of events to come.

If the world had stopped changing on that spring day in 1984, Reagan's "evil empire" would still exist. Eastern and Western Europe would remain divided. Terrorism would be a local and national phenomenon and Islam merely a religion. Globalization was not yet a part of the public vocabulary.[6] Old Europe, the agglomeration of political ideologies and practices, institutional arrangements and national political cultures, would remain largely unchanged from their consolidation in the nineteenth century. In 1984, it would have been as difficult to imagine that the Italian and European left would cease to be a potent oppositionist force to the march of markets as it would have been difficult to imagine that Islam would be a force in European politics. In 1984, Europe was national. It would have been difficult to imagine then that if one wrote about domestic contestation in Italy, or France or Germany or the Netherlands, one would also have to incorporate the larger entity of Europe into the analysis.

In 1984, European public discourse did not connect routinely the words "neo" and "liberalism." At that point, neoliberalism evoked Margaret Thatcher and Ronald Reagan – not something that characterized continental or Nordic Europe.[7] The signs of something new were nonetheless apparent in the halls of public policy as well as in the streets. Across the Alps in France, on May 10, 1984, French President François Mitterand gave an interview to *Libération* newspaper on the occasion of the third anniversary of his election. The socialist President surprised his constituency by announcing his plans to create "a society with a mixed economy, a state closer to the people and a market more accommodating to the creators of businesses [*enterprises*] and aware of the aspirations of workers" (*L'Année Politique* 1984, p. 45). On June 17, 1984, the French National Front acquired ten seats in the European Parliament. In December 1984, Bernard Stasi, who in 2003 headed the commission that restricted the wearing of religious symbols in public places, published a report entitled, *Immigration, a Chance for France* (1984) that defended the contribution of immigrants to French life. The contours of future change were becoming visible.

---

[6] Fiss and Hirsch (2005) show that the term "globalization" only began to take off as a concept in the early 1990s and did not achieve widespread usage until the late 1990s.

[7] Harvey's (2005) brief historical introduction to neoliberalism identifies Sweden as an example of "circumscribed neoliberalism" (p. 115). On the introduction of neoliberalism to the French as well as European polity, see Fourcade-Gourinchas and Babb (2002) and Prasad (2005; 2006).

Old Europe, new Europe and the postwar "world of security"

In 1984, old Europe was on the verge of becoming new Europe. It was one of the last years of the postwar "world of security" – a term that Stefan Zweig, the Austrian essayist and novelist, popularized in the context of World War II. He began his autobiography with a description of the prewar "World of Security": "When I attempt to find a simple formula for the period in which I grew up, prior to the First World War, I hope that I convey its fullness by calling it the Golden Age of Security. Everything in our almost thousand year old Austrian monarchy seemed based on permanency, and the State itself was the chief guarantor of this stability ... The feeling of security was the most eagerly sought-after possession of millions, the common ideal of life. Only the possession of this security made life seem worthwhile" (Zweig 1943, pp. 1–2).[8]

Zweig's description of the "world of security" and the collective emotional attachment that it implied resonated as much with post-World War II Europe as with the interwar period. Tradition and hierarchy governed Zweig's "world of security." He invoked the Austrian monarchy as its infelicitous primary symbol. Yet the differences between the two periods were differences of degree, not of kind. Arguably, after witnessing the horrors of World War II and the Nazi genocide, security was paramount in the minds of European citizens and rulers alike.

Postwar European security was a material, as well as an emotional, state of collective well-being that was socially solidaristic, economically redistributive and international (Alesina and Giavazzi 2006). High productivity and growth were the economic pillars of postwar security. The Cold War and the threat of nuclear proliferation did little to undermine the basic feeling of security that permeated postwar European society. Eichengreen's (2006) exhaustive history of the postwar European economy describes the period as a "golden age." The French have labeled the same period the *Trente Glorieuses* – the Thirty Glorious Years. The German and Italian economies were "economic miracles."

By 1984, the social safety net associated with the postwar social contract was beginning to fray. The "end of ideology" politics associated with neoliberal economic policy that was unthinkable in Europe in 1984 is now more the norm. Europeans either stay away from the polls – abstention rates have increased – or vote in a volatile fashion that suggests no deep cultural or ideological commitments. The Muslim students who

---

[8] Zweig, a Jewish émigré, wrote his autobiography, *The World of Yesterday* (1943), as he fled the Nazis. He committed suicide in exile in Brazil shortly after completing this work.

seemed mysterious in 1984 are now a constitutive feature of the urban landscape of contemporary Europe and a potent political force.

Since 1984, the collapse of communism in Eastern Europe coupled with the twin and interconnected processes of Europeanization – the expanding process of European integration – and globalization have altered the social and political landscape of contemporary Europe (Berezin 2003). Insecurity in both the public and private domains has been one response to these processes. Fear – of immigrants, crime, disease, unemployment – has become a recurrent theme in European public discourse. Europeanization and globalization have fueled social and cultural anxieties that imbue the rhetoric of fear with emotional resonance as well as political salience.[9] Rightwing populist parties and movements, a label of classificatory convenience rather than strict analytic precision as these parties and movements have as many differences as commonalities, have thrived in the European climate of insecurity. Although the European right is not alone in its evocation of insecurity, it has arguably been the most effective in bringing the emotion of fear to the foreground of political discourse. The events of September 11 in the United States and the increased possibility of terrorist activities in Europe have solidified the rhetoric of fear and insecurity as a legitimate political stance.[10]

Rightwing populism and European integration gained momentum during the 1990s – a temporal coincidence that matters. European integration, an instance of enforced transnationalism, challenges the standard prerogatives of the territorially defined nation-state. The accelerated pace of European integration disequilibrates the existing mix of national cultures and legal norms that governs those nation-states. An unintended consequence of disequilibration is the weakening of the national social contracts that threatens to make the national space "unfamiliar" to many of its citizens. "Unfamiliarity" is more than simply a feeling of disorientation: it has practical consequences.

The modern nation-state is the institutional location of a relation between a polity and a people that provides security for its members. Legal institutions of the modern nation-state, such as citizenship requirements, structurally inscribe individuals in the polity and society. National cultural practices from common language to shared norms cognitively and emotionally inscribe individuals in the polity and society. *Experience,*

---

[9] Anderson and Pontusson (2007) use OECD data that distinguish between the fact and perception of economic insecurity.

[10] Robin (2004) discusses "fear" as a political idea and emotion. Berezin (2002) explores the interaction between the emotions of security and insecurity and their effect upon political institutions and behavior.

individual and collective, is a temporal and cognitive phenomenon that consciously or unconsciously draws upon the past to assess the future.[11] Experience creates a tension between imagined possibilities and perceptions of constraint. Social, cultural and monetary capital draws the boundaries of experience that permit individuals and groups to negotiate between institutions and culture. Postwar Europe, for the most part, minimized tensions between national culture and national institutions. The postwar European nation-state was an arena that adjudicated risk for its members. Capital in all its dimensions was national. "Social Europe" and the need to preserve it, a *pro-forma* comment built into integration discourse, is an acknowledgement of postwar social solidarity.

The collective and individual experience of old Europe was national *and* solidaristic; the evolving experience of "new" Europe is individualistic, albeit with a dose of ambivalence and nostalgia. In terms of the argument of this book, "new" Europe, writ large, can be conceptualized as an opportunity space primarily for individuals and groups who are able to compete in trans-European economic, social and cultural markets – the "eurostars" that Favell (2008) chronicles. For a host of reasons, this is a restricted group, as evidenced by the 2005 defeat of the referenda on the European constitution in France and the Netherlands. In the month before the referendum on the European constitution in France, *Le Monde* described the typical "convinced European" as a "male, citizen of less than thirty-nine years, educated, of the center left or center right."[12] The living exemplar of *Le Monde*'s dry statistical profile emerged in an interview given to the *International Herald Tribune* on the day after the referendum. A thirty-six-year-old male who "works in an Internet Company" claimed "I am embarrassed for France ... I travel a lot for work and have a lot of friends across Europe. My Italian and my Spanish friends just don't understand what is happening in France – I don't either."[13]

---

[11] Historians (for example, Scott 1996; LaCapra 2004, Chapter 1; Jay 2005) who privilege experience as an analytic category tend to focus on individual subjects. Their approach is inductive and contrasts to the deductive and collective conceptualization of experience that this book offers. See Throop (2003) for a critique from the perspective of anthropology.

[12] Nicholas Weill, "En trente ans, l'euroscepticisme n'a cessé de croître sur tout le continent." *Le Monde* (Paris) April 4, 2005. Citations to newspapers are referenced by publication name, place of publication, author where appropriate and date of publication. If a page number is available, it is noted. Many of the citations from the French newspapers came from the Dossiers de Presse, a clipping file, at the library of Science-Po in Paris, France. Unfortunately, the page numbers of articles were often cut off and replaced with an official "date stamp." Many of the articles from the more mainstream French newspapers may also be found on the web where page numbers are also not noted.

[13] Katrin Bennhold, "France Turns Out for Vote on the EU: Political Class Braces for Rejection." *International Herald Tribune* (Paris), May 30, 2005.

In contrast to the bewildered mobile male Internet consultant and his trans-European colleagues, the experience of the ordinary European is still national – that is, their cultural and social capital, as well as their economic possibilities, are still firmly tied to the national state (Díez Medrano 2003). The disconnection between past experience and a European future that is oriented to the market rather than to the collectivity is fueling a reassertion of nation-ness that characterizes the rightwing populist moment.

Early theorists of modern democracy understood that feeling safe in one's political space was a cornerstone of democracy that enabled citizens to empathize with others. In the beginning of the *Politics*, Aristotle underscored the link between security and democracy among citizens when he emphasized the need of "common safety" among members of the polity – the "rulers and ruled" (Aristotle 1979, p. 29). Contemporary discussions of democracy have elided the discussion of security that was crucial to earlier formulations. Europe as a fully realized political and cultural space, as institutionalized in the European Union of now twenty-seven member states, has compromised the link between democracy and security, broadly conceived as social, political and cultural, that was the cornerstone of the postwar settlement. By moving the center of political gravity from the polity to the person, from the state to the market, Europeanization has compromised the bonds of democratic empathy and provided an opportunity for rightwing populists to articulate a discourse of fear and insecurity.

The rightwing populist moment as historical surprise: the argument in brief

The accelerated process of Europeanization that includes political, economic and cultural integration is the core trans-European context, I suggest, within which the rightwing populist moment emerged. Synergy exists between "new" Europe's rightwing populist moment and the transformation, if not outright disappearance, of the postwar "world of security."[14] Despite the presence of political terrorism in Italy and other parts of Europe during the student agitations of the 1960s and early 1970s, no one – academics, journalists or politicians – would have imagined in 1984 that rightwing populist parties would become a significant presence in

---

[14] The debate over security has often taken the form of the debate over welfare and social Europe. See Pontusson (2005), Mares (2003) and Offe (2003) for recent discussions. With the exception of Offe (2003), most of these authors work with a more restricted material conception of security.

European politics. Yet, today this is the case. The fluctuating electoral success of rightwing political parties is the most salient empirical indicator of an emergent rightwing populist moment. Rightwing parties are not new to European politics. A majority of European nation-states have such parties – some dating back to the 1930s (Pettigrew 1998; Eatwell 2000).[15] What is new is that parties that analysts had viewed as extremist and fringe now attract sufficient numbers of votes to sometimes become part of legally constituted governing coalitions.[16]

An analytically sensible starting date for the rightwing populist moment is March 1994 when Gianfranco Fini's "post-fascist" National Alliance became part of an Italian governing coalition. The short-lived 1994 Silvio Berlusconi government was the first instance in the democratic parts of postwar Western Europe where the right so visibly emerged as a legitimate political actor (Ginsborg 2003, pp. 285–324). In 1994, the genre of political parties to which the National Alliance belonged appeared as an exception to the prevailing political rules. From the vantage point of today, these parties appear more as fixtures than as fissures on the European political landscape.

In March 1998, Jean-Marie Le Pen's National Front made a significant showing in the French regional elections (for analysis see Perrineau and Reynié 1999). In April 2002, the first round of the French presidential elections gave Le Pen enough votes to have become President of the Republic – if he had won the second round. In February 2000, Jörg Haider's Freedom Party became part of an Austrian governing coalition – that unraveled, and reemerged periodically. International alarm and public outcry in the national and international public spheres followed these events in Italy, France and Austria.[17] In the Austrian case, the European Union applied sanctions. In addition to these more prominent cases, fringe parties have posed significant parliamentary threats in Switzerland, Belgium, the Netherlands and Denmark.[18]

---

[15] I make this observation to underscore that in some cases there is a degree of formal continuity between old and new rightwing parties, not to imply that there is substantive similarity between the past and the present.

[16] Norris (2005, p. 8) reports a graph of mean votes for seven radical rightwing parties in Western Europe that displays an unbroken curve from 1980 to 2004. This curve begins to level off in 2002 and the figure, although striking, should be interpreted with caution.

[17] Van de Steeg (2006) has analyzed the trans-European component of the reaction to Haider's electoral victory. Haider died in a car accident in October 2008.

[18] Hossay (2002) provides profiles including electoral data of rightwing parties in eleven European nation-states. Eatwell (2000, p. 408) provides a list of rightwing political parties and the percentage of the vote that they captured between 1996 and 1999. Norris (2005, p. 59) covers the same ground but takes statistics to 2004 in a much more visually compelling way.

Despite exceptions such as Holmes' (2000) anthropological account and Art's (2006) historical analysis, the rightwing populist moment lacks an analytic and theoretical narrative that situates it within the changing political, social and cultural context of contemporary Europe.[19] Noisy cadres of militants expressing extremist positions of various sorts distract from nuanced analysis of rightwing populist parties. The recurrent popularity of the genre of parties that constitute the rightwing populist moment suggests that they are expressions of deeper social phenomena that the explanations of mainstream political science based on party strategy, electoral behavior and public opinion surveys only partially capture.

Wide fluctuations in electoral politics and outcomes suggest that the salience of rightwing parties represents *thin* rather than *thick* commitments on the part of a volatile European electorate. *Thick* commitments characterize party militants with a deep commitment to xenophobia and a simple-minded ethnic nationalism. These are the activists that Klandermans and Mayer (2006) have recently profiled. While political extremism of all stripes may generate violence and hatred, it tends not to make large electoral inroads. Skinheads do not win political campaigns. The ever variable *thin* commitments of disgruntled citizens are sociologically and culturally more interesting and politically more important. *Thin* commitments make urgent the recalibration of the standard categories that analysts typically deploy to discuss the right.

Social scientists who study rightwing populism in contemporary Europe frequently explain it as a xenophobic response to the increased presence of non-Western immigrants in diverse nation-states. In these formulations, rightwing populism is morally unfortunate but politically unsurprising. This book takes a different stance. It starts from the position that contemporary rightwing populism represents a historical surprise, not a political and social certainty. Migration, whether for employment, family reunification or political asylum, is an undeniable fact of past, as well as present, European experience. Immigrants may be a necessary but not a sufficient condition to account for the contemporary right. As Hall (2003, p. 398) cautions, "correlation is not causation."

This book views the emergence of the rightwing populist moment in the 1990s in various European venues as an unexpected, rather than an expected or natural, event. It asks whether there would be a rightwing populist moment in the absence of Maastricht and the subsequent intensification of Europeanization. This formulation suggests compelling

---

[19] One reason for the lack of nuanced writing on the right is that ethnic conflict and nationalism have captured the scholarly space that such studies would normally occupy.

contextual issues that a single-minded focus upon migration elides. Rightwing populism poses a challenge to prevailing social science and commonsense assumptions about transnationalism and cosmopolitanism. Viewing the rightwing populist moment through the lens of the social science literature on political institutions, culture and democracy provides analytic leverage on the puzzle that rightwing populism represents. By analyzing the rightwing populist moment in relation to the broader context of Europeanization and globalization, this book attempts to, first, unpack the political and cultural processes that evoke the *thin* commitments that characterize citizen support, and, second, signal that we cannot make sense of rightwing populism independently of the historical legacies and practices, both national and international, within which it arises. In a multicultural Europe of acknowledged social and political integration and increased cultural contact, rightwing populism represents a recidivist contraction and turning inward that is puzzling. Unraveling this puzzle requires historical, that is contextual, exegesis that looks primarily at *events*, and secondarily at individual and collective actors.

The rightwing populist moment refracted through the prism of culture and history

Method and meaning

The increasing salience of rightwing populism in Europe as a political phenomenon manifests itself, among other ways, in electoral behavior and party politics. This book departs from standard practice and does not focus on party strategy, voting behavior or political attitudes. Focusing simply on rightwing parties and voting behavior presents a danger of sampling on the dependent variable – that is, explaining the phenomenon of interest in terms of itself without reference to a broader temporal and spatial context. Party politics and voting studies dominate the literature on rightwing populism. This book draws upon these many important studies. Yet, because they rely on univalent methods of analysis, these studies attenuate the significance of the phenomenon itself.

The method of this study is historical and narrative. It shifts the unit of analysis from political actors, whether voters or party operatives, to events that marked turning points in collective national perceptions. Contingent events, events that were unexpected and that emotionally engaged the national collectivity at all levels from the average citizen to political elites, are at the center of this analysis. The focus upon events as a unit of analysis breaks with standard party-centric approaches to rightwing politics as well as analyses grounded in social movement theory (for example, Kriesi 1999). Historical sociologists (Sewell 2005; Abbott 2001) have recently argued that events as units of analysis may yield robust forms of political cultural explanation. For example, Sewell's (1996a) thick description of the storming of the Bastille as a unitary event permits him to develop a nuanced account of a larger phenomenon, the French Revolution, than traditional analyses that limit themselves to causes and consequences.[20]

Events as sites of analysis offer a substantive as well as methodological advantage. First, events are cross-sectional. They incorporate structure and culture, institutions and actors. In this regard, events are methodologically similar to open-ended interviews of stratified random samples of subjects. For example, Lamont (2000) asked a sample of working-class men in France and the United States how they drew moral boundaries. Their answers to Lamont's open-ended interview script ranged widely across issues and permitted her to develop a rich comparative account of the interplay of culture and inequality in the United States and France. Second, events permit the researcher to hear the voices of multiple subjects at the same time. Third, events are embedded in social and political relations, so they situate the right in its immediate national venue as well as in the wider context of European politics. Fourth, though the meaning of events is open to interpretation, events as actions in time and space are transparent. Borrowing from sociologist Émile Durkheim ([1895] 1966), events constitute "social facts" – phenomena with sufficient identity and coherence that the social collectivity recognizes them as discrete and important. Lastly, an event-focused account encourages engagement with recent methodological moves in historical and cultural sociology that explore the relation between narrative and explanation.[21]

Sites of analysis

Selected events primarily in France, and secondarily in Italy, between 1994 and 2005 are the empirical core of this analysis. The broader scope of the book is Europe between 1980 and the present day. The book has three time frames that intersect with the analysis. The first time frame focuses upon France and the National Front in the years between 1997 and 2005 – the

---

[20] This approach differs from path dependence which also relies on events as a unit of analysis but views them as causally connected in a temporally linked sequence. See Pierson (2004); Bates *et al.* (1998).

[21] See Adams *et al.* (2005) and Steinmetz (2005) for discussions of theory and method in comparative historical sociology. Polletta (2006) and Tilly (2002), from divergent perspectives, have analyzed how narrative or "stories" contribute to political explanation.

year that French citizens rejected the European constitution. In 1997 the National Front held its party congress in Strasbourg and took as its mandate to insert itself into French politics as a "normal" and legitimate political party – *banalisation* as the French describe it. The second time frame that serves as a context for the rightwing populist moment begins in 1994, the year of the first Silvio Berlusconi government in Italy. The Italian case is not a fully developed comparison, rather it serves as a shadow case that provides a contrast for France and the more general phenomenon of the European right. The broader time frame of the book departs from the early 1980s when the postwar social contract began to unravel and serves as a reference point for discussing the European context more generally.

France and Italy are paradigmatic cases in discussions of European populism. Political analysts view Jean-Marie Le Pen's French National Front as the textbook case of the new European right. The National Front is the only European rightwing party that has had an electoral presence on the local, national and European level (Mayer [1999] 2002, p. 289). Italy's National Alliance falls under the rubric of the right because it has its roots in a party, the MSI (Movimento Sociale Italiano), with direct links to the Fascist Party from the period of the Salò Republic. The French National Front has never become part of a national governing coalition whereas the National Alliance has twice become part of an Italian national governing coalition. Its leader Gianfranco Fini became Italy's Minister of Foreign Affairs in November 2004.

Plan of the book

The book divides into three interrelated parts. The first part situates the rightwing populist moment in time and space. Chapter 1 contains a general discussion of the electoral salience of the contemporary right as well as an elaboration of the term "populism." Chapter 2 lays out the contours of a new approach to the right that melds political and cultural analysis. The second part, Chapters 3 through 7, describes the political trajectory of the National Front in France. These chapters explore a series of significant events – the 1997 National Front party congress in Strasbourg, the March 1998 regional elections, the World Cup victory in July 1998, the 2002 presidential elections and the 2005 constitutional referendum – that became part of a French public narrative that challenged collective national perceptions. These chapters also discuss trans-European extra-parliamentary movements that emerged during the same period, particularly anti-globalization protestors who added their voice to an emerging public narrative against neoliberalism. The third part situates the rightwing populist moment within the context of Europeanization. Chapter 8 views the trajectory of the National Front within the context of French and European politics. Chapter 9 measures the French case against the trajectory of the right in Italy. The Conclusion synthesizes the empirical materials, draws out the broader implications of the analysis and theorizes a relation between democracy and security.

Note on sources

Multiple data sources inform this analysis. The Italian material that speaks to the Resistance narrative was gathered at the Biblioteca Nazionale and the Institute for the Study of the Resistance in Florence during 1995–1996 while I was a visiting fellow at the European University Institute in Fiesole, Italy. Between 1998 and 2002, I spent extensive periods of time in France where I attended rallies for and against the National Front. A systematic analysis of various texts supplemented the ethnographic material. First, I constructed a chronology of events in Europe, France and Italy and where applicable beyond (i.e., Gulf War, Chernobyl, Kosovo) for the years between 1984 and 2004. I used standard sources: Pinder (2001, pp. 174–181); *Storia d'Italia* (1991); Fhima (2000); and the annuals: *Italian Politics: A Review* (Istituto Carlo Cattaneo); *L'Année Politique*. This chronology yielded a total of 482 events.

In addition, I constructed a newspaper archive for France in the years between 1996 and 2002 using "Les Dossiers de Presse" at the Centre de Documentation Contemporaine, Fondation Nationale des Sciences Politiques, Paris, France. The French newspaper archive consisted of 960 entries.[22] Both newspaper archives were supplemented with official documents, films, books, and an extensive review of secondary literature.

---

[22] See Earl *et al.* (2004) for the use of newspapers as a data source. Even though this article focuses upon social movement research, it makes useful points for when it is necessary to rely on newspaper sources. Smith (2005, pp. 50–55) makes a cogent argument for the value of newspapers as data sources when trying to map collective public perceptions. In contrast to the American press, European newspapers including the French have never espoused the norm of neutrality. The principal newspapers used in the French chapters represent distinct points of view. *Le Monde* is the journal of record for the French elite; *Libération* emerged from the tumult of May '68; *L'Humanité* is the daily of the French Communist Party; *Le Figaro* is the oldest French daily newspaper, founded in 1854, with a decidedly conservative bent. In contrast to American newspapers, these media serve as chronicles of daily events. French academics regularly contribute as they serve as public intellectuals and commentators. For a survey of the French press, see Thogmartin (1998).

PART I

Situating the rightwing populist moment

1

Cinderella in the polis: rightwing populism as historical phenomenon and political concept

The European right in time and space

Extremist political parties and movements have been a constituent feature of European politics since the early twentieth century. These parties and movements often share the formal property of being outside the prevailing political mainstream. However, they vary according to temporal and national specificity. With the exception of the 1920s and 1930s, these parties and movements have remained for the most part extreme and at the margins of normal politics.[1] The spectacular disaster of World War II overshadowed the fact that, even in the 1920s and 1930s, the Italian fascist regime was tepid. Mussolini met his downfall through his alliance with Hitler; and Spain's Franco prudently avoided war and alliances.[2] Despite the fascist regime's commitment to the March on Rome as its founding moment, the procedures of parliamentary democracy, and not a coup d'état, brought Mussolini, and later Hitler, to power.[3]

The European right did not disappear at the end of World War II. Although the postwar constitutions of Italy and Germany outlawed fascism and Nazism, rightwing and extremist parties and movements existed in the crevices of postwar democratic nation-states.[4] On the most

---

[1] *Who Were the Fascists?* (1980) is a classic anthology that maps the presence of the right during the interwar period in Eastern and Western Europe. "Right-Wing Extremism in Western Europe" (1988) covers the right in Italy, West Germany, France, Great Britain and Spain in the postwar period as marginal political actors. Pettigrew (1998) provides a summary of xenophobic parties.

[2] Berezin (1997a) reiterates this point which other historians have made.

[3] Departing from an older liberal historiography that viewed the 1920s and 1930s as an aberration, recent scholarship (Capoccia 2005; Bermeo 2003; Berman 2006) addresses the interwar period in Europe as a problem in the political development of European democracy.

[4] The German Basic Law did not operate as a fully developed modern constitution until the reunification of Germany in 1990.

elementary level, ordinary citizens who were committed Nazis or fascists were simply not important enough to be rounded up and submitted to war tribunals. They remained in their villages and towns and nursed nostalgic yearnings for a fascist or Nazi past (Tarchi 1995; Goldhagen 1996) as well as forming the nuclei of fringe parties.

The Italian and German responses to fascism and Nazism were clear cut. France as a nation did not begin to come to terms with the Vichy regime until the early 1970s. Events such as Max Ophuls' 1969 film, *The Sorrow and the Pity*, and the French translation of American historian Robert Paxton's *Vichy France: Old Guard and New Order, 1940–1944* (1972) placed the issue of collaboration firmly in the French public sphere (Rousso 1991, pp. 251–256). From 1940 to 1972, the year that the National Front was founded, a mélange of rightwing parties and organizations existed in France – some of which had roots in the French revolutionary period (Rémond 1969; 2005). With the exception of Pierre Poujade whose movement of nationalist shopkeepers won 11 percent of votes in the legislative elections of 1956 (Hoffmann 1956), the extreme right, while present, exercised virtually no political power.

The Movimento Sociale Italiano (MSI) was the only European rightwing party in the interwar period with direct links to a fascist past. Founded in 1946, the MSI consisted of remnants of the Repubblica Sociale Italiana (RSI) – the name of Mussolini's government in exile in the years between 1943 and 1945. Although fascism was outlawed, fascists were not. RSI militants who had escaped prosecution were available to reconstitute a party that was national, anti-monarchist, anti-clerical and anti-NATO. The party polled 2 percent of the votes and earned six seats in the 1948 Italian parliamentary elections. As the MSI was militantly anti-communist, the postwar Italian governing coalitions ignored the party's fascist past when it was convenient to do so.[5] Although the MSI was always disreputable among Northern elites, Christian Democrats and left-leaning intellectuals, the Vatican welcomed its participation in the political debate because of its anti-communist stance (Ferraresi 1996, p. 23).

The MSI had its greatest level of support in the South, which had never been part of the fascist or anti-fascist project (Caciagli 1988, p. 21). It was always on hand to engage in violence and in acts of destabilization. By the 1970s, the major goal of its aging leader Giorgio Almirante was to market the MSI to voters as a respectable conservative alternative to the Italian Christian Democrats. In the years between 1953 and 1994, the MSI polled

---

[5] Tranfaglia (1996) dissects the consequences of this official moral flexibility in *Un passato scomodo: fascismo e postfascismo* (*An Inconvenient Past: Fascism and Postfascism*).

between 5 and 7 percent of the vote in parliamentary elections. It reached
8.7 percent showing in the parliamentary elections of 1972 (Ignazi 2003,
p. 40).

Recidivist rightwing parties and movements left over from the 1920s and
1930s did not dominate either the European public conscience or the
political agendas of national politicians. As Benedict Anderson observed
([1983] 1991, pp. 187–206), "forgetting" is constitutive of new beginnings.[6]
The Cold War notwithstanding, ordinary citizens experienced the years
between 1945 and 1980 in Europe as a period of social security and spreading affluence.[7] The social contract forged during those years, known as the
"postwar settlement," was social democratic, repudiated the fascist past,
was committed to social welfare and firmly anti-communist despite the
presence of strong communist parties in many European nation-states. In
1945 when the war ended, European leaders were determined that the
European future would not include any unpleasant residue from the
past. International institutions such as the United Nations and initiatives
such as the Marshall Plan and the North Atlantic Treaty Organization
(NATO), spearheaded by the United States, emerged to secure the peace
(Milward 1984). European integration in the form of the European
Economic Community was central to a common European commitment
to intra-continental peace. The signatories of the Treaty of Rome in 1957
imagined a limited community of six nation-states committed to peace
through prosperity.[8]

Against this background of hope and optimism, rightwing parties
seemed to exist as thread-like fractures in a smooth and democratic
European political and social landscape. The dissidence that attracted
political attention came from a new generation of leftwing political activists. Beginning in the late 1960s and continuing in some instances into the
mid-1970s, New Left agitation dominated European public space. May '68
in France and the "hot autumn" of 1969 in Italy were exemplars of protest
mobilization among a generation born during, or immediately after,
World War II. In their rediscovery of Marxism, militant middle-class
students and intellectuals joined with workers in a renewed form of
"class struggle." This period of protest is well documented (for example,

---

[6] It was not until the 1990s, the period covered in this book, that memory of the war period
became a political and academic obsession in Europe. For example, see discussions in Olick
and Robbins (1998) and Fritzsche (2001).
[7] De Grazia (2005) describes much of this period through the lens of Americanization. Judt's
(2005) magisterial *Postwar* captures the years between 1945 and 1989 in all their variation.
[8] This is a vast simplification of a complicated history with an enormous historiography. For
a cogent and comprehensive account see Moravcsik (1998).

Tarrow 1989; Eley 2002, pp. 341–383). New Left agitation sometimes degenerated into organized political terrorism, such as the activities of the Red Brigades in Italy and the Baader-Meinhof Group in Germany. Political violence captured the attention of the international news media and generated years of public chaos and insecurity (Della Porta 1995).[9]

In the 1980s, Green parties, environmental parties, anti-nuclear and feminist movements drew more attention than either the right or the left. The German Greens were founded in 1980. By 1989, virtually every East and West European nation-state had a variation of a Green party (Eley 2002, p. 484). In 1977, Inglehart identified a shift in European politics from the class orientation of the 1950s and 1960s, that focused on the material interests of groups, to a post-materialist politics based on culture and values. Students of social movements coined the term "new social movements" to distinguish between materialist and post-materialist political mobilization. In 1985, an issue of *Social Research* was devoted to "new social movements" in Europe. Cohen's (1985) lead article, which announced that identity had replaced strategy as the basis of collective action, became a quasi social science classic.

In contrast to leftwing parties and extra-parliamentary movements, rightwing parties drew little attention in national and international media or in academic journals. Nonetheless, they commanded a steady if small constituency of thickly committed members who shared their political values. Rightwing parties had leaders and stable, if fractious, organizations. As the 1980s drew to a close, rightwing parties still appeared more fringe than mainstream, with the exception of two events that occurred in France which attracted attention and academic scrutiny. In 1983, the French National Front achieved a breakthrough in Dreux, a small city in the north of France, when a party operative was elected mayor. This was the beginning of a series of electoral inroads (Schain 1987; Mitra 1988; DeClair 1999). At the time, the French media and political establishment viewed Dreux as local and the event drew little international attention (Gaspard 1995, pp. 120–135).[10] In 1988, Jean-Marie Le Pen received 14 percent of the votes in the first round of the French presidential elections. Viewed as aberrant events at the time, both elections reflected subtle shifts

---

[9] Political analysts often failed to draw a distinction between extremist movements and extremist parties. Terrorism was often merged with leftwing and rightwing forms of political organization; see Stoss (1988) for example.

[10] Sixteen years later, Tribalat (1999) offered a radically different view of Dreux as a laboratory of modern France, "Dreux, planted in the middle of fields, escaping the stature of a city or a ghetto of a large metropolis, appeared at once singular and exemplary, of the excessive form that many actual ills of French society have taken" (p. 7).

in the political landscape of France and of Europe more generally. In 1988, the journal *West European Politics* published a "special issue" devoted to "Right-Wing Extremism in Western Europe." A striking feature of the volume from the vantage point of today is that, with the exception of the French National Front, none of the parties or movements that the volume discusses were meaningful political actors even as little as ten years after its publication.

In 1989, the Berlin Wall fell and the Cold War, long on its deathbed, officially ended. With communism gone, other threats emerged to take the place of the "evil empire." As my opening introductory narrative suggested, signs of transition were beginning to appear well before the collapse of communism. Beginning in the early 1980s in France and following in the 1990s in Germany, political violence reemerged, but in contrast to the 1960s and 1970s, this time the violence was directed against immigrants.

In 1992, skinheads on the loose in northern German towns burned down an immigrant Muslim apartment complex. Jane Kramer chronicled these events for the *New Yorker*. She eventually published these articles in a volume on the *Politics of Memory* (1996). Kramer describes the life of a skinhead who is on probation for "sidewalk cracking," which is finding a Turkish immigrant, knocking him down and kicking him in the head. Kramer's subject is marginally literate and employed, and spends his spare time listening to Oi! music and describing the "chaos in the head" that he experiences. The Turkish immigrant in Kramer's narrative thinks he has had a good day if he has not experienced any random acts of verbal abuse – despite the fact that the grocery store, in which he had invested his hopes and dreams, was burned to the ground by local skinheads.

German social scientists documented 276 acts of antisemitic and extreme rightwing violence in Germany between 1989 and 1994 (Erb and Kurthen 1997). A recent study of rightwing violence in Germany (Koopmans and Olzak 2004) reported that acts of xenophobic violence were correlated with public discourse about "problems" with immigrants, particularly asylum seekers, and not with the number of immigrants or the unemployment rates in a site of violence. The study found a steady level of violence directed against immigrants to Germany between 1990 and 1999. Violence peaked in the years of 1991 and 1992 when asylum seekers were on the public agenda.

By the early 1990s, scholars as well as the European public were beginning to associate xenophobia and violence against immigrants with the right. In August 2002, an Associated Press dispatch proclaimed, "Europe's Skinhead Movement Grows." Typical of much sensationalist journalism on the subject, the author made no distinction between the disenfranchised youth who make up the core of skinhead culture and the legally incorporated right. But as this section describes, the right was not new and it was simply awaiting its moment. France and Germany were sites of racist violence and xenophobic activity in the 1980s and early 1990s, but the European right had its breakthrough moment on the national level in Italy. Ironically, in 1994 when the first Berlusconi governing coalition formed, an immigrant might still mean a Southern Italian, as well as a foreigner, and the principle source of violence was still the Mafia.

Italian elections March 1994: a pivotal event
for political legitimacy

In Italy in March 1994, the unthinkable occurred. A party with roots in the Italian fascist past, the Movimento Sociale Italiano (MSI) under the direction of its relatively young leader Gianfranco Fini, became part of a legally constituted Italian governing coalition – the first Silvio Berlusconi government. The MSI, which became the National Alliance (Alleanza Nazionale) in 1995, has moved considerably toward the center since 1994 (Ignazi 2003, p. 52). Yet, the Italian elections of 1994 were a pivotal event at the national and the European level. First, they opened up the Italian political space to include a range of new parties and political actors (Diamanti and Mannheimer 1994). Second, they signaled at the European level the emergence of a new European right as a legitimate political force. The MSI was a direct descendant of the old Italian Fascist Party and its inclusion in a governing coalition sent shock waves throughout Europe and the world.

In 1994, in order to obtain the majority required to form a governing coalition, Berlusconi allied himself with Fini and the regional separatist movement the Northern League (Lega Nord) under the leadership of Umberto Bossi. The political name for the coalition of Berlusconi, Bossi and Fini was the Polo delle Libertà (Pole of Liberty). Journalists and scholars refer to it as the Italian right, which is something of a misnomer as it is more accurately described as "everything but the left." Berlusconi is and remains a successful entrepreneur; Bossi is an erratic regional chauvinist whose movement has caught on sporadically outside of his home base in the North. Fini was the most politically questionable member of the coalition. Although Fini described his party as "post-fascist," it was hard to erase its connections to the fascist past. Fini did not help matters when he proclaimed that Mussolini was the greatest statesman of the twentieth century – a statement he has since disowned. In 1995, at Fini's insistence, the old MSI ceased to exist and the National Alliance became the official party of the Italian right.

The first Berlusconi government was short-lived – lasting only from May to December 1994. In May 2001, Berlusconi returned as the Prime Minister of Italy. The second Berlusconi government lasted until spring 2006 – making it the longest lasting governing coalition in postwar Italian history.[11] The length of time that Berlusconi managed to keep his coalition in office evoked consistent comparisons to Mussolini. Certain segments of the public sphere consistently referred to Berlusconi and his governing coalition as rightwing. Berlusconi was a source of deep embarrassment to various segments of the Italian intelligentsia and governing strata, yet, as a brash entrepreneur, he was more of a Donald Trump than a Benito Mussolini.[12]

The 2006 issue of *Forbes* magazine listed Berlusconi's personal fortune at 11 billion dollars and ranked him thirty-seventh on its list of the richest people in the world. Berlusconi made his fortune by developing a private market for television transmission – a market that he expanded into other forms of mass media. Questionable financial practices, originally tied to his involvements with Bettino Craxi and the Italian Socialist Party, that have kept him continually under indictment for fraud and tax evasion have no doubt also helped his accumulation of capital. Berlusconi's party founded in 1994 was Forza Italia (Go Italy), named after the cheer for the national soccer team (Ginsborg 2004). His 2001 party platform, the *Contract with Italy*, eschewed ideology in favor of the market rationality which he champions in private and public.[13]

Berlusconi's second coalition collapsed in spring 2006. By the end of their second tenure, the meaning of the Berlusconi, Bossi, Fini coalition had altered radically. In November 2004, Fini assumed the post of Minister of Foreign Affairs. He had traveled a long way toward normalizing his position in Italian, European and international politics. Fini no longer described himself or his party as post-fascist and had backpedaled from his 1994 statement that praised Mussolini as the greatest statesman of the twentieth century. When the French National Front achieved a significant breakthrough in the March 1998 regional elections, Gianfranco Fini immediately gave an interview to the French newspaper *Le Monde* to underscore the point that the National Alliance in its earlier incarnation,

---

[11] The essays in Newell (2002) provide an analysis of what in the end was a fairly close election.

[12] For a less benign view, see Stille (2006); for a nuanced account of Berlusconi's political career, see Shin and Agnew (2008).

[13] "Contratto con gli Italiani" www.forza-italia.it/silvioberlusconi/contratto.pdf.

the MSI, had broken with the National Front in 1989 when it formed an alliance with the German rightwing party the Republikaner.[14]

Despite the presence of Bossi and Fini, it is difficult to categorize the second Berlusconi governing coalition as anything other than center right. The Catholic Church has had a more conservative effect on recent Italian politics than the Berlusconi coalition. For example, the Catholic Church supported a December 2003 law that banned in vitro fertilization in Italy. On June 13, 2005, the Italian referendum to reverse the law failed because only 25.9 percent of the Italian electorate turned out to vote, and Italian referenda require a 50 percent rate of participation.[15] Fini supported the repeal of the law and placed himself in public opposition to the Pope who wanted the law retained.

In January 2008, the center left government of Romano Prodi that had succeeded Berlusconi collapsed. In response, the President of Italy dissolved Parliament in February 2008 and called for new elections in the spring. To the surprise of many observers, Berlusconi's center right coalition received enough votes in the April 2008 general election to return him as Prime Minister. Between 1994 and 2007, Berlusconi changed the name of his coalition three times. The 1994 Polo delle Libertà became the Casa delle Libertà (House of Liberties) in 2001 and reemerged in 2007 as Il Popolo della Libertà (The People of Liberty). Despite the name changes, the core members of the coalition were the same in 2008 as in 1994. The 2008 election enhanced Gianfranco Fini's political résumé. In the election's aftermath, he was elected President of the Chamber of Deputies, the lower house of the Italian Parliament. Umberto Bossi returned as a Cabinet minister without portfolio in charge of federal reforms.[16]

Today, within the context of European politics, the Berlusconi coalition is not as remarkable as it was when it first emerged. Yet, the 1994 Italian election remains pivotal in an analytic and empirical sense. First, the 1994 Italian election and the subsequent reemergence of the coalition in 2001 and again in 2008 serve as a shadow case against which social scientists can assess other rightwing populist parties. Second, the Italian election of 1994 had meaning that extended beyond Italy. For the first time in postwar European politics, the Italian state and public acknowledged the right as a

---

[14] Gianfranco Fini, "Pourquoi nous avons rompu avec le FN." *Le Monde* (Paris) June 26, 1998, pp. 1 ff.

[15] *La Repubblica* (Rome) published a graph of participation rates in Italian referenda from 1974 to the 2005 referendum (June 14, 2005, p. 2). Participation rates began falling in the late 1990s. In 1974, 87.7 percent turned out to vote on divorce; in 1981, 79.4 percent turned out to vote on abortion. Both of these referenda passed.

[16] Agnew (2002) describes the relation between Bossi's League and Italian regional politics.

legitimate political actor by allowing it to become part of a legally constituted governing coalition. Thus, the 1994 Italian elections endowed the
European right with the political legitimacy that it had lacked in the
postwar period. For this reason, the 1994 Italian election drew international attention and criticism.

Italy was not alone. Across the Alps in France, the French right had
slowly and more insidiously begun inserting itself into French politics. If
the Italian elections of 1994 were a defining moment in European as well as
Italian politics, then spring 2002 marked another turning point in the
development of the European right. In April 2002, Jean-Marie Le Pen
advanced to the second round of the French presidential elections. His
success, no matter how unwelcome to vast segments of the French citizenry, signaled that the French right had significantly extended its constituency. Less than a month later, the Dutch populist Pim Fortuyn, who
had questioned whether Muslims were capable of acquiring Dutch and
European values, was gunned down in Amsterdam in the midst of a
political campaign (Bruff 2003; Van Holsteyn and Irwin 2003).

In March 2002, the Italian economics professor Marco Biagi, who was
negotiating the revision of Article 18 of the Workers' Statute, was shot and
killed in the streets of Bologna. The Berlusconi government wanted to
repeal Article 18 of the Italian Labor Code that only permitted workers to
be let go for "just cause." Article 18 created rigidities in the Italian labor
market that made it difficult to meet the conditions of the European
Union's 1997 Stability and Growth Pact. While the French were busy
protesting Le Pen between April 22 and May 6, 2002, the Italians took to
the piazza in Rome and Milan to protest the repeal of Article 18.[17] On
April 16, 2002, the Italians staged a general strike that lasted eight hours.
Some parts of Europe were becoming more violent. Southern Europe was
returning to its workerist roots.

In 1994, rightwing populist parties appeared as exceptions to normal
national politics. Today, they are entrenched in the European political
scene and represent a trans-European political process that had roots in
the 1980s and flowered in the 1990s. This process took different forms in
different European nation-states and has had different trajectories and
political outcomes. By spring 2002, Europeanization, directly and indirectly,
was at the core of events in France, the Netherlands and Italy, suggesting
that the increasing pace of European integration coupled with shifting
demographics had fueled a new political culture of legitimate populism.

---

[17] Accornero and Como (2003) provide a discussion of the reform of Article 18. Chapter 9 of
this volume discusses these events in greater detail.

The populist moment: an excursus on political nomenclature

The class of political phenomena that includes events such as the electoral inroads of Le Pen, Haider and the Italian trio of Berlusconi, Bossi and Fini is of analytic and political significance because they carry the penumbra of legitimacy. Yet as a class of political phenomena, these parties and movements elude easy classification. Analysts recognize that they represent a departure from typical postwar European political practice. Beyond the empirical fact that these electoral breakthroughs – the term favored by political scientists – occurred during roughly the same time period, it is difficult to ascribe meaningful commonalities to them.[18]

When academics and journalists began to take notice of these movements and parties, they initially labeled them as rightwing. But it soon became clear that this nomenclature was problematic for two reasons: first, the parties and movements were too different among themselves; and second, they were not "right" in the traditional sense of the term. In addition, a counter-trend of extra-parliamentary political extremism muddied the analytic waters. In the suburban slums of major European cities from Stockholm to Paris, bands of youthful neo-Nazis and skinheads engaged in acts of racist violence (Fort 1994; Hagan *et al.* 1995; Rainer and Kurthen 1997; Pred 2000).

From roughly year 2000 onwards, populism has begun to emerge as a default term in public discourse and in the scholarly literature to describe the political phenomena that comprise the class of events constituting the right. In November 2003, the Italian newspaper *La Repubblica* ran a four-page spread on populism for which it enlisted academic authors. Headlines from the articles read: "Populism the Ghost that Haunts the World"; "Many Followers No Maestro."[19] The article located the phenomena in diverse parts of the world and in many time periods, and included an eclectic mix of exponents from Thomas Jefferson to Lech Wałęsa. The French intellectual press – as good a bellwether as any of political idioms – published an article in May 2003 on the "Permanence of Populism." Academic studies of populism also began to emerge, such as Hermet's *Les populismes dans le monde* (2001) and Mény and Surel's anthology, *Democracies and the Populist Challenge* (2002).[20] On May 29, 2006, *Newsweek International* (web edition, May 30, 2006) ran an article

---

[18] Chapter 2 addresses the voluminous secondary literature on this phenomenon.
[19] Remo Bodei, "Populismo lo spettro che si aggira per il mondo." *La Repubblica* (Rome) November 12, 2003, pp. 1, 41; Marco Tarchi, "Molti seguaci nessun maestro." *La Repubblica* (Rome) November 12, 2003, p. 39.
[20] Other works include Taguieff (2002; 2004), Tarchi (2003a) and Ihl *et al.* (2003).

entitled "March of the Populists" that declared that populism was spreading beyond its Latin roots and becoming a global phenomenon.[21]

Dézé (2004) labeled populism the "unfindable Cinderella," suggesting its ambiguity as a default analytic category. The *SAIS Review* of Johns Hopkins University recently devoted an entire issue to populism that began by describing it as an "amorphous concept" that is "insufficiently understood" (Carlucci *et al.* 2007). The entry on "populism" in the 1933 edition of the *Encyclopedia of the Social Sciences* refers the reader to "agrarian movements" and the "Russian Revolution." Analysts view populism as anti-intellectual and anti-ideological. Populism is a Cinderella theory of ill repute. It conjures images of a faceless mass, such as Gustave Le Bon's (1982) crowd, under the sway of a demagogic figure whose personal charisma seduces the people. Hitler and Eva Peron as well as numerous other twentieth-century figures fit the category. Contemporary European populists such as Jean-Marie Le Pen, Jörg Haider and Umberto Bossi appear pale and listless, whatever electoral appeal they may hold in time and space, in contrast to Eva Peron in Argentina.

Unlike other political terms, populism has an uncertain pedigree. There is no major political or social theorist attached to it. Canovan's (1996; 1999) sustained analysis of populism argues that it can be easily confused with democracy as democracy promotes popular sovereignty. Yet, populism, as Taggart (2002) notes, is also a "pathology" of democracy, as its tendency to reject authority imbues it with a general lack of toleration. Urbinati (1998) argues that in a pre-democratic environment populism is a progressive force and leads to the creation of a *demos*; whereas the form of populism that emerges in an existing democratic polity contributes to the breakdown of mediating institutions and the creation of an *ethnos*. Mudde (2004, p. 562) defines populism as an ideology that pits the "pure people" against a "corrupt elite." While this definition in some respects fits the distrust of "Europe" that is gathering force in some European nation-states, its essential rationality (i.e., distrust of elites) fails to capture the cultural contradictions at the heart of contemporary populism.[22] In short, populism when it emerges underscores the fact that democratic sentiments and democratic procedures may not always cohere.

An uncomfortable feature of populism is that it has a leftwing and rightwing variant. The anti-globalization movement which developed in

---

[21] Scholars did not associate populism with Europe until recently. In a 1969 anthology, Ionescu and Gellner assembled authors who discussed populism in North America, Latin America, Russia, Eastern Europe and Africa. Western Europe was notably absent.

[22] On the issue of "Euroskepticism," see the essays in Tiersky (2001).

Europe at the same time as the rightwing populist moment is populist in orientation and formulation.[23] Leftwing and rightwing populists focus on normative issues – that is, the right to be secure in their heartland, the nation-state they inhabit. Rightwing populists articulate their claims against perceived enemies – immigrants, Eurocrats; leftwing populists focus on the threat of global capital to national social security. Rightwing and leftwing populists have different popular imaginaries of good and evil, making them on the surface appear quite different. Rightwing populists deploy racist rhetoric; their positive image is the family. Leftwing populists may appear anarchical when their rallies end up in confrontations with the police; their positive image is their empathy with the sufferings of the global poor. Rightwing populists tend to identify with the nation; leftwing populists articulate their claims in terms of social justice. In some instances right and left converge on issues, as they did in France in 2005 during the campaign against the European constitution.

The ephemera of nomenclature and the landscape of European populism

The paradox of populism is that the people are not always populist. A people and peoplehood are hallmarks of modernity – even if their relation to democratic process is complex. Smith (2003) and Lie (2004) argue that peoplehood is germane to all nation-state projects and that coherent visions of peoplehood are necessary for coherent democratic nation-state projects. Conceptualizing populism as a process, rather than a static entity, occurring within particular historical moments, and grounding these moments in the flow of politically and socially salient events, transcend the ephemera of nomenclature that often stall discussion.

French political scientist Pascal Perrineau (1997, p. 12) has used the term "political syndrome" – signs and symptoms of large-scale social recalibration – to describe populist politics in contemporary Europe. The populist moment has emerged in the interstices of several long-term secular trends that have altered the European political landscape dramatically since 1984 where I began my narrative. Any meaningful analysis of the populist moment needs to take into account the shifting gradations of this landscape: first, the changing nature of European political parties; second, the interconnection of immigration and demographic decline; third, Europeanization, neoliberalism and the fraying of social solidarity; and

---

[23] The collection of essays in Della Porta and Tarrow (2005) provide a multifaceted view of these movements.

lastly, the emergence of Islam as a political force. These elements do not stand in direct causal relation to the emergence of a new European populism; rather, they are factors that exist in relation to each other and combine and recombine to produce a new European political, social and cultural space. The following sections briefly sketch the contours of recalibration.

The changing nature of political parties

A history of European political parties is beyond the scope of this chapter. However, certain facets of European political parties, past and present, require highlighting. In general, European political parties were nineteenth-century institutions with more or less coherent political ideologies (Eley 2002) that evolved in connection with the development of the modern nation-state (Caramani 2004). These political parties attracted relatively stable constituencies based on variable combinations of geography, religion and fairly rigid labor market positions.[24] The historical context that produced political parties also, until recently, produced remarkably stable patterns of political behavior over a relatively *longue durée* (Bartolini and Mair 1990). This is not to suggest that the same parties existed from the nineteenth century to the last twenty years of the twentieth century, but rather that the same *types* of parties with the same *types* of constituencies existed.

Signs of emerging fissures in the European political landscape include the appearance of fringe and new parties, voter apathy and electoral instability. The emergence of "fringe" political parties on the right such as the National Front, and new parties on the left such as the Greens, as well as confusion among old political parties as to their political identities, were tremors that indicated larger shocks to come.[25] The phenomenon that Patterson (2002) labels the "disappearing voter" has plagued European, as well as American, politics. Unprecedented rates of abstention on the local, national and European level have produced fluctuations in what had previously been fairly predictable electoral results.[26] In short, political

---

[24] Lipset and Rokkan (1967) is the benchmark anthology; Manza and Brooks (1999) have followed this tradition with respect to the United States.

[25] The renaming and reorganizing of the Italian Communist Party is a salient example (Kertzer 1996).

[26] Voter apathy is by no means limited to Europe. See Eliasoph (1998) for a micro-level cultural analysis of what produces such apathy in the United States that may or may not be generalizeable to the European context.

parties and politicians can no longer count on their previously taken-for-granted constituencies – or the preferences of those constituencies.[27]

The April 2002 presidential vote in France is a prominent example of this phenomenon that this book discusses in depth in later chapters. The abstention rate of 28 percent in the first round contributed to the previously unimaginable result – National Front leader Jean-Marie Le Pen in second place in the first round of voting. The fear of Le Pen actually becoming the President of France led to Jacques Chirac's reelection with 82 percent of the vote in the second round. But, electoral politics in contemporary Europe are unstable and unpredictable.[28] Two years later in the March 2004 French regional elections, public dissatisfaction with the center right led to the unexpected consequence of a Socialist Party sweep. French political scientist Dominique Reynié warned that the resurgence of the Socialist Party did not signal the end of the National Front. He argued that in some elections the National Front would continue to be the voice of French workers – it would just depend upon *which* election.[29]

One expects fluctuations in a democratic polity with free elections. What is remarkable is not that parties win and lose, but the extent to which political analysts view electoral results as unexpected and unpredictable (Swyngedouw 2000). Some of this comes from the fact that the media plays a much greater role in the dissemination of political information than it did in the past. Old-style European party politics were firmly embedded in ideological commitments and were transmitted at sites of sociability such as party cafés and festivals and in tightly knit neighborhoods and communities where everyone knew who you were and where you stood (Kohn 2003; Kertzer 1980). In short, Europe is experiencing a variation of the "end of ideology" politics that sociologist Daniel Bell (1962 [2000]) first identified in the 1960s in the United States. Third Way politics espoused by politicians of various stripes signal that European politics is experiencing not so much the "end of ideology" as the end of ideological commitment (Pasquino 2002).

---

[27] Schmitter (2001, pp. 70–72) makes the point that political parties are part of a trio that includes interest associations and social movements. In the past, political analysts privileged political parties because they did in fact translate the preferences of citizens into political outcomes. Today, there is no reason to assign them a special place in the trio.

[28] On these points, see "The Future of Parties," *Parliamentary Affairs*, special issue 58 (3) July 2005, particularly Catherine Needham's introduction (pp. 499–502), "Do Parties Have a Future?"

[29] Dominique Reynié (Interview), "La France au fond des urnes," *L'Express* March 22, 2004, pp. 52–57.

Immigration and demographic decline

Europe has always been a continent of movement for its peoples (Moch [1992] 2003). Since the beginning of the 1980s, immigration has been perceived as a political and social problem in Europe. This is in part because the character of immigration has undergone a transformation. For example, countries such as Italy that had previously been sending countries have become receiving countries in recent years.[30]

The story of contemporary European immigration is familiar. World War II created a class of European political refugees and displaced persons that put the issue of asylum on the political agendas of core European nation-states. Aside from political refugees, contemporary European immigration began in earnest in the affluent postwar period with a system of guest workers. France, Switzerland and Germany recruited guest workers from Mediterranean Europe – Italy, Spain and Portugal – to meet the demands of their flourishing postwar economies. The workers were "guests" because they came on temporary labor contracts and would return to their homelands when their work was completed. The wave of decolonialization that occurred in the 1950s and 1960s also contributed to immigrant flow within Europe. Immigrants to Great Britain were not strictly "foreign" as many were from former British colonies, as were the immigrants from North Africa who flocked to France in the 1960s. In the 1970s, immigrants from Turkey began to migrate to France and to Germany. From the perspective of the host countries, the Turkish immigration, as well as to some extent the North African immigration, was qualitatively different from the guest worker generation of immigrants. The Turkish immigrant population was relatively large, not European, Islamic and – most importantly due to family reunification policies – not returning home.[31]

The shift from European to non-European immigrants has made religion a salient and contested feature of contemporary European society and politics.[32] Muslim immigrants who are now in their second and

---

[30] Social scientists have produced an extensive literature on European immigration in all of its dimensions. Massey, Arango, Hugo *et al.* (1998, Chapter 4) provide the best short demographic summary. Although their focus is not primarily Europe, Cornelius and Rosenblum (2005) assess the political implications of immigration. The essays in Guiraudon and Lahav (2006) provide the most current summary of immigration in Europe.

[31] Brubaker (1992) and Kastoryano (2002) provide cogent accounts that contrast French and German policies toward immigrants.

[32] Bail (2008) provides a detailed analysis of the factors, including religion, that contribute to the symbolic exclusion and inclusion of immigrants in twenty-one European countries.

sometimes third generation on European soil may willingly acquire the citizenship and language of their new nation-states, but they are not willing to give up their religion. Europe with its armory of medieval churches now has to cope with the demands to build mosques in major cities.[33] An unexpected consequence of the increased presence of Muslim immigrants has been the growth of Islamic community groups that serve not only the purposes of integration but also as sites for the recruitment of extremist and dissident youth. This became increasingly urgent in the aftermath of September 11 (Zolberg 2002).

Until recently, European politicians as well as social scientists have viewed immigration and fertility as two separate issues (Livi-Bacci 2000, pp. 163–189).[34] These two structural variables increasingly shape the political development of the European Union and the labor market structures of member states. Increasing rates of immigration (legal immigration has leveled off in recent years) in the core of Europe corresponded to a decline in birth rates among the native born. In Germany and Italy, birth rates have dropped below what demographers label as "replacement" (United Nations 2000).

Rising participation rates of women in labor markets do not appear to be the principal variable contributing to declining birth rates. The majority of European nation-states (and there are exceptions) have policies that are supportive of motherhood and childbearing. Birth rates are declining independently of the level of social support for maternity – suggesting that, rather than demographic decline, there is a long-term secular trend toward "demographic refusal" among the non-immigrant populations (Teitelbaum and Winter 1998). Demographic policies, from which European politicians had distanced themselves because they evoked the eugenics and genocidal policies of the 1920s and 1930s, have begun to appear attractive to center and leftwing politicians. Declining birth rates combined with an aging population have begun to threaten the economic foundations of the European welfare state – a traditional focus of the European left (Esping-Andersen 1997).

Nation-states need replacement populations to sustain the labor force as well as to contribute to the pension funds that support the aging populations. Without replacement populations, the entire European social

---

[33] Klausen's (2005) study of Muslim elites and community leaders in six European countries takes up some of the pragmatic issues involved in creating a Europeanized Islam. Warner and Wenner (2006) provide an institutional analysis.

[34] After borders, population is the core of any territorial unit. Robust natality is essential to any nation-state project – whether it be democratic (Watkins 1991) or state socialist (Gal and Kligman 2000).

welfare system, already under siege, is in danger of collapsing. Ironically, immigrants and their communities are an important factor in salvaging the welfare state. Immigrants to established European nation-states, for cultural and economic reasons, reproduce at a higher rate than the native born. Full incorporation of immigrants on the territory, that is citizenship, will allow their participation in the types of labor markets that typically provide the tax base for the welfare state. By the year 2050, according to United Nations' (2000, p. 25) projections, over 60 percent of the populations of France, Germany and Italy will be descendants of non-native born.

Europeanization, neoliberalism and the fraying of social solidarity

Early accounts attributed the electoral emergence of rightwing politics, particularly Jean-Marie Le Pen's National Front, to xenophobia in the face of increased presence of immigrants. This claim may describe the presence of the right in the 1980s but it is a less compelling explanation for the increasing presence of the right that occurred in the 1990s.[35] There are theoretical as well as practical reasons to look beyond immigration. First, on the theoretical level as Alba and Nee (2003) have demonstrated for the American case, immigrants do over time assimilate. There is no evidence as yet to suggest that this is not, or will not be, the case in Europe today – especially in a country such as France where assimilation is the cornerstone of French Republicanism.[36] On the practical level, in the 1980s and 1990s European nation-states began to tighten borders and redefine nationality codes (Withol de Wenden 2004; Feldblum 1999).[37] Analysis of the November 2005 riots in the French *banlieues* pointed out that poverty generated by long-term unemployment among second- and, in some instances, third-generation immigrant youth fueled the violence.[38]

Illegal immigration, rather than immigration *sui generis*, has become the pressing transnational issue. Particularly problematic was the issue of political asylum and the claiming of refugee status in the absence of human rights violations.[39] In the spring of 2002, the European Commission issued a Green Paper with the intent of combating illegal

---

[35] Many of these studies written in the 1990s were based on data collected in the 1980s.

[36] On the perception of assimilation, among French working-class men, see Lamont (2000, pp. 178–198).

[37] Weil (2002) provides the definitive history of nationality law in France.

[38] For brief, contemporaneous accounts and commentary, see "The Riots in France" www.ssrc.org.

[39] Levy (2005) provides a comprehensive introduction to the issues of asylum and human rights in the post 9/11 period.

immigration which was at an all-time high. While, as Schain (1996) argues, the National Front helped to put immigration on the French political agenda, immigration and movement have always been a part of European political cultural (Zolberg 2002).

Sniderman *et al.*'s study (2000) of anti-immigrant sentiment in contemporary Italy, *The Outsider*, is a suggestive corrective to studies that suggest that immigrants and xenophobia always go hand in hand. As a terrain new to immigration but not to color prejudice (Italians viewed Southern Italians as non-white), Italy was the ideal research venue to develop an "integrated" account of why groups become prejudiced against other groups. Contrary to Sniderman *et al.*'s expectations, race did not seem to matter in the Italian case. Bluntly put, Italians disliked Eastern Europeans more than sub-Saharan Africans. The initial findings suggested prejudice was more a perception than a fact of difference.

To interpret results that were at first puzzling, Sniderman and his collaborators developed a "Two Flavors Model" of prejudice. The first "flavor" drew upon psychological accounts of prejudice that were long out of favor in studies of race and ethnicity. The focus on social psychology, Sniderman *et al.* argued, needed to be refined, rather than abandoned. This refinement required a "second flavor" with a more rational taste. Prejudice would reflect an instrumental group struggle over scarce societal resources, that is, we dislike immigrants because they take our jobs. Both "flavors" rely on categorization – who is like us and who is not – but with an important caveat. At any given historical moment, differences of race, ethnicity, nationality or whatever are always more or less present in a modern society.

Exogenous shocks to the social, economic and political system transform difference from a social fact to a social exacerbation. This transformation of the social weight of difference has the potential (as is shown in contemporary Europe) to contribute to the parliamentary success of rightwing parties that organized around it. Sniderman *et al.*'s data further showed that ordinary constituents of the leftwing and rightwing parties may espouse different ideological positions but they share a common commitment to authority. When exogenous threats to the system occur, most people, independently of the ideological labels they espouse, are likely to retreat to "authority," or, more colloquially put, pleas for law and order. The political party that exploits that commitment, whether leftwing or rightwing, is likely to garner electoral support.

If, as Sniderman *et al.* suggest, exogenous, rather than endogenous, shocks tend to create the forms of insecurity that give rise to xenophobia, then the tendency to categorize others as different, agents of dis-order, is likely to increase, not decrease, in contemporary Europe.[40] Drawing on this perspective, we can view Europeanization, the term that encapsulates the accelerated process of European integration, as an exogenous shock that produces such issues as threats to nationality, unemployment and even crime that fuel social unrest, as well as fear and insecurity.[41]

Europe today is more than simply a cognitive frame for fear. Europe as a political and cultural entity is a far more salient reality today than it was in 1984 or 1994. Recent work on public opinion has shown that Euroskepticism and anti-immigrant sentiment are highly correlated (Lahav 2004). This is not surprising but it does not explain why they are correlated. As of January 1, 2002, Europe acquired a single currency. On May 1, 2004, Europe expanded its member states, including eight countries from the former Eastern Europe. On January 1, 2007, Romania and Bulgaria joined the European Union – bringing its total membership to twenty-seven nation-states.

As of June 18, 2004, Europe had a constitution in draft. Less than a year later, in spring 2005, the constitution suffered a defeat after popular referenda in France and the Netherlands rejected it.[42] A week after the constitution's apparent setback, political scientist Andrew Moravcsik, writing in the *Financial Times* (June 13, 2005), argued that the constitution was unnecessary and that Europe could continue its institutional development "without the grand illusion[s]" of citizens' support. While Moravcsik was correct in his assessment that it was difficult to excite the citizenry about a bureaucratic document, he underestimated the broader significance of the popular rejection of the constitution in France and the Netherlands. Three years later, on June 12, 2008, the Irish electorate rejected a revised version of the constitution, the Lisbon Treaty. Despite the best efforts of European political elites, the people – when asked to decide – often decided against Europeanization.

---

[40] Berezin (2006d) draws on Sniderman *et al.*'s analysis to discuss the relation between xenophobia and "new" nationalisms in Europe.

[41] Borneman and Fowler (1997) provide the best short discussion of the process of Europeanization. Jürgen Habermas presents a strong counter-position that Europe is a space of cosmopolitan democracy. This is an important position that this book implicitly engages because it focuses on empirical events that suggest that Europe is not a wellspring of toleration. On May 7, 2005, Habermas published an essay in French in *Nouvel Observateur* warning of the dangers of voting no on the European constitution in the French referendum and chiding the left for advocating a no position. The English translation, Jürgen Habermas, "The Illusionary 'Leftist No': Adopting the Constitution to Strengthen Europe's Power to Act," appeared on the website www.signandsight.com/features/163.html.

[42] The French vote took place on May 29, 2005; the Dutch vote on June 1, 2005.

Europe and the institutional redesign that it mandates are driving sectoral changes at an ever accelerating pace. Neoliberalism and accompanying globalization, permanently wed French *bêtes noires* (Gordon and Meunier 2001), are rewriting the postwar European social contract. Europeanization is arguably a variant of globalization. Anti-globalization activists on the left vociferously shout – "Another Europe is possible." Anti-globalization and anti-Europeanization are not solely issues for the left. In the 2005 campaign to vote "Non" on the European constitution in France, the extreme left and extreme right were virtually united – voting 95 percent and 96 percent respectively against the constitution.[43]

Whether left or right, the meaning of social solidarity is undergoing transformation in the European case. Significantly, "neither left nor right" has become a staple of European political (and sometimes academic) discourse.[44] The norms of reciprocity and trust among peoples who were (or became) fundamentally like each other created the European nation-states that are mutating if not entirely dissolving. The assortment of phenomena that populism embraces as its own is a *cri de coeur* over social assumptions that were hard won and developed in the nineteenth century, fully institutionalized in the twentieth century – but that appear to be approaching obsolescence in the twenty-first century.

---

[43] "Référendum: la question sociale au coeur du refus," *Le Monde* (Paris) May 5, 2005.

[44] For example, Giddens (1994) wrote *Beyond Left and Right*. He followed this with *The Third Way* (1998), which was a plea for a new form of social democracy. The irony that these phrases served as rallying cries for the interwar European right could not have escaped Giddens.

2

Experience and events: reformulating the rightwing populist moment

Why reformulate?

The terms "rightwing" and "populist" either combined or individually tend to conjure up images of racist violence, xenophobic extremism, neo-Nazi skinheads and charismatic politicians with authoritarian tendencies. These images, while undeniably real, are only partial illuminations of a complex political and social landscape. The rhetoric and sometimes colorful antics of rightwing party leaders such as Jean-Marie Le Pen in France, the late Jörg Haider in Austria and the late Pim Fortuyn in the Netherlands distract from the fundamental social fact that the right in all its national variation has become part of a normal electoral presence in several European nation-states.[1]

As Chapter 1 described, rightwing parties were a marginal feature of European politics for much of the post-World War II period.[2] Three features of the current rightwing populist moment suggest deeper salience and set it apart from its postwar iterations: first, electoral results for the right are quite variable which suggests that analyses that focus strictly on the role of minority parties have limited explanatory value; second, the rightwing populist moment points to the existence of broader social problems that just happen to manifest themselves in the political arena, that is,

---

[1] Eatwell (2002) takes the position that the "charisma" of the leader is a factor in the political success of contemporary rightwing movements and parties.

[2] The electoral success of European rightwing populist parties has reawakened social science interest in *historical fascism* (for example, Prowe 1994; Paxton 2004; Mann 2004). Precise conceptualization eluded past exegeses of historical fascism (see literature discussion, e.g. Berezin 1997a, pp. 11–29; Berezin 2007a). Theories that were inconclusive in the 1950s are not likely to serve as useful starting points for contemporary analysis. Mann (2004) has recently helped to clarify many of the ambiguities in past approaches to fascism by specifying an affinity between a weak state aspiring to strength and groups who view a developing state as a source of political and social opportunity.

voting behavior signals rightwing populism's existence but does not define it; third, rightwing populism is a trans-European political phenomenon that manifests itself variably among different nation-states and in different political moments within those nation-states.

The principal task of this chapter is to specify the conceptual parameters of an alternative approach to the right that informs the narrative of the National Front and the contrasting Italian case. After discussing the rationale, the "why," for a reformulation of the right, this chapter moves forward in three stages. First, it provides a synthesis of prevailing social science approaches to the right that explores their strengths and limitations. Second, this chapter lays out the analytic contours of an alternative account that is interdisciplinary and historical, and draws from cultural and political sociology. Building upon the literature on nationhood, political institutions and identities, this chapter develops a concept of *national experience* (as articulated in the Introduction) and *consolidation regime* that speaks to the political effects of the relation between a people and a polity. Third, this chapter proposes a methodological shift from a variable-centered to an event-centered approach to the right. *Events*, I suggest, are public sites of collectively recognized social, political and cultural salience that involve cross-cutting constituencies.

From party to polity: recasting the analytic angle of vision

The official beginning of Jean-Marie Le Pen's 2007 presidential election bid provides an entry to the analytic reformulation that follows. On September 20, 2006, Jean-Marie Le Pen announced that he would become a candidate in the 2007 French presidential election in Valmy – the town where, on September 20, 1792, French troops drove back the Austrians and secured the revolution. On the day after the battle of Valmy, the National Assembly abolished the monarchy and proclaimed the First French Republic. Because of its connection to the revolution, Valmy has meaning in French political and national culture.

Le Pen's speech identified the battle of Valmy as the "last victory of the monarchy, the first victory of the Republic."[3] If he became President of France, Le Pen promised that he would restore the Republic of the revolution which was under threat from globalization, Europeanization, multiculturalism and, not least of all, French politicians. Le Pen closed his

---

[3] www.frontnational.com/doc_interventions_detail.php?id_inter=43 (accessed March 21, 2007).

speech with the proclamation: "Yes, all of us, not only the native born or naturalized French, but the French of heart and spirit, we can reconstitute tomorrow, in a great spirit of national union, that odd army of soldiers of Valmy assembled around the same idea – of France, which is first an idea – that of the Republic, one and indivisible, proud of its history and assimilated, respectful of liberty and solicitous of the lowly, and above all in love with justice and equality, that of the Republic, according to our Constitution: Secular, Democratic and Social."

Pundits, intellectuals and politicians of all stripes proclaimed that Le Pen's choice of Valmy to open his campaign was a provocation. The media declared that Le Pen violated everything for which the French Republic stood and that he had no right to usurp its symbols.[4] Political scientist and expert on the National Front, Pascal Perrineau struck a more sanguine note when he told *Le Monde* that it was not unusual for politicians of various ideological persuasions to invoke French political symbols.[5]

Le Pen's choice elicited hostile response and public outcry because Valmy was more than simply a material symbol – such as the flag, or the Bastille, or Marianne. Valmy invoked the tradition of Republicanism that signaled a historically specific relation between a people and a polity that political and cultural elites institutionalized in the nineteenth century and that had endured throughout the twentieth. The relationship between people and polity is not unique to France. Every modern nation-state institutionalized a relation between its people and its polity even if they did so at different times and in different ways.

Modern political parties developed in parallel with the nation-state (Caramani 2004; Bartolini and Mair 1990). Independent of their national specificity and ideological particularity, whether left, right or center, political parties shared the common task of mediating between the people and the polity. Standard analyses of the rightwing populist moment typically focus upon the rightwing political parties and assign little analytic status to the relation between people and polity that political parties mediate. For the most part, political scientists have defined the analytic approaches to the rightwing populist moment. The tenor of these approaches is positivist and concentrates narrowly on survey data that tap into political attitudes, voting behavior and party strategy. While there is much of value in these

---

[4] Jean-Baptiste de Montvalon, "Jean-Marie Le Pen accommode à sa façon le symbole républicain de Valmy" Le Monde.fr (accessed September 21, 2006).
[5] If Perrineau had been a cultural sociologist, he might have pointed out that Valmy was a plastic political symbol – infinitely malleable to fit a multiplicity of meanings.

approaches, there is also much that they do not capture.[6] In short, a narrative that explores why Europe is experiencing a rightwing populist moment is available only in attenuated form.

A cogent and nuanced account of rightwing populism requires *both* analytic *and* methodological reformulation. An analytic lens focused on the legacy of the relation between people and polity that parties mediate serves as a scaffold for a reformulation that is conceptually novel and theoretically rigorous. Historically sensitive conceptual terms that we apply to other forms of politics – such as nation, state, democracy, identity – capture the legacy of the relation between a people and a polity and open an interpretive window on the rightwing populist moment.[7] Legacies speak to content and history; relations speak to formal processes. Combining the historical and the formal allows for two analytic advantages. First, the historical grounds the rightwing populist moment in the particular moment that it emerges in the interstices of the democratic nation-state. Second, the formal renders transparent the social mechanisms underlying modern democracy. Specifically, the combination of historical and relational permits us to specify analytically, as well as empirically, the processes that come into play that relate increasing Europeanization and the rightwing populist moment.

Comparing social science approaches to the contemporary European right

The literature on the contemporary European right, as well as the right itself, eludes easy definition and categorization. In general, analytic approaches to the contemporary right are predicated on *thick* commitments. For this reason, they do not account well for *thin* commitments. This section assesses the various approaches and attempts to demarcate their strengths and weaknesses (see summary Table 2.1).

---

[6] For example, see the essays collected in Perrineau (2001) and Schain *et al.* (2002). Mudde (2007) ends his exhaustive account of the European right on a pessimistic note. He claims that there have been no conceptual advances in the study of the right since the 1990s and concludes: "One of the main hindrances towards further progress is the lack of originality in terms of approaches, cases, data, and methods. If this book has at least triggered some interest in exploring new venues and breaking out of the more comfortable studies of the usual suspect on the basis of the usual data sets, it has achieved its aims" (p. 304).

[7] By "historical" and "historically sensitive" I do not mean to imply that the right today is a continuation of the right in 1920s' and 1930s' Europe. Nor do I wish to suggest that history is about to repeat itself. "Historical" underscores the national context and institutions in which the right is embedded. Somers (1995) captures this process in what she labels "a historical sociology of concept formation."

Table 2.1 *Analytic approaches to the new European right*

	Institutional			Cultural		
	T1	T2	T3	T4	T5	T6
	Organization	Agenda setting	Labor market	Post-materialist	*Ressentiment*	Legacy
Core assumptions	Bureaucratic rationality	Political rationality	Economic rationality	Values	Emotion fear/ anger	History memory
Parameters	Strategy efficiency	Legitimacy	Welfare	Anomie or commitment	Prejudice scapegoating	Power of the past
Expectations from theory	Efficient party organizations = electoral success/ capacity to form coalitions	Rightwing party raises issues ahead of mainstream parties	Employment data correlated with support	Fluctuation in political preferences	Fear of immigrants correlated with rightwing support	*Parties appear in same venue as 1930s*
Explains	Regional success	Political salience of issues	Correlation	Instability	Correlation xenophobia	Tradition
Does not account for	National success	Public perception	Why a leftwing response does not develop	Extreme nationalism	Social mechanism absent	Past does not map onto present-day parties

Recently, political scientists (for example, Eatwell 2003; Rydgren 2007) have synthesized the available literature on the contemporary right along the analytic axes of "supply" and "demand." "Supply" variables describe the availability of a rightwing party, and "demand" variables speak to voter characteristics and preferences. In contrast, this chapter uses "institutions" and "culture" as analytic axes on the grounds that they capture nuances and empirical complexities in the existing literature that the "supply" and "demand" axes tend to miss. The cultural classification encompasses meaning in the broadest sense – although some of the approaches are psychological, others are historical. The legal system underlies institutional approaches.

The assumption of rational calculation defines the institutional category that encompasses organization, agenda setting and labor market approaches. Cultural approaches, on the other hand, assume non-rationality and include theories based upon post-materialist values, *ressentiment* and historical legacy. The concept of rationality deployed here is broadly Weberian, in that it assumes that instrumental rationality is congruent with behavior oriented toward a goal. Thus, a means–end link is the basis of the causal flow of action on the part of either individuals or collectivities. Whereas non-rational implies behavior oriented toward a value or sentiment.

Organization theories that deal with the right have an implicit notion of efficiency built into them as they prioritize strategy. The choice theoretic variation of these theories assumes that marginality is a mark of strength and not weakness. Political scientists examine the logic of rightwing party coalitions and focus upon the right's ability to become strategic players in electoral politics (Meguid 2005; Givens 2005; Norris 2005). Organizational approaches tend to describe the right as "radical" and to discuss this political phenomenon in terms of "anti-statist" parties. Organization theories do a good job of explaining the regional success of rightwing parties because they can point to the intersection of local-level bargaining and political strategy. They provide a conceptual framework for analyzing the reasons that mainstream parties on the local level would be willing to enter into bargaining coalitions with the right. Organization theories do a less good job of explaining rightwing success and failure in national elections where electoral breakthroughs have occurred.

Agenda setting approaches assume political rationality with an underlying normative critique. The argument is that the "right" is garnering political legitimacy by bringing marginal issues into the electoral arena ahead of mainstream political parties (Schain 1987). Agenda setting theories confuse issues of perception and timing and conflate causes with effects. For example, in the case of France, the French state placed immigration on its agenda before the National Front identified it as a political issue (Schor 1985). Agenda setting approaches, when deployed in this context, assume that Europeans are becoming less tolerant and more xenophobic. However, the empirical evidence contradicts this assumption. For example, Lamont's (2000) research shows a complex interaction between civility and exclusion among French and North African workers. Agenda setting theories capture the salience of political issues for the citizenry writ large, the spreading *thinness*, not *thickness*, of political commitments, rather than an increasing rightward turn of the populace.

Long-term sectoral changes in the class structure of post-industrial society have structured labor market explanations of the rise of the right (Betz 1994; Ignazi 1994a; 2003; Kitschelt 1995). These arguments assume that inefficiencies in the labor market and subsequent unemployment due to structural obsolescence lead to the propensity to vote for a rightwing party.[8] Among these studies, Kitschelt's (1995) political economy model of rightwing success is the most influential. He argues that the new occupational structure of post-industrial society has pushed traditional left/rightwing parties toward an undifferentiated center and left behind an ideological void that "extremists" fill. He also assumes that the right is a proponent of free market capitalism – an assumption that as Schain (1997) and Ivarsflaten (2005) pointed out does not fit the French case. Holmes (2000) approaches labor market theories from the disciplinary perspective of anthropology. Rather than focus on the structure of employment markets, Holmes argues that it is capitalism itself, the "fast capitalism" of globalization, that has given rise to rightwing impulses across the European continent. Holmes' study focuses on the French National Front, the Italian Northern League and British skinheads.

Labor market theories assume economic rationality; *ressentiment* theories assume emotional rationality, that is, fear of immigrants leads to support for the right. The German philosopher and social theorist Max Scheler ([1915] 1992) identified *ressentiment* as a problematic social emotion in pre-World War I European society. Betz (1993; 1994) was the first to appropriate the concept to discuss the European right. Others have employed various iterations of the idea. Crudely put, *ressentiment* as a social concept posits that losers in the competition over scarce social goods and material resources respond in frustration with diffuse emotions of

---

[8] Klausen (1999) is not primarily interested in the right but she points to the obsolescence of male workers and the gendering of the European labor market. These men made redundant by structural change presumably form a core of the constituency of rightwing parties.

anger, fear and, in the extreme case, hatred. *Ressentiment* theories fall under the rubric of behavioral approaches to politics that studies of political attitudes and voting behavior capture.

While labor market theories are structural and *ressentiment* theories are psychological and emotional, they share the assumption that an observed correlation between unemployment and immigration is causal with respect to rightwing ascendance. *Ressentiment* theories relate to class-based theories of political behavior that look to characteristics of groups of persons (such as Lipset's "working-class authoritarianism") who seem to be attracted to rightwing parties. For example, Mayer ([1999] 2002) has developed profiles of typical French National Front supporters and mapped how these profiles have changed over time. Klandermans and Mayer (2006) have recently developed profiles of extreme rightwing activists in diverse national venues.

The relation between xenophobia and immigration policy has dominated labor market and *ressentiment* approaches to the European right (for example, Schain 1996; Lafont 2001; Karapin 2002; Jackman and Volpert 1996). The fall 2005 and 2007 riots in the *banlieues* of Paris remind us that increased numbers of unemployed and disenfranchised second- and third-generation immigrants present a social problem. Xenophobia is a contingent and not a necessary response to the social problems that immigrants pose. Labor market theories establish a correlation between the presence of the right and unemployment. They fail to account for why a hyper-nationalist movement should be the outcome of the fear of unemployment. Widespread unemployment could as easily trigger a reinvigorated European left as an emergent European right.

The contradictions in accepting a correlation between support for the right and fear of unemployment as causal emerged in spring 2005 when the French turned down the European constitution in a national referendum. Parties of the extreme left and right, coupled with Socialist Party defectors, voted "No" to the constitution. Fear of unemployment was the leading reason that voters gave for their decision. *Ressentiment* theories share the weakness of labor market theories in that they predict a correlation but fail to predict an action. They also fail to take into account that studies have demonstrated that the presence of immigrants, xenophobic sentiments and a vibrant local right do not always map perfectly onto each other (for example, Quillian 1995).

Cultural theories that pertain to the right focus on the non-rational elements of political behavior (Antonio 2000). Drawing inspiration from Inglehart's (1977) concept of post-materialist values and new social movements theory, analysts describe the right as protest parties and movements with anti-system goals that are not easily identified as leftwing or rightwing (for example, Kriesi 1999). Party family is another term that analysts working in this mode employ. Cultural theories sometimes echo mass society theory from the 1940s as they focus on persons who due to the dislocation of advanced capitalism become anomic and feel an attraction for political parties and movements that offer certainty. For example, Perrineau (1997) describes the French National Front as a "political syndrome."

In sum, organization and agenda setting approaches, based on different forms of means–end rationality, are formal theories that fail to capture the content of politics as they are equally applicable to leftwing, rightwing or center parties. Labor market and *ressentiment* approaches point to correlations between social phenomena but fall short of explaining the social mechanisms behind those correlations. Post-materialism describes a political reality but does not account for left/rightwing variation. It identifies anomie or commitment fluctuation as well as accounting for a variety of political parties. Post-materialism describes the instability of political preferences but it does not capture the form that those preferences take. In short, the post-material claim does not account well for extreme nationalism.

National experience: the legacy of a relation between people and polity

Legacy theories that invoke the power of the past fall under the classification of "cultural" approaches. The typical form of the argument is that nation-states that had fascist regimes and movements in the past are more likely to have fascist-type parties and movements again. Art's (2006) study that focuses upon how German and Austrian politicians use national memory to influence public debate is a notable exception to this general tendency.[9] Legacies have been somewhat discredited as causal mechanisms. Analysts tend to invoke them if only to dismiss them (Kitschelt 1995, pp. 203–239; Eatwell 2003, pp. 62–63; Martin 1996, pp. 25–28; Capoccia 2004, pp. 83–107). Legacy theories that suggest that the past will repeat itself are empirically weak as contemporary rightwing parties and movements do not map neatly onto interwar rightwing parties and movements.

Yet, as the beginning of this chapter argues, legacies have value but not as a simple one-to-one mapping of the past onto the present. A robust

---

[9] Art (2008) shifts his angle of vision to explicitly theorize historical legacies.

account of the rightwing populist moment that incorporates the acceleration of *thin* commitments requires an approach that is historical – meaning an account that situates the right in the broader social and political changes outlined in Chapter 1. The "legacy" that matters in thinking about the rightwing populist moment is not the power of a narrowly specified past – whether or not a country had a fascist party or regime – but the legacy of the particular national iteration of the relation between people and polity.

This analysis conceptualizes nation-states as *consolidation regimes* as well as locations of individual and collective *national experience*. Geographically situated and territorially bound – even in a transnational context – nation-states are material entities. Nation-states are also experiential entities, that is, they give cultural form to collective interpretations of the past and evaluations of the future. Alterations in the configuration of the nation-state such as the expansion of European integration pose challenges; national experience affects whether those challenges appear as threats or opportunities. The next section discusses the political implications of national experience and sketches the contours of a consolidation regime, the heuristic that informs the empirical analysis in the book.

Calhoun (2007) has recently reminded us that "nations matter." Amending Calhoun's exhortation to include the state is particularly urgent within the context of Europeanization. Nation-states matter, not because they have intrinsic merit as a form of political organization, but because they are constituted as moral ontologies, collectively defined ways of being in the world, as well as political categories. Moral ontology is a shorthand term for the body of unspoken assumptions that nation-states deploy to address the normative issues that they regularly encounter as they organize political and social security for their members. Citizenship law defines and limits membership in the nation-state and confers rights as well as obligations on members.[10] Events such as the French, followed by the Dutch, rejection of the 2004 draft of a European constitution, suggest that the expanding project of European integration challenges the moral, as well as

---

[10] Marshall (1964) provides the classic account of modern citizenship that Somers (1993) among others has challenged. For a summary and critique of the burgeoning literature, see Turner (2001). On the problems that transnationalism and globalization pose to citizenship rights, see Kymlicka (1995) and Sassen (2006). Non-members, such as immigrants, may make claims on the state (Koopmans and Statham 1999; Soysal 1997) but have limited rights.

political, authority of individual European nation-states as well as the social and emotional security of citizens.[11]

Nation-state: the "daily plebiscite"

Max Weber's ([1922] 1978) ideal type of "political community" (pp. 901–926) provides a vocabulary from which to begin to theorize why changes in the form of the polity, such as those that Europeanization presents, might pose a collective challenge. According to Weber, "political community" is not reducible to economics (i.e., market activity) or politics (i.e., territorial control); rather it is a form of association that governs social actions among "inhabitants of the territory" who share culture and bonds of solidarity. The "belief in group affinity" that creates a sense of "ethnic honor" and "sentiments of likeness" (pp. 389, 390) is crucial to the formation of political community. In practice, a common language and a monopoly on closure, both territorial and cultural, are the vehicles of honor, sentiment and community, as well as national sovereignty and power. The willingness to sacrifice one's life for one's community based on the belief in a fictive collective past imbues the "political community" with its "enduring emotional foundations" (p. 909). "Political communities" wherever they form are powerful emotional collectivities. Weber never argued that the modern state harnessed the emotional energy of the political community, but it is a useful analytic leap to make when discussing the political development of historically specific nation-states.[12]

Nation-states were the political and cultural projects that characterized the nineteenth- and twentieth-century polity.[13] They are modern and they

---

[11] Pérez-Díaz (1993) and Miller (1995) among others make the argument that the nation-state has a moral or ethical imperative as well as a purely bureaucratic function. Much of the discussion of the nation-state in Europe and beyond has focused on it as an epistemology – a category of political governance – and has taken the form of whether or not the nation-state has "declined" (see, for example, Mann 1997; Weiss 1998; Paul *et al.* 2003) in the wake of a "new world order" (Slaughter 2004) or regionalization (Katzenstein 2005).

[12] See Spillman and Faeges (2005) for an alternative Weberian reading of "nations."

[13] The discussion of the state and nationalism has a long history. In the 1980s, social scientists turned their attention to the formation of the state (for example, the essays in Evans *et al.* 1985). By the 1990s, interest in the state was rechanneled into a focus on institutions as mediating organizations. "New" institutionalists focused their attention on laws, associations and public policy. March and Olsen (1989) wrote the landmark article on "new institutionalism." See Clemens and Cook (1999), Hall and Taylor (1996), Immergut (1998) and Thelen (1999), who provide analytic summaries of debates and theories. State theorists and "new" institutionalists tended to macro- and meso-level structural analysis. Historical events forced culture to the forefront of social science analysis. The resurgence of ethnic chauvinism in the former Eastern Europe post-1989 fueled an interest in nationalism (for example, Calhoun 1997) and national identity (for example, Kumar 2005) as a category of experience.

are Western in the sense that they flourished in post-1789 Europe.[14] The term "project" signals the dynamic nature of the process that governed political development. Two features of this project deserve emphasis in view of the arguments that this book advances. First, the modern nation-state is the end result of two processes – a nation-building and a state-building process – which developed along separate and sometimes overlapping trajectories. With the exception of Italy and Germany, much of the state building took place in the eighteenth century and much of the culture building took place in the nineteenth century (Ziblatt 2006). The modern nation-state is a marriage of culture and structure. Second, modern nation-states do not have to be democratic. There is no necessary correlation between the form of the state and the type of governance. Procedurally democratic nation-states can engage in practices that might not ordinarily be associated with democracy – what Zakaria (2003) labeled as "illiberal democracy" and Holmes (1993) defined as "antiliberalism." In short, democratic institutions and democratic sentiments do not always cohere.

The state is a modern technology of rule governed by bureaucratic rationality. As a political form, the rational bureaucratic state accommodates a range of political ideologies and regimes.[15] States may be efficient or inefficient, the trains may or may not run on time, but they are a modern and Western apparatus of political organization. The nation-state until recently has been the principal vehicle to give form to modern politics. Much of the emphasis in the literature on state making has been on territorial consolidation through either war (Tilly 1985) or networks of elites (Mann 1993).[16]

The networks of elites who promoted the modern state understood that cultural consolidation was a necessity for political consolidation. Communities of people who were like each other (or who thought that they were like each other) were essential to providing the emotional identification that encouraged individuals to pay taxes and to go to war in the name of the state. The cultural community of the nation provided that reason. Cultural consolidation was secular in that it aimed to break the moral authority of religion and replace it with the moral and legal authority of

---

[14] Bell (2001), Greenfeld (1992) and Gorski (2003) among others argue that nationalism existed prior to 1789, but there is a distinction between nationalism and nation-states.

[15] Again, this is a strictly Weberian conception of the term "rationality." Weber ([1927] 1981, pp. 338–351) identifies the "rational state" as a purely Western form of political organization.

[16] See Ikegami (2005) for examples of a non-Western case; Centeno (2002) for a Latin American study.

the state. In practice this meant controlling the power of the Catholic Church or absorbing Protestant Churches into the state structure.[17] Benedict Anderson's (1983 [1991]) "imagined community" was based on linguistic consolidation and the establishment of a vernacular facilitated by a material advance – the invention of the printing press.

The nation was not merely an imaginary entity. It was as Renan in his classic essay "What is a Nation?" argues, "a large-scale solidarity, constituted by the feeling of the sacrifices that one has made in the past and of those that one is prepared to make in the future. It presupposes a past; it is summarized, however, in the present by a tangible fact, namely, consent, the clearly expressed desire to continue a common life. A nation's existence is ... a daily plebiscite, just as an individual's existence is a perpetual affirmation of life."[18] In short, national experience is a committed and committing phenomenon, a part of daily life that lies dormant within the collective and individual consciousness – until an internal or external force threatens that experience and makes it manifest.

Consolidation regimes: describing the fit between the state and the national culture

Every European nation-state accomplished political and cultural consolidation in different time periods and with different degrees of "fit" between culture and the polity. In formal terms, the nation-state is a dyad linked by territorial consolidation on the one hand and cultural consolidation on the other (Berezin 1999b). In practice, nation and state, culture and structure, are enmeshed inextricably. But, separating the nation and the state is an analytic move that provides conceptual leverage. It lends clarity to the issue of Europeanization, where scholars often discuss institutions and identities as if they were independent of each other, It permits rigorous conceptualization that may be brought to bear upon the relation between rightwing populism and the advancing European project.

This section unpacks the nation/state dyad. By breaking up what is a deeply contextual and dynamic process into formal components, it allows us to think analytically about the relation between the state and the

---

[17] Ozouf (1963) and Curtis (2000) document the relation between school and Church for France.
[18] Renan ([1882] 1996, p. 53).

Table 2.2 *Consolidation regimes (analytic heuristic)*

State-nation relation	Consolidation regime type	Dominant collective identity	Vulnerabilities	Cases
Strong state / strong nation	*Hegemonic*	National (unique or consociational)	External threat	France, Netherlands
Strong state / weak nation	*Flexible*	Sub-national (multiple)	Internal conflict	Italy, Spain
Weak state / weak nation	*Brittle*	Sub-national (ethnic)	Internal conflict and external threat	Former Soviet Union and Eastern Bloc countries

Strong state: Established parliamentary democracies. A state in the process of transition, or that is engaged in building new institutions, would fall into the conceptual category of "weak."
Strong nation: In the context of the polity, national cultures are "strong" or "weak" to the degree that the "political community" has subsumed ethnic and regional cultures and enforced a single national language.

culture.[19] If we approach the nation-state as a dyad, then either of its component parts – state or nation – can be more or less strong (Table 2.2). In this context, the term "strong state" refers to established parliamentary democracies and does not speak to its efficiency or form. Any state in the process of transition, or that is engaged in building new institutions, would fall into the conceptual category of "weak."[20] In the context of the polity, national cultures are "strong" or "weak" to the degree that the "political community" has subsumed ethnic and regional cultures and enforced a single national language.

Nation-state conceived as a dyad presents four possible combinations: first, strong state/strong nation; second, strong state/weak nation; third, strong nation/weak state; and fourth, weak state/weak nation. All categories require qualification. The strong/weak distinction suggests a degree of "fit" from tightly to loosely coupled between state and nation – culture and

[19] While many scholars have looked at nation through nationalism and state structures, the field of scholars who have taken the historical approach and looked at nation-states as processes is relatively limited. The field of scholarship is restricted and France dominates, see, for example, Weber (1976), Brubaker (1992) and Hazareesingh (1998). Berezin (1997a, b) has analyzed this in the case of the non-democratic instance, fascist Italy. For a recent account of the Soviet Union, see Hirsch (2005).
[20] Moravcsik (2000c) uses different language to make a similar distinction in his discussion of "human rights regimes."

organization. *Consolidation regime* as a term captures the process of territorial and cultural consolidation that the "fit" describes.

Weak state/weak nation is a pre-modern category as modern persons do not live outside of institutions and culture. If we exclude it from discussion, three possibilities for consolidation regimes exist. A tight fit between culture and the state (strong state/strong nation) implies strong national identities with a state institutional structure that supports those identities. Hegemonic consolidation regimes suggest that the territorial and cultural trajectories coalesce. However, the paths to coalescence will vary depending upon the specific nation-state. This configuration is internally adaptable, but is susceptible to external threats. France is the paradigmatic case of constructed hegemonic consolidation, although, as Eugen Weber (1976) discusses, "peasants" did not "become Frenchmen" until much after territorial consolidation. Ethnically and linguistically homogeneous nation-states such as Sweden (Ringmar 1996) followed different processes than multilingual France. Consociations that have legislated the existence of multiple national cultures (i.e., Switzerland) or religions (i.e., the Netherlands) also fall under this rubric.

A loose fit between culture and the state (weak national culture/strong state) implies weak national identities, with a state structure that does not at least initially support strong identity-forming institutions, that is, school, national language. This is not to say that the polity lacks identities (or for that matter schools or a national language) just that all identities are not exclusively tied to the national state. Extra-national identities may be tied to religion or region. Flexible consolidation regimes are internally less coherent and given to internal conflict, but externally flexible and much more able than hegemonic consolidation regimes to respond to external threats or exogenous factors. Flexible consolidation regimes are susceptible to separatist movements. Italy and Spain fall into this category.

Hegemonic and flexible consolidation regimes describe states where modern political institutions are in place, and it is only the relation to the national culture that varies. The fit between nation and state, culture and polity in established states is the focus of this analysis, so the distinction between hegemonic and flexible consolidation regimes is one of degree on a continuum. These types of regimes are the principal focus of this book, but it is worthwhile for analytic reasons to examine the third strand of the conceptualization. A strong ethnic culture tied to a weak or developing state yields a brittle consolidation regime that has the potential for strong internal conflict (particularly if the territorial state is not ethnically homogeneous), as well as violence and, in the extreme, genocide. Brittle consolidation regimes are also subject to intervention from external states. This category captures the former states of Eastern Europe as well as the former Soviet Union.

Secure states: identity practice and the adjudication of risk

The above section focused upon how the polity situates citizens within it. This section focuses upon how citizens situate themselves within the polity. Its principle focus is to theorize why the relation between people and polity is substantively consequential. It shifts attention to the conditions under which citizens feel heightened identification with the polity, in this instance the modern nation-state. The "business of identity," to borrow from Poggi (1978), is a component feature of the "business of rule." The strength or weakness of national identity is one measure of the degree of fit between a national culture and the state. Scholars of identity, social constructivists (for example, Brubaker and Cooper 2000; Cerulo 1997; Somers 1994), psychologists (Tajfel 1981), modified essentialists who emphasize emotion (Suny 2001) and political scientists (Abdelal *et al.* 2006) tend to view identity as a property of individuals or groups. The discussion that follows continues an approach to identity developed in earlier work (Berezin 1997a; 1999a, b; 2001; 2003) that views identity (whether national or otherwise) as located between the constructed and the emotional. There are three features to identity that are salient for political cultural analysis: first, identity is a bifocal concept; second, law is constitutive of identity; and third, identities are contingent.

Identity is a bifocal concept. Identity has the dimension of "identified as," a categorical or epistemological concept, as well as "identifying with," an ontological or emotional concept. Identity in both dimensions maps onto the nation-state dyad. Scholars, even the most perceptive, often conflate "identified as" and "identified with" leading to conceptual as well as terminological slippage. Law is constituent of identity because it creates the categories of "identified as." In the case of the nation-state, national constitutions defined the parameters of the state. National citizenship was the standard legal mechanism that nation-states used to bind individuals to the polity and to bridge the gap between a categorical conception of identity and an emotional attachment (Marshall 1964). Language consolidation was essential to creating the citizens who could communicate with each other and who were a potentially receptive audience for the political communications of the nation-state (Deutsch 1953).

"Theatre states" – to borrow Geertz's (1980) felicitous term – were necessary to the extent that societies were pre-literate or quasi literate. Modern monarchies are a residue of pre-modern ritual events.[21] In conjunction with language consolidation, the modern state developed a series

---

[21] Hobsbawm's (1983) "invention of tradition" is the classic articulation.

of institutions that required participation from all of its citizens to assure that citizens experienced themselves as "identical to each other." The educational system and the military, particularly the practice of conscription, were the standard institutions that mediated the relation between the citizen and the nation-state (Weber 1976, Chapter 17; Levi 1998; Finer 1975). Identity was a byproduct of the compulsory nature of these institutions. Compulsory school attendance and military conscription generated solidarity among citizens. These institutions aimed to generate emotional identification with the nation-state – to transform a feeling of "I am" to "We are" which is the essence of peoplehood (Lie 2004; Smith 2003).

Identity in the sense of "identified as," the epistemological or categorical, is legally fixed; whereas identity in the sense of "identifies with," the onto-logical or emotional, is contingent. By legally fixed, I do not mean to suggest that these categories of identification were not contested in their formation or that all legal frameworks are identical. As sociologists have recently demonstrated, there is much national variation in laws that seek to regulate similar processes.[22] By contingent, I simply mean that we all are embedded in a field of social categories, and only under some conditions do identities become salient for us. In other words, we do not feel all of our categorical identities with the same emotional intensity at all times. Most identities lie dormant and function as a kind of habit until they are challenged either positively or negatively in some way.[23]

National identities, of all possible identities, are the most difficult to evoke since they are, under most circumstances, remote from everyday experience.[24] It is the remoteness, not the closeness, of the nation which forces states to create identity rituals such as national holidays and symbols. In a classic essay, Tilly (1985) has argued that war made states. He was speaking about struggling over resources and setting territorial boundaries. But war or threat also makes collective identities – "us vs. them" is bonding. Threat is an efficient mechanism for creating a common identity, whether national or European. Threat makes cultural communities because it forces groups to define boundaries and argue about who is

---

[22] See, for example, Beckert (2008) on inheritance law; Saguy (2003) on sexual harassment law; Soysal (1994) on citizenship.

[23] See, for example, Laitin's (1998) description of identity as a "tipping" phenomenon and Gould's (1995) conception of identity as place-based, which speak to the issue of contingency. Berezin (1997a, pp. 19–23), using ideas drawn from Connolly (1991), first elaborates the idea of "contingent identity."

[24] Berezin (1997a) demonstrates this via the case of fascist Italy. More recently, Brubaker's (2006) ethnographic account of Cluj, a border town in Transylvania, also confirms this fact.

different and who is the same.[25] Threats are also potentially egalitarian as they touch everyone – not just the elite.

Poggi (1978) has argued that a unique virtue of the modern state was that it created loyalty by managing the balance between internal security and external threat, friend and enemy, taxes and war. Poggi's insight, borrowed from Carl Schmidt, suggests that the modern state was a political community that adjudicated risk for its members. Poggi's implicit argument is that a byproduct of the state's "business of rule" is the "business" of creating a common identity and culture that produces loyal, solidaristic and secure members. In short, identification in the broadest terms is the linchpin of internal and external security – taxes and war.

Postwar Europe lived with the threat of the Cold War balanced against the internal security of its various welfare states. To identify with one's nation-state was easy because solidarity gave everyone a stake in the state where people helped like-minded citizens – who also culturally and legally (and sometimes physically) resembled them. In the formulation developed in these pages, national identity is not simply something that resides in people's heads, or as some would have it in their daily talk, but it is intimately connected to the security of the state in which they live. National identity has a practical as well as cultural dimension and it remains quiescent until it is threatened – but although citizens might articulate the threat as an identity threat, it is in practice a security threat.

Shifting the methodological focus: events as templates of possibilities and sites of collective evaluation

The preceding section has argued for analytic reformulation. This section argues for methodological reformulation. In contrast to previous studies of the right that typically focus upon variables from party organizations to voter preferences and attitudes, this study is historical and cultural and based upon comparative "thick descriptions" of salient *events* within specific temporal and national contexts. Its focus is on social, political and cultural process. Events, both large and small, tap into these processes.[26]

Recently, historical sociologists have turned their attention to events.[27] Much of this theorizing views history as a causal process and events are

---

[25] Lamont and Molnar (2002) address the issue of boundary formation as a vital social process.

[26] As a concept, *event* engages the current concern with narrative theory in comparative historical sociology (Sewell 1996a, b; Somers and Gibson 1994; Somers 1996; Tilly 2002; Büthe 2002).

[27] For a review of recent work, see Clemens (2007).

seen as crucial conjunctures on a causal trajectory. Path dependence is the term that encapsulates the intersection of events and trajectory (Mahoney 2000; Pierson 2004). Borrowed from economic theory and economic history, path dependence assumes that at crucial moments collective decisions or events push collective actors down particular routes or "paths." Once a path is taken it precludes others, makes course corrections difficult, if not impossible, and sets the course of future choices. Thus, the path taken, the choices made, are of critical importance for historical outcomes. The path and the choice are in effect causal with regards to the next set of choices. Path dependence is at the core of the concept of analytic narrative developed by economic historians (Bates *et al.* 1998). Path analysis is amenable to counterfactual analysis because it permits formulations such as, if this choice had been made and not that. Path dependence is subject to the criticism of, first, being overly deterministic and, second, of being difficult to operationalize. Rigorous causal reasoning demands a focus on extremely discrete events if one is to be able to specify all the steps in a path with confidence.[28] Yet, historical sociologists have recognized its central insights and built upon it in important ways.

Historical sociologists have focused upon *events* to counter some of the more problematic claims of path analysis. Sewell (1996a,b) is the leading exponent of the sociological theory of events.[29] He argues (1996b) that classic path analysis is not capable of dealing with change because it assumes that "causal structures are uniform through time" (p. 263). Sewell posits an "eventful temporality" that recognizes that the "radical contingency" of some events allows for social change and transformation. Sewell's (1996a, p. 844) refinement of his argument defines a historical event as "(1) a ramified sequence of occurrences that (2) is recognized as notable by contemporaries, and that (3) results in a durable transformation of structures." The event that Sewell discusses is the storming of the Bastille in Paris in 1789 – an event that historians agree was pivotal to the series of events that constituted the French Revolution. Sewell's theory of *events* has several characteristics. Events are the subject of narrative and are recognized as significant when they occur. Events reveal "heightened emotion"; collective creativity; take ritual form; and – most importantly – generate more events.

Sewell's elaboration of events is subject to critique on multiple levels. He is, for one thing, interested in events that change the course of history. But

---

[28] The comparison of Griffin (1993) versus Mahoney (2003) illustrates this dilemma.

[29] Sewell, who acknowledges a debt to Marshall Sahlins (1991), reformulated these theories in *Logics of History* (2005).

arguably there are many events that occur and recur in political life that are not as iconic as the storming of the Bastille, however constituted, that still have importance for the overall national political narrative. Patterson (2007) has critiqued precisely this part of Sewell's argument as well as its neglect of causality. Steinmetz (2008) has challenged Sewell's insistence on recognition. Whether or not the course of history is altered in the short or the long run, Sewell elaborates salient features of events (particularly his emphasis on collective recognition, emotion and narrative) that transpose well to political cultural analysis.

Building upon Sewell's insights, we can argue that events are *templates of possibility*. Events are sociologically and politically important because they permit us to see relations and interconnections that speak to broader macro- and micro-level social processes. Events speak to collective resonance, present possibilities, and offer visions of possible paths – even if those paths are not pursued. Events make manifest what *might* happen, rather than predict what *will* happen. Public political events, the empirical focus of this book, engage the collective imagination and have the capacity to alter public perceptions that *may* in the future alter political actions. Because they make manifest the possible, they have the power to engage collective emotions from fear to collective euphoria and the range of emotions that lie in between these polarities.

Events, evaluation and narrative are intimately connected. Occurrences constitute events, but not all occurrences are events. Most occurrences are routine. Events have a varied time line. Some events are over in a matter of days; some events in weeks; and some events, such as the Vietnam War, in years. The death of a President may or may not be an event; an election may or may not be an event. What distinguishes an event from a mere occurrence is the collective evaluation that it generates. Collective evaluation borrows from Boltanski and Thévenot's ([1991] 2006) theory of justification and moral evaluation. Their central argument is that social actors continually employ a recognized language of evaluation to ascribe moral worth to public and private actions and situations. Boltanski and Thévenot developed their theory with respect to the economic realm, but their emphasis upon collectively shared practices of justification suggests that the theory is equally applicable to the political realm. Collective evaluations are public narratives about *meanings that matter* that emerge in response to contingent, that is unexpected, events. Emotional resonance distinguishes a collective evaluation from the myriads of narratives that float around in the public sphere and fall on collective deaf ears. Events and their collective evaluation are not causal or explanatory in and of themselves. They lead in the directions of causes, explanation and relations that often elude structurally oriented approaches.[30] Collective evaluation gives a narrative and cultural structure to events. As Polletta (2006) and Alexander (2004) have recently argued, without "stories" or "social performance," events would appear as inchoate. Identifying collective evaluations in *narrative* terms permits the reformulation of events in historical and analytical terms.

By taking an eventful, and hence novel, methodological approach to the study of rightwing populism, this book is able to look at parts of the European social and cultural structure that standard explanatory methods obscure. Scholars of events have for the most part been more interested in a theory of history and causality, and less in the more mundane aspects of event selection. But the empirical core of this book is built around events, and these events were not randomly chosen but rather manifested themselves as important in a flood of occurrences. These events – the 1997 Strasbourg congress and the public demonstrations against it, the 1998 regional elections and the World Cup victory, the 2002 presidential elections and the defeat of the European constitution in France, played against the presence of the Italian willingness to absorb Gianfranco Fini into its legitimate politics – form the core of the book.

Public narratives that emerged in response to these contingent events in French, and secondarily Italian, politics reveal a public conversation about institutional change in the European nation-state and the relationship between those changes and its citizens. It is to those events and narratives that we shall now turn.

---

[30] See, for example, Alexander (1987, pp. 281–301) on the "hermeneutic challenge."

PART II

The trajectory of thin commitments: France and the National Front

3

Beginning on the margins:
the French first!

Ascendance (1983–1994): early successes and outrageous remarks

This chapter begins an "eventful" analysis of the trajectory of Jean-Marie Le Pen and the French National Front. The events discussed fall within five analytically distinct time periods from 1983 when the National Front made its first electoral breakthrough in Dreux to 2002 when Jean-Marie Le Pen came in second in the first round of the French presidential elections. In the years between 1983 and 1994, *Ascendance*, the National Front began to win local elections. During this period, Jean-Marie Le Pen made the outrageous public statements that would define his persona as xenophobic and racist. Although he still has difficulty resisting an outrageous remark, the Le Pen of today is considerably toned down from the Le Pen of 1987 when he said that the gas chambers were a "detail" of the history of World War II. During this early period, the National Front was most vociferous on the subject of immigration. Much of the social science literature that links Le Pen to xenophobic sentiment relies on data from this period. During the late 1980s and early 1990s, political actors in the state and civil sphere began to realize that they needed to take Le Pen seriously.

The second period, *Mobilization* (1995–1997), incorporates the 1995 presidential elections, the mayoral elections in the south and the tenth National Front party congress in Strasbourg. Le Pen's campaign to insert himself and the National Front into legitimate French political space began during that period and continued through 1999. *Banalisation* (1998–1999), the process of making commonplace, characterizes the third period. The salient events of this period are the March 1998 regional elections, the 1998 rupture between Bruno Mégret and Jean-Marie Le Pen that resulted in the 1999 division of the National Front into two separate parties and the National Front's crushing defeat in the June 1999 European elections. By the beginning of 2000, it was difficult to imagine Le Pen or the National Front as significant political actors. *Climbing Back* (2000–2002) characterizes the years between the National Front's defeat in the European elections and the 2002 presidential election. Between 2000 and 2002, Le Pen campaigned tirelessly in the face of strong opposition to secure a place on the 2002 presidential ballot. He also began to articulate a new vision of France and the National Front. The last period, *Dédiabolisation*, rehabilitation, began in 2002 with Le Pen's first-round triumph in the presidential elections. In the aftermath of the 2002 elections, a peculiar dynamic came into play which became visible in the 2005 French rejection of the European constitution. Le Pen's ideas, which had expanded to include a vociferous anti-Europe agenda, began to become detached from him and his party and to gain general currency.

This chapter sketches the early days of the National Front and ends with its "city strategy" of the mid-1990s. It serves as background to Chapters 4 through 7 that focus on selected events that mark the trajectory of the National Front as it intersects with national and international events in the years between 1997 and 2005. As discussed in Chapter 2, events – and the emotional valence that the National Front and the wider French public attached to them – serve as "templates of possibilities" that render analytically transparent a range of collective commitments and contradictions. As argued in Chapter 2, such events are interdependent rather than path dependent. What relates them is the collective emotion that they generate. Viewing the trajectory of the National Front through the lens of events allows us to make new arguments and see new connections. These intersecting trajectories underscore the central claim of this book that the rightwing populist moment is a product of the disjuncture between culture and structure that the project of Europe promotes.

"With Us, Before It Is Too Late"

The National Front came together in October 1972 from an agglomeration of French organizations on the right that had been in existence from the post-World War II period.[1] Jean-Marie Le Pen emerged as the leader from the founding moment and he has held on to that position tightly to the

---

[1] An expanded lineage of the National Front begins in 1894 with Charles Maurras's Action Française. DeClair (1999, pp. 11–58) describes the parties that evolved into the National Front. Camus's (1996) comprehensive history ends with the presidential elections of 1995. Shields (2007) begins his account with Vichy and follows Le Pen and the National Front through the 2002 election.

present day. On its thirtieth anniversary, the National Front produced its own abbreviated history for its website. For the same anniversary, it issued a video *The National Front at 30 Years*. The video is amateurish and not well produced. A large part of the video consists of National Front politicians speaking to the camera. The video provides a visual sense of the trajectory of the National Front. It shows that every time the National Front made a breakthrough the political classes as well as the mainstream media referred to it as a "shock."

While the Front has become associated in the popular press with xenophobia and racism, the perceived societal threat of May '68 and Marxism was the impetus behind its formation. The Front's initial motto, "With Us, Before It Is Too Late," addressed the threat of communism, not immigration. Referring to the barricades in the streets of Paris in 1968, the Front's organizational narrative notes that the "Marxist subversion" has undermined "the heart of education," dominated the "world of culture," and infiltrated the "Church."[2] In the early 1970s, the morale of the far right was down due to the experience of Algeria, the departure of de Gaulle and the failure of the Jean-Louis Tixier-Vignancour presidential attempt (Perrineau 1997, pp. 19–20). One theme that has persisted in the Front is its attack on the ruling political class of the moment. In its early days, the Front attacked French President Georges Pompidou for "tottering under financial scandals." The Front leveled similar charges against Jacques Chirac in 1997 when he assembled his government of "cohabitation."

During the first ten years of the Front's existence, it was consigned to the fringes of French politics. The Front ran in various local and national elections but gained little support (Perrineau 1997). In 1973, the Front listed 104 candidates who obtained about 1 percent of votes. In the 1974 presidential elections, Jean-Marie Le Pen received less than 1 percent of votes cast. In 1981, Le Pen was unable to obtain the 500 signatures required to be on the French presidential ballot. This state of affairs rapidly changed. As the 1980s progressed, the National Front began to achieve electoral breakthroughs and to attract the attention of politicians and political analysts (Schain 1987; Mayer and Perrineau 1992; Veugelers 1997; Perrineau 1997).

The year 1983 was an important one for the Front. Le Pen was elected a councilor in the 20th *arrondissement* of Paris and Jean-Pierre Stirbois, Secretary General of the National Front, received 16.7 percent of the vote in Dreux (Perrineau 1997, p. 34). The National Front developed so incrementally in Dreux that it was not until the election itself and the victory of Stirbois that the left understood how deeply rooted it had

[2] www.frontnational.com/historique.php (accessed April 2, 2007).

become in this small city located one hour west of Paris (Gaspard 1995; Tribalat 1999).

Beginning in 1984 with its showing of 10.95% in the European elections, the National Front maintained a steady 10–15% share of the national vote until the European elections of 1999. Le Pen ran as a candidate for the presidency in 1988 and in 1995. He received 14.39% of the vote in 1988 and came in fourth place behind Raymond Barre, Jacques Chirac and François Mitterand. Seven years later, he received 15% of the vote and came in fourth place behind Édouard Balladur, Lionel Jospin and Jacques Chirac. Given Le Pen's steady state in the first round of the previous two presidential elections, his 17.02% in 2002 should not have been the shock that made the French political landscape tremble. Table 3.1 summarizes these figures.[3]

In the 1980s as its electoral presence was growing, the National Front became more vociferous and began to establish itself as an anti-immigrant party, one associated with racism and xenophobia in public discourse. In the fall of 1983, Muslim youths were killed in a series of incidents with policemen in the housing projects, *banlieues*, on the outskirts of Paris. SOS Racisme, an association whose members had ties to the French Socialist Party, was created in response to the violence in the *banlieues*. Throughout the 1980s, the group organized demonstrations against racism.[4] In June 1985, SOS Racisme mobilized 300,000 for a rock concert in the place de la Concorde in Paris. They printed their motto, "Don't touch my buddy," on a badge that they distributed widely in Paris (Veugelers and Lamont 1991, pp. 143–149). Despite this mobilization against racism, incidents continued to occur. Prominent among these incidents were the murder of a Muslim teenager in Marseilles and the murder of an immigrant youth and the dumping of his body in the Seine (Ardagh 1999, pp. 219–243; Birnbaum [1998] 2001, pp. 246–247).[5] Although the National Front was not directly implicated in any of these events, some segments of the French public viewed Le Pen's anti-immigrant rhetoric as creating the climate of intolerance that contributed to these racist and xenophobic attacks.

---

[3] These figures must be interpreted with caution. They do demonstrate a steady state from the early 1980s. However, much of their electoral impact depended on whether the Front was able to engage in bargaining and form coalitions with the center right parties.

[4] Waters (2003) documents SOS Racisme and a number of other groups, such as Ras l'Front and Le Manifeste, that arose in French civil society to combat the far right and other forms of social injustice and racism. In 1995, researchers at the Center for the Study of Political Life attached to Science-Po in Paris formed an intellectual collective against the Front with the explicit purpose of supplementing and providing research support to anti-Front movements in civil society (Mayer 1995a, b).

[5] Bleich (2003) documents state response to race in Britain and France.

Table 3.1 *Performance of National Front in French elections, 1974–2007*

Year	Percent vote	Type of election
1974	<1	Presidential
1984	10.95	European
1986	9.65	Legislative
1988	14.39	Presidential
1988	9.65	Legislative
1989	11.73	European
1992	13.90	Regionals
1993	12.52	Legislative
1994	10.51	European
1995	15.00	Presidential
1997	15.24	Legislative
1998	15.27	Regionals
1999	5.69	European
2002	17.02	Presidential, 1st round
	17.79	Presidential, 2nd round
2002	11.12	Legislative
2004	15.11	Regionals
2004	9.80	European
2007	10.44	Presidential, 1st round

Source: www.frontnational.com/lefn_resultats.
php (accessed January 14, 2007).

Ugly details

From its inception, the National Front aimed at public provocation. Its newspapers, *France d'Abord* (*France First*) and the *National Hebdo*, subtitled "The Politically Incorrect Journal," were designed to generate controversy and attract attention. Le Pen developed a repertoire of statements that were racist, xenophobic and antisemitic that the French media liberally quoted whenever he made a political breakthrough.[6]

Le Pen's most frequently cited remarks date from the late 1980s. These remarks were antisemitic, but not anti-immigrant. The most notorious

---

[6] Gerber (1998) argues that Le Pen played to the press and they took the bait. On the same point, see Le Bohec (2004). Scholars and media intellectuals often underestimate the attraction of Le Pen's tendency to give an extreme formulation to a value that is already a part of what Lamont and Thévenot (2000) have described as the national cultural repertoire.

remark was his offhand comment in September 1987 that the gas chambers were a "detail of the history of the Second World War."[7] In September 1988, Le Pen made a pun on the name of the Jewish government minister Michel Durafour. He called him "Durafour crématoire." In English, the French "four crématoire" translates as "crematory oven" (Rousso 1991, p. 197). In December 1989, the European parliament rescinded Le Pen's immunity from prosecution. As an elected member of the European Parliament without customary immunity, his antisemitic remarks could now be prosecuted as "crimes against humanity."

Le Pen made his remarks in the wake of a series of antisemitic attacks that were as dramatic as later attacks against Muslim immigrants. These antisemitic attacks began with the 1982 bombing of the Jewish delicatessen on the rue des Rosiers and culminated in May 1990 with the desecration of a Jewish cemetery in Carpentras in the south of France. Two hundred thousand people turned out in Paris to protest the acts of desecration.

The memory of Vichy was the other national context that informed Le Pen's remarks. In 1940, France surrendered to Germany and Marshal Pétain set up an authoritarian French state in the south of France. Whether the majority of the French resisted or collaborated is a contentious issue in postwar French history. In May 1987, the trial of Klaus Barbie, the Vichy collaborator, was occurring in Lyons. Six years after the Barbie trial, the French state began to implicitly acknowledge its role in the fate of French Jews when it made the date of the 1942 roundup of the Jews in Vél' d'Hiv a national day of commemoration. On July 16, 1995, fifty-three years after Vél d'Hiv, Jacques Chirac publicly atoned to the Jews of France and admitted national complicity during the Nazi occupation (Carrier 2005, pp. 49–98; Conan and Rousso 1998, pp. 16–45). The French public viewed Le Pen's antisemitic remarks as especially heinous in the context of the Vichy past and the new controversies over the memory of that past. Le Pen exacerbated matters when he accused the French ruling class of cynicism on the subject of collaboration.[8]

On the occasion of the desecration of the cemetery, Le Pen gave a speech in which he called the desecration "large" (grand).[9] Le Pen argued that French patriots must always respect the dead, "The *patrie* is the earth of our fathers, the earth of the dead. Because we are believers and patriots, we believe that respect is due to the buried body." He expressed fear that acts of "psychological terrorism" would be waged against the Jewish community

---

[7] On the press and the "detail," see Rajsfus (1998).
[8] Judt (1992, pp. 45–74) takes up the issue of the betrayal of the intellectuals; Rousso (1991) deals with the issue of memory and betrayal more broadly.
[9] Jean-Marie Le Pen, "Declaration sur Carpentras, 11 mai." Pp. 33–41 in Le Pen (1991).

that might "isolate" or "intimidate" them or lead to escalation. Le Pen listed a number of desecrations of Jewish cemeteries throughout France in the late 1980s. He argued that the government was trying to blame the National Front for these desecrations in order to rally support for anti-racist legislation.[10] Le Pen proclaimed that the Front was neither racist nor antisemitic and challenged the ruling elites to find an "appeal to hate" in any of his speeches. He also underlined the fact that by focusing on the Front, the government permitted the perpetrators to go free and to turn this heinous action into a ruse to discredit "political adversaries."

When Le Pen came in second in the first round of the 2002 presidential elections, the French leftwing newspaper *Libération* published a glossary of his words of "hate."[11] The newspaper excerpted his comments on the rights of women and abortion, immigration and race. Le Pen argued that it was ridiculous for women to think that their bodies were their own – a standard nationalist argument that views women as part of the national patrimony because they produce the next generation of citizens.[12] With the exception of his anti-abortion rhetoric, the spirit of Le Pen's pro-natalist remarks are not far removed from a traditional French social policy that heavily subsidizes the family and women as mothers (Morgan 2006; Pedersen 1993). Recent statistics suggest that Le Pen's fears of "demographic decline" among the French may be off the mark. Demographic data from 2005 revealed that the index of fecundity in France was 1.9, which placed it above the European average of 1.4 and ahead of every other European nation-state except Albania, Ireland and Iceland.[13]

On May 1, 1996, Le Pen characterized immigration as: "This agonizing phenomenon that imposes its costumes, its habits, its religion on us and steals our souls. The ocean of immigration seeks to submerge us and to leave us in ruins." In a remark that came back to haunt him after the French soccer team won the World Cup in 1998, Le Pen argued that immigrants and children of immigrants should not be allowed to play on the national soccer team because they did not know how to sing the French

---

[10] This was the Fabius-Gayssot law that was passed on July 13, 1990 and made it a crime to dispute the existence of crimes against humanity (Conan and Rousso 1998). Le Pen called for its repeal in 1997. Mayer (1992) points to the role that the French media played in making Le Pen a scapegoat for the desecration.

[11] "Verbatim: les mots pour dire la haine." *Libération* (Paris) April 26, 2002, p. 7. Citations to Le Pen in this paragraph come from this source.

[12] Le Bras (1991) has labeled this phenomenon the French "demographic obsession." See also Le Bras (1998). Lesselier and Venner (1997) have produced an anthology on women and the right in Europe. The essays are historical as well as contemporary and several address issues of France.

[13] Editorial, "Fécondité française." *Le Monde* (Paris) July 7, 2005, Le Monde.fr (accessed July 21, 2005).

national anthem. In September 1996, Le Pen's speech on race delivered at the National Front's summer university for training new party activists was the *coup de grâce*. Giving the press endless fodder for commentary, Le Pen said: "Yes, I believe in the inequality of races ... At the Olympic Games, there is an evident inequality between the black race and the white race, it is a fact. I contend that the races are unequal. It is a banality."

By April 2002 when *Libération* published the list of quotes, Le Pen had already backtracked from many of his earlier remarks. But even in 1996, his remarks were extreme for a politician whose goal was to normalize his presence in French politics. Le Pen's public persona as a pariah was difficult to overcome. Despite his electoral successes, journalists and survey researchers often found it difficult to find citizens, except among the most *thickly* committed, who would admit that they had voted for Le Pen.

Pour la France*: "national preference"*

Political parties develop program statements at major junctions in their careers. The National Front was no exception to this general rule. In the 1980s, Jean-Marie Le Pen published three books that combined personal memoir with programmatic statements. In 1984, Le Pen wrote *Les Français d'abord* (*French First*), a series of short essays that ran through many of the Front's early themes in epigrammatic fashion. In 1985, he wrote *Pour la France* (*For France*) – a systematic statement of the Front's program and principles. *L'espoir* (*Hope*) (1989) was a series of interviews between Le Pen and two journalists.

Le Pen described *Les Français d'abord* as a "message of hope" (p. 24). The book is full of joyful pictures of the Le Pen family. Le Pen's narrative combines political and personal biography. He describes his youth in a small fishing village in Brittany, his first trip to Paris as a student at the Faculty of Law and his service in the Algerian War. He vehemently denies charges that he is a fascist and says that as far as he knows fascism died with Mussolini in 1945. In 1984, communism not fascism is the true menace. Le Pen describes 1968, the year of the student revolts in France, as "nausea," poking fun at Jean-Paul Sartre who protested with the students and whose first novel, *Le nausée*, shared that name. Le Pen described the events of May 1968, the general strike, the student revolts, the new barricades, as a "gesture of despair and disenchantment" (p. 54).

By 1972, when Le Pen founded the National Front, it was clear that it was necessary to "reconquer derailed spirits and anesthetized consciences" (p. 54). The metaphor of the "weakened spirits," best understood in English as "failure of will," runs through much of National Front propaganda. In time, Le Pen came to identify the ideal French spirit with himself. But in 1984, he was content to rail against communists at home and in Moscow who had led France astray. In a chapter entitled, "The Game of Truth," he answers many of the charges typically leveled against him. He begins "Am I a racist?" And in the same rhetorical format goes through antisemite, fascist extremist, anti-communist, reformist or revolutionary, elitist or democrat. Of the various tropes, the two most interesting for his style of reasoning and subsequent political development are his responses to whether he is a racist and a democrat.

His response to charges of racism reflects his position on control of immigration and "national preference." Le Pen begins his self-defense, "I am surely not a racist" (p. 167). He points to a "fundamental confusion" that did not beset the men who framed the Declaration of the Rights of Man and of the Citizen. Le Pen argues that the framers of the Rights of Man proclaimed that "men were equal before the law. In law. That is to say that one should apply their same dispositions. Citizens are equal in law, not men" (p. 168).

When addressing the question as to whether he is a democrat, Le Pen compares himself to Winston Churchill, "I am a democrat of the Churchill type in the sense that I refer to that remark of Churchill: 'Democracy is without doubt a very bad system, but I do not know any other.' The Mission of a political man is first to assure the interpretation of popular aspirations but also at the same time [to provide] information to people, not only daily information, that which is in the press, the television and the radio, but also information for the medium and long term" (p. 177).

In contrast to *Les Français d'abord* (1984), *Pour la France* (1985) is strictly programmatic and establishes the Front's positions on issues as it was beginning to attract serious national attention and a stable constituency. In 1984, the Front campaigned for the European parliamentary elections (and won ten seats) on the slogan, "French First." The general argument of *Pour la France* was that a corrupt class of politicians, technocrats and media operatives governed contemporary France. A "protected and sclerotic political class" had "confiscated" French democracy. Invoking the French constitution at the beginning of *Pour la France*, Le Pen pointed out that in France sovereignty belongs to the people. Le Pen claimed that an elite that touted "ready-made thoughts" (*prêt-à-penser*) drowned out the people's voice. Le Pen's insult invokes the French ready-to-wear clothing industry (*prêt-à-porter*) which is a degradation of *haute couture* where individuality was regarded as the *sine qua non* of French style and fashion (DeJean 2005).

Le Pen renamed the Thirty Glorious Years (*Trente Glorieuses*), the term that French political commentators use to describe the French economy in the period between 1945 and 1973, as the Thirty Decadent Years (*Trente Decadents*). According to Le Pen, the "takeoff" years in the French economy were the years that France as a nation declined. During this period, the birth rate declined so native French were fewer in number. The education system weakened, the culture fell victim to "Americanization" and "fast food," crime rates increased and France's position in the world declined. Le Pen blamed the French left and the appeal of international communism for this decline.

To combat the agents of decay, Le Pen and the National Front aimed to "renew" France. The National Front had "principles of action: national claims, respect for tradition, a preoccupation with freedom, a concern for justice. It also has a strategy: to rely on the vitality of the nation and on the assemblage of the people" (Le Pen 1985, p. 33). Le Pen identified the heads of small and medium-sized businesses, independent professionals and workers who work "conscientiously" in their industries or enterprises – the little people at the heart of the "true France" – as agents of renewal.[14]

Unlike the left or, more precisely, the National Front's vision of the left, Le Pen wanted to restore "power" to the people before the law and not in the streets. Le Pen justified his proposals by citing Article Six of the Declaration of the Rights of Man and Article Three of the French constitution. Article Six describes the "general will" and Article Three states that "National sovereignty" belongs to the people "who shall exercise it through their representatives and by means of referendum." Le Pen proposed to extend the power of popular referenda. Defending the principle of subsidiarity (Føllesdal 1998; Holmes 2000), Le Pen wanted governance to be local and the central state to intervene only when it was necessary.

Pour la France offered a well-articulated position on immigration and "national preference" that became a rallying cry for *and* against the National Front. "National preference" argues exactly what the term implies. French nationals should be given priority for a range of social goods from housing to education to welfare. The opposition to the National Front claimed, and claims, that "national preference" is inherently racist because it violates the French commitment to the "rights of man" and later to "human rights." The logic of the opposition suggests

---

[14] On the concept of "true France," see Lebovics (1992). The National Front received financial contributions from a host of small businesses that ranged from gas stations to cafés to hotels (Fourest and Venner 1998). On the social composition of the National Front, see Mayer and Perrineau (1992); Martin (1996); Mayer ([1999] 2002).

that no one can, or ought, to receive "national preference." Opponents of the National Front from the President of the Republic to the most rowdy street protester consistently drew the connection between "national preference" and violation of human rights.

Dominique Schnapper (1995) summarized this perspective in an essay written for a collection entitled *To Combat the National Front* (*Combattre le Front national*): "To adopt a politics of 'national preference' consists of fundamentally questioning well enough the actual positive rights of the international engagements of France. It is a project of rupture with an old political tradition of many centuries that France herself has powerfully contributed to elaborating intellectually and institutionally. It is in the proper sense of the term a revolutionary project" (p. 209). "Family preference" (préférence familiale), a conceptual kin of "national preference," is the descriptor that the Front developed to capture its defense of the traditional French family values – marriage, childbirth, adoption not abortion, and social welfare.

Social security and security from criminality are central to the well-organized state. According to Le Pen, immigration challenges national security on multiple levels. Le Pen argued that France was being overrun by a new kind of immigrant – Maghrebis and immigrants from "Black Africa." He argued that the link between immigration and "insecurity" is "not contestable" (p. 111). Le Pen said that immigration is challenging national identity because the immigrants have a higher birth rate than the native French. He cited statistics demonstrating that by the year 2085 France will have a vast contingent of Arabs and Muslims. According to Le Pen, in districts in Marseilles and around Lyons, there is such a high proportion of immigrant children that the schools cannot fulfill their role in ensuring the transmission of the bases of French citizenship – national language, history and geography.

According to Le Pen, the problem of immigration was aggravated in the years between 1974 and 1983. He cites large numbers and high birth rates – among legal and illegal immigrants. Le Pen's solution is to abandon the notions of multiculturalism he imputes to French politicians of the left and center right and "remain faithful to the French tradition of assimilation" (p. 116). The first "headscarf affair" (*l'affaire du foulard islamique*) occurred in France in 1989 (Beriss 1990): three young French Muslim schoolgirls wore a headscarf to school in Creil and the principal expelled them. The girls were later reinstated. The expulsion of the three girls from school marked the first time that the headscarf and the issue of *laïcité* – the strict separation of Church and state mandated since 1905 by French law – became an issue in public education (William 1991).

The "headscarf affair" became a *cause célèbre* in France, but remained essentially unresolved (Kaltenbach and Tribalat 2002, pp. 88–235). After months of public debate the Council of State came up with a non-decision. Headscarves did violate the separation of Church and state, but to forbid them violated the rights of the girls to education and of religious toleration. Young Muslim women were allowed, although not encouraged, to wear headscarves to public schools. Lionel Jospin who was then Minister of Education was deeply involved in this decision which would later come back to haunt him. In response, Le Pen argued that the French state should offer immigrants a choice, "to become fully French or to leave." Assimilation according to Le Pen did not exclude remaining faithful to one's origins and traditions, such as wearing the "headscarf" outside of school, as long as those traditions were compatible with "French cultural norms and law" (p. 117).

In *Pour la France*, Le Pen described French immigration policy as incoherent, and proposed: "the revision of the nationality code, abandoning multicultural pedagogy in school, the end of family reunification, the expulsion of undocumented immigrants [*sans-papiers*] and delinquents, the return of the unemployed to their country of origin, the reservation of family subsidies and social aid to French nationals, a stricter application of the Geneva Convention on refugees, putting in place a veritable priority of employment for nationals, the beginning of a plan to return immigrants" (p. 117). From the 1980s to the present the French state has engaged in continuous redesign of its immigration laws. Le Pen's influence on the increasingly restrictionist tenor of French immigration policy is difficult to dispute (Hollifield 1991, 2004; Weil 2001b; Hargreaves 2007).

Le Pen ends *Pour la France* with strong support of Europe as a cultural ideal. In 1984, Le Pen was elected as a deputy to the European Parliament. The abstention rate in the second European parliamentary elections was 43.2 percent suggesting that Le Pen and the Front made a serious showing. Le Pen described France as the "motor of Europe." Aside from advocating a common policy on immigration in the European Economic Community, Le Pen envisioned Europe as an independent identity that recognizes the "rights of peoples" who are "faithful to their roots." In 1985, Le Pen was strongly anti-American, an emotion that did not separate him from other French politicians then or now, and surprisingly pro-Israel.[15] In contrast to Le Pen's later opposition to European integration, his 1985 critique was

---

[15] On anti-Americanism in general with special reference to France, see Judt and Lacorne (2005); Meunier (2007).

aimed against European institutions, including the Parliament, and warned against the danger of a soulless bureaucratic Europe. He argued:

The European Parliament too often offers the spectacle of an assembly sensitive to the Marxist dialectic and attentive to third world ideology. The Commission in Brussels is an organ influenced by bureaucratic socialism. No Europe! Europe is not that, not only the Europe of merchants, unions, theoreticians and technocrats! It is a community of destiny more than a thousand years old, of which the construction, the last great design of the twentieth century, may give our youth a future worthy of their legitimate ambitions.   (p. 189)

Pour la France was the cornerstone of the Front program in the 1980s as well as the motor of its increasing influence. From the vantage point of 1985, Le Pen and his party did not appear to have much to offer. In 1985, France was simply France – its identity did not appear under siege. The Soviet Union and Marxism were the Front's twin *bêtes noires*. Europe was a continent and not a bureaucratic project. The 1980s was the period in which the European Union was beginning to consolidate. Jacques Delors took control of the European Commission in January 1985 (Ross 1995); the Schengen Agreement which allowed work across borders was passed in June 1985; and the European Council passed the Single European Act in 1986 paving the way to full integration in 1992. However, in 1985, it was hard to foresee the fall of the Soviet Union and the Eastern Bloc and all that these events would imply for France and Europe – as well as for Le Pen and his party.

The city strategy

"The worst was that I failed to cry ..."

In the 1990s, the National Front's opponents began to take them seriously and the National Front began to take itself more seriously as well. The 1990s made Le Pen hopeful that the National Front could expand and play a significant role in French politics. During this period, the National Front began to develop something that resembled a political strategy rather than a series of proclamations. A sign of this change was that party platforms were issued under the name of the National Front and not Jean-Marie Le Pen, thus shifting the focus from the person to the organization.[16]

---

[16] For example, *300 mesures pour la renaissance de la France* (1993) was issued under the corporate authorship of the National Front. It officially replaced *Pour la France* (1985) (Perrineau 1997, p. 75) as the National Front position statement.

The National Front's recognition of its viability among citizens who were attracted to its positions on specific issues pushed the party in new directions.

The increasing salience of Europe as a political issue was among the most important developments within the National Front during this period. As the pace and extent of European integration increased, Europe provided the National Front with an issue that had broad public appeal and transcended the narrow scope of racism and xenophobia. In addition, it was legal to resist Europeanization. Anti-Europe rhetoric did not have the same moral valence as antisemitic or anti-immigrant rhetoric. To be against an expanded process of European integration might represent an extreme form of nationalism but it was not inherently racist. Europe and Europeanization provided an unanticipated political opportunity for the National Front as the 1990s progressed.

During this period, Le Pen and the Front began to think in terms of a national strategy that would insert the Front into the political mainstream (Schain 1987; Camus 1996, pp. 47–74). Bruno Mégret, second in command at the Front, was Le Pen's partner in the legitimation strategy. Unlike Le Pen, Mégret was a product of the French establishment and was never a member of groups on the far right. He studied at the École Polytechnique and held a masters degree from the University of California at Berkeley. The French press dubbed Mégret "the ambitious." He was as technocratic in orientation as his generational compatriots on the left.

The "city strategy" was the core of the national strategy. The National Front was from the beginning a regional phenomenon – that is it was stronger in some regions than others. The "city strategy" targeted cities and towns in key National Front regions and aimed to control them through electing National Front mayors.[17] These cities would then become "laboratories" for National Front strategies. This is also the period that Mégret introduced the "University of the Summer" held in August each year to train new recruits.

The Front became firmly entrenched in the southeast corner of France, in the region Provence-Alpes-Côte d'Azur, known as PACA, when it won mayoral elections in the cities of Orange, Toulon and Marignane in 1995.[18] The Front added the city of Vitrolles to its coterie when Bruno Mégret's wife Catherine was elected mayor in February 1997. These four cities are in

---

[17] Christiane Chombeau, "Le Front national se vante d'appliquer son programme dans 'ses' villes." *Le Monde* (Paris) June 15, 1996, p. 8.

[18] There exists a body of narrative accounts on Toulon (Samson 1997; Martin 2002); Orange (Martin 1998); and Toulon, Orange and Marignane (Viard 1996).

Provence – the heart of tourist France. The romance of tourism and the sheer natural beauty of the region mask serious social problems that the National Front was able to exploit.

PACA (Provence-Alpes-Côte d'Azur) is third in population density among France's twenty-two regions. Its population is aging and youth unemployment is high. In 2002, the population over sixty years of age was 23.4% which was 3% higher than the French average.[19] Given the centrality of the tourist industry, it was not surprising that 79.6% of the population was engaged in services and only 16.4% in industry. Although unemployment was 11.5%, only slightly higher than the French average, for those under twenty-five, the unemployment rate was 27% – one of the highest rates in the country. PACA has always been a National Front stronghold. In the legislative elections of 1997, the National Front polled 23.9% in the first round – nine points above its national average of 14.9%. In 1992, PACA voted 55% against the Maastricht Treaty in contrast to 49% in the rest of France. In the first round of the 2002 presidential elections, Le Pen received 23.4% of the vote; Chirac trailed in second place with 18.9%. In 2005, PACA voted 58.9% against the European constitution.

Orange is a classic Provençal town and site of one of the most well-preserved Roman amphitheaters. Toulon, the largest of the four, is an old port city. Marignane and Vitrolles were developed for industrial purposes. Vitrolles has a population of 36,784. Its principal industries are Shell and Eurocopter which employ a large number of its sizeable North African population. Vitrolles consistently voted for National Front candidates until the split in the party in 1999 when the city switched its loyalties to Bruno Mégret and his National Republican Movement Party (MNR).[20] Vitrolles voted for Le Pen in 2002 and rejected the European constitution with a vote of 70.2 percent. When Catherine Mégret, Bruno Mégret's wife, became the mayor of Vitrolles in February 1997, *Le Monde* ran a series of articles, entitled "La France du Front." The reporter captured the angst of the citizenry of Vitrolles. The first article, "The Silences of Vitrolles," began with a quote from a citizen who voted for Mégret but did not wish to discuss it.[21] Citizens embarrassed to have voted for the Front and also deeply angered by the French political establishment often refused to discuss their voting behavior.

---

[19] Cordellier and Netter (2003) and Dupoirier (1998) provide the statistics for the descriptions that follow.

[20] Perrineau (1997, pp. 90–94) discusses the ripple effect of Vitrolles.

[21] Dominique Le Guilledoux, "Les silences de Vitrolles." *Le Monde* (Paris) March 18, 1997, p. 8.

The second article, "Vitrolles, the Angry in Solitude," spoke to a growing hostility toward the French establishment. One citizen described his feeling of having been betrayed by the left: "Mitterand [former socialist President who died on January 8, 1996], fourteen years, a million and a half unemployed and more, and the last thing, the summer of Tapie, the worst was that I failed to cry at the death of Mitterand."[22] Most poignant here is the anger combined with the recognition that he no longer felt an emotional attachment to the Socialist Party or its representatives. In the third article, a socialist activist articulates the pervasive despair among citizens at the cynicism of politicians: "Politicians are constituted as a caste essentially focused upon themselves. Personal ambition replaces collective ambition." The article concludes on a hopeless note when another socialist organizer claims, "No one can even help us exist – let alone mobilize."[23]

Culture wars

In PACA, the National Front tapped the despair of citizens who were unemployed and without hope. The party attracted negative national attention to the cities Le Monde described in February 1997 as National Front "laboratories" when local Front politicians engaged in a French variant of "culture wars." Even the Catholic newspaper Témoignage Chrétien, in an obvious reference to Nazi Germany, accused the National Front of engaging in "the culture of the bunker." Critics of the "culture wars" that the National Front initiated in its city "laboratories" often cited Goebbels, Hitler's Minister of Propaganda, who made the infamous statement, "When I hear the word culture, I reach for my gun." In September 1995, the mayor of Orange rescinded, ostensibly for economic reasons, a 1.5 million franc annual subsidy to the Mosaic Cultural Center that put on an annual "Night of Antique Theater." The same mayor denied the Chorégies, a famous lyric art festival held in Orange, its annual 1 million franc subsidy. In Marignane, the public library ended its subscriptions to the leftwing newspaper Libération and substituted National Front newspapers and journals. In Toulon, Gérard

---

[22] Dominique Le Guilledoux, "Vitrolles, les colères en solitaire." Le Monde (Paris) March 19, 1997, p. 7. Tapie was the president of the soccer club of Marseilles which became champions of France and won the European Champions League. He was also outspoken in his criticisms of the National Front and had run as a legislator in Marseilles (Reinhard 1991). In the year that the club won the title, Tapie was accused of match fixing. His club was stripped of its title. Tapie was put under criminal investigation and in 1995 he was sentenced to two years in prison.

[23] Dominique Le Guilledoux, "Vitrolles: et maintenant?" Le Monde (Paris) March 20, 1997, p. 8.

Paquet, the director of the Chateauvallon theater, was fired and the festival of books was renamed, "The Festival of the Liberty of Books." The mayor opened the new festival with readings from books written by members of the National Front. In Vitrolles, Catherine Mégret fired the director of the municipal cinema for refusing the mayor's order to ban the film, *Love Reinvented, Ten Love Stories in the Time of AIDS.*[24]

The artistic community organized against the Front's assault on freedom of expression that occurred in these small cities in Provence. But the tipping point in terms of public outrage occurred in January 1998 over the issue of family, and not cultural, policy. On January 1, 1998, Catherine Mégret announced a "National Preference" policy in Vitrolles. (Toulon did the same.) The city government would award 5,000 French francs to French mothers giving birth to pure "European" children. Catherine Mégret's policy was consistent with National Front policy on the family. In a propaganda pamphlet, *The Family: For a Family Politics* (Baeckeroot 1992), the Front warned that demographic decline, that is the decline in births of persons who are French by blood, was one of the leading problems facing contemporary France, arguing that "The Family is the Cornerstone of the City" and pointing out that Marxists and socialists have brought "totalitarian and inhumane" ideas to France such as abortion, euthanasia and sexual promiscuity, as opposed to the National Front that advocates "the profoundly human sentiment of an infant born and raised by its mother, protected by its father, developing among those of its own blood. It is necessary as the twentieth century ends, to rediscover the vitality and the eminent role of nations as opposed to totalitarianism, [and] to rediscover equally the family as a privileged cadre of individual blossoming" (Baeckeroot 1992, p. 45).

The critics of Catherine Mégret and "national preference" expressed public outrage and described it as "shameful discrimination" and a "provocation." A French court fined Catherine Mégret for stirring racial hatred. This was the second time in a year that she had been censored. She had been sentenced earlier to three months in prison for racist statements made in Berlin. The French press claimed that corruption in the form of appointing family members to political office was the principal strategy of "national preference" that the Front employed. The left argued that the National Front's true vision of the family was to relegate women to the kitchen.

---

[24] Antoine Guiral, "La culture, cible preferée du lepénisme." *Libération* (Paris) October 7, 1997, p. 3.

Summary

"Real problems ... bad answers"

The National Front's electoral strength began to increase in 1983 and continued at a more or less constant level until the French presidential elections of 1995 when Jean-Marie Le Pen came fourth in the first round. These years coincided with the presidency (1981–1995) of the former head of the Socialist Party, François Mitterand. Le Pen's 15 percent of votes cast suggests that his political claims were beginning to resonate with a public that extended beyond his band of *thickly* committed adherents. The Front was drawing upon the thin commitments of citizens disturbed by a host of social and political issues that the French state appeared incapable of addressing. In the course of a debate with Jacques Chirac in 1985, Laurent Fabius, then the youngest minister in Mitterand's government, made the frequently cited remark, "M. Le Pen raises real problems, but gives bad answers" (Le Bohec 2004, p. 257).

In 1985, Le Pen placed the immigration issue on the political agenda, tying it to social issues around unemployment, security and support for the family.[25] Europe was on Le Pen's agenda as early as 1985. Europe in 1985 had very different meaning than it had in 1995 or 2005. Europe was not a cause for general concern and did not touch the lives of ordinary citizens in any but the most abstract of ways. In 1985, Europe was still divided between East and West. A public claim that communism was a moral, if not a political or military, threat might still appear plausible – especially if one conflated the socialists and the communists as Le Pen often did. While the National Front sought to keep the political issue of communism alive as late as 1998 to lure French workers, many of the Front's other issues such as immigration and unemployment were at least being addressed if not solved by the French state. For example, between 1981 and 1998, the French state amended its immigration laws seven times (Withol de Wenden 2004, pp. 289–290). With each additional law, immigration policy was becoming increasingly restrictive.

By the beginning of the 1990s, Europe began to emerge as an issue in its own right. The National Front also was beginning to change, but it was still viewed as fringe, a nuisance rather than a threat, and immigration was being handled by administrative measures. Youth protest groups such as SOS Racisme dealt with the Front. Of all of Le Pen's early issues, Europe as a homeland was the strongest remaining one and it was being fueled every day not only by the presence of immigrants who were not being assimilated but also by the increasing presence of a new kind of European Union.

---

[25] On immigration, see the essays in Baldwin-Edwards and Schain (1994).

4

"Neither right nor left: French!" The campaign for political normalcy

Mobilization: Strasbourg March 1997

"The Transformation": the National Front party congress

With the city strategy well underway, the Front turned its attention to its campaign for the regional elections in spring 1998. The National Front began its campaign for the March 1998 regional elections with its party congress in March 1997 in Strasbourg. A red, white and blue banner proclaiming, "10th Congress of the National Front, the Transformation [*le changement*]," adorned the front façade of the Congressional Palace in Strasbourg. The banner signaled the beginning of the congress and the Front's launching of its new image as a legitimate political actor. The National Front's slogan for the congress was, "Neither right nor left: French!" The National Front began to use the phrase in the summer and fall of 1995. At the Front's summer university in August 1995, Le Pen declared that the National Front would be an "alternative to the system" and in a "position to justify the slogan, 'neither right nor left'" (Perrineau 1997, pp. 84–86). By December 1996, Le Pen and Mégret were regularly employing 1930s' political language. They described the National Front as offering a "third way" that was "neither socialist nor capitalist" (Perrineau 1997, p. 88).

The tenth congress merged political and religious symbolism. First, it took place on Easter weekend from the 29th to the 31st of March – Good Friday to Easter Sunday.[1] The Christian holy days that celebrated the resurrection of Christ also celebrated the resurrection of the National Front. Jean-Marie Le Pen had no difficulty during the course of the

---

[1] On the political strategy of blending sacred and secular practices, see Berezin (1997a, pp. 87–88) and Kertzer (1980).

weekend comparing himself to Charles de Gaulle and to Pope John Paul II. He did stop short of comparing himself to Christ. Resurrection was not only on the mind of the National Front. It was also on the agenda of the French left that mounted a large "citizens" campaign against the congress and hailed the mobilization as the "birth of a new political generation."[2]

The party congress generated controversy from the moment that the Front announced that Strasbourg would be its location. Strasbourg is the capital of Alsace – a region with a history of cultural and political division that goes back to the Middle Ages. From the 1980s, Alsace, particularly its rural areas, was becoming a center of National Front support. Crime was increasing in the larger Alsatian cities. In the mid-1990s, incidents occurred in which native and immigrant youths got into skirmishes where they overturned and burned cars. Despite the unusual violence in the cities, it was rural Alsace that was voting National Front.[3]

The residues of a volatile history dominate Alsatian politics and culture. Located in northeastern France, Alsace is on the French–German border and has been subject to the issues of mixed identity that characterizes border regions (Gras 1982; Mayeur 2006). The French national anthem, *La Marseillaise*, was written in 1792 in Strasbourg (Weber 1976, 439). The region was tossed back and forth between France and Germany for much of the nineteenth and twentieth centuries. The Germans took over the region in 1870 and the French reclaimed it after World War I. The Nazis occupied it during World War II. Its border position between two great national powers has given Alsace a distinct regional identity (Le Roy Ladurie 2001). Catholicism is strong in Alsace and, unlike the rest of France, Church and state are not separate. The schools are French, yet the area is multilingual. Older generations speak French and German. French citizens regularly cross the border to work in Germany. Surnames are as likely to be German as French. There is a spoken Alsatian (Elsässich) dialect and a regional autonomy movement. The medieval cathedral and university were the principal jewels in the city's crown – until the European Parliament moved to Strasbourg.

---

[2] Laurent Joffrin, "Naissance d'une génération militante." *Libération* (Paris) March 31, 1997, p. 3.

[3] Boswell (2005) describes the developing relation between the National Front and Alsace. Alain Bihr, "Exception alsacienne," *Le Monde Diplomatique* (Paris) May 1998, pp. 16–17, provides the statistics on the National Front and elections in Alsace: Le Pen received 25.4% of votes in Alsace as compared to 15.1% in France in the 1995 presidential first round; in the June 1997 legislative elections the Front polled 21% in Alsace as compared to 14.9% in France; and in the regionals of 1998 the Front polled 20.6% in Alsace as compared to 15.2% in the rest of France.

Charles de Gaulle came to Strasbourg in March 1947 to found his Rally for the French People Party that aimed to challenge the postwar political establishment. The region has been traditionally center right. Although the National Front is strong in many areas, its strength does not always translate into popular support for its policies. Unlike PACA in the south of France that consistently followed the National Front on all issues, Alsace supported the Maastricht Treaty by 65.6 percent in 1992 and the European constitution in 2005 by 53.4 percent. In 1992, Strasbourg elected a socialist mayor, Catherine Trautmann.

Alsace is a land of acknowledged contradictions. In 1997, workers were angry in Alsace, and disinclined to follow the line of the political establishment. In an interview with the communist newspaper *L'Humanité*, an Alsatian worker explained his grievances and why he and other workers were finding the National Front attractive.[4] He began by saying, "I am French. I want to be an ordinary French person." He pointed out that the French political establishment treated Alsace as an "exception" – using it and ignoring it as it chose. Politicians from the center came to Alsace and viewed it like a "visit to a zoo." When Alsatians voted for Le Pen, the establishment reminded them of the Nazi occupation and their complicity with the Germans. When Alsatians voted for Maastricht, they were "patriots" and "focused on the future." Having helped with Maastricht, Alsatians with all their special regional issues wanted the government to realize "before it's too late" that, "Alsatians deserve to be treated as ordinary Frenchmen with all that implies."

From the moment that Strasbourg was announced as the location of the congress, a core of intellectuals, artists, writers and university professors requested that the mayor prohibit the conference – by refusing to provide the necessary permits.[5] The choice of Strasbourg was an "inadmissible provocation" because it underscored the fact that Alsace was voting National Front and evoked the memory of the Nazi occupation. Furthermore, the congress "degraded the image of Strasbourg." Of particular irritation to this group of intellectuals was the location of the congress in the palace that was also the site of the annual "Meetings of Strasbourg" – a democratic experiment in the public sphere where citizens gathered to discuss issues.

The collective of intellectuals argued: "The choice of Strasbourg by the National Front is not innocent. Strasbourg is a powerful symbol of liberation, of reinvigorated democracy, of Europe, of the Rights of Man, of a

---

[4] Michel Muller, "Colère d'un Alsacien." *L'Humanité* (Paris) May 12, 1995, p. 9.
[5] Varié, "Grands élus alsaciens, dites 'non' à Le Pen." *Le Monde* (Paris) December 14, 1996.

city that mobilizes daily to renounce social privilege and defend the values of meeting, tolerance and respect, a true bulwark against the resurgence of old ideas." The authors of the *Le Monde* article later published a collection of anti-National Front articles in a book called *The Call of Strasbourg: The Wake-up Call of Democrats* (Reumaux and Breton 1997).

Joan of Arc protests the congress

Catherine Trautmann, the socialist mayor of Strasbourg, considered banning the congress. In the end, she decided that it would be of greater political value to allow the congress than to ban it. She published the reasons for her decision in *Le Monde* a week before the congress. She argued that Strasbourg was indeed a symbol – both of French history and of the history of the new post-World War II Europe. Rejection of war and commitment to peace was the cornerstone of postwar Europe. Emphasizing that Strasbourg was the site of the European Parliament and of the European Court of Justice, Trautmann argued that it was the ideal location to fight Le Pen by underscoring the values of the Republic. Trautmann's reasoning was threefold: first, if Le Pen were banned he would simply view this as another example of his being martyred at the hands of the establishment; second, prohibition would violate Le Pen's civil right to speak; and third, his more extreme formulations such as his affirmation that he believed in the "inequality of races" were more usefully combated in the public sphere than in the courts.[6]

Trautmann argued that Le Pen and the National Front required a "citizen response."[7] According to Trautmann, "M. Le Pen is a danger for France, and the National Front takes its place as a party that threatens the social pact." Trautmann observed that, "Since the FN announced that it would hold its congress in Strasbourg, a powerful citizen mobilization has emerged in the city. In a few weeks the city has been transformed into an immense forum of debates and initiatives. This mobilization demonstrates that popular engagement is necessary to preserve republican values. We are all accountable for our liberty and our dignity … M. Le Pen will find himself face to face with determined citizens and not passive spectators. It is they who will conduct the great demonstration of March 29. It is they who will carry out the offensive awaited by the majority of the French."

---

[6] Catherine Mégret as newly elected mayor of Vitrolles cited Le Pen on the "inequality of races" in an interview that she gave to the German newspaper *Berliner Zeitung* and in September 1997 was fined in a French court for these comments.

[7] Catherine Trautmann, "La riposte citoyenne de Strasbourg." *Le Monde* (Paris) March 22, 1997, p. 16.

In an act of symbolic protest, Trautmann ordered that the cast-iron statue of Joan of Arc in the town square be removed for the duration of the Front's congress.[8] Joan of Arc is a symbol for the National Front. Jean-Marie Le Pen often gives his speeches in front of the statues of Joan of Arc that dot the urban landscapes of France. Le Pen has famously proclaimed that he had "a great affection for Joan of Arc" (Le Pen 1984, p. 196). In reporting on the congress, the National Front's newspaper the *National Hebdo* complained about the kidnapping of Joan of Arc. The newspaper accused "Cathy the Red," referring both to her hair color and to her politics, of resorting to provocation and harassment. Since she was unable to "legally" stop the National Front from coming to Strasbourg, Trautmann, according to the *National Hebdo*, encouraged demonstrations to "intimidate and provoke" the Front. Removing the statue of Joan of Arc from the city center was a provocation because Trautmann knew that it was Le Pen's favorite stage prop when he addressed crowds of supporters.[9]

Civil society responds: "The Springtime of the Anti-FN"

Trautmann's call to arms was opportune. A new spirit of militancy seemed to be engaging French civil society. A month before the Front's party congress, Bruno Mégret's wife, Catherine Mégret, was elected mayor of Vitrolles. The addition of this fourth city to the Front's arsenal of municipal strongholds provided a rallying cry for a new generation of activists. Protest groups labeled Strasbourg the "anti-Vitrolles," and rallied behind the slogan, "From Toulon to Vitrolles, never again!"[10] French intellectuals were prepared to join this new generation of protesters. In December 1996, the French National Assembly passed the Debré law – the most restrictive and punitive on immigration to that point (Hollifield 2004). By February 1997, the law generated public protest in the streets of Paris. One hundred and fifty prominent French artists and writers signed a petition written by the League of the Rights of Man against the Debré law – dubbed the "anti-hospitality law" (Gotman 2001, pp. 42–45). Artists, such as the French actress Catherine Deneuve, protested the law that required French citizens to register immigrants even if they were guests in their home.

---

[8] Christophe Barbier and Romain Rosso, "Branle-bas de combat contre le Front national." *L'Express* (Paris) March 27, 1997, p. 32.

[9] Jean Roberto, "Les trois jours du FN à Strasbourg." *National Hebdo* (Saint-Cloud) April 3–9, 1997, no. 663.

[10] David Dufresne, "Strasbourg, un rempart contre le Front national." *Libération* (Paris) March 29–30, 1997, p. 2.

From the Debré law to the Strasbourg congress was a short step for these artists and writers. On March 28, 1997, the day before the Front's congress, authors and writers of all stripes descended on Strasbourg for a symposium organized by the group Culture and Liberty. Salman Rushdie joined the French writers in a defense of cosmopolitanism against censorship. While the Front's congress was the immediate cause of activism among French authors, the broader context was the ongoing cultural suppression that mayors in Toulon, Marignane and Orange were inflicting on freedom of expression. The authors were particularly concerned about the suppression of opinion in the books permitted in the public libraries. Comparing the Front's banning of books to the Catholic Church's *Index Librorum Prohibitorum*, the writers argued: "In France itself, the lists of books circulate. To be put on the index, a word suffices: globalism, cosmopolitanism, a Jewish name, an Arab tale."[11]

Citizens of Strasbourg as well as a coalition of leftwing and center right groups from all over France heeded Trautmann's message and mobilized against the National Front's congress. Echoing Trautmann's desire for a citizen response to Le Pen, the public sphere was exuberant and breathless in its recounting of events in the language of citizenship. On March 24, *Libération*'s headline declared "The Springtime of the Anti-FN" and noted that protests were growing.[12] A day later, *Le Monde*'s headline proclaimed, "The Left and the Right Mobilize at Strasbourg Against the Congress of the FN."[13] On the weekend of the congress, *Libération*'s front page proclaimed, "Strasbourg, the Citizens' Battle"[14] and provided an eight-page supplement on the "FN machine." Inside the issue, an article proclaimed that this is a "citizen mobilization without precedent against the extreme right" and a "jumpstart," or a citizens' wake-up call. Listing the protest against the Debré law and the mayoral victory in Vitrolles, the author argued that citizens are realizing that France's position in the world as a democratic country demands that the National Front not be allowed to slip into political legitimacy – which was the Front's stated goal. The "February movement" must progress and political parties must be shaken up.[15] An editorial on the same page argued that the Front is not a "normal party." Similar to the right in the 1930s, the National Front was nourished by

---

[11] Catherine Bedearida, "Salman Rushdie se joint aux écrivains qui défendent le cosmopolitisme." *Le Monde* (Paris) March 29, 1997, p. 4.

[12] "Le printemps des anti-FN." *Libération* (Paris) March 24, 1997, front page.

[13] "La gauche et la droite mobilisent à Strasbourg contre le congrès du FN." *Le Monde* (Paris) March 25, 1997, front page.

[14] "Strasbourg, la bataille citoyenne." *Libération* (Paris) March 29–30, 1997, front page.

[15] Jean-Michel Thenard, "La cristallisation du sursaut citoyen." *Libération* (Paris) March 29–30, 1997, p. 3.

"passions, anguish and obsessions." Invoking a history of rightwing tendencies in France, the article concluded that it is better to fight the Front in Strasbourg, capital of Alsace, where a "certain idea of liberty holds."[16]

"Citizen waves" wash over Strasbourg

The major French newspapers printed the plan of attack on Strasbourg.[17] On Saturday, March 29 special trains from Paris, Le Havre, Lille, Poitiers, Toulouse and Germany were scheduled to arrive in Strasbourg with protesters who would participate in three days of demonstrations. The majority of the demonstrations were staged by coalitions of the left, the collective Justice and Liberty, a loose association of ninety-seven local groups and unions, and the National Committee of Vigilance composed of parties of the left, Socialists, Communists and Greens. Trautmann asked her deputies to collect 17,890 signatures against the Front – the year 1789 multiplied by ten: 1789 was the year that the French wrote the Declaration of the Rights of Man and of the Citizen. Trautmann's deputy ended up with 32,000. The symbolism of the number was an affirmation of democracy and the French Revolution and its values against "a man and a party that believes in the inequality of races."

The principal protest march began on Saturday at three in the afternoon at the place de l'Étoile on the outskirts of the city and marched into the place Broglie in the center of Strasbourg arriving three hours later at six in the evening. A special delegation of demonstrators from Marignane, Orange and Toulon followed the marchers from Justice and Liberty and the National Committee of Vigilance – followed by citizens' groups. After the march, at eight in the evening, there was a dance of resistance as well as an opera. For those not inclined to protest with dance, there were evening colloquia on the history of racism and integration. On Sunday, there was a citizens' breakfast as well as a hip-hop festival. On Monday evening, there was a "grand" public picnic to bid the demonstrators goodbye.

Neither/nor: the "liberal-nationalistic cocktail"

Le Monde ran a cartoon of Le Pen as a hot-air balloon, "The balloon of Alsace," dressed in a Nazi-esque uniform, with protesters trying to punch

---

[16] Laurent Joffrin, "L'autre idée de la France." *Libération* (Paris) March 29–30, 1997, p. 3.
[17] This description comes from David Dufresne, "Strasbourg, un rempart contre le Front national." *Libération* (Paris) March 29–30, 1997, p. 2. All the national newspapers carried the plan for the day.

the balloon with their signs.[18] The headline read, "At the Congress of Strasbourg, the National Front Claims it is Capable of Winning Power." In Strasbourg, Le Pen defined his mission to "save" France from "chaos." He emphasized his position as a legitimate member of the French political scene and pointed out that the Front had done nothing illegal in its career. The National Front viewed the congress as the "congress of maturity" – a sign that they were at the point where they could step into mainstream French politics. Bruno Mégret argued that the Front's program was "an economic and social third way, neither liberal nor socialist."[19]

The French leftwing liberal newspaper *Libération* quipped that the Strasbourg event was the congress of the "neither nor." The Front's slogan, "Neither right nor left, French," evoked the Vichy regime that often defined itself with those terms (Sternhell 1986). The communist French newspaper *L'Humanité* (April 1, 1997, p. 6) described the Front's platform as a "liberal-nationalistic cocktail, with a taint of the social." Ironically, the Front's social program contained echoes of that of the center left. *Libération*, the leftwing newspaper, headlined with "The Mad Program of the National Front" and promised its readers a "measure by measure" analysis. *Libération* described the program as "catchall and unrealistic" followed by the comment that the "first party of workers" dashed a drop of the "social" in its "liberal water."[20]

The proposals that the Front put forward at the Strasbourg congress were a reiteration of its 1993 program, *300 Measures for the Rebirth of France* (National Front 1993). The *300 Measures* argued that France should be governed by three levers: courage, liberty (which not only included freedom of expression and markets but also "direct democracy through referendum") and justice, by which Le Pen meant justice for the French and national preference (pp. 19–20). In contrast to previous Front documents, the *Measures* was professional and reasoned in its style of argumentation.

The *300 Measures* took up "Prosperity, fraternity, security and sovereignty." Its section on "Identity" proposed to "reverse the current" of

---

[18] The descriptions in this section come from Christiane Chombeau, "Au congrès de Strasbourg, le Front national se dit capable de conquérir le pouvoir." *Le Monde* (Paris) March 29, 1997, pp. 1, 6; Christiane Chombeau, "Jean-Marie Le Pen se dit investi de la mission de 'sauver' la France du 'chaos.' " *Le Monde* (Paris) April 2, 1997; Christiane Chombeau, "Le Front national cherche à se donner une image légaliste." *Le Monde* (Paris) April 1, 1997.

[19] Mégret's pronouncement resembled the "third way" program that Tony Blair and Gerhard Schroeder announced in spring 2000 (Barkan 2000).

[20] Varié, "Radioscopie d'un programme attrape-tout et irréaliste." *Libération* (Paris) April 1, 1997, pp. 4–5.

immigration, to defend the "roots of French culture," to safeguard the natural environment, to provide a social France without communists and to promote a "Europe of *patries*." On the issue of institutions, the Front wanted to return "power to the people." It concluded with some areas for immediate action. These included "national preference," reform of the code of nationality, shortening the duration of the *carte de séjour* from ten to five years, maternal or paternal subsidies, reinstitution of the death penalty and increasing the reach of popular referenda.

The National Front printed its own abbreviated version of its program in the *National Hebdo*. The Front newspaper version was more strident than the version reported in the general press. The Front proposed to reform the constitution to include the idea of "national preference" in its preamble and to refuse to transfer any form of sovereignty to Europe. The Front demanded the return of proportional voting, which favors minority parties, and the expansion of popular referenda. The program attacked globalization, and supported a minimum social wage and the creation of apprenticeships. To impose "national preference" on employers, the Front wanted to rescind Articles 122–145 of the French labor code that prevents firing or discriminating against anyone for their "sex, racial, ethnic or national belonging, or political opinions." While all of the proposals outraged the opponents of the National Front, the French state revised immigration law in the late 1990s in ways that were consistent with some of the Front's proposals (Hargreaves 2007, pp. 24–31).

"Do Not Be Afraid": appropriating which past?

The National Front and its opponents dipped into the archive of French history and the arena of contemporary events to fashion a string of political metaphors that would sharpen the ideological battles that they waged to capture the hearts and votes of the public. In the spring of 1997, the following events were in the immediate future: the passage of the thirty-five-hour bill that would shorten the work week; the signing of the Amsterdam Treaty that extended and clarified the jurisdictions of the Maastricht Treaty; the dissolution of the National Assembly and the beginning of "cohabitation" between Chirac and Jospin; and the trial of Maurice Papon.

Vichy and the issue of collaboration was always a contested and uncomfortable memory in postwar France. In the 1990s, contestation flared up over Vichy in multiple venues in French society (Rousso 1991; Conan and Rousso 1998). In this context, the Front's choice of "Neither right nor left, French!" as its congress slogan could not be regarded as innocent. During the 1990s, Le Pen fanned the flames of the contestation over the Vichy past with numerous incendiary remarks. The congress in Strasbourg coincided with two Vichy-related issues. First, in February 1997, Le Pen repeated his proposal to repeal the Fabius-Gayssot law that eliminated the statute of limitations on persecution of hate crimes defined broadly but with a particular focus on Holocaust denial. Second, the trial of Maurice Papon for collaboration was scheduled to begin in October 1997. Papon had spent the postwar years as a French government minister. In the early 1980s, a French newspaper revealed that he had been involved in the deportation of French Jews to concentration camps. Papon did not decide policy, he merely carried it out, and he was charged with "crimes against humanity." It took sixteen years for the charges to stick and the trial was a *cause célèbre*. In spring 1997, Papon's impending trial was part of the background noise of general anti-fascist sentiment and another exposed wound on the French collective psyche that preferred to think of itself as victims of the Nazis and not as collaborators (Rousso 1991; Conan and Rousso 1998).

To counter the memories of Vichy, the National Front also evoked the memory of Charles de Gaulle who came to Strasbourg on April 7, 1947. Faced with a factionalized party system in postwar France, de Gaulle chose Strasbourg to give the speech that would found his party, Rally of the People of France (RPF), that would later evolve into the Rally for the Republic (RPR) Party of Chirac.[21] Charles de Gaulle's speech, aimed at restoring the "grandeur" of France, ended: "It is time for the French women and French men who I am certain feel and think this way, that is to say I am sure the overwhelming majority of our people, to gather together in order to prove it. It is time for the Rally of the People of France to take form and get organized. Within the framework of laws and rising above differences in opinion, it will both promote and make triumph the common good and far-reaching reforms of the state. Thus, tomorrow, with action and will aligned in harmony, the French Republic will build the new France!"[22]

De Gaulle saw himself as providing the vision to save France from sectarian party politics in the immediate postwar period, although it took eleven more years before de Gaulle's accession to power and the creation of the Fifth Republic in 1958. Likewise, Le Pen viewed himself as

---

[21] Mayeur (2006, pp. 436–440) describes the relation between Charles de Gaulle and Alsace. Agulhon (2000) analyzes the figure of de Gaulle as a political cultural emblem.

[22] http://mjp.univ-perp.fr/textes/degaulle07041947.htm (accessed October 4, 2006).

overcoming the sectarian tendencies of the mainstream French left and right. Despite the show of unity in their moral outrage against Le Pen, both the left and right were attempting to use his growing support to their advantage.

The demonstrations against the National Front in Strasbourg were also a site of center right and leftwing political competition. Not to be outdone by the French left that had organized the protest marches, Jacques Chirac, President of France, and representatives of the center rightwing parties, the RPR and the UDF (Union for French Democracy), attended a commemorative ceremony on Saturday morning in Strasbourg at the site of a synagogue that the Nazis had burned to the ground in 1940.

The UDF, a small center rightwing party, used the Strasbourg congress as an opportunity to attack both the National Front and the French socialists. François Léotard, a UDF leader, in the days before the Strasbourg congress, equated the National Front with the Popular Front of the 1930s, in which Communist and Socialist Parties worked in alliance with one another. Catherine Trautmann expressed the moral outrage of the Socialist Party when she accused Léotard of "dar[ing]" to put the Popular Front and the National Front on the "same level." To counter Léotard, she reminded her audience that the Popular Front had brought them the "paid vacation" and the "forty-hour work week."[23] She also reminded Léotard that his party brought the Debré law that prevented immigrants from being houseguests without registering. Trautmann hoped to repeat in Strasbourg the "civil disobedience" and large demonstrations in Paris that had characterized the left's response to the Debré law.

The mayor of Digne-les-Bains, a town of 16,000 in Provence noted for its thermal baths, lavender cultivation and grassroots socialism in the midst of National Front territory, indignantly responded to Léotard. The mayor argued that the way to combat the Front was to be "morally irreproachable," referring to the corruption scandals that were plaguing Jacques Chirac's governing coalition. He argued that the entire French left should follow the example of Digne-les-Bains where we "listen to our citizens." The mayor of the tiny town had a less than favorable view of

---

[23] There is coyness in Trautmann's reference to the forty-hour work week because in October 1997 the socialists introduced the thirty-five-hour bill to solve the problem of unemployment, and the reduced hours did not benefit the average worker. See Gordon and Meunier (2001, pp. 35–37) for a succinct explanation of the thirty-five-hour bill and its implications for French labor.

Europe and called for a new Maastricht Treaty. Yet, he spoke to the left side of *France profonde* and called on the French to "rekindle hope, pride in the nation, confidence in the future."[24]

The Strasbourg congress ended on a sacred rather than secular note. Le Pen invoked Pope John Paul II in his closing speech. *Le Monde* excerpted Le Pen's speech with the headline "Do Not Be Afraid!" Pope John Paul II used this phrase in his installation address and in 1979 when he visited his native Poland after he had been elected to the papacy. "Do not be afraid!" was a call to hope and action and became a hallmark of John Paul II's papal reign.[25] Besides the hubris attached to Le Pen's use of the term, it suggests that he was speaking to the traditional Catholic element among his constituency as well as trying to appropriate the charisma of the Pope. Le Pen implored his audience:

I wish that you would understand in these days, to say to France and to the French ... To everyone, to all races, to all religions, to all colors, to all opinions, I say, as Pope John Paul II would say it: Do not be afraid! Because you do not find dangers on the side of the National Front, you find dangers in front of it ... We are a grand, national, popular, humanist movement, working ... to provide for those on our soil, and only our soil, a little less pain; for men, a little less danger and fewer risks, and greater hope and well-being.[26]

Counter-mobilization: the lessons of Strasbourg

"Occupy yourself with the National Front, or else it will occupy you!"

Intellectuals and politicians declared that the Strasbourg protests signaled a new generation of citizen engagement in France and an end to the self-absorption and greed of the 1980s. On Monday, March 31, *Libération* jubilantly proclaimed on its front page that Strasbourg was flooded by a "citizen wave" and "Strasbourg has not known such a demonstration since the Liberation [of France from the Nazis] and the National Front has never sustained a similar stomping [*déferlement*]: some 50,000 demonstrators of all

---

[24] Jean-Louis Bianco, "Le vrai combat contre le FN." *Libération* (Paris) March 21, 1997. Voting patterns on key elections in this small city suggest the contradictions in French politics. Digne-les-Bains voted 25 percent for Jospin in the first round of the presidential elections in 1995 although Jospin came in second in 2002 and Chirac first. The city voted 56 percent "no" in the referendum on the European constitution.

[25] The Pope's recurrent use of this biblical phrase has both God and man in mind (John Paul II 1984).

[26] "N'ayez pas peur!" *Le Monde* (Paris) April 1, 1997.

ranks, of all origins, of all regions paraded on Saturday in the streets of the Alsatian capital to say no to the racism of the National Front."[27]

A *Libération* editorial praised the fact that Strasbourg signaled the "birth of a militant generation." Citizenship not age united this generation and it was a historic period rather than a birthdate that drove persons into the streets. The generation of 1968 determined the struggles of the 1970s. A tepid fight against racism characterized the 1980s. The 1990s would be different. Engaged citizens and not factions would fight a vast array of social problems from globalization to racism to generalized poverty.[28]

The more centrist *Le Monde* echoed the message of *Libération* in its Tuesday editorial, again pointing to the 1980s as a time that brought not only "lepénisme" but also a culture of individualism. This is a reference to the privatization of French industry that began under socialist Prime Minister François Mitterand.[29] The 1990s and the millennium would hopefully be the years of "antilepénisme." French citizens "disenchanted not by political discourse but by the discourse of politicians, the words of civil society confiscated for a long time by the National Front, that takes the privilege of saying in the open what the French think in private" would reclaim the public sphere. The French should not be divided us against them, it should be all us and us against the National Front. In short, the National Front was a French problem. One banner carried by a protester cautioned, "Occupy yourself with the National Front, or else it will occupy you!" The virtue of Strasbourg according to the *Le Monde* editorial is the realization that "The National Front's most beautiful victory announces perhaps its defeat; society takes the National Front seriously. Nothing worse could happen to it."[30]

In 1997, the rallying cries of citizenship and civil society had supplanted the language of class oppression that had distinguished previous French public politics. The protest against Le Pen was an example of new civic movements that were dominating European and American politics.[31] The coalition of groups that mobilized in Strasbourg and continued to mobilize against the National Front was far more amorphous than traditional

---

[27] "La vague citoyenne." *Libération* (Paris) March 31, 1997, front page.
[28] Laurent Joffrin, "Naissance d'une génération militante." *Libération* (Paris) March 31, 1997, p. 3.
[29] On industrial policy during the 1980s and the beginnings of privatization, see Hall (1986, pp. 137–226), Schmidt (1996) and Prasad (2006, pp. 235–279).
[30] Editorial, "Yapakapari." *Le Monde* (Paris) April 1, 1997, p. 13.
[31] Waters (2003) describes the range of these movements in France.

protest groups of the 1960s and earlier. They were not institution-based and were frequently diffuse cadres of like-minded spirits.

The three that received particular attention in the Strasbourg demonstrations were Ras l'Front, Le Manifeste and SOS Racisme. SOS Racisme was founded in the early 1980s and large music events were their favored mode of protest (Veugelers and Lamont 1991; Mayer 1995a, b). SOS Racisme was part of the tepid 1980s' protest against emerging racism in France. Ras l'Front, founded under the auspices of the Trotskyist League of Revolutionary Communists (LCR), categorized the National Front as a fascist party. Le Manifeste saw the National Front as a "voice of fascistification." Le Manifeste, according to one of its principal intellectual spokespersons, Pierre-André Taguieff, described the National Front as "national-populist." Jean-Christophe Cambadélis founded Le Manifeste in 1990. In 1997, when he was a deputy member of the national secretariat of the French Socialist Party, Cambadélis viewed Le Manifeste as representing the sensibilities of the left, if not the extreme left.

The combination of the elections of 1995 and the Vitrolles election of February 1997 pushed the Le Manifeste group and the Ras l'Front to the forefront of mobilization against Le Pen. Ras l'Front had neither a spokesperson nor a president. It operated from a postal box address in Paris and printed a journal which sold between 4,500 and 15,000 copies in the first six months of 1997. Le Manifeste had an email membership list of about 1,500 members and 80 percent of them were also members of the French Socialist Party.[32]

The mobilization against the National Front did not end with the Strasbourg congress. A small but visible opposition to Le Pen, "The France that says no," kept the Front as a threat before the French public by organizing events such as symposia at the Sorbonne. Twelve hundred persons attended the first Sorbonne event – enough to keep the issue of opposition to Le Pen alive.[33] *L'Événement du Jeudi* published a *Guide anti-FN* as a supplement, arguing, "They say everything and do not care how. Learn to answer them!"[34] The *Guide* was a point-by-point rejoinder to the Front's *300 Measures*.

---

[32] Ariane Chemin, Nathaniel Herzberg and Michel Noblecourt, "Ras l'Front, le Manifeste et SOS Racisme vivent différemment leur combat anti-FN." *Le Monde* (Paris) March 29, 1997, p. 7.

[33] Jean Daniel, "Le siècle de l'étranger." *Le Nouvel Observateur* (Paris) April 30, 1997, pp. 100–101.

[34] *Le guide anti-Fn* (special supplement) *L'Événement du Jeudi* (651) April 14, 1997.

Place as symbol and the meaning of Strasbourg

Social scientists (Berezin 2003; Kohn 2003; Tarrow 2006; Gieryn 2000), geographers (Entrikin 1991) and historians (Sewell 2001) are beginning to argue that the places of political events are as salient as the events. Strasbourg as a political event had multiple layers of meaning: to the Front, to the politics of the city, to the protesters who arrived from all over France, to ordinary French citizens who were neither rightwing nor leftwing. The interpretation of Strasbourg as a political place was connected to the way one interpreted Strasbourg as a political event.

For the anti-Le Pen contingent, the citizens who mobilized to fight against the National Front, the focus was on Strasbourg as the site of the European Court of Justice. Their symbolism revolved around the Declaration of the Rights of Man and the human rights accords signed in Geneva after World War II. From a human rights perspective, it was a short mental step to the Nazi period. The Nazis annexed Alsace during World War II. To the protesters who composed the "citizen wave," Strasbourg as a place underscored the racism and antisemitism of Le Pen and the Front. To "official" Strasbourg as articulated by its principal spokespersons, Trautmann the mayor and various civil society groups, the concern was also that this French–German city with its Nazi past was in danger of becoming a National Front electoral bastion. In March 1997, national and regional opposition to Le Pen revitalized Alsatian civil society and infused public discourse with a narrative of hope and regeneration.

Strasbourg is also the seat of the European Union's Parliament. A large part of the Front's Strasbourg strategy was to present itself as a legitimate political actor. The Front's choice of Strasbourg was more blatantly aimed at the threat of expanding European integration than as a challenge to human rights and justice. Holding their congress in Strasbourg allowed the National Front to challenge the Europe of "Eurocrats" rather than the Europe of immigrants.

Fête des Bleu-Blanc-Rouge: *1997*

Jean-Marie Le Pen formally opened his campaign for the March 1998 regional elections on July 13, 1997 in Marignane – one of the four National Front cities in PACA. He wanted the Front to control the entire region.[35] The Strasbourg congress was a relative success for Le Pen and the National

---

[35] Christiane Chombeau, "Le Front national prepare les élections régionales de mars 1998." *Le Monde* (Paris) July 15, 1997, p. 5.

Front but trouble was brewing within the party. A debate was arising within the National Front as to who would replace the aging Le Pen at the head of the organization. Bruno Mégret who had been his loyal spokesperson and second in command began making policy statements that ran counter to Le Pen. The Front's annual summer university was held in Orange, another Front city, in 1997. His theme was "For France, regional combat."[36] Amid the concern within his own party about succession, Le Pen had more than the regionals with which to contend. His summer university was greeted with organized protest by a variety of leftwing associations who vigorously organized against Le Pen and the Front.[37]

Le Pen designed his speech in September 1997 at the annual party *Fête des Bleu-Blanc-Rouge* to smooth over internal conflict and external attacks. His speech aimed to capitalize on the gains of the Strasbourg congress and to establish himself and his party as France's principal party of opposition.[38] The National Front stood between the corrupt government party of Chirac and the flaccid opposition of Jospin's Socialist Party. The 1997 *Fête* was also the twenty-fifth anniversary of the founding of the National Front. A coalition of leftwing organizations organized a rally against the National Front on the Saturday of the *Fête*. In the center of Paris, groups marched from the place de la Bastille to the place de la République. The papers reported between 10,000 and 15,000 protesters. Hoping to regain the spirit of Strasbourg, one organizer told the communist weekly, *l'Humanité*, "A demonstration is always a good thing."[39]

In the period between the Strasbourg congress in March and the party *Fête* in September, two events enabled Le Pen to bring into sharp focus his role as leader of the opposition party. First, in April 1997, unable to keep his government together Chirac dissolved the French National Assembly and called for new elections. In the June elections, the leftwing coalition parties of Socialists, Communists and Greens did surprisingly well and Chirac was forced to assemble his second government of "cohabitation" with the socialist Lionel Jospin as his Prime Minister. The June elections were widely perceived as a crisis for the center right politicians. Jospin and his carefully assembled leftwing coalition, La Gauche Plurielle, did not

[36] Christiane Chombeau, "La lutte d'influence au sein de sa direction pèse sur l'université d'été du Front national." *Le Monde* (Paris) August 27, 1997, p. 5; Olivier Pognon, "Le FN parie sur les régionales." *Le Figaro* (Paris) August 28, 1997.

[37] Raymond Massoni, "Orange: une semaine de mobilization contre le FN." *L'Humanité* (Paris) August 25, 1997, p. 6; Rafaele Rivals, "À Orange, la gauche se mobilize avant l'université d'été du FN." *Le Monde* (Paris) August 25, 1997.

[38] Christiane Chambois, "Le Front national veut devenir le principal parti d'opposition." *Le Monde* (Paris) September 30, 1997, p. 7.

[39] "Paris descend sur le pavé contre le FN." *L'Humanité* (Paris) September 27, 1997, p. 3.

involve compromises with anti-system or extremist parties or candidates. In order for Chirac and the center right to accomplish the same type of coalition building as the left, the party would have had to strike deals with Le Pen and the National Front. As this was untenable, cohabitation resulted (Knapp 2004, pp. 49–57; Schain 1999). That the extreme left could join a leftwing coalition without moral censure, and the extreme right could not, advantaged the center left. The issue of coalitions became particularly salient in the 1998 regional elections.

The second event of this period was the initiation of the Amsterdam Treaty which European leaders ratified in June 1997 in Brussels and which the French signed in October 1997 (Ross 1999, pp. 100–114). The Amsterdam Treaty completed the Maastricht Treaty (Moravcsik and Nicolaidis 1999). In contrast to Maastricht, France signed the document without submitting it to a popular referendum. By the end of 1997, it was clear that the French could not put the treaty into practice without modifying its own constitution.

In September 1997, Le Pen began his *Fête* speech by attacking the government of "cohabitation." According to Le Pen it was Chirac's corrupt government which had brought France to an "electoral *bérézina*" that was reminiscent of Napoleon's defeat at the Battle of Berezina in 1812 by the Russians. Quoting Victor Hugo, Le Pen accused Chirac of being "the void awaiting chaos." According to Le Pen, Chirac's new government represented "decomposition" and not "recomposition." The National Front was "the single force bearing hope."

According to Le Pen, Chirac was a devious as well as a corrupt politician for having signed the Amsterdam Treaty without consulting the French people. The National Front has always been against an expanding bureaucratic Europe and the Amsterdam Treaty fueled its opposition. Pointing at the beginning of his speech to the fact that in four months the Front had gained 600,000 votes, Le Pen argued:

This victory was above all yours, a victory of *France profonde*, of France the militant, of France the resisting, a victory of France that refuses Maastricht, hyper-speculation and globalization ... If the National Front is excluded from the airwaves, the television and newspaper columns, it is because it is the only one to propose solutions to the various issues that worry the French in their daily lives: unemployment, insecurity, immigration, illiteracy, fiscalism, moral laxity, lack of births, denatalization, delusion of France in the globalist Europe of Maastricht, abandoning national sovereignty.[40]

---

[40] The quotations are from "Discours de Jean-Marie Le Pen, 17ème Fête des Bleu-Blanc-Rouge 1997" www.frontnational.com/doc_interventions_detail.php?id_inter=2.

In 1997, Le Pen began to identify forcefully the National Front as the party of France. His speech at the 1997 *Fête des Bleu-Blanc-Rouge* began to signal a new national enemy – Europe. The National Front's original enemies were Marxists and communists. By 1997, communism was no longer effective as a threat. Many French citizens were leftwing in orientation if not stridently devoted. Communism was by the end of the twentieth century as arguably part of the French political culture as Catholicism. They were both part of the substratum of everyday life – whether one was a devout believer or not. Europe was new. The original rationale for European Union as a peace project was fading fast in post-communist political space where it was unclear where the next enemy would emerge. What was clear was that Europe was growing and accelerating in the 1990s at the same time as the French socialists were privatizing the state. Europe was a tangible enemy – tangible because it affected everyday life for ordinary French people.

Pierre Giacometti, the director of the French public opinion poll Ipsos, made this point cogently after the Strasbourg weekend. Writing in *Le Monde*, he argued that the Front would always have a constituency of committed militants with, in my terms, "thick commitments." Giacometti located the National Front's threat in its capacity to attract citizens with *thin* commitments to its overall agenda but who would respond to the National Front's "foreign representations (Europe, globalization, the euro, immigrants)." Giacometti pointed out that the increasing attraction of the National Front forced "traditional parties" to mount an "aggressive and concrete political discourse on the 'European front' capable of preserving their electoral foundations."[41] To this end, Giacometti argues that the mainstream French parties needed to develop a program that addressed collective fears of external forces – a tricky proposition since both Chirac's party and Jospin's socialists supported Europeanization and globalization.

Summary

Provocations: "the political horror that menaces us"[42]

Before Strasbourg, a poll conducted by Sofres, the French polling organization, found that by March 1997, 75% of the French viewed the National

---

[41] Pierre Giacometti, "Front national, l'objectif de 1998." *Le Monde* (Paris) April 2, 1997, p. 12.
[42] Denis Jeambar, "FN: l'horreur politique nous menace." *L'Express* (Paris) December 11, 1997, pp. 27–36.

Front as a "danger to democracy" and only 19% perceived them as no threat.[43] This represented a dramatic if gradual change from 1983, when the National Front had become an electoral presence. At that time, the response on the Sofres question, "Does the Front represent a danger for democracy?" versus "Does it not represent a danger for democracy?" were more or less even with 43% seeing no danger and 38% seeing a danger in the Front in 1983. The gap between those two positions reversed in 1984 and widened through the 1980s and 1990s until it reached its peak in 1997.

French intellectuals and leftwing politicians viewed Le Pen as a "political horror." In 1997, the parity of the traditional left and right that "cohabitation" represented, coupled with unresolved social problems, placed Le Pen at an advantage. When Le Pen said that he wanted to "save France from chaos," the average person could tend to agree. Le Pen and the National Front kept advancing despite negative public opinion. The force of political events in France, coupled with the declining social situation and the expansion of European integration, contributed to Le Pen's momentum. Despite gains, Le Pen ended 1997 on a sour note due to his inability to resist an opportunity to provoke.

In December 1997, Jean-Marie Le Pen visited Munich and declared that the "gas chambers were a detail of the history of the Second World War." The German courts, in response, threatened to lift his parliamentary immunity and prosecute him for inciting racial hatred; a French court in Nanterre fined him 300,000 francs (about 50,000 dollars) for crimes against humanity. Le Pen had made the same remark ten years earlier and had received the same fine.[44] The French press declared that this "detail" would "cost" Le Pen "dearly" in the coming regional elections.[45] A socialist European parliamentary deputy called to exclude him from his position, declaring, "I am ashamed to be seated in the same amphitheater as him." His ability to take his seat in the European Parliament was revoked for one year.

In the May 1997 legislative elections, black, Jewish and Muslim candidates stood with the National Front suggesting that the party was in fact undergoing somewhat of a transformation.[46] By the end of 1997, Le Pen became more focused on European integration and began to emphasize

---

[43] Gerard Courtois, "Trois Français sur quatre perçoivent le Front national comme un danger." *Le Monde* (Paris) March 20, 1997, p. 6. See Chapter 8 below, Figs. 8.1 and 8.2, for the evolution of these opinions.

[44] Marc Pivois and Vanessa Schneider, "Le 'detail' de Le Pen: même faute, même punition." *Libération* (Paris) December 28, 1997.

[45] Acacio Pereira, "Jean-Marie Le Pen est à nouveau condamné dans l'affaire du 'détail.'" *Le Monde* (Paris) December 28–29, 1997.

[46] Jonathan Steele, "National Effrontery." *Guardian* (London) May 24, 1997.

assimilation in his discussion of immigration. French civil society organized protests against Le Pen and his xenophobic ideas while the French state was quietly embracing ever more restrictive immigration policies. The unpopular Debré law was an example of this restriction. The National Front's rhetoric on identity coupled with its electoral success suggest that it was the perceived threat of Europeanization embodied in the European Union, and not fear of immigrants per se, that was resonating with the National Front's expanding constituency. The National Front's rhetorical and symbolic strategies deployed during the March 1998 regional election campaign supports the claim that the Front was broadening its vision as well as its base of support.

5

The paradox of defeat: the rise and fall and rise of the French National Front

La Fête des Bleu-Blanc-Rouge: September 1998

September 19, 1998 was a beautiful sunny fall day in Paris. The French National Front was out in force. Members and supporters of the Front took the twenty-minute Metro ride to the outskirts of Paris to the pelouse de Reuilly, a park on the northern side of the bois de Vincennes that was frequently a site of political demonstrations as well as an annual gathering place for circuses. Named after the colors of the French flag, the *Fête des Bleu-Blanc-Rouge*, or BBR as the Front refers to it, began in 1981 as a symbolic challenge to the French Communist Party's *Fête de l'Humanité* that takes place every year in early September in the park of the Courneuve on the outskirts of Paris. Party festivals common to Mediterranean Europe provide an opportunity for local party leaders to fraternize with national party elites. Party festivals are, to borrow from sociologist Georg Simmel ([1908] 1971), sites of "sociability," a "play-form" of politics with equal parts food, drink, party propaganda and public discussion (Berezin 2006b). The Front uses its annual *Fête* to entertain its base – or at least as much of its base as can afford the trip to Paris.[1]

Bruno Gollnisch, a Front party functionary, triumphantly told a reporter for the *National Hebdo*, the Front's weekly newspaper, that "Today, the BBR draws more French than the *Fête de l'Humanité!*" According to Gollnisch, "year after year, the fête BBR has become the 'French meeting place [*rendez-vous*].'"[2] By September 1998, the French

---

[1] The account of the *Fête* is from the author's field notes recorded September 19, 1998. Harris (2000) provides an introduction to the place of popular festivals in contemporary France. Kertzer (1980) describes the role of festival among Italian communists in the 1970s.

[2] Benoit Duhamel, "La Fête des Bleu-Blanc-Rouge." *National Hebdo* (Paris) September 10, 1998, p. 2.

Communist Party was no longer seen to be a threat by either the National Front or any other French political party. In contrast, the National Front in the wake of its successes in the March 1998 regional elections seemed to be on an upward and menacing trajectory. In September 1998, the National Front was gaining, not losing, supporters.

On that particular September day, the Front's security guards dressed in black patrolled the entrance to the *Fête* and hand searched the bags and backpacks of people as they entered. The park grounds were densely packed with throngs of Front supporters who socialized among themselves and visited the numerous booths that sold National Front memorabilia as well as local craft items. The mood was congenial but not in any way emotionally charged. The park was filled with men and women who appeared to be in their sixties and older as well as a surprising contingent of young people of university and high-school age. Men and women were equally present. The attendees at the *Fête* were not dressed in the manner of urban Parisians. Visitors to the *Fête* had a slightly staid appearance that resembled the 1950s rather than the 1990s. With the exception of the skinhead contingent in attendance, clothes and hairstyles on both men and women seemed vaguely out of date. No one appeared rich but no one appeared poor either. The people who were committed enough to come to the *Fête*, or who could afford the trip to Paris, resembled what Front supporters supposedly were – the petite bourgeoisie of non-urban France: the butcher, the baker and the office functionary (Fourest and Venner 1998; Mayer [1999] 2002; Lamont 2000).[3]

Food stands representing the cuisines of France's regions that offered "traditional" French food as well as political tracts filled the park. Stickers and tee shirts were on sale that bore the Vichy slogan, "Neither right nor left: French!" There was a poster with a National Front emblem, the French flag as a flame superimposed on the map of Europe with the caption, "Europe peoples and nations." One popular poster displayed the caption, "Communism, 85 million deaths!" over pictures of Robert Hue, then National Secretary of the French Communist Party, Stalin, Lenin and Marx. Underneath the pictures were the words, "The National Front against the left." Given that the French Communist Party, as well as other European Communist parties, had been in decline across Europe since the 1970s, the diatribes against the communists had

---

[3] Hoffmann's (1956) study of the Poujadist movement is the classic account of the politically regressive French lower middle class.

the nostalgic feel of fighting the last war.[4] In addition to the posters, there were tables of medieval regalia with swords and shields on sale, as well as pictures and statues of Joan of Arc, the culture heroine of the National Front, and Clovis, the first King of France.[5] Unlike the high culture view of the Middle Ages available in the tourist culture of France, the Front seemed to promulgate a 1950s' Hollywood B movie version of the period.

The food was traditional, the tracts benign and the medieval artifacts bordered on kitsch, and yet there were disturbing images. Some of the youths who meandered through the exhibits resembled skinheads rather than retro university students. There were several booths devoted to the trans-European right such as the Belgian Vlaams Blok and a far-right Italian group Forza Nuova. There was an organization called Roots of Europe whose president, Martin Peltier, also managing editor of the *National Hebdo*, described himself and his group as "Sons of France, brothers of Europe." The organization linked geography to race in an attempt to identify common European themes. When asked whether his organization was racist, Peltier responded that this is a "regrettable confusion" and his purpose is "to research in a common history the roots of our national identity. This is the best way to preserve French unity." The founding principles of the Roots of Europe defend "family, Christianity and our land."

There were folk songs and performances during the day; dances in the evening; and a Roman Catholic public Mass on Sunday morning. The high point of the *Fête* was Jean-Marie Le Pen's entry to the park grounds, preceded by drum-beating militia and stout security guards. After working the crowds, Le Pen ascended a wooden platform to deliver his annual BBR speech. This speech is comparable in importance to the annual speech that Le Pen delivers on May 1 – a French and European holiday that celebrates labor. The Front uses May Day to celebrate itself and Joan of Arc, patron saint of France. Since Joan of Arc's official feast day is on May 30, the appropriation of Joan on May 1 is a symbolic political move on the Front's part to undercut the traditionally leftwing holiday.

Le Pen gave his speech in 1998 from a large makeshift stage with a black screen as background. The audience was modest with approximately half of the assembled chairs empty. Three monumental colorful images stood in sharp contrast against the black. Yellow letters ran across the top of the

---

[4] The National Front had been attracting members of the working classes who had traditionally formed the constituency of the French Communist Party (see Schain 1996, pp. 176–182; Platone and Rey 1996; Viard 1997).

[5] On the cult of Clovis in the 1990s, see Terrio (1999); on Joan of Arc and the National Front see Hainsworth (2000), Apter (1999) and Tumblety (1999).

5.1 Fête des Bleu-Blanc-Rouge, *September 19, 1998*

black that said, "For the blue, white, red: a flag, a flame, a hope." The images are of *France profonde*, which signifies the deep heart of rural, as opposed to urban, France.[6] A bright blue panel displayed an image of the monastery of Mont Saint-Michel jutting out from the sea and signaling the Christian roots of France; the white panel displayed an image of the Alps, the southeastern border of France; the red panel was somewhat less decipherable in terms of standard National Front iconography as it was an image of a rocket shooting into space (Fig. 5.1).

Le Pen's 1998 speech was a diatribe against the expansion of the European Union.[7] The speech marked the continuation of Le Pen's anti-Europe discourse that began with his 1997 speech and was becoming more acerbic. Lashing into every member of the political class, regardless of their position on the left–right political spectrum, Le Pen argued that the public debate over the Maastricht Treaty was a "masterpiece of disinformation" with the press keeping negative opinions from the public. As in 1997, Le Pen again directed his ire against the Treaty of Amsterdam.

---

[6] On the importance of the "local" to French national identity, see Gerson (2003); for an introduction to the French government's promotion of the "rural," see Rogers (2002).

[7] Jean-Marie Le Pen, "18ème Fête des Bleu-Blanc-Rouge 1998" www.frontnational.com/doc_interventions_detail.php?id_inter = 6.

While ranging from domestic issues such as the *Pacte civil de solidarité* (PACS) (non-marital cohabitation arrangements) to the genocide in Rwanda (he was against it), Le Pen's main point was that every French politician had chosen "against France for the Europe of Brussels."[8] According to Le Pen the mistakes of the political class would bring an end to a "French France, the death of the French Republic, the submission of the French people to the New World Order." The National Front wanted to "reconquer our independence, in another Europe, that of nations, that of fatherlands, with our difference and our particularisms, [to] practice the fraternity of the destiny that geography, history, culture, politics and even the economy design for us."

Le Pen drew upon a specific strand of nation-ness at the end of his talk that blended Catholicism with secularism (Bell 2001). Speaking of the French nation, Le Pen continued: "She is rich with our Christian and humanist culture ... It [the nation] is the blood of our fathers that runs in our veins ... the landscape, preserved and embellished that is the bulwark of our life ... the language that we speak. When we eat the products of the earth, symbolized by bread and wine, we commune with them, in the warm, sentimental part of the nation body and spirit, and when our souls depart the earth, it is in the maternal earth that we rest." He invoked Catholicism with a reference to "bread and wine," the standard Catholic Eucharist.

An open-air Roman Catholic Mass traditionally closes the *Fête des Bleu-Blanc-Rouge*. Le Pen emphasized the earthiness of the nation – the fact that it is literally the land that we pass on from generation to generation. He ended with the first iteration of a message that would become a theme in his speeches in the years to come: "Long live the free nations of a European Europe, long live the nationals of Europe, long live the National Front, long live France!"

At the end of his speech, Le Pen awarded gold medals, the *Flamme d'honneur*, to longstanding members of the Front who had displayed exemplary service and devotion. Although Le Pen was seventy-one years old at the time, he was (and still is) jovial and energetic and had a slight bounce to his step that made him appear younger. In contrast to the bland blue suits that most French politicians wear, Le Pen wore a houndstooth-check sport jacket with a yellow tie. He stood in sharp contrast to the medal recipients who were white-haired and gave the appearance of their seventy-plus years.

---

[8] On the PACs, see Scott (2005, pp. 100–123).

In September 1998, Le Pen and the National Front were gaining momentum. By September 1999, this momentum had been lost and with it the Front's capacity to influence political outcomes. Social analysts viewed the Front as so reduced in influence as to be gone from the political scene. A conflict between Le Pen and his deputy and presumed heir apparent Bruno Mégret over the direction of the Front led to a rupture in the party. In January 1999, Mégret founded his own version of the National Front called the Mouvement National Républicain (MNR). With the party split neither could garner the votes necessary to maintain electoral bargaining power. In June 1999, the National Front secured 5.69 percent of the votes in the European parliamentary elections – the lowest vote that they had received since 1974 when Le Pen ran in the presidential elections.

This chapter follows the National Front from the March 1998 regional elections through the 1999 European elections. Le Pen generated fear among French citizens as he seemed to threaten the values upon which the Republic was built. The emotions that the National Front evoked in French citizens are the thread that unites the three segments of this chapter. The chapter begins with the regional elections and then describes the euphoric national reaction to the unanticipated World Cup victory. It ends with Le Pen's defeat in the European elections and points to the harbingers of his April 2002 first-round victory.

Banalisation (1998–1999): anyone can be French

March 15, 1998: the régionales*: losing the sense of things*

The National Front did not actually "win" the regional elections of 1998. In raw numbers, the election belonged to the French left. The Front did however manage to split the French center right and for the first time make its presence felt as a serious bargaining force in French politics. The French regional elections of March 1998 produced the same type of seismic political shock as the Italian elections of March 1994. Alarm was not limited to France. Europe itself seemed alerted to the fact that Le Pen, who most had taken as a vulgar extremist buffoon, was, in concert with his party, a threat to the spirit of French and European democracy. The Vice-President of the European Parliament, in an opinion piece for *Libération*, pointed out that Europe itself was a peace project that was founded in opposition to racism and xenophobia. He exhorted all Europeans not only the French to voice opposition to Le Pen.[9]

---

[9] Jean-Pierre Cot, "L'Europe contre Le Pen." *Libération* (Paris) April 2, 1998, p. 8.

The regional elections began in 1986 in response to France's decentralization laws of 1982 (Sa'adah 2003, p. 322). In March 1998, France consisted of twenty-two regions. The Front had polled a steady 10 to 15 percent of the vote from 1988 onwards in various elections (Ysmal 1999, pp. 161–172). In 1995, there were National Front mayors in the towns of Toulon, Marignane, Vitrolles and Orange. In short, March 1998 should not have come as a complete surprise to the French left and center right. In the first round of the March elections, the Front held the majority in Île de France (the Paris region), the *banlieues*, the suburbs outside of Paris, PACA, Rhône-Alpes, another southeastern region, and Alsace. As the previous chapter described, citizens of Alsace often vote in anomalous ways. For example, contrary to expectations, Alsace voted "yes" on the Maastricht Treaty and the European constitution.

In the regional elections of March 15, 1998, the Front increased its presence to 15.27 percent of the vote. More significant was its capacity to control the outcome of who would actually become regional presidents. The socialists and leftwing coalition had only one clear win out of a possible twenty-two regions. Who would control the most regions, center right or a leftwing coalition, La Gauche Plurielle, depended on whether the center right would collaborate with the National Front. Le Pen and his party held the balance of power in the outcomes of eighteen of twenty-two regions in France. In the past Chirac had warned center right politicians representing the UDF and RPR parties not to form a pact with the devil in order to hold on to regional power (Ysmal 1999, pp. 173–182: Reynié 1999, pp. 83–87).

Le Pen proposed a "minimum program" to the center right regional candidates to facilitate coalition building. He agreed to drop or to downplay his "national preference" program in the interest of assuring that sufficient consensus on the right could be developed so as to defeat the socialists.[10] Chirac firmly rejected forming any coalitions with a party that he denounced as "racist and xenophobic." He went on television to address the French people on the evening of March 23, 1998.[11] Beginning by saying that such an address was beyond the scope of his role as President, he nonetheless felt obliged to comment because he felt that the French were perhaps "on a train that had lost the sense of things"; that "passion might

---

[10] Christiane Chombeau, "Le Front national propose à la droite un 'programme minimum.'" *Le Monde* (Paris) March 18, 1998, p. 7.
[11] "Allocution de Monsieur Jacques Chirac Président de la République à l'occasion des élections régionales" www.elysee.fr/elysee/elysee.fr/Français/interventions/discours_et_declarations/1998/mars/allocution_de_m_jacques_chirac_president_de_la_republique_a_l_occasion_des_elections_regionales-palais_de_l_elysee.2976.html.

substitute for reason"; and that France's "values" and "image" might be damaged in the public eye. The theme of how France would be viewed by the rest of the world is powerful in French political discourse. Chirac exhorted French politicians not to "prefer political games to the voice of their conscience." Chirac made this normative argument repeatedly in the years between 1998 and 2005 – most notably in 2002 after Le Pen came in second place in the first round of the presidential elections and in 2005 after the French rejected the constitution.

Jacques Chirac was not alone in the mobilization of political emotion. In an attempt to kindle the same intense emotions that citizens had displayed in Strasbourg at the National Front congress the year before, the left called for public demonstrations on the weekend of March 22 and 23 – the weekend between the first and second round of the elections. On the Saturday before the second round, March 28, demonstrations blanketed France (Fig. 5.2).[12]

Libération's front page on March 28–29 proclaimed "Republic to the Heart." This was in response to a comment by Le Pen that the National Front spoke to the heart of France. French artists and writers produced a supplement to *Le Monde* (March 28, 1998) entitled, "Where Madness Prowls, Writers Confront Hate." Thirty-one well-known French intellectuals contributed to the supplement. *L'Humanité* featured a picture of a father carrying his young son on his shoulders. In the son's hand was a placard that said, "Yesterday Papon, today Millon, enough collaboration!!!"[13] Many protesters carried banners labeling Le Pen as a French fascist and his movement as fascism. This was exacerbated by the fact that the Maurice Papon trial for collaboration with the Nazis in Vichy – a trial that began in 1997 when the Front was in Strasbourg – had just concluded. Papon was found guilty on April 2, 1998, and condemned to ten years in prison, but escaped his sentence due to old age (Rousso 1991).

On March 30, *Libération* claimed a "second wind [*souffle*]" of "anti-FN" mobilization.[14] Organizers claimed that there were 150,000 demonstrators

---

[12] This map (Fig. 5.2) was prepared using the times and places of demonstrations listed as "Tour de France des principales manifestations aujourd'hui." *L'Humanité* (Paris) March 28, 1998, p. 3. We have drawn circles with a 100-kilometer radius to demonstrate that on March 28, 1998 a demonstration was frequently less than 100 kilometers (60 miles) from whatever town or city a protester happened to be located in. Most French citizens would not have to travel more than that distance to attend a demonstration. The demonstrations were also timed in such a way that one could travel from one to the other.

[13] "Rien ne va plus á droite." *L'Humanité* (Paris) March 30, 1998, p. 8. Charles Millon was a candidate of the center right who accepted support of the National Front to become president of the Rhône-Alpes region (Martin 1999, pp. 230–237).

[14] Nicole Gauthier, "Mobilisation anti-FN: le deuxième souffle." *Libération* (Paris) March 30, 1998, pp. 2, 3.

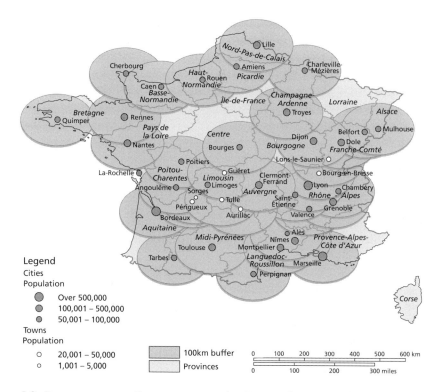

5.2 Protests across France against the National Front's showing in the March 1998 regional elections

in the streets. Newspapers carried pictures of mostly young people bearing banners saying "Non!" Yet, the living memory of the Nazis and collaboration was dying with Papon who represented the end of one stage of French history. Despite the outcry against Le Pen from left and right, the fact that Le Pen could advance as far as he did suggests that something profound was changing in French society. As the correspondent for the *International Herald Tribune* put it, "France's bugbear" was its inability to recognize and deal with change in any meaningful way.[15]

By April public opinion polls were suggesting that despite the outrage on the part of the "plural left," the Front was becoming normalized (*se banalise*) among the electorate who were less ideologically driven as

[15] John Vincour, "France's Bugbear: Change, not the National Front." *International Herald Tribune* (Paris) March 25, 1998, pp. 1, 8.

they voted and more concerned with their own well-being.[16] Chirac's plea not to bargain with the National Front went partially unheeded. In the end, seven regional presidents saved their presidencies by accepting National Front votes (Knapp 2004, p. 228). Le Pen drove a wedge through the center right that persisted through the presidential elections of 2002 and ultimately resulted in the reconfiguration of center rightwing parties.

Europe: "the new slavery of today"

May 1, 1998 was particularly exuberant for the National Front fresh from its March regional electoral victory and looking ahead to the European elections of June 1999. The date is part of the repertoire of celebratory days in European political culture as it is Labor Day for Socialist and Communist parties and often a day of demonstrations and counter-demonstrations.

Typically, the Front marches from the Palais Royal up the rue de Rivoli past the statue of Joan of Arc at the place de la Pyramide to the steps of the old Paris Opera House where Le Pen gives his annual speech. On May 1, 1998, the National Front claimed 40,000 supporters (the police estimated 11,000) in front of the Paris Opera House. A banner hung from the steps with a picture of Joan of Arc on her horse. The mantra of National Front values dominated the speeches: "honesty, family, fraternity, resistance, liberty, sovereignty, harmony, security, patriotism, fidelity, truth, courage, nation, devotion, identity, grandeur, honor, justice, determination, respect, work."

Le Pen's May 1 speech is always topical – linked to the issue of the year. In 1998, the issue was Europe and globalization. Le Pen drew on four recent political events to craft his speech. The first two events were European. In June 1997, the European Council approved the Amsterdam Treaty which expanded the competencies of the Maastricht Treaty to include a common immigration and security policy. The French state ratified it on December 31 without submitting it to a popular referendum even though the treaty required amending the French constitution. It took until December 1, 1998 for the French National Assembly to vote on the constitutional amendment that was necessary to allow the treaty to take effect in France.

---

[16] Gérard Courtois, "Le Front national se banalise aux yeux de l'électorat de droite." *Le Monde* (Paris) April 28, 1998; Christiane Chombeau, "Le Front national s'incruse dans le paysage politique." *Le Monde* (Paris) March 17, 1998.

On May 3, 1998, France was one of eleven EU member states that agreed to adopt the euro as a common currency on January 1, 1999. (The currency was not widely used until January 1, 2002.) In June 1998, a European Central Bank (ECB) was established in Frankfurt. The history of the National Front that was posted on its website in June 1998 identified the increased pace of European integration which Amsterdam and the euro represented as the principal enemy of France and condemned the complicity of the "global vision of the political establishment." The Front in 1998 defined itself as the "party of France" that aimed for a "French France in a European Europe."

Events in France gave Le Pen an emotionally potent frame of collaboration in which to recast the Treaty of Amsterdam and the single currency. The first event was the sentencing of Maurice Papon who had been a prefect during the Vichy period and was responsible for the arrest and deportation of Jews to Nazi concentration camps. The second event was Chirac's address to the French people on April 23, 1998 that commemorated the 150th anniversary of France's abolition of slavery. With the March 1998 elections in mind, Chirac reminded his audience that the principal lessons of the "spring of 1848" were, "To keep alive, or relive our model of integration. To be faithful to the values of our Republic. To lead, without relenting, everywhere in the world, the fight for liberty and dignity. To assume fully our duty of memory that is equal only to our duty of vigilance."[17]

On May 1, 1998, Le Pen gave an hour-and-a-half speech that began by comparing the Maastricht Treaty to the "infamous" Treaty of Troyes that brought the English to French soil. By analogy, contemporary France required its own Joan of Arc to drive out the "Eurocrats." Le Pen then shifted his focus to the celebration of labor – the remembrance of "bloody struggles." According to Le Pen, "euroglobalization" was reigniting those struggles as evidenced by high unemployment figures. Immigration, particularly clandestine immigration, exacerbated the problem by adding new workers to the French labor supply.

The villains in Le Pen's narrative are French politicians of the left and right who view globalization as "irresistible" and "unavoidable." The French political establishment has sold France into "modern slavery." The immigrants are also victims according to Le Pen as they arrive in France with "the golden chain of the occidental dream" promoted by

---

[17] www.elysee.fr/elysee/elysee.fr/Français/interventions/discours_et_declarations/1998/avril/ discours_de_m_jacques_chirac_president_de_la_republique_lors_de_la_reception_pour_ le_150e_anniversaire_de_l_abolition_de_l_esclavage.2821.html.

perfidious media such as CNN or NBC. Le Pen pursued this point relent-lessly: "In truth, ladies and gentlemen, the new slavery of today is the New World Order, and the new slave drivers are the big cheeses of international finance, of anonymous and itinerant finance that wants to destroy nations. This new slavery enslaves people of the entire world. The New Legal Tablets are the Chicago Stock Exchange or the Dow Jones index, their great priests are the GATT, the IMF, the OECD, their prophets are CNN and the *Washington Post*. And these obscure forces are in our midst, their Trojan horse, the eurocracy of Brussels."

Le Pen described the euro, the common currency, as "illegal and uncon-stitutional" because it was not in the Treaty of Maastricht, which the French ratified in 1992. The European Central Bank was going to be located in Frankfurt.[18] Le Pen did not waste the opportunity to draw a connection between the German occupation of France during Vichy and, by extension, the German reoccupation via the common currency. Le Pen called the "ignoble" euro the "money of occupation" and called on the French to "refuse to collaborate." He described Chirac as "a super collab-orationist" by signing on to the currency and accused the French President of carrying off French gold to Germany.

Le Pen said that Chirac had signed the death warrant of France and that he was worse than Hitler or Marshal Pétain. Le Pen called the euro an "economic error," a "conduit of social disaster" and a "political betrayal." In the aftermath of the Papon trial and a 1995 statement by Chirac that the French (perhaps) had not taken sufficient responsibility for their complic-ity in the fate of French Jews, "collaboration" with the Nazis was an emotionally charged political trope in France – as in fact revisionist histories are suggesting that many more collaborated than one would have imagined (Rousso 1991). *Libération* declared that Le Pen "indexed the euro to hatred" and described "resistance rhetoric" as an example of the "mobilization of all the classical semantics of the French right."

Le Pen ended his talk by reminding his followers that they needed to spend the next year mobilizing for the European parliamentary elections. These elections, which began in 1979, are held every five years and provide European citizens with the opportunity to elect directly representatives to the European Parliament. Le Pen has held a seat since 1984. The Front had elected ten deputies in 1984; ten deputies in 1989; and eleven deputies in

---

[18] On May 3, 1998, the European Council decided that eleven states, including France, were ready to adopt the euro as its currency. On June 1, 1999, the European Central Bank was established; and on January 1, 1999, the euro became the official currency of these eleven states, including France (Pinder 2001, 180).

1994. Le Pen was hoping that 1999 would be a banner year for the Front. Le Pen and the National Front planned to campaign for a year to send deputies to the European Parliament who would promote a "Europe of *Patries*, of Nations, of States." He would form a "resistance" drawing from "all political horizons," "all races, all religions to defend a *Patrie* in danger." As Joan of Arc had defended France 600 years earlier, the National Front would defend "patriots" and France from the "betrayal of unworthy leaders."

World Cup victory: "a France that wins together"[19]

In the wake of Le Pen's "success" in the regional elections, public despair and international embarrassment gripped the French public and political class. In the post-election period, the dilemmas of French identity and nationhood occupied the partners of the governing coalition. Four months after the regional elections, on July 12, 1998, the French soccer team won the World Cup. The French soccer victory set off a wave of collective public euphoria.[20] The government seized the victory as an unanticipated political cultural opportunity to redress the shame of Le Pen and burnish France's international image.

In contrast to their European neighbors who had greater expectations of victory, such as Germany and Italy, the French were not overly excited about the World Cup. The state had constructed a new Stadium of France with 80,000 seats on the outskirts of Paris in Saint-Denis for the occasion. The French team had never won a World Cup since the Cup's inception in 1930 and was not expected to win in 1998. As France advanced through the rounds to the finals, what most interested the press was the fact that for the first time French women were also interested in soccer. French philosopher Gilles Lipovetsky said that French women embraced soccer with "an aesthetic appropriation and emotional participation."[21] Newspapers of all political persuasions displayed pictures of young women in the streets with French flags painted on their faces.

---

[19] "Intervention télévisée de M. Jacques Chirac Président de la République à l'occasion de la fête nationale (Palais de l'Elysée)" www.elysee.fr/elysee/elysee.fr/frahtncais/interventions/interviews_articles_de_presse_et_interventions_televisees./1998/juillet/intervention_televisee_de_m_jacques_chirac_president_de_la_republique_a_l_occasion_de_la_fete_nationale-palais_de_l_elysee.3100.html.

[20] The essays in Dauncey and Hare (1999) describe the impact of the 1998 World Cup in France. Markovits (1998) and Lebovics (2004, pp. 136–142) go over much of the same terrain with slightly more attention to the political context.

[21] "Tout foot, tout femme." *Libération* (Paris) July 14, 1998, p. 8.

As France advanced, the collective excitement began to take on a life of its own. When it became clear that France would be in the finals against Brazil, the entire country gave way to a seemingly endless outpouring of public emotion. The press did not hesitate to pick up on the collective euphoria. *Libération*'s headlines after France advanced to the final round read: "All of France is Converted to the World Cup!"; "Everything is Ablaze! Everything is Soccer!" That day's edition emphasized how the French path to the finals "transcended all social cleavages."[22] The star player on the French team, Zinédine Zidane, was the son of Algerian immigrants (Markovits 1998). The press cited his career as reflecting glory on a new multicultural France. His stardom would erase the taint of the recent National Front electoral victory that had tarnished France's image in the world. Zidane, Zizou as he was affectionately called, was described as an "icon of integration." The team consisted of all races. *Libération* intoned: "The exploits of the Blues [the team name] converted France into a cult of soccer, men, women, blacks, whites, *beurs* [slang for second-generation North African immigrants], the World Cup finals' team is a model of integration."[23] *L'Humanité* proclaimed, "We are all soccer players!"[24] In anticipation of the final match, an editorial in *Le Monde* echoed Ernest Renan's famous essay, "What is a Nation?," and asked "What is a nation, if not joy, fear, common trembling?"[25]

When the French team won, a "miraculous victory" as one commentator put it, "historic ecstasy" ensued. A popular celebration broke out that was "unprecedented since the Liberation."[26] The police estimated that over a million and a half people spent the night of July 12 partying on the Champs Élysées. Coincidentally and conveniently, the victory occurred two days before July 14, Bastille Day, the traditional French national holiday. The combination of the victory and the national holiday initiated an emotionally charged celebration and public debate over the meaning of nationalism and multiculturalism in France.

On Bastille Day 1998, 500,000 people attended the annual parade on the Champs Élysées to celebrate the national holiday and the World Cup victory. *Le Monde* proclaimed, "A July 14 of a Galvanized France!"; *Libération* carried an eight-page centerfold and, with a picture of the

---

[22] "Tout feu, tout foot." *Libération* (Paris) July 10, 1998.
[23] Renaud Dély, "Zidane, icône de l'integration." *Libération* (Paris) July 10, 1998. Silverstein (2004, pp. 127–129) discusses Zidane's iconic status among *beur* youth.
[24] "Nous sommes tous des footballeurs." *L'Humanité* (Paris) July 11, 1998.
[25] Daniel Schneidermann, "Le maillot 23." *Le Monde* (Paris) July 13, 1998.
[26] "La France en liesse célèbre sa première coupe du monde." *Le Monde* (Paris) July 14, 1998, front page.

team among the crowds and flags, proclaimed, "A Holiday" and that a month of the World Cup had revealed a "blended France" (*la France en fusion*).[27] As the star player on the soccer team was the son of Algerian immigrants, the French state seized the victory as an opportunity to celebrate a multicultural France. Both the socialist Prime Minister, Lionel Jospin, and President Jacques Chirac exploited the soccer victory for their own political ends when they stood together on the reviewing stand to sing the national anthem.

Jacques Chirac took the opportunity of his annual televised Bastille Day address to the nation to use the soccer victory as a crucible of all that was worthwhile in French society and culture. His speech, as well as the panoply of events around the World Cup victory, was aimed at repairing the damage that France's image in the world had suffered due to the ascendance of Le Pen and the National Front.[28]

When the reporter asked Chirac about the significance of the World Cup victory, he said that "a people" needs "in a certain moment, to rediscover, to rediscover together, an idea that makes them proud of themselves." The Cup demonstrated "solidarity, cohesion" and showed that France had "a soul." When asked about the issue of racism in France, Chirac pointed out that France has from its origin been a "plural" society making "integration" a historic necessity. Emphasizing the image of France, Chirac shared his thoughts and emotions as the French soccer team passed the reviewing stand in the traditional parade, "it is true, this team at the same time tricolored [the blue, white, red of the French flag] and multicolored gave a beautiful image of France in which she is humane, strong, together."

When asked about the regional elections and whether he thought that the World Cup victory would erase some of the "disaffection" in French society that contributed to Le Pen's victory, Chirac said that he hoped that it would. When asked about whether the soccer victory might heal the national dissension over the Amsterdam Treaty, Chirac reaffirmed his support for the role of France in Europe. He said that the France that was dancing in the streets on the evening of July 12 was a "modern" and a "European" France. He argued that the only way France could play a role in the new international order was to become an integral part of Europe. According to Chirac, full participation in Europe is the only way to "defend our values, our standard of living, our lifestyle" and in the long

---

[27] "Le 14 juillet d'une France galvanisée." *Le Monde* (Paris) July 15, 1998, front page; "Jour de fête." *Libération* (Paris) July 14, 1998, front page.
[28] See footnote 19.

run the French version of democracy and the "Rights of Man." The idea that Europe would preserve France – a direct attack on Le Pen – was the theme that Chirac would return to as Euroskeptics on the left and right took center stage in French politics.[29]

Chirac's appropriation of the World Cup energy was widely viewed as a political coup for himself and his party. But Le Pen was not to be left on the sidelines even though the soccer victory was being widely interpreted as a repudiation of Le Pen and his beliefs. Le Pen seized the opportunity to put a National Front slant on events. Two years earlier, in 1996, Le Pen had attributed the resounding defeat of the French soccer team in the European games to the fact that many of the players were from immigrant families. In 1996, Le Pen claimed that the "foreign" players did not even know how to sing the national anthem (Marks 1999, p. 50). Confronted with the World Cup victory, Le Pen proclaimed that the team's success could be viewed as a "victory of the National Front which had animated the cadres." He pointed to the team's singing of the national anthem, *La Marseillaise*, to show that even the immigrants had finally come round to being good French men and declared a "lepénisation" of players' minds.[30] Reversing his earlier position, in what the press called a "new provocative diatribe," he said, "The National Front always recognized that French citizens can be of different races and religions as long as they share a common love of country and will to serve it." Invoking his infelicitous "gas chamber" remark, the ever provocative Le Pen described the multicultural French team as an outgrowth of post-colonial conflict and the World Cup as "a detail of the history of war [this time the Algerian War and not World War II] that drives peoples to the terrain of sport."[31]

On first glance, Le Pen's claiming the soccer victory appears farcical; a second glance suggests he may have not been so far off the political mark. The very public World Cup celebration not only served to distance the French nation/state from what they saw as the shame of Le Pen but also to appropriate the National Front's theme of nationhood with an honorable multicultural slant. National identity was not only on the mind of the

---

[29] This would be the government's central argument in the 2005 campaign for the European constitution, and it was Chirac's failure to call a referendum on the Treaty of Amsterdam which led to the referendum on the constitution and its ultimate defeat.

[30] *Lepénisation des esprits* was a phrase that Le Pen employed to describe the diffusion of his ideals among French citizens who were not members of the National Front.

[31] Envoyé spécial, "Le Pen: 'la Coupe du monde est un détail de l'histoire.'" *Libération* (Paris) July 13, 1998.

National Front. The editorial staff of the French news weekly *L'Express*, in a post-Cup special edition entitled, "The World Cup that Changed France," captured the combination of nationalism and multiculturalism that dominated both the representation of the victory and its collective emotional valence.[32] *L'Express* journalists emphasized the inclusiveness of the team and praised the immigrants as "team players," as opposed to the egocentric French players of old. A quote from a German newspaper that described its team as "white, old and tired," suggested that Germany, a traditional soccer power who had last won the World Cup in 1990, was looking to French multiculturalism as a model of how to improve its soccer team. A German sociologist seconded that opinion when he said that he "regretted" that Germany did not have a more inclusive citizenship law which would allow non-Germans on the team and maybe then Germany would be playing better soccer! – showing that the line between soccer and citizenship politics is thin.

According to *L'Express* the five weeks of the World Cup gave France an "improvised fraternity" that was reminiscent of May '68 – but with a difference. In contrast to May '68, springtime '98 was: "A revolution in the heads. But a revolution without barricades. A May '68 for everyone. People of the left as of the right, young and old, secure or unemployed. Surely, it is not only football. But when football makes one forget a country's ancestral cramps [as in "muscle" – a play on words] and renders it more tolerant, more generous and even – we dare the word – more intelligent, one asks for more [*on en redemande*]."

The emotional energy around the soccer victory generated a narrative around the French nation – a narrative that had been part of Le Pen's rhetorical repertoire. The soccer victory and the public response to it underscored the collective anxiety about France as a distinct and majestic nation-state that the National Front had frequently tapped with its generalized anti-immigrant and anti-Europe rhetoric.

In the end, the World Cup energy benefited everyone. It gave the French a collective feeling of joy and accomplishment that lifted the national mood. Le Pen appropriated the mood to the National Front. Not to be outdone on the multicultural terrain, Le Pen made sure that he created a photo opportunity at the 1998 *Fête des Bleu-Blanc-Rouge* to show that he and the National Front loved immigrants – if they became French. As the photograph suggests (Fig. 5.3), at the appropriate moment Le Pen and the National Front were willing to embrace the "other."

---

[32] Henri Haget *et al.*, "Ce mondial qui a changé la France." *L'Express* (Paris) June 16, 1998.

5.3 *Jean-Marie Le Pen and an unnamed person*, Fête des Bleu-Blanc-Rouge, *September 19, 1998*

The end of the beginning: 1999

The schism and the European parliamentary elections

In the summer of 1998, looking ahead to the European elections of June 1999 and buoyed by the Front's success in the regional elections, Le Pen, echoing Louis XIV, declared, "The Europeans are me!" His goal for the National Front was 20 percent of the available French seats in the European Parliament. Le Pen's goal was ambitious in the best of circumstances, as the Front had managed to send only eleven members to the European Parliament in 1994, and Le Pen faced other problems besides his lofty ambitions.

Bruno Mégret, second in command of the National Front, was Le Pen's heir apparent. The two men were opposites on virtually every dimension except in their commitment to a hyper-nationalist vision of France.

Mégret, educated at Berkeley and the *Grandes écoles*, was a cool, calculating technocrat. Eschewing the hyperbolic language and outrageous remarks that characterized Le Pen's public political persona, Mégret tended to be focused and reasoned.

For example, Mégret published his views on European Union in *The New Europe: For France and a Europe of Nations* (1998). He described European Union as "constructed" in Brussels – a "utopian scheme of Eurocrats who dream of a super European state occupied by all, but in reality, they destroy nations." In 290 pages, Mégret argued that Europe represented a common civilization but that each of its national cultures has individual integrity based upon years of tradition and governance. He advocated: "A Europe of nations [which] is conceived in effect as a political expression of the civilization that constitutes the families of Europe." He argued that economic merging is no reason to destroy identity and that to make Europe move forward it must preserve its past.

Mégret is widely considered the architect of the Front's "national preference" policy of jobs and houses to the native French first. And in February 1997, Mégret had installed his wife Catherine as mayor of Vitrolles. From the Front's Strasbourg convention of 1997 onwards, Mégret was making attempts to undermine the absolute leadership of Le Pen in the National Front. In the period after the regional elections in March 1998, when the Front did poorly in the cantonal elections, receiving only 7.4 percent in the second round, Mégret began to become more aggressive in his confrontations with Le Pen. He viewed Le Pen and his excesses as a political liability to the continuing advance of the National Front. In the late spring, Le Manifeste, one of the groups that organized public resistance to the National Front, described Mégret as "He is Le Pen at his worst [*C'est Le Pen en pire*]."[33] In the beginning of January 1999, the group around Le Manifeste believed that Mégret on his own posed a more serious threat than Le Pen. Mégret required a more disciplined and focused opposition movement. The rupture that was brewing between Mégret and Le Pen when Le Manifeste put out its January 16, 1999 position paper became final between January 23 and 24, 1999. On those dates, Mégret and his supporters organized an opposition party congress in Marignane and founded another rightwing party, the Mouvement National Républicain (MNR).

On the evening of the 1999 European elections, Le Pen gave a speech in which he said that the French clearly did not care about Europe or else there would not be an abstention rate of over 50 percent. He said that the

---

[33] Le Manifeste, "La déchirure," Paris January 16, 1999 (web document).

National Front suffered several handicaps in the election: first, the "cata-strophic betrayal" within the party; second, the blockage of their bank accounts and withdrawal of their annual subsidy; and third, Le Pen's continuous complaint that the French media did not provide equal time for the National Front so that its message could reach the French people. Le Pen described the media blackout as "unjust and profoundly anti-democratic treatment in the domain of information."[34]

As expected, the split in the National Front damaged the extreme right showing in the June 13 European elections. The National Front received only 5.7% of votes. Mégret's party received 3.3%. Charles Pasqua and Philippe de Villiers combined forces during the European elections to form La Rassemblement pour la France (RPF) as opposed to Chirac's Rassemblement pour la République (RPR). Philippe de Villiers was the head of Mouvement pour la France (MPF) – which continues to this day and which Le Pen viewed as his principal opposition for the nationalist vote. The Pasqua and de Villiers union received 13.1% of the vote in the 1999 European elections, elected thirteen delegates and captured much of the French anti-Europe sentiment. The combined French left of the Socialists, Greens and Communists – Gauche Plurielle – actually sur-passed even the center right in this election and received 38.4% of the vote.

Le Pen's analysis of the election results asserted that, without the "betrayal" of Mégret, the National Front would have come in second or third. By June 14, the political bureau of the Front issued the following communiqué on the elections, "Success finally and above all of the polit-ical voice opened by the National Front to change the Europe of unem-ployment, precariousness and technocracy. Millions of electors, some scattered among many lists cloned from the National Front program [a reference to Pasqua–de Villiers RPR list], have confirmed in effect on June 13 their adhesion to the ideas of sovereignty and identity of which Jean-Marie Le Pen assured the defense for two decades."

From July 2 to 4, 1999, the Le Manifeste group organized a public conference at the Sorbonne in Paris to assess "fifteen years of struggle against the extreme right."[35] Le Manifeste took credit for mobilizing 50,000 people to march in Strasbourg and for a public campaign to warn people of the dangers of a "true national right." Le Manifeste viewed the

---

[34] "Déclaration de Jean-Marie Le Pen" (June 13, 1999) www.frontnational.com/actualites. php.

[35] Le Manifeste, "Les rencontres du Manifeste contre le FN" (undated web document, internal dating after the European elections of June 13, 1999). I attended these meetings, which were subdued and resembled an academic conference rather than a mobilization event.

weak showing of both Mégret and Le Pen in the European elections as a serious obstacle to the continued advance of the extreme right in France. It gathered together a group of intellectuals, politicians, journalists and trade unionists to discuss the future of the right and the struggle against it. The group that came to the Sorbonne that day consisted of many of the prominent academics and public figures who had written, researched or mobilized against the National Front. The mood was cautious, but in general the group was of the mind that the split in the party had halted the forward momentum of the National Front.

Europeanization and globalization: challenges from right and left

The expanding project of European integration raised questions about national sovereignty and globalization that were becoming increasingly Le Pen's issues as 1998 slid into 1999. Le Pen's racist anti-immigrant rhetoric risked being seen as anti-French because it violated the principles of the Republic and the Rights of Man. In contrast, Le Pen's anti-Europe and anti-globalization rhetoric was becoming increasingly a French rhetoric – and a French leftwing rhetoric. At the end of his May Day speech in 1998, Le Pen staked out the National Front's claim to anti-Europeanization and anti-globalization. He argued:

Let us be clear. We are not enemies of Europe, but we do not want just any Europe, not a global Europe that wants to make us slaves.
A Europe of Maastricht, that is a Europe of Capital, for Capital, by Capital.
Yes to a Europe of *Patries*, of Nations, of States.
Yes to a common money, symbol of fraternal cooperation of Europeans.
But frankly, very frankly, No, a thousand times no, to a single currency.
No to globalization.
No to the euroglobalization of stateless capitalism.

Le Pen's anti-Europe and anti-globalization rhetoric gave voice to a national mood that lacked a public forum. In the spring of 1997, before the Front's Strasbourg congress, *L'Express*, the French weekly, asked Pierre-André Taguieff, a vocal scholar of racism in France, whether Le Pen was profiting from the lack of clear distinctions between the center left and center right on economic issues. Taguieff replied, "Absolutely, the National Front occupies a space that was abandoned [by the left]: that of resistance to turbocapitalism."[36] Taguieff gave this interview in spring

---

[36] Pierre-André Taguieff: "La droite me fait penser à un pachyderme effondré." *L'Express* March 4, 1997, p. 34.

1997; by December 1997 a leftwing popular opposition to "turbocapitalism" in France had emerged.

In December 1997, Ignacio Ramonet, editor in chief of *Le Monde Diplomatique*, wrote an editorial, "Let's Disarm the Markets," and fired the first shot in this round of the leftwing war against global capitalism.[37] Seven months after Ramonet's call to arms, Bernard Cassen, director general of *Le Monde Diplomatique*, and an assortment of trade unionists, intellectuals and human rights activists, founded ATTAC (*Action pour une Taxe Tobin d'Aide aux Citoyens*) in Paris in June 1998.[38] The Tobin Tax was named after James Tobin the Nobel Prize-winning economist who recommended a tax on international monetary transactions to moderate the effects of exchange speculation. ATTAC named its weekly email newsletter *Sand in the Wheels* after Tobin's metaphor that an international finance tax would, like sand in the wheels of a car, slow the advance of global capitalism (Eichengreen *et al.* 1995). The ATTAC group uses the % sign as their logo. They became active in Paris in the late 1990s with meetings and publishing. In 1999, their collective published a small didactic book called *Against the Dictatorship of Markets* (Cassen *et al.* 1999).

In this early period, ATTAC was overshadowed by a colorful compatriot, the French farmer José Bové, who in March 1999 dismantled a McDonald's in the French town of Millau and became a martyr to the anti-globalization cause as he valiantly agreed to stand trial and go to prison. Bové, who had lived in Berkeley with his parents as a child, was an activist farmer who founded a Farmers' Agricultural Union in the French countryside where he lived and worked when he was not involved in transnational protest events. In 2001, Verso published the English edition of Bové's manifesto, *The World is Not for Sale: Farmers Against Junk Food*.

ATTAC was founded two years before the mobilization in Seattle in the United States against the GATT talks. ATTAC spent much of 1998 and 1999 disseminating its ideas. Its first large anti-Europe mobilization occurred in December 2000 in Nice at the meeting of the European Council of Ministers. ATTAC's target was the European Union's Charter of Fundamental Rights. The slogan "Another Europe is possible" that

---

[37] See Ignacio Ramonet, "Désarmer les marchés." *Le Monde Diplomatique* (Paris) December 1997, p. 1. For a summary of the general antipathy of French intellectuals to globalization, see Leruth (2001).

[38] On ATTAC, see Ancelovici (2002) and Waters (2003); on anti-globalization movements more generally, see Wieviorka (2003); on transnational movements, see Keck and Sikkink (1998) and Tarrow (2005).

ATTAC created for this event bore a resemblance to Le Pen's rhetoric on May Day 1998.

Defending sovereignty and the Republic

The defense of national sovereignty is the flip side of the attack on Europeanization. The Amsterdam Treaty, which the French had ratified in December 1997 and was scheduled to go into effect in May 1999, provided the focus of Le Pen's anti-Europe rhetoric in 1999. The Amsterdam Treaty, which was an amendment to the Maastricht Treaty, completed the process of European integration by calling for a common immigration policy and a common security policy. On both of these issues, the treaty could be said to challenge the boundaries of the nation-state and pose a threat to national sovereignty (Krasner 1999, pp. 9–25).

Le Pen's first speech in 1999 was a diatribe against the Treaty of Amsterdam. Speaking from the place de la Loi (Plaza of the Law) in Paris, Le Pen pointed out that January 17 was the 206th anniversary of the day that Louis XVI was condemned to death. Le Pen drew a parallel between the end of monarchical sovereignty that the King's death brought and the end of the "sovereignty of the French people, the sovereignty of the Nation" that Europe, Maastricht and Amsterdam threatened. Le Pen argued that the Treaty of Amsterdam violated the French constitution, particularly Article 3 which defines sovereignty as resting with the French people. The treaty also violated Article 5 which speaks to the issue of executive powers.

Passing the Amsterdam Treaty in France required a constitutional revision on which the French Constitutional Council was set to vote on the day after Le Pen's speech. Earlier the Council had determined that the treaty met the minimum conditions for maintaining national sovereignty. Le Pen, never at a loss for rhetorical flourish, described the French constitution as a patient with Parkinson's disease (*le Parkinson constitutionnel*) that "trembled" when "Brussels spoke." He claimed that the constitution was revised eleven times to accommodate the Europeanization process.[39] Le Pen continued his theme of the defense of national sovereignty in his annual May 1 speech as well as in his speech that closed the *Fête des Bleu-Blanc-Rouge*. His speech at the National Front's summer university in September was entitled, "French Hope at the Dawn of the Third Millennium." Undaunted by the split in the party and the defeat in the

---

[39] www.frontnational.com/doc_interventions_detail.php?id_inter=10 (accessed October 9, 2006).

European elections in June, Le Pen told the assembled cadres of future leaders that the "totalitarian project" – by which he meant Europe – views the National Front as its "principal target." According to Le Pen, the National Front, in order to "save France," must "carry out a decisive and prolonged reconstruction of fundamental values." A "renovated, reorganized, dynamised" National Front would play a decisive role in future battles against the "enemies of the *Patrie*."[40]

In April 1999, Le Pen authored a pamphlet entitled, *Lettres françaises ouvertes*. The book consisted of eight essays in the form of letters to French public figures. The letters were addressed to Marie-France Garaud, Philippe de Villiers, Charles Pasqua, Charles de Gaulle, Jean-Pierre Chevènement and Lionel Jospin. The popular author Max Gallo and the film star Alain Delon were included. What united the politicians was that they had all questioned or placed limits on the project of Europe. For example, Garaud had broken with her party and campaigned against the ratification of the Maastricht Treaty in 1992. The popular-culture figures represented Frenchness. Le Pen described the letters as similar to "letters in a bottle" that are then cast off to sea. Someone might find them and they might have an effect. They might also simply toss in the ocean. Whether or not the addressees or anyone else read the letters, they did demonstrate that Le Pen and his party were beginning to cast a wide net around the issue of sovereignty and Europe.

The "Actualities of the National Front," the press notices that the National Front issued between January 1, 1999 and the European elections in June, reveal a party that is engaging in public debate on a wide range of French and European issues. The National Front's positions on various issues were not idiosyncratic to the party. In seventy-three dispatches, Le Pen's statements ran from comments on increasing crime rates in France to the war in Kosovo (in which he sided with the Serbs), European integration, the upcoming European elections, the contaminated blood affair in France, the PACS unions that were destroying the French family and not surprisingly diatribes against Bruno Mégret.

While Le Pen and the National Front were visibly and vocally defending national sovereignty against a panoply of threats, a less flamboyant defense came from the French state in the summer of 1999. Jacques Chirac refused to permit France to ratify the Council of Europe's European Charter for Regional or Minority Languages (Oakes 2001, pp. 116–125). This was a document aimed at protecting minority languages. Metropolitan France itself has ten such languages – Occitan, Breton, Basque,

---

[40] www.front-nat.fr/discours (October 22, 1999).

Catalan, Flemish, Alsatian, Corsican, Frankish, Franco-Provençal and Öil. Lionel Jospin as Prime Minister signed the Charter, which is a convention in effect since 1992. Signatories must sign thirty-five of the document's ninety-eight articles and France had signed thirty-nine.

When the Charter became an issue in the spring of 1999, Chirac commissioned Bernard Cerquiglini, Director of the National Institute of the French Language, to look into the matter and prepare a report.[41] Chirac sent the report to the French Constitutional Council for review to determine whether it would be necessary to amend the French constitution in order to ratify the language charter. The Council articulated a tension embedded within French constitutional law and political culture. On the one hand, ratifying the Charter violated Article 1 of the French constitution that claims that the French people are one and sovereignty belongs to the nation. This is the principle of Republicanism. Article 2 of the constitution says that, "The language of the Republic is French." On the other hand, not approving the language charter violated the spirit of Article 11 of the Declaration of the Rights of Man that guarantees "freedom of expression." Similar tensions would emerge four years later in 2003, when the French government took up the question of the wearing of the Muslim headscarf in public.

The Council decided that the Charter violated the constitution because its provisions, "confer specific rights on 'groups' of speakers of regional or minority languages within 'territories' in which these languages are used, undermine the constitutional principles of the indivisibility of the Republic, equality before the law and the unicity of the French people." In addition, France had already implemented practices that promoted regional languages.

Based on these reports and recommendations, Chirac decided not to ratify the Charter because it required an amendment to the French constitution. Chirac's public argument was that ratifying the Charter would destroy national cohesion. In some leftwing circles, the refusal to ratify the Charter produced, as *Libération*'s headline so coyly put it, "Open mouths." Situated within the general stream of events in 1999, the Charter ruling was a relatively understated issue – a soft iteration of the national sovereignty issue.[42] Chirac's decision came three weeks after the European elections. His rejection of the Charter and his defense of

---

[41] "Les langues de la France, April 1999" www.culture-gouv.fr/culture/ (accessed October 7, 2006); www.culture.gouv.fr/culture/dglf/lang-reg/rapport_cerquiglini/langues-france.html.

[42] "Langues régionales: les bouches s'ouvrent." *Libération* (Paris) July 5, 1999, front page. Viaut (2004) provides a cogent account of the history of the Charter as well as the French position on it.

the French constitution – a defense of law and culture – was a harbinger of things to come. The difference of opinion between the left and center right on the European Charter for Regional or Minority Languages foreshadowed the ambivalence toward Europe that was paradoxically not only a rightwing and center right emotion, but a more general collective emotion, shared by French citizens and the French state – which was in theory one of the strongest advocates of a new Europe.[43]

Summary

Turning point: the paradox of defeat

In May 2000, French academics who studied the National Front announced to *Le Monde* that they had redirected their research agendas to more general European issues of racism.[44] In short, they had written off the National Front as a political threat. The evidence of this chapter suggests that the "rupture" in late fall 1998 between Mégret and Le Pen, followed by the National Front's weak showing in the European elections, was the end of the beginning and not the beginning of the end for the National Front.

The year 1999 was pivotal for the National Front – but not for the reasons that analysts typically provide. The year marked a turning point – a moment of departure from which the entity under consideration charts a new path for itself.[45] The first obvious point is that Le Pen and the National Front did not disappear from the political landscape. The second point is that Mégret and his breakaway party never developed the widespread voter appeal that Le Pen, for better or worse, managed to maintain until the 2007 presidential elections.

By focusing upon events as *templates of possibilities*, my analysis identifies three tendencies that came together in 1999 that standard accounts of the National Front overlook. First, Le Pen's issues were becoming increasingly French issues. Second, independently of Le Pen, an anti-Europe position was forming in civil society that linked Europeanization and globalization. Third, the French state itself began to give mixed signals on the issue of Europe and the program of Europe. From mad cow disease, to Kosovo to the euro, to domestic security, to the Charter for Regional or Minority Languages, Le Pen tapped the national *esprit*.

---

[43] On ambivalence as a social emotion, see Smelser (1998).
[44] Nicolas Weill, "Les universitaires analysent l'ampleur du déclin de l'extrême droite en France." *Le Monde* (Paris) April 30–May 2, 2000, p. 8.
[45] Abbott (1997) theorizes the analytic significance of turning points.

Upon closer examination, much of the National Front's official platform from the *300 Measures* in 1993 to the millennium was anti-liberal and
conservative rather than xenophobic and racist. The platform among
other things called for a restoration of family values, was anti-abortion,
tough on crime and sought to strengthen traditional French institutions
such as the military and the courts. Many of the Front's purely economic
positions such as agricultural subsidies were also in line with French
cultural ideals (National Front 1993).[46]

In the summer of 1999, the National Front was ever more ingrained in
the French political landscape because Le Pen's issues were becoming
more manifestly French issues. Events were forcing the French state and
its politicians to find "good answers" to the "real problems" from unemployment to immigration that Le Pen had raised. A paradox emerged from
the National Front's defeat in the European elections and the rupture
within the party. Le Pen and the National Front were becoming more
salient and influential just at the point at which politicians and academic
analysts assumed that they were in terminal decline.

---

[46] France has been the strongest supporter of the EU's Common Agricultural Policy as well
as one of the largest beneficiaries. On the history of France's involvement in the CAP, see
Moravcsik (2000a, b).

6

The 2002 presidential elections: the fabulous destiny of Jean-Marie Le Pen

Amélie and ennui: popular culture and political mood in summer 2001

The early summer of 2001 was sleepy in France. Unemployment was down for the first time in years but crime was up. A lackluster political campaign for the spring 2002 presidential elections was beginning between the socialist Prime Minister Lionel Jospin and sitting President Jacques Chirac. Revelations that Chirac had been involved in bribes and corruption punctuated the otherwise politically somnolent early summer. Mainstream political life in France and elsewhere seemed uneventful.

The French anti-globalization group ATTAC had planned protest events for June in Gothenburg, Sweden at the time of the biannual European meetings, and for July in Genoa, Italy, at the annual G8 summit meetings. Violence erupted during these events. In early summer 2001, opposition to globalization and Europeanization was emerging as a left-wing and rightwing populist issue, but it would have been hard to view the mobilizations in Sweden and Italy as harbingers of significant political trends. Lionel Jospin's *My Vision of Europe and Globalization* ([2001] 2002), written in preparation for the 2002 presidential campaign, supported the Treaty of Nice, an expanded social Europe and a European constitution. In the summer of 2001, Jospin's book appeared on target; by spring 2002, it would prove off the mark as a document of popular political persuasion. The French presidential elections of April 2002 and the European constitutional referendum of May 2005 suggested that attacks on globalization and Europe resonated with the political perceptions and instincts of French citizens and were not simply the idiosyncratic outbursts of fringe groups.

During the summer of 2001, it would have been difficult to imagine September 11 and the renewed acts of religious violence and global conflict that it would generate. In France, it was difficult to imagine that Jean-Marie Le Pen could come in second place in the first round of the 2002 presidential elections. As the summer of 2001 began, French intellectuals and political commentators were principally thinking and talking about popular culture. That popular culture would matter is not surprising in France. A recent Eurobarometer (European Commission 2004a) survey that asked, "Which three of the following are most important to you?" from a range of entities from family to work to friendship revealed that 8 percent of the French, and only the French, chose "arts and culture." They were 4 percentage points above (twice as high as) the European average on the valuation of culture.[1]

French pundits discussed the television reality show *Loft Story* as an example of the degradation of French culture. Until the "shock" of Le Pen's second place in spring 2002, the biggest cultural "shock" among French intellectuals was the memoir, *La vie sexuelle de Catherine M.* (Millet 2001). Written by a prominent member of the French art establishment, *Catherine* detailed the author's twenty years of prodigious sexual exploits and was a bestseller in France in summer 2001.[2] Meanwhile, the French flocked en masse to see the film *Le fabuleux destin d'Amélie Poulain*, about a lower-middle-class waitress who develops a capacity to see into the souls of those around her. Amélie magically makes her co-workers' dreams come true, their phobias disappear and she herself finds true love. The film is a whimsical romance shot in the Paris subway stations, cafés of Montmartre and the countryside.

In less than a month, *Amélie* made more money at the box office than the majority of French films made in a year.[3] The film's resounding popularity drew the attention of the cultural and political establishment. *Amélie* had trans-cultural appeal. The American entertainment newsletter *Variety* called *Amélie* "an event in the history of cinema." But *Amélie* was a French production with French actors and French settings, and French intellectuals could not ignore its impact. The popularity of the film triggered a protracted debate in the pages of the French leftwing newspaper *Libération*. The debate began with an article by two founding members of Génération République, the youth division of Pôle Républicain, a splinter

---

[1] This figure must be placed in context of the entire list of valuations which were scored on a scale. In general, the top three entities that Europeans valued were family (82%), health (58%) and work (39%).

[2] The memoir had an English translation. But its main draw was the gossipy portrayal of the French art world – devoid of that context, the memoir did not fare that well in the American market.

[3] "Café Society." *Sight & Sound* review, August 2001, www.bfi.org.uk/sightandsound/feature/15/.

leftwing group founded by Jean-Pierre Chevènement in April 2001 in preparation for the presidential elections in spring 2002. In this article, the authors argued that the "secret" of the film's success was that *Amélie* spoke to the "little people" with "tenderness and respect." It was only the "snobs" who had refused the film a place at the Cannes film festival who had described *Amélie* as "populist." The authors attributed the film's popularity to the fact that *Amélie* gave its audience "hope."[4] Hope is a resonating political trope in French political discourse. Charles de Gaulle entitled his autobiography *Memoirs of Hope*. French communists made hope their theme when they campaigned against the European constitution. Even Le Pen published a book of interviews entitled simply *Hope* (*L'espoir*) (1989).

Serge Kaganski, a Parisian film critic, responded to the initial comments in *Libération* a few days later and said that the world of *Amélie* depicted a reactionary vision of Paris that was an ideal fit as a piece of National Front propaganda: "if the demagogue of La Trinité-sur-Mer [Le Pen's home-town] was seeking a clip to illustrate his discourse, promote his vision of people and his idea of France, it seems to me that Amélie Poulain would be an ideal candidate." Kaganski argued that the film resembled a postcard of a France long gone – "totally disconnected from contemporary reality."[5] *Amélie* represented Paris as a "village" with a "profoundly reactionary" ideology. Kaganski's Paris is multicultural and filled with persons of diverse sexual orientations: "The Paris of Jeunet [the director] is meticulously 'cleaned' of all of its ethnic, social, sexual and cultural polysemy." Not to be outdone by Kaganski, a film correspondent for *Libération* responded that *Amélie* is free of ideology and speaks to the "contemporary social and affective misery" of the middle classes.[6] The writer defines the experience of *Amélie* not as "lepéniste" but rather as similar to a night spent watching television. In *Amélie*, Montmartre resembles Euro-Disney.

French politicians became involved with this *bonbon* of a film.[7] President Jacques Chirac had the film screened for himself and his wife at his official residence. He came to the showing tired and left revitalized and asked to buy his own copy. Lionel Jospin and other prominent social-ists also viewed the film. A critic characterized the politicians as "surfing the wave" of the film's popularity and argued that *Amélie* had "the

---

[4] David Martin-Castelnau and Guillaume Bigot, "Le secret d'Amélie Poulain." *Libération* (Paris) May 28, 2001.

[5] Serge Kaganski, "'Amélie' pas jolie." *Libération* (Paris) May 31, 2001.

[6] Philippe Lançon, "Le frauduleux destin d'Amélie Poulain." *Libération* (Paris) June 1, 2001.

[7] Didier Perón, "Quatre millions d'adhérents au parti d'Amélie Poulain." *Libération* (Paris) June 2, 2001.

perfume of opportunism, seen by demagogues as if the film held in the secret of its seduction a sacred particle of the spirit of the nation, despite its political cleavages." Pundits joked that both Chirac and Jospin were mining the film for ideas as to how to rekindle the collective effervescence that the French felt when they won the World Cup in 1998.

Libération concluded its series by interviewing a group of politicians of diverse political perspectives.[8] A center right politician argued that the film displayed a "demand for a profound humanity in our society." He would call his political project, "The Humane France." The socialist mayor of the *arrondissement* where the film was shot said that *Amélie* depicted life perfectly in her quarter – the blend of the "natural with the extraordinary." The Communist Party representative said that the film demonstrated the "need to dream." Finally, an RPR deputy argued that political strategists who sent the presidential candidates to view the film to learn what to feel or say were profoundly misguided, "*Amélie Poulain* neither merits the indignity of being compared to a National Front film nor the honor of the Presidents. Amélie has the attraction of an 'adorable child' that one sees on the street and loves for its innocence."

Amélie was fantasy, but in the end, all of Amélie's dreams and desires come true. As such, *Amélie* is a dubious model for life and an even more dubious model for politics. This film is not an obvious object of interest for a political cultural analysis. An overtly apolitical film, it only gained political significance when it attracted the attention of French politicians and intellectuals. Chirac and Jospin viewed it to discover a political mood which they were incapable of ferreting out on their own. In this regard, the film stands as a kind of perverse political metaphor. Politics by the tone deaf misses the mark.

In *Ces Français qui votent FN* (*The French Who Vote for the National Front*) ([1999] 2002), political scientist Nonna Mayer says that the National Front attracts people who succumb to the "force of simple ideas" and who view the world in "black and white" (p. 73). Successful politicians of all political persuasions know that complexity does not win elections. Even before contemporary soundbite political culture, simplicity won the electorate. In the summer of 2001, French mainstream politicians weighed down with complex intellectual arguments and intricate analyses were in search of simple ideas. In contrast to their colleagues in other political parties, the National Front, for better or worse, always knew what it wanted and said it without nuance.

---

[8] Gilles Bresson, Renaud Dély and Didier Hassoux, "Un besoin de bonheur simple." *Libération* (Paris) June 3, 2001.

On May 1, 2001, Jean-Marie Le Pen targeted the 2002 presidential elections saying, "It will be 2002 or never!"[9] He told his supporters that it is time to engage in the "battle of France for France" and to "break up the plot against France."[10] The "battle of France" is the name for the German and Italian invasion of France in 1940, after which France fell to the Axis Powers and was occupied until 1944. In Le Pen's metaphor, the National Front is invading France to save it from a new genre of internal and external enemies. Le Pen railed against a "veritable plot against the Nation and consequently against the Republic which is in the institutional cadres." A central component of the plot against France is the "globalist revolution" that aims "to destroy" national "political, social and moral structures" and replace them with a "New World Order." The center of this conspiracy on the European scale is:

Federal Europe of Brussels, that of the Treaties of Maastricht, Schengen and Amsterdam, that which has already imposed 60% of the laws that govern us and takes from us progressively all the attributes of sovereignty: the control of our frontiers, regional politics, monetary independence, defense ... [and] from 2004 will be the guardian of our immigration policy. An anticipated method to denationalize us, is massive immigration from the population of the Third World with whom it is strongly recommended that we physically, culturally and religiously crossbreed [*métisser*]. The American General Wesley Clark, commander in chief of NATO, declared in July 1999: "There is no place in Europe for non-mixed peoples."

Le Pen complained that he was unjustly labeled a "racist" and "xenophobe" because he has always pointed to the problems inherent in mass immigration. He considers this an unfair charge as he argues that immigration has consequences for which the French establishment has failed to account. Of course, in this May 1 speech, he is linking United States' imperialism to the threat to French nationality posed by both Europe and transnational organizations such as the International Monetary Fund (IMF) and NATO.[11] Le Pen says that in 2002, he will be the one who "With you men and women, young boys and girls of my country, will engage as the head of a grand National Reunion in the battle of France, for France, for its independence and its sovereignty, for identity, security and liberty of the French people."

As discussed in Chapter 5, spring 1999 marked a turning point for Le Pen and the National Front – the end of the beginning. Fall 2001 and the campaign for the presidency marked a turning point in French politics

---

[9] Oliver Pognon, "Le Pen joue 2002 ou jamais." *Le Figaro* (Paris) May 2, 2001.
[10] www.frontnational.com/doc_interventions (accessed June 21, 2005).
[11] On anti-Americanism and French political culture, see Revel (2002).

more generally. Contingent events, such as the attack on the World Trade Center, combined with the push for a more expanded version of European integration, not only changed the landscape of international politics, but also reverberated within the politics of individual nation-states. France did not escape the effects of contingent events. Le Pen rode the wave of events.

In short, contingent events made Le Pen's issues French issues and he capitalized on the twists and turns of national and international politics. This chapter follows Le Pen and the National Front from its party congress in April 2000, where he first declared his intention of running for President, to the 2002 election and its aftermath. It describes the "shock" of April 21, 2002 when Le Pen came in second place after Jacques Chirac in the first round of the presidential elections. Chapter 7 turns to the 2005 defeat of the referendum on the European constitution. The thread that connects these events, the 2002 presidential elections and the 2005 referendum, is an intensifying collective French assertion of nation-ness in the face of increasing Europeanization and external security threats. Le Pen did not win any national elections. Given his age and setbacks in the 2007 presidential elections, it is not likely that he ever will. But it was never likely that he would win a national election. His significance lay in his capacity to elicit collective emotion and to force the French to reevaluate their national self-perceptions. In that respect, Le Pen's political trajectory, as it intertwined with contemporary French history, has been as fabulous as Amélie's destiny.

Climbing back (2000–2002)

"Let's liberate France!"

In April 2000, the National Front had its eleventh party congress in Paris – the first since Strasbourg and the first since the rupture with Mégret. In general, the press and the social scientists who studied Le Pen considered him and his party weakened to a point where they could not possibly be a political threat. For example, when *Libération* interviewed Nonna Mayer, leading scholar on the social composition of the National Front, they asked her whether she thought the Front had the capacity to bargain for outcomes as they had done in the regional elections of 1998. Her answer was definitive: "They are considerably weakened. The National Front will find it much harder to maintain itself in a second round and to impose the triangulations which often lead to the defeat of the moderate right. And it will weigh less heavy in the general matter of political debate."[12]

---

[12] Interview with Nonna Mayer, *Libération* (Paris) April 30, 2000, p. 15.

Alluding to the break with Mégret, *Libération* described Le Pen as the "uncontested head" of a "weakened Front."[13] The French communist newspaper *l'Humanité* described Le Pen at his congress as so weakened as to be "ravaged."[14] Le Pen had had a series of setbacks in addition to the break with Mégret and the division of the party. In November 1998, Le Pen's eligibility to run for public office had been suspended for a year because of a physical confrontation that he had with a socialist woman candidate in 1997. After the January 1999 split, Le Pen retained legal control of the name "Front national." In June 1999, he received public aid in the amount of 41 million francs for the Front as a political party, but this was the same June that he received only 5.69 percent of votes in the European elections. In February 2000, he was deprived of his mandate as regional councilor in PACA; and in April he was deprived of his mandate as a European deputy for a year as a result of his attack on the socialist deputy. Thus, it was not surprising that many analysts and political opponents considered him and his party weak and ineffective.

But to underestimate Le Pen was a mistake. His vision had broadened and if his language had not exactly softened he was, at least, sometimes managing to contain his more outrageous remarks. Although he does not characterize it as such, much of his rhetoric is a version of "épater la bourgeoisie," only this time it is "épater le politically correct," as he likes to call everyone that he views as an ideological opponent. In the 1980s, characterizing Le Pen as a single-issue anti-immigrant candidate was apt. By the late 1990s and beginning of the millennium, this frame failed to capture the expansiveness of his political ideas. Le Pen's shift in emphasis to Europe, globalization and unemployment attracted broad constituencies in an increasingly insecure France.

A popular National Front slogan about French nationality was that one had to "inherit or merit it." Thus, the National Front was opposed only to those immigrants who steadfastly refused to be French. It is difficult to refuse to be French in France. The nation-state has an assimilationist policy that is reinforced through its commitment to Republican tradition. Frenchness is uniformly imposed in the French state school system from the earliest age. And as the Charter of Regional Languages issue illustrated even the President was reluctant to do anything to compromise the constitutional mandate that declares French as the national language.

The theme of the party congress was "Let's liberate France!" (*Libérons la France*). Le Pen's speech at the congress draws a rhetorical line in the sand

---

[13] Christophe Forcari, *Libération* (Paris) April 30, 2000, pp. 14, 15.
[14] "Extrême droite: la draguée est en noir." *l'Humanité* (Paris) April 28, 2000, p. 10.

between the past and the present of both the Front and France.[15] Ignoring the real and perceived weakness of the National Front, Le Pen speaks with exuberance of new projects and goals. He announces that the Front's "next battles" will be "electoral." He lists threats to French society as follows: "globalization, communism, Europeanization, decline (*décadence*), decline in natality, unemployment, immigration, insecurity, corruption, political and cultural colonization" (a swipe at American popular culture). Acknowledging that change in the world is "a reality that cannot be contested," Le Pen proposes a new National Front to meet the challenges of change. He argues that in contrast to communism, which at least sought to benefit the poor, globalization aims to benefit the rich. He accuses French "pseudo-elites" of being in the camp of globalists when they support Europe.

Le Pen argues that "insecurity" is a consequence of globalization because "social instability" results when many civilizations "are installed" on French soil and generate "everyday confrontations" that are the "first signs of nascent barbarism." There is a national need to liberate France from globalization and to "dare to say no to Europe." Le Pen argues that the National Front should no longer be viewed as an old "political for-mation," but rather, that the congress must be understood as "the point of departure for a movement of national resistance, a veritable union of defense of the French first and the sole possibility of a renaissance for our *patrie*." The National Front of the congress of 2000 is on a "historic mission to liberate France, Europe and even the world."

Despite the characteristically inflated language, the National Front's "program for government" as outlined in the 423-page *Pour un avenir français* (*For a French Future*) (2001) is sober – with policy prescriptions under each of the numerous topics that range from identity to sovereignty to security. The document reads like a textbook and it lacks the free-floating propagandistic tone and looseness of the earlier position books. The six themes of the book emerged from the work of twenty-one sub-commissions that formed around different sub-themes. Forty-two National Front operatives and three administrative staff put the book together for the party congress. *Pour un avenir français* was a professional document and signaled a new dimension to National Front operations. Despite covering all the social and economic issues that were affecting France, Europe and the rejection of Europe were at the center of the Front's program. In his introduction, Le Pen argues that the "Europe of Brussels is a prison for its peoples" (p. 8). The opening chapter places

---

[15] www.frontnational.com/doc_interventions (June 21, 2005).

France in a field of universalism, memory and the sacred. The book then plunges into discussion of identity that addresses immigration.

In a section labeled, "No to the Islamization of France," the book points out that France had 50 mosques in 1974 and in 1999 (when the book was researched) there were 1,536 (p. 58). The argument in this section is a harbinger of things to come – asserting that the Islamic notion of community is intrinsically opposed to the French notion of Republicanism and that the *umma* (the closed community of Muslims) is a daily threat to French sovereignty because it creates a system of "dual allegiance."[16] In the pre-9/11 period, this seemed like a xenophobic remark. Post-September 11, it takes on a different color. According to this book, the Front respects the religious practice of those Muslims who risked their lives to choose France in the Algerian War, and the policy solution is to place mosques under the French law of association so that they can be monitored for political subversion. The other policy suggestions on immigration (pp. 67–73) aim at tightening the laws for acquiring French citizenship, being less lenient toward illegal immigrants (*clandestines* and *sans-papiers*) and being stricter about family reunification.

The severest section of the Front's program is devoted to the issue of sovereignty. There is a picture of a map of France in chains. Cartoons of Uncle Sam make it clear that the United States is the chief of the New World Order and that it is promoting supra-nationalism to further its interest in world domination at the expense of smaller nation-states. The expanding process of Europeanization is by extension another arm of the United States and globalization that must be resisted at all costs. One of the downsides of Europe according to the Front is that it will submerge France in the "culture of Hollywood." Europe with its "judicial totalitarianism" will mean the end of "social protection" and the sacrifice of the nation to the regions.[17] The major proposal on this score is the most extreme – France must exit the European Union. The program also points out that the various treaties of the EU violate Article 55 of the French constitution that "does not permit international treaties to have a superior authority to French law."

When Le Pen began to make Europe and globalization his issue, he entered an area that directly touched more French people than immigration. Europe was a more universal issue since it did not rely on having direct negative contact with immigrant groups. It was less an emotional

---

[16] See Warner and Wenner (2006) for the strengths and limitations of this argument.
[17] Le Galès (2002) takes up the issue of urban governance and regionalism in contemporary Europe.

issue, even though Le Pen frequently couched it in the language of emotion, than a rational issue. Europe and globalization could be pointed to as bringing unemployment and threatening the French social welfare system – in short, touching just about everyone. Less charged with the language of intolerance and hate, anti-Europe sentiment could be respectable. It was also a sentiment that had a history in France – as de Gaulle had warned against becoming too involved in Europe.[18]

Defending sovereignty/ATTAC-ing markets

Two events that buttressed the National Front's April congress placed in relief the increasing significance of the party. In February 2000, Jörg Haider's rightwing Freedom Party achieved enough votes to become part of a governing coalition in Austria. The second event was the mobilization that ATTAC staged in Nice in December 2000 to protest the Charter of Fundamental Rights that was an addendum to the Maastricht and Amsterdam Treaties and known as the Treaty of Nice. The Haider event and the ATTAC mobilization worked in two ways to benefit the National Front by giving its issues greater visibility.

In Austria, the Haider event brought the issue of national sovereignty to the forefront of European public debate. Wolfgang Schüssel, the leader of the conservative People's Party, asked Haider and his Freedom Party to join his governing coalition after the election results revealed that he could not form a government without Haider. The European political community responded with alarm and moral outrage. In the past, Haider had made violent statements against immigrants. He justified the Holocaust by saying that members of his parents' generation were not to blame for Nazi atrocities. To ensure that his party would become part of the government and to block the calling of new elections, Haider quickly "apologized" for past mistakes and immediately stepped down from his position as party leader. Haider retreated to his base in the border province of Carinthia.

Despite Haider's retreat, there were international calls for Austria to redo the election. The European Parliament, which had no authority in this matter, placed sanctions on Austria as a member of the EU. Austrians perceived these sanctions as a violation of national sovereignty. A democratic national election had brought the Freedom Party into the government. On one level, the sanctions backfired: first, they increased the popularity of the Freedom Party among Austrians who resented "foreign"

---

[18] Moravcsik (1998, pp. 176–197) provides a nuanced account of de Gaulle's actions after 1958.

interference in their national election; and second, they raised the issue of an organization without a democratic mandate attempting to undercut the authority of a nation-state. The sanctions had no juridical force and were, in practice, rather pallid, amounting to little more than snubs to Austrian diplomats and ministers at an international forum. A cynical interpretation might be that the European Parliament perceived the Austrian elections as an opportunity to show that, even if they had a "democratic deficit," they did not suffer from a moral deficit. By May 2000, members were already speaking of lifting the sanctions.[19]

The Haider event put national sovereignty on the European agenda in a very public way (Van de Steeg 2006). But it also put the issue of a spreading populism before the European public. Just as Gianfranco Fini, head of the Italian National Alliance Party, had done in June 1998, Haider disavowed Le Pen and called him a racist, whereas he himself was merely a free market populist. Le Pen, in turn, disavowed Haider claiming that he was merely trying to reinforce the conservative People's Party, whereas Le Pen had a genuinely new agenda for France.[20] When asked during the electoral campaign for the 2002 presidential elections whether he saw Silvio Berlusconi of Italy and Jörg Haider of Austria as models, Le Pen indignantly replied: "I am the model! Me, who was the first to be a national force of opposition in Europe, it was not them [Berlusconi, Haider]. I prefer to be in power for my ideas rather than in power for those of others. There are people who want to be in power at any price, like Mégret. He is an opportunist."[21] The question as to who was the more original political persona was moot. The Haider event forced before a European public the idea that a populist moment was emerging in response to broader social and political recalibrations than the mere number of immigrants in a country. The ubiquity of that moment was apparent even if its exponents were as diverse as they claimed as they busily disavowed each other.

The growing presence of ATTAC in France and in Europe is germane to the forward movement of the National Front. Members of ATTAC recognized the connection between the rise of rightwing populism in Europe and the encroaching presence of globalization or neoliberalism. In an article in ATTAC's newsletter, *Sand in the Wheels*, written after the 2002

---

[19] I base this discussion upon a broad reading of the European and American press at the time. See, particularly, Judt (2000); Roger Cohen, "Six Nations Seem Ready to Ease up on Austria." *New York Times* (New York) May 10, 2000.

[20] Christiane Chombon, "Le FN et le MNR espèrent être banalisés grâce à 'l'effet Haider.'" *Le Monde* (France) February 13, 2000.

[21] Christiane Chombeau, "Interview with Le Pen." *Le Monde* (Paris) April 18, 2002.

French presidential elections, the author argued that Le Pen was the "chief beneficiary" of globalization.[22]

The European Union's Charter of Fundamental Rights and the opposition to it were the first tangible signs of the "unbundling" of an institutionalized European form of social solidarity. Participants in a February 1999 meeting of the European Commission on Employment, Industrial Relations and Social Affairs decided to design a document that outlined fundamental rights in the European Union (European Commission 1999). Union expansion to the countries of the former Eastern Europe, demographic changes, globalization and even rising crime rates suggested that the time was propitious to come up with a set of common European principles. On the surface, affirmation of rights is laudable. From the perspective of politics, the action was puzzling. The 1996 revision of the European Social Charter, originally passed in 1961, had already accounted for changes in the structural positions of women and the influx of immigrants (Harris and Darcy 2001).

A sequential reading of the European Social Charter of 1961 and its 1996 revision followed by the Charter of Fundamental Rights of the European Union (2000) places in bold relief how much, and in how short a time, the political culture of Europe has changed. The 1961 Charter was written with the view that full employment was a goal. The International Labour Organization was a party to the Charter. And it firmly supported the idea that the family was the basic unit of society. Socialist or not, the 1961 Charter was a collectivist document. The 1996 Amendments kept the basic spirit of the 1961 Charter while bringing it up to date with contemporary issues such as gender discrimination, informed consent, the right to housing and the rights of the disabled. Work and family, labor and community were at the core of the Social Charter in both its iterations.

Read against these two previous documents, the Charter of Fundamental Rights represents a striking departure from an earlier political culture. The sense of the social is absent from the new Charter. It is replaced with an affirmation of the individual. The new Charter is individualist because it replaces entitlement with a neoliberal version of freedom that shifts responsibility from the polity to the person. A few examples from the Charter serve to illustrate this point. The individual has the right to freely seek employment; society is not responsible for creating jobs (Article 15). Women have the right to be free of harassment and discrimination – once they have found their market niche (Articles 21, 23). The family as the basic unit of society has been

---

[22] John Bunzl, "Le Pen is Chief Beneficiary of Corporate Globalisation." *Sand in the Wheels* Newsletter 126, pp. 8–10.

replaced by the guarantee that the family has an absolute right to privacy (Article 7).

The European Council unveiled the Charter of Fundamental Rights at its biannual meeting in December 2000 at Nice, France. ATTAC mobilized 50,000 people to travel to Nice to engage in three days of public protest against the Charter. ATTAC described the mobilization as a *euromanifestation*. The Nice mobilization consisted of two days of conferences, forums and marches. It was an extra-parliamentary attack on the expanding process of Europeanization that leftwing *and* rightwing populists viewed as a form of globalization.

ATTAC campaigned against the Charter with the slogan, "Another Europe is possible." Proclaiming that the European Union has become a "motor of liberal globalization," ATTAC argued that the new Charter was fundamentally anti-labor, anti-social and anti-national. The weakening of social rights was among ATTAC's principal concerns – specifically Article 15 that ensures only the right to look for work. ATTAC was not alone in its antipathy to the Charter. Although it was signed unanimously, representatives of the member states were not united in their enthusiasm.

From the vantage point of today, it is easy to forget that solidarity in the old Europe was not only leftist. It was embedded in the collective mentality of long defunct aristocracies as well as in bourgeois networks of family capital and national firms. Global capital depersonalizes capital transactions. In the United States with its individualist ethic, the de-socialization of capital is hardly noticed – until its economic effects are felt. In Europe, de-socializing capital sends shock waves through the political and social system. From that perspective, the new Charter protects individuals against the abuses that are constitutive of unbridled market forces. But as this strategy focuses upon the individual rather than the collective, it represents a distinct rupture with past practices in Europe and a challenge to – if not the complete repudiation of – European versions of social solidarity.

Looking toward the 2002 presidential elections

As the year 2001 opened, it appeared that anti-globalization movements such as ATTAC would be defining the field of public discourse in France and that they would be the center of political interest. Le Pen and the National Front were viewed as weakened and a public nuisance. The mobilizations across Europe, Gothenburg in June and Genoa in July, coupled with the colorful antics of José Bové the French farmer who dismantled a McDonald's in the south of France made it appear that anti-globalization rhetoric and movements were the principal voice of a new campaign against Europe and neoliberalism. ATTAC and its kindred organizations put globalization in public space and on the Internet. *Sand in the Wheels*, its electronic newsletter, offered weekly email updates on the international spread of the movement to an ever growing cadre of youthful supporters.

Yet, ATTAC remained an extra-parliamentary organization and had limited capacity to put pressure on the system that they wished to change. Members of ATTAC could protest and mobilize as much as they wanted but they were not a political party. They could not run for office or mobilize an electorate around a party platform. Paradoxically, with the exception of the National Front, the mainstream French political parties were pro-Europe and, by extension, pro-globalization even though they too protested and declared publicly that they wished to maintain the French social model. The discussions that began in Millau in June 2000 when José Bové dismantled a McDonald's, the ever present symbol of American "soft power," continued on the promenade at Nice in December and erupted in the spring of 2005 when the French voted against the European constitution in a popular referendum. Although the National Front and ATTAC were never allies in the standard sense of the term – the left finding the Front morally and politically repulsive – they nevertheless led the charge against the constitution that many would describe as "neoliberal."

During the summer of 2001, crime and security seemed the only way that Jacques Chirac could distinguish his campaign from the campaign of socialist candidate Lionel Jospin. On September 11, 2001, terrorists attacked the World Trade Center in New York and the landscape of political discourse changed in Europe and the world. Suddenly security was no longer a local issue focused on petty crimes but an international problem that occupied a transnational political space. *Le Monde*'s headline on September 12 read, "We are all Americans." This was a landscape that Le Pen was positioned to take advantage of. The events of September 11 signaled a change in international perceptions of security and many other politicians repositioned themselves.

September 11 worked politically for Le Pen although he was astute enough not to say so explicitly. On September 13, he offered his condolences to the United States and "to the victims of these crimes" and condemned terrorism. However, in contrast to Chirac who said he would support the United States in whatever measures they took, Le Pen warned that "France was not an American protectorate" and that the French nation should tread carefully before it engaged in American battles. On September 21, 2001, Le Pen told his followers at the annual *Fête des*

Bleu-Blanc-Rouge that "Opportunity has never been so great, the events have came to rescue our will, to make our ideas triumph." September 11 provided an opportunity for Le Pen to reiterate his longstanding claim. Radical Islamist cells were operating in Europe through legitimate Islamic organizations. And as he had said many times before, immigrants were indeed dangerous.

The link between security and immigration became very real after the events of September 11 in the United States. Even though France was not a site of any known terrorist cells, the longstanding Muslim community, living in the impoverished *banlieues*, provided an opportunity for such cells to develop. By November 2001, there was a "surprise" in a poll taken by the French polling agency Sofres. Although it was widely assumed that Le Pen and the Front were politically marginalized, this poll showed that 11 percent of the French would vote for Le Pen in the upcoming presidential elections in 2002. An editorial in *Le Monde* entitled, "Silent Le Pen [*Le Pen en silence*]" described the "bad surprise" of the autumn that Le Pen, who was seventy-four years old, largely ignored by the media and considered too weak after the 1999 party split, had benefited from the international situation.[23] By that point the United States had invaded Afghanistan. Chirac had spoken in front of UNESCO on Afghanistan. Jospin had answered questions in the National Assembly. Both appeared weak in their responses. Whereas the editorial argued, "Le Pen maintains a calculated silence. He turns the international crisis to his benefit. He exploits the fears that may arise, or rearise in a segment of [public] opinion. It is a winning triptych for the extreme right: Islam, immigration, insecurity. Jean-Marie Le Pen can profit more than the President of the Republic or the Prime Minister who are not very eloquent on this crisis and the large questions that it elicits."

In the spring of 2002, Le Pen was fighting to accumulate the 500 signatures required to get on the presidential ballot. At the end of March and the beginning of April, militant Muslim groups vandalized synagogues in Lyons, Strasbourg, Marseilles and Montpellier. In addition to generating protest events in Paris that were pro-Israel and pro-Palestine, the attacks on the synagogues created a climate that supported Le Pen's claims about crime. At the very last moment, he managed to get a place on the ballot.[24] Chirac and Jospin were running neck and neck. No one took Le Pen and his candidacy seriously. But the world had changed in

---

[23] Editorial, "Le Pen en silence." *Le Monde* (Paris) November 6, 2001, p. 21.
[24] Mayer (2003), Miguet (2002), Ysmal (2003) and Shields (2006) provide compressed narratives of the pre- and post-election period.

the time that had passed between the rupture within the National Front of January 1999 and the spring of 2002. French citizens may not have wanted Le Pen as their President, but events were turning France and the French in Le Pen's direction. The stage was set for the "earthquake" of April 21, 2002.

Shock and shame: the first round of the 2002 presidential elections

The earthquake

On the evening of April 21, 2002, Jean-Marie Le Pen came in second in the first round of the French presidential elections. He received 16.9 percent of the vote, just ahead of Lionel Jospin's 16.2 percent. Le Pen's second place assured that Chirac would be elected President in the second round and ended the political career of Lionel Jospin who promptly announced his retirement as the results became known. Le Pen's position was experienced as a seismic shock – a political earthquake that overtook France and a source of national shame and profound international embarrassment.

Shame and shock – horror and disbelief – swept over France in the aftermath of Le Pen's success and Jospin's failure. The iconic image of the election that ran in global media outlets from print to the Internet featured workers at Jospin's headquarters staring at a screen as the election results were coming in. As it became clear that Le Pen had come in ahead of Jospin, the men and women clutch their heads in disbelief. Their mouths are open. Some are crying. All appear stunned (Fig. 6.1).

On the evening of the election, Jacques Chirac dramatically addressed the French people. He argued that the results of the election were a "profound attack" on the "values of the Republic." Chirac appealed to all French men and women to gather together to "defend the Rights of Man, to guarantee the cohesion of the Nation, to affirm the unity of the Republic and to restore the authority of the State." This was of course an argument to assure that citizens voted in the second round and that they voted for him. Chirac promised that he would do a better job in his second term of listening to the voices and heeding the anxieties of the French people. Chirac played off the shock of the French when he equated a victory for him with the salvation of the Republic and democracy itself. He closed his speech with the following dramatic words:

I appeal to French men and women, to everyone among you, because democracy is the most precious good. Because the Republic is in your hands.

6.1 *Campaign operatives at Lionel Jospin's headquarters watching election results, April 21, 2002*

This evening, my dear compatriots, France has a need for you; I have a need for you. I hope that, over the next few days, everyone will prove their responsibility, tolerance and respect!

Long live the Republic! Long live France![25]

Chirac's speech captured the emotion of the moment. The idea, as much as the reality, that Le Pen would be a contender for the presidency of the French Republic sent shock waves throughout France and the international community: "le choc," as the French referred to it. Spontaneous mobilization occurred in the streets of Paris and throughout France. The specter of Le Pen as President of France led to many political oddities. Socialists and leftists of all stripes ended up voting for the center right, even

---

[25] "Déclaration de M. Jacques Chirac au soir du premier tour de l'élection présidentielle" www.elysee.fr/elysee/elysee.fr/francais/interventions/discours_et_declarations/2002/avril/declaration_de_m_jacques_chirac_au_soir_du_premier_tour_de_l_election_presidentielle-campagne_electorale_pour_l_election_presidentielle.2688.html (accessed July 6, 2006).

if some did it literally with clothespins on their noses. On May 5, 2002, Chirac who had been the center of a corruption scandal and was popularly referred to as a "crook" was returned to office with a vote of 82.21 percent – the highest ever for a President in modern French history.

The first round generated an outpouring of words – but the words were more expressive than denotative. Emotion, not reason, characterized the national response to the election of 2002. The possibility that Le Pen could represent the French nation-state as its leader generated spontaneous and visceral revulsion. This revulsion convulsed through enough of the French population to bring record numbers of protesters into the streets of large and small French cities in the two weeks between the first and second rounds.

The presidential election of 2002 began, as all elections do, in the realm of politics; it ended as a template of national identity and emotion. The first round placed in bold relief what French citizens felt, *not* what they thought. The second round would underscore what was valuable to the ordinary French citizen – the Republic and its image abroad; as well as what they were willing to give up – partisan politics. The French valued the reputation of the nation in the international arena more than they valued internal political rivalries or ideological positions. Those values and political attachments brought Chirac back to office with a resounding 82.21% of the vote. The election of 2002 began in unbounded emotion and ended in stark rationality as people of all political parties and persuasions voted with their heads and not their hearts.

The election of 2002 triggered a crisis of national self-perception and a reassertion of nation-ness. It also revealed fissures in the political landscape that were mended but not fully repaired, as evidenced three years later when the French rejected the European constitution.[26] For these larger reasons, the presidential elections of 2002 bear scrutiny. French social science has analyzed the institutional dimensions of the election. The next section will focus primarily on its emotional dimensions and only secondarily on the institutional dimensions to the extent that they interact with the latter.

Insecurity and indecision: running on fear and evoking ambivalence

By spring 2002, the press and public had ceased to take the National Front seriously as a political threat.[27] A cartoon published in the French

---

[26] For a narrative account, see Cohen and Salmon (2003). Baverez (2003) in *La France qui tombe* took up the issue of French decline and generated a national debate.

[27] On the "complicity" of the mass media, see Lemieux (2003) and Gunthert and Delage (2003) in Declert *et al.* (2003).

6.2 *Political cartoon, May 2002*

communist daily *L'Humanité* illustrates the tunnel vision that permitted French elites to underestimate the continuing allure of the National Front (Fig. 6.2). As the cartoon suggests, the public sphere had assumed that the party rupture in 1999 had inflicted irreparable damage on the National Front. In addition, the 1998 World Cup victory was engraved in the national consciousness as a sign of collective cohesion (Lebovics 2004, pp. 136–142). The cartoon headline reads "Remember ... 1998: France wins the World Cup." The average person expresses the confidence of the French public, "We are in good shape thanks to this genial melting pot of a team." Juxtaposed against the ordinary French citizen wearing a "we are the champs" tee shirt is the pipe-smoking, well-dressed academic analyst, waving a French flag and declaring, "The National Front is over."

The cartoon captured the general view of the Front that dominated traditional media sources as the election campaign was getting underway. News magazines such as *L'Express*, which during the 1997 Strasbourg congress and the regional elections of 1998 ran somber articles on the danger of Le Pen, published an almost playful article in January 2002 entitled "Help, Le Pen revives!"[28] The author pointed to the "implosion" of the Front in 1999, Le Pen's advanced age (seventy-three years at the time) and the fact that he had been around French politics for so long. Le Pen was elected for the first time in 1956, which the article viewed as a sure sign that at best Le Pen could come in third in the first round of the presidential elections. The author did point to the boost that September 11 gave to the National Front. But he added that Le Pen's "national preference" idea, which argued for an amendment to the French constitution so that naturalized French people would receive preferential treatment with respect to jobs, housing and social welfare, was offensive to the majority of French citizens. The author concluded that 2002 would probably be the "swan song of Jean-Marie Le Pen" which is after all a "redoubtable scuffle of honor."

In a similar vein, *Le Monde* ran a cover of Le Pen dressed as a genie blowing into a water pipe with the number 2002 wafting out in smoke rings. *Le Monde* claimed that even though Le Pen wanted to be "respectable" and a man of the "center right," he had not changed at all. Le Pen at that point had gathered 600 signatures – 100 beyond what was required to get on the ballot. But Chirac had disqualified some of Le Pen's signatures on various grounds making Le Pen retort that Chirac was "not only a thief but a liar."[29] In the end, Le Pen squeaked onto the ballot at the last moment, but not without a loud debate in the press that ironically kept him in the public eye and made his struggle to collect signatures the most interesting electoral story in a lackluster campaign.[30]

An editorial in the *Financial Times*, written three days before the first-round vote, called the election a "poll without passion" that fed the French public a "diet of deliberate dullness."[31] The writer reflected: "The French want to be

---

[28] Romain Rosso, "Au secours, Le Pen revient!" *L'Express* (Paris) January 31, 2002, pp. 26–27.

[29] "Comment Jean-Marie Le Pen veut devenir respectable." *Le Monde* (Paris) February 4, 2002, p. 1.

[30] Suzanne Daley, "French Far-rightist Faces Early Defeat." *International Herald Tribune* (Paris) March 28, 2002.

[31] Editorial, "France's Poll Without Passion." *Financial Times* (London) April 18, 2002.

protected. Chief among their concerns is crime. But there is also a strong sense of economic and cultural vulnerability in the face of global capitalism – a proxy for Americanization in all its forms."

Institutional features of the French electoral system combined with a lack of focus on the part of the major candidates and a basic inability to consider Le Pen as a serious contender fed into the outcome of the evening of April 21. The institutional factors that are repeatedly emphasized in the voluminous secondary literature are fourfold: first, the large number of candidates that ran in the first round; second, the failure to differentiate between the positions of not only Chirac and Jospin but of the other candidates as well; third, the first-round/second-round rule that allowed citizens to cast a protest vote in the first round, saving their "real" vote for the second round; and lastly, the high rate of abstentions – 28.4 percent in the first round.[32] In general, explanations of the outcome focused more on this odd combination of factors, than on either the shifting constituency of the National Front or the evolving political geography of Front strongholds.

Sixteen candidates ran in the first round of the presidential elections (Table 6.1). These candidates represented parties of the extreme left and extreme right, and everything in between. With the exception of Le Pen, many of their positions shaded into each other. Examination of three salient issues – security, immigration and Europe – reveals a troubling lack of differentiation among the various parties. Even a cursory perusal of Table 6.1 reveals that if one or two of these candidates had not run, the outcome could have been favorable to Jospin.

On the issue of security, Le Pen and Mégret had the harshest position – zero tolerance for crime and restoration of the death penalty. The other parties either advocated reforms of various sorts or educational programs aimed at prevention. Democratic Liberal Alain Madelin joined Mégret and Le Pen in advocating a very strict immigration policy that called for tightening of borders and repatriation of illegal immigrants. The other candidates favored inclusive policies, from legalizing the *sans-papiers* to allowing immigrants to vote in local elections. In the case of European integration, there was more variety. Only the National Front, Mégret's party and the French Communist Party were against a constitution for Europe and advocated pulling out of Europe entirely. Other parties took a more cautious approach and advocated renegotiating existing treaties or concentrating on a new design. Chirac and Jospin were firmly in favor of a

---

[32] See essays in Perrineau and Ysmal (2003), Cautrès and Mayer (2004) and Lewis-Beck (2004).

Table 6.1 *French presidential elections 2002: candidates and positions on selected issues*[1]

Candidate	Party	% of vote first round	Positions on selected issues		
			Security orientation[2]	Immigration[3]	Europe[4]
Jacques Chirac	**Rassemblement pour la République (RPR)**	**19.88**	**Reform/Prevention**	**Expansive**	**Pro**
Jean-Marie Le Pen	**Front National (FN)**	**16.86**	**Penalty**	**Restrictive**	**Con**
Lionel Jospin	**Parti Socialiste (PS)**	**16.18**	**Reform**	**Expansive**	**Pro**
François Bayrou	Union pour la Démocratie Française (UDF)	6.84	Reform	Expansive	Pro
Arlette Laguiller	Lutte Ouvrière (LO)	5.72	–	Expansive	–
Jean-Pierre Chevènement	Mouvement des Citoyens (MDC)	5.33	Reform	Expansive	Cautious
Noël Mamère	Les Verts (Green Party)	5.25	Prevention	Expansive	Cautious
Olivier Besancenot	Ligue Communiste Révolutionnaire (LCR)	4.25	Reform	Expansive	Cautious
Jean Saint-Josse	Chasse, Pêche, Nature et Traditions (CPNT)	4.23	Prevention	–	Con
Alain Madelin	Démocratie Libérale (DL)	3.91	Reform	Restrictive	Pro
Robert Hue	Parti Communiste Français (PCF)	3.37	Reform	Expansive	Con
Bruno Mégret	Mouvement National Républicain (MNR)	2.34	Penalty	Restrictive	Con
Christiane Taubira	Parti Radical de Gauche (PRG)	2.32	Prevention	–	Pro
Christine Boutin	Forum des Républicains Sociaux (FRS)	1.2	Penalty	Expansive	Cautious
Corinne Lepage	Citoyenneté Action Participation pour le XXIe Siècle (CAP21)	1.19	Prevention	Expansive	Pro
Daniel Gluckstein	Parti des Travailleurs (PT)	0.47	–	–	–

[1] Source: *Le Monde* (Paris) April 11, 2002 *Demandez le programme!* (Supplement); www.conseil-constitutionnel.fr.

[2] Penalty = death penalty, imprisonment; Reform = 1945 law, public service; Prevention = education

[3] Restrictive = strong border control, repatriation of undocumented; Expansive = regularize undocumented "sans-papiers," vote in local elections

[4] Pro = favors European constitution; Con = pull out of Maastricht Treaty or restrict it; Cautious = Europe with alternative design

Europe with a constitution. Many of these configurations not surprisingly repeated themselves in 2005 during the French referendum on the constitution.

Chirac and Jospin were not very far apart on the issues of security, immigration and Europe. By spring 2002, only negative issues distinguished them. In summer 2001, the press revealed that Chirac was involved in a fiscal corruption scandal and that Jospin had, in his youth, been a member of a Trotskyite group. To overcome this negative publicity, Jospin gave a series of interviews to the journalist Alain Duhamel that were published in book form entitled, *The Time to Respond* (*Le temps de répondre*) (Jospin 2002). In May 2001, Jospin had given a speech that supported workers and workers' rights. He was trying to identify himself with the traditional left constituency that was moving increasingly to the right. Quoting Jean Jaurès, founder of the French Socialist Party, Jospin (2001) promised to follow "the flame not the ashes." Trying to argue that Europe could be both global and social, Jospin argued, "Europe is made up not merely of regulations, directives and disputes. It is first and foremost a project of the mind, a social model, a world view … The Europe that I love, that I and countless others want to achieve, has a social program, a world view and a political architecture." Wanting to ensure that Europe would not be "one more market in a sea of globalization," Jospin continued, "There is such a thing as a European *art de vivre* [way of life], a specific way of doing things, of defending freedoms, of fighting inequality and discrimination, of organizing and handling labor relations, of ensuring access to education and health care, a European peace" (p. 6).

The similarity among the platforms of the various candidates played into the hands of Le Pen, who had clear, if extreme, ideas. The biggest problem for Jospin was the large number of leftwing and left-leaning candidates who took votes away from the Socialist Party. If Jospin had received even a fraction of these leftwing votes, the first round would have turned out differently. As Bruno Gollnisch, a general delegate of the National Front, quipped, the large number of candidates on the left virtually gave the first round to the Front. Combined with this was the first- and second-round electoral structure that allowed individuals to cast a protest vote. Most French citizens were sanguine about the outcome of the election and assumed that the final pair would be Jospin and Chirac. They viewed the two-stage process as an opportunity to use their initial vote to express their discontent with the cohabiting government. The last factor that neither party could have predicted that worked in Le Pen's favor was the high abstention rate. A bored and disaffected populace stayed away in droves. The election had the highest rate of abstention in the first round than in any post-1958 French election. The abstention rate was 28.4 percent higher than in any previous French election since 1969, when the abstention rate was 22.4 percent in the contest that ultimately elected Georges Pompidou as President.

As many commentators noted, even though September 11 was in the background, in general international issues were left out of the election discussion. Europe and Europeanization, one of Le Pen's major issues, were not present in the first round. The electoral results mapped onto the Maastricht referendum results. Twenty-one of the twenty-five departments where Le Pen was strong had voted against the Maastricht Treaty.[33] The rejection of the European constitution in 2005 suggested that Europe did matter to the French voting public.

As a sitting President, Chirac had advantages that a series of strategic errors turned to disadvantages. He made Le Pen's issue of security and insecurity his major campaign issue. Insecurity narrowly defined in terms of crime was Le Pen's issue.[34] The French public had experienced much of that in the period before the election while also suffering from the general malaise that Chirac as President had done little to address. Chirac also made a mistake when he went to the European economic summit in March 2002 in Barcelona and made three economic decisions that would increase social insecurity in France: to increase the retirement age by five years; to reduce the budget deficit to zero by 2004; and to open the French energy company EDF to capital markets.[35] Le Pen exploited the Europe issue and the crime issue.

Just as Chirac in the period between the first and second round was able to equate a vote for himself with a vote for democracy and Republicanism, Le Pen in the period before the first round was able to argue that a vote for him was a vote for France. In his last message before the election to his supporters, published in the party newspaper, the *National Hebdo*, Le Pen made the following plea:

On Sunday April 21, 2002, French nationals can create an event. This presidential election is the last chance to save our liberty. After a Europeanist President [this would be either Chirac or Jospin], it will be very difficult to exit the globalist order ... The presidential election of 2002 is the last meeting place that permits us to assure our security ... If a radical change does not take place on Sunday, the

---

[33] Thomas Ferenczi, "Le Pen se met à l'avant-garde du camp de la société fermée." *Le Monde* (Paris) April 28–29, 2002, p. 20.

[34] See Mayer and Tiberj (2004) on crime and the election; on the general French concern with issues of security, see Roché (1998) and Robert (2002); on the 2002 election, see Castel (2003).

[35] Serge July, "L'insécurité politique." *Libération* (Paris) April 18, 2002, p. 8.

French will have to resign themselves to a destiny as slaves of the new world order where the power of the strongest replaces the French genius, made of exemplariness, equilibrium and liberty ...

For a sovereign France, respected, united and prosperous, do not hesitate, or hesitate again: VOTE LE PEN![36]

On the Saturday before the first-round voting, *Le Monde* headlined with "Indecision of Electors" and claimed that "4 out of 10 French voters are undecided." It published a cartoon with a picture of a blind man leading electors into the voting booth. *Le Nouvel Observateur* on April 18 described the election as the "Sunday of indecision." It quoted figures from a Sofres poll that had Jospin and Chirac running neck and neck. Jospin ran 2 percentage points ahead of Chirac for the entire month of March until April, when the figures reversed and Chirac ran 2 percentage points ahead of Jospin.

No one took Le Pen into account in discussions of the election and the polls. When a journalist wrote an article for the *International Herald Tribune*, saying "Voter anger at the choice could set off an explosion," nowhere in his article did he mention Le Pen.[37] However, if analysts had paid slightly more attention, they might have noticed in the Sofres polls that Le Pen was the only political candidate who consistently gained votes during the March and April polling period – setting the stage for an upset.[38] Le Pen himself did not plan for an upset. In an interview with *Libération*, he indicated that he did not expect to come in second. His political power was that he was planning not to aid Chirac or the center right in a runoff between Chirac and Jospin. Le Pen with more than a touch of *Schadenfreude* told a reporter, "I will not bargain. If Jospin qualifies for the second round, he will beat Chirac. The Chiraciens have said that they would ask nothing of Le Pen. Chirac will commit suicide."[39]

The wound

Le Pen's second place generated an intense collective emotional response. The newspapers on the morning of April 22, 2002 only partially captured

---

[36] Jean-Marie Le Pen, "Le vote national, c'est le vote Le Pen." *National Hebdo* (Paris) April 18, 2002.

[37] William Pfaff, "The French Election." *International Herald Tribune* (Paris) April 16, 2002.

[38] Robert Schneider, "Le dimanche de l'indécision." *Le Nouvel Observateur* (Paris) April 18, 2002.

[39] Service politique, "La fin d'un marathon couru à l'allure d'un sprint." *Libération* (Paris) April 21, 2002, p. 5.

6.3 *Political cartoon, April 2002*

the shock that a plurality of French citizens felt at what had occurred. The headlines of *Le Monde* and *Libération* editorials mapped the intense passions, a combination of moral outrage and will to fight, that consumed France in the period between the first and second rounds.

Libération had a big bold "NON" etched across the face of Le Pen on its cover. "Frightful" was the title of their editorial essay. On the front page of the April 23 edition of *Le Monde* the newspaper's editorial director, Jean-Marie Colombani, wrote an essay entitled "The Wound" that began: "France is wounded. And a number of the French humiliated." France which had once been a powerful force for European integration, has "politically crowned a sinister demagogue." Instead of the model European country, France, with the victory of Le Pen, gives "the image of a closed, constrained country, haunted by its own decline, even a country that fears its children, particularly those who live in the *banlieue*. Yes, alas, times are spoiled for France."[40]

Le Monde's front page also featured a cartoon that underscored the trauma and humiliation that Colombani's editorial described (Fig. 6.3). The cartoon depicted Le Pen and the National Front as a small Nazi fighter plane crashing into the twin towers of Chirac and Jospin. The Eiffel Tower with a French flag stands in the foreground. A French citizen with a flag coming out of his head watches in horror as the little plane steers into the twin towers of French politics. The towers and the flames

---

[40] Jean-Marie Colombani, "La blessure." *Le Monde* (Paris) April 23, 2002, front page, p. 15.

jutting out of them bear a strong resemblance to the World Trade Center buildings in New York City. The comparison to September 11 and the attack on the World Trade Center may seem extreme to the American sensibility, yet it has to be interpreted in the European context where the memory of Nazism and genocide was not so distant. Le Pen's constant reference to "work, family, *patrie*," the slogan of the Vichy regime, heightened rather than softened the memory. Le Pen, who was vocally and unequivocally anti-Europe, was a reminder of the fact that the European Union was originally conceived as an antidote to the horrors of World War II.

The French could not have been pleased to have Silvio Berlusconi, Italian Prime Minister and head of the center right coalition that the French had frequently dubbed rightwing, remind them of the original purposes of European integration. But Berlusconi wasted no time in telling the French, "Populism is in your house." Berlusconi pointed out that Umberto Bossi's programs were far apart from those of Le Pen. He argued that the election demonstrated two points: first, that the French and, by extension, the European left had lost ground; and second, that the French were endangering the project of European integration.

Gianfranco Fini, head of the Italian National Alliance, carefully marked his distance from Le Pen as well as his own neo-fascist past when he said, "a rightwing response that is opposite of *lepénisme* is necessary: more of a united Europe of nations and not chauvinism, stricter and integrated toward foreigners and not xenophobia, more social economy of markets and solidarity and not populist statism and egoism, more legality and not authoritarianism, solid values and not nostalgic myths."[41] The press both in France and abroad wanted to draw comparisons between Le Pen and a host of other populist politicians, such as Jörg Haider in Austria, Umberto Bossi in Italy, Pia Kjærsgaard in Denmark and Pim Fortuyn in the Netherlands.

From April 21 to May 5, the two weeks between the first and second rounds, France was in a frenzy. There was embarrassment as the international arena turned a critical eye on France, and there was a sense of humiliation that Le Pen, who many regarded as a crude racist, could be even in the running as President of a nation-state that prided itself on its refined political traditions – as well as its commitment to the Rights of Man. As criticism began to pour in from Europe and abroad, an April 24 *Le Monde* editorial entitled, "Humiliation" cried out: "Rarely, has the

---

[41] "Berlusconi critica i francesi, 'Il populismo è in casa vostra.'" La Repubblica.it (web page), April 22, 2002.

disgrace that touches France been so universal. Rarely, will the image of France to the foreigner be so weakened. And it is difficult to imagine that this phenomenon will not have lasting repercussions."[42] With criticism pouring in from Asia, Africa and Latin America as well as the United States, it was hard for the French to imagine how they would restore their position of authority in international politics.

On the editorial pages of the liberal Italian newspaper *La Stampa*, the link between Le Pen, Europe, genocide and September 11 was made forcibly. Writing in the form of an open letter to the European Convention, particularly Valéry Giscard d'Estaing who was its president and former President of France, the editorial made an explicit link between the project of Europe, the past and the attack in New York. Its central argument was that Europe needed a single constitution so that it could react in moments such as these. The editorial began, "The presence of Jean-Marie Le Pen in the last round of the French presidential election has taken Europe by surprise, and the same Parisian elite that had not intuited the force of his ascent." The author pointed to the fact that "nationalism and xenophobic populism" had already taken hold in a number of European countries. The construction of a "political Europe" had the potential to combat the "state of emergency" that the Le Pens of Europe as well as the terrorists had created. Only a "United States of Europe" would "avoid the dangerous forces" that "threaten to conquer [Europe's] civility, laws, liberal order." The editorial concluded, "Not only will Europe perish, but [also] the democratic traditions and civil liberties that our fragile nation-states have sought to protect themselves, from generation to generation, and it will do so at the hands of our own monsters or demons."[43]

As the days went by, criticism of Le Pen increased in the public sphere. Prominent French intellectuals such as the sociologist Alain Touraine, Yves Mény, then President of the European University Institute in Florence, as well as Anthony Giddens, wrote opinion pieces on the editorial pages of the major French newspapers. Unanimously, they bemoaned the results of the first round and urged the public to put aside partisan concerns and vote for Chirac in the second round in defense of French democracy. French Catholic bishops in cities where Le Pen did well and religious associations, in view of the fact that 19 percent of French Catholics voted for Le Pen, issued a call to Catholics to vote according

[42] Editorial, "L'humiliation." *Le Monde* (Paris) April 24, 2002, p. 19.
[43] Barbara Spinelli, "Fate presto l'Europa è a rischio." *La Stampa* (Turin) April 23, 2002. Website.

to the values of tolerance and Catholic universalism in the second round.[44] Zinédine Zidane, the star of the 1998 French World Cup victory of Algerian heritage, issued a public statement denouncing, "a party that does not correspond to all the values of France."

On April 24, Chirac refused to enter a public debate with Le Pen, which would have been expected of the candidates between rounds. On April 25, elected members of the European Parliament in Brussels stood up for a collective moment of protest against Le Pen, holding placards marked *NON*. On April 26, Lionel Jospin with some difficulty issued a statement telling voters that in the second round they should "refuse the extreme right and the danger that it represents for our country and those who live there."

The spaces of national emotion

Collective expressions of national emotion fused time and space in the two weeks between the first and second rounds. Demonstrations, expressions of public outrage, speeches and written commentary filled the hours, days, the temporal space of France between April 21 and May 5. An outpouring of public emotion and protest, particularly among French youth, occurred throughout France. The ever "contentious" French took to the streets in record numbers.[45] There were daily demonstrations against Le Pen in Paris and Strasbourg. Medium-sized cities, Lille, Brest, Nantes, Caen, Rouen and Montpellier, with populations between 100,000 and 500,000 also staged daily events, as did Vannes and Poitiers – smaller cities in the west. There were smaller mobilizations in the northeast of France, in the center, in PACA and in Alsace. The daily protests covered the regional or provincial capitals of France and the site of the European Parliament, as well as strategic points in the south and the north.

Libération published a daily column "Front against the Front" that listed demonstration sites and schedules as well as Internet sites that provided calendars and instructions as to how to move from event to event. Saturday, April 27 was a day of mass protest. On that day, one did not have to travel further than 100 kilometers to locate a demonstration site (Fig. 6.4).[46] Protest blanketed the geographical space of France.

---

[44] "Un front religieux contre Le Front national." *La Croix* (Paris) April 26, 2002, p. 8.
[45] The phrase comes from Tilly (1986).
[46] This map (Fig. 6.4) was created from information in *Le Monde* as to time and place of protest events. 100-kilometer buffer zones were drawn around the sites of protest to map the proximity of events.

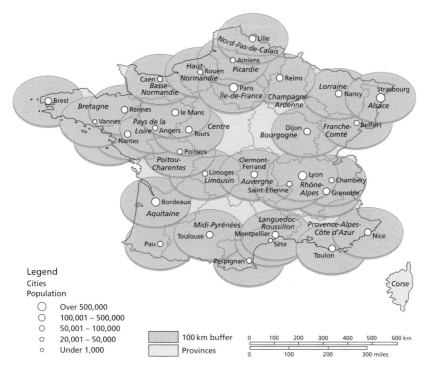

6.4 *Protests across France against Jean-Marie Le Pen, April 27, 2002*

This *tour de force* occurred four days before the second round of the presidential elections on May 1 – the traditional leftwing European labor holiday, as well as National Front celebration day. The timing as well as the historical significance of the date provided an opportunity to make a forceful and emotional statement against Le Pen. As the day is also a public holiday with time off from work, people from all spheres were available to participate in protest events (Fig. 6.5). Sixty political parties, trade unions and civic associations – virtually all French political actors – mobilized to make this May 1 a day against Le Pen. In the end, concerted mobilization was unnecessary as the French public poured into the streets of Paris and beyond to express their horror at a Le Pen presidency. The May 1 demonstrations were so successful that Jean-Pierre Raffarin (who would later replace Jospin as Chirac's Prime Minister) voiced his concern that the intensity of the anti-Le Pen demonstrations might backfire and encourage undecided voters to support Le Pen in the second round.

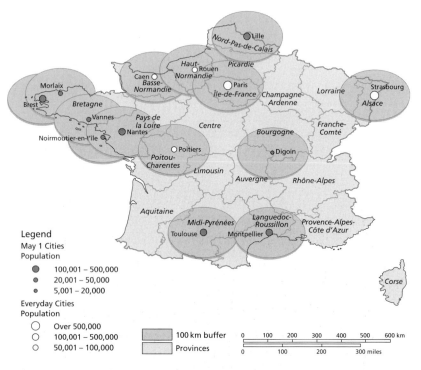

6.5 *Protests across France against Jean-Marie Le Pen, May 1, 2002*

Paris was the site of the largest demonstration against Le Pen. But there were three marches in all including the march of the National Front.[47] The parade routes used the topography of the city of Paris to etch the emotion of revolt on the ancient streets and monuments. The anti-Le Pen march occupied the heart of revolutionary Paris and disrupted public space for an entire afternoon. The spatial arrangements as well as the timing of the marches were designed so that the National Front and its opponents would be far away from each other, so as to avoid confrontation in the streets. The French state placed 3,500 policemen on duty in the city of Paris to keep order.

The National Front began its May 1 march as it traditionally did at the place du Châtelet at 9:30 in the morning (Fig. 6.6). The Front marched up the rue de Rivoli, stopped at the statue of Joan of Arc and then proceeded up the rue des Pyramides, ending at the place de l'Opéra by noon, where Le

---

[47] Pascal Ceaux, "3500 policiers pour éviter les débordements le 1 mai." *Le Monde* (Paris) April 30, 2002, p. 2.

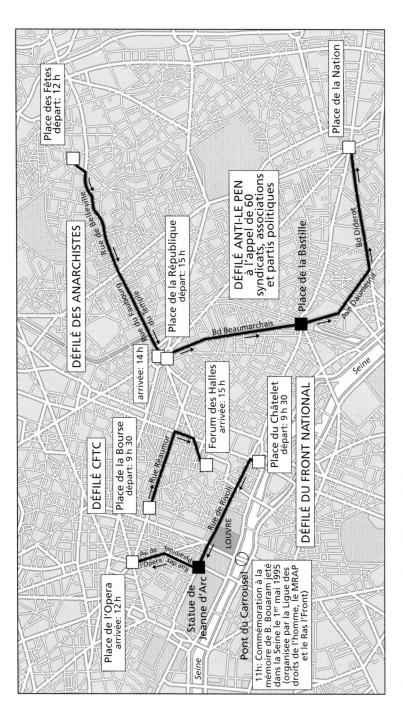

DÉFILÉ DES ANARCHISTES

Place des Fêtes
départ: 12 h

Rue de Belleville

Rue du Faubourg
du Temple

arrivée: 14 h

Place de la République
départ: 15 h

DÉFILÉ ANTI-LE PEN
à l'appel de 60
syndicats, associations
et partis politiques

Bd Beaumarchais

Place de la Bastille

Ave Daumesnil

Bd Diderot

Place de la Nation

Seine

DÉFILÉ CFTC

Place de la Bourse
départ: 9 h 30

Rue Réaumur

Forum des Halles
arrivée: 15 h

Place du Châtelet
départ: 9 h 30

DÉFILÉ DU FRONT NATIONAL

Rue de Rivoli

Place de l'Opera
arrivée: 12 h

Ave de l'Opera
Rue des Pyramides

LOUVRE

Statue de
Jeanne d'Arc

Pont du Carrousel

Seine

11h: Commémoration à la
mémoire de B. Bouaram jeté
dans la Seine le 1er mai 1995
(organisée par la Ligue des
droits de l'homme, le MRAP
et le Ras l'Front)

6.6 *Protest routes in Paris, May 1, 2002*

Pen gave his May Day speech. The CFTC (French Confederation of Christian Workers), a politically marginal but often vocal Catholic trade union, organized a second march midway between the space that the Front occupied and what would later be the principal anti-Le Pen parade route. The CFTC march began at the place de la Bourse at 9:30 and ended up at the old place Bourse. At 11 in the morning, there was a ceremony organized by the League of the Rights of Man (LDH) and the Ras l'Front to commemorate the death of an Arab youth who had been thrown into the Seine by National Front members and drowned on May 1, 1995. The location of the commemoration on the pont du Carrousel on the Seine was perilously close to the Front march. Le Pen warned his adherents to beware of provocation, as he thought that his opponents would want to get National Front adherents to engage in acts of violence.

The anti-Le Pen march began with the march of anarchists who assembled in the 19th *arrondissement* of Paris at the place des Fêtes and marched down the rue de Belleville to the place de la République, where groups brought together by the trade unions, political parties and associations joined the march which proceeded down the boulevard Beaumarchais to the place de la Bastille and then on to the place de la Nation. Citizens joined the march as it ambled through the streets of the historic right bank of Paris.

On May 1, over a million people took to the streets of Paris – the only demonstration that had been larger was the 2 million that flowed into the streets when Paris was liberated from the Nazis in 1944 (Table 6.2; Fig. 6.7). In more recent history, the crowd was as large as the masses that poured into the Champs Élysées when France won the World Cup in 1998. The crowd was orderly but filled with passion and raw disgust at the thought of having Le Pen as President. College students, senior citizens and young families with children marched. They held placards that read: "I am ashamed to be French"; "NO to Hate!" "F like fascism, N like nazism." The demonstrations embodied an almost physical determination to overcome what many perceived as a shameful moment in French politics.

The rational choice: "Better a crook than a fascist!"

Even after the emotional outpouring of May 1, the opposition to Le Pen did not assume that Chirac would win. In the press and in campaign posters, they continued to ply the public until the very last moment with the message that a vote for Chirac would be a vote against Le Pen, as they did not want to run the risk of the left staying home and refusing to vote. Comments made at the last moment by José Bové, the anti-globalization

Table 6.2 *Largest political demonstrations in Paris since the Liberation:*
August 1944 to May 2002

Date	Event	Estimated no. of people	Place
Aug. 26, 1944	Liberation Day	1–2 million	Champs Élysées
May 28, 1958	The left against the return of Charles de Gaulle to power	200,000–300,000	Place de la Nation Place de la République
Feb. 13, 1962	Protest against OAS and victims of torture in Algeria	Thousands	Père Lachaise cemetery
May 13, 1968	May '68 solidarity with students	1,000,000	Place de la Nation Place de la République
May 30, 1968	May '68 solidarity with de Gaulle	800,000	Champs Élysées
Mar. 4, 1972	Funeral of Pierre Overney	Over 500,000	
Oct. 7, 1980	Protest against attack on synagogue on rue Copernic	200,000	Place de la Nation Place de la République
Jun. 24, 1984	Defense of private education	1,500,000	
Dec. 4, 1986	Lycée students protest Devaquet university reforms	1,000,000	
May 14, 1990	Protest against desecration of Jewish cemetery at Carpentras	200,000	Place de la République and the Bastille
Jan. 16, 1994	Defense of public schools against Falloux law	1,000,000	
July 12, 1998	World Cup celebration	Over 1,000,000	Champs Élysées
May 1, 2002	Mobilization against Le Pen's second place in 2002 presidential elections	Over 1,000,000	Bastille

Source: "Un des plus grands défilés parle plein depuis la libération." *Le Monde* (Paris)
May 3, 2002, p. 3.

activist and radical farmer, who blamed "20 years of neoliberalism" for Le
Pen's success, were typical of the remarks that the anti-Le Pen coalition
hoped to avoid. Alain Juppé, former RPR minister, responded to Bové's
remarks by accusing him of being an "accomplice of Le Pen."

The less dignified slogan that had emerged in the street protest early on –
"Better a crook than a fascist" – was repeated over and over on the streets

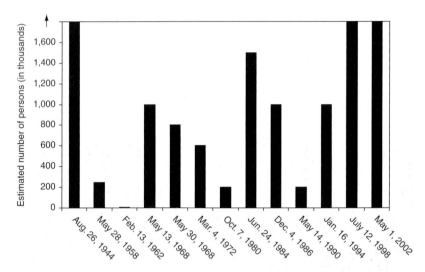

6.7 *Largest political demonstrations in Paris since the Liberation: August 1944 to May 2002*

and in some of the press until the day of the election. *Le Monde*, *Libération* and *Le Figaro* hammered home a more rational version of the chant. On May 3, *Le Monde*'s editorial stated flat out, "Vote Chirac." *Libération*'s editorial gave the opposition to Chirac some emotional space when it began "Who wants Chirac?" The answer of course was that everyone must want Chirac or the French would be left with Le Pen. On May 9, three days after the election, *Paris-Match* printed a cartoon that showed a drowning French citizen jettisoned off the ship of French politics that was sinking and reaching out to a life raft that said "Vote Chirac" (Fig. 6.8).

The message that surrounded French citizens as they approached the second round was that a vote for Chirac was a vote for France, for the Republic, for democracy. On Saturday, May 4, the eve of the election, *Le Monde* published a subdued front page with an opinion piece by Robert Badinter, former Minister of Justice and President of the Constitutional Council.[48] He argued that Le Pen's ideas violated the Rights of Man – the founding principles of the French Republic. If Le Pen were to be elected,

[48] Robert Badinter, "Point de vue: une autre idée de la France." *Le Monde* (Paris) May 4, 2002, pp. 1, 16.

6.8 *Political cartoon, May 2002*

according to Badinter, it would be a counter-revolution that would over-
turn 200 years of struggle for human rights and Republicanism.

Libération's cover on May 4 displayed in bold letters "OUI" and the
phrase "For the Republic" with an image of a vote with Chirac's name on
it (Fig. 6.9). The most dramatic image of the day was on the cover of *Le
Figaro*, the morning conservative newspaper (Fig. 6.10). While it is not
surprising that *Le Figaro* would be a strong supporter of Chirac, its cover
image was imbued with patriotic emotion. The headline read in bold
letters, "For France." Underneath the headline was the map of France
superimposed upon a picture of the crowds of young people who had
gathered to protest against Le Pen. To the right of the image, the editorial
headline read, "Chirac, Of Course."

6.9 *"Yes, For the Republic." May 2002*

On the evening of May 5 when it was clear that Chirac had won, he addressed the French people.[49] He said that "Tonight we celebrate the Republic ... As always faced with a test, the Republic stands, proud, faithful to its values, present, strong and assembled. It refused to give in to the temptation of intolerance and demagoguery." Telling the French that he had in the first-round results observed their discontents and listened to them he would go on a second term that would "reinforce the cohesion of the Nation and solidarity between all the French." He argued, "Strong in our unity, we will put France in motion, drive her onto a new path of youth, of growth and employment, make Europe advance, and carry our message of peace, liberty and fraternity all over the world." After expressing his gratitude to all, Chirac concluded, "In the weeks, in the months and in the years to come, I will need you to guide the Republic and to defend its values."

---

[49] www.elysee.fr/elysee/elysee.fr/francais_archives/interventions/discours_et_declarations/2002/mai/discours_de_m_jacques_chirac_au_soir_du_second_tour_de_l_election_presidentiel le_de_2002.1784.html.

6.10 "For France." May 2002

Summary

Turning points: the end of an illusion

The World Cup games in soccer began a month after the election. On June 11, 2002, the French soccer team was eliminated in the first round. French intellectuals immediately drew a connection between the previous soccer victory, the current defeat and the presidential elections of 2002. In 1998 after the World Cup victory, as discussed in the previous chapter, the French were euphoric. They experienced the soccer victory as an affirmation of the French system of assimilation and Republican values. The Blues (the name of the French soccer team), the French state and the French people were "world champions." The Republic worked. The presidential elections of 2002 challenged those beliefs and feelings. A *Le Monde* editorial, borrowing its headline from Sigmund Freud's classic treatise on religion, described the soccer defeat and the electoral season as signaling "the end of an illusion." The belief that France worked as a democratic and tolerant society and that its soccer team was still world champions was nothing but an illusion in spring 2002. The editorial began, "On April 21, France, which imagined itself champion of the world of democracy, discovered that 16.95% of electors in the presidential cast their votes for Jean-Marie Le Pen, head of the extreme right. On June 9, France, which thought of itself as world champion of engaged citizens, discovered that 35.6% of the electoral body decided not to participate in the first round of the legislative elections."[50]

Jean Baudrillard published a scathing critique in the aftermath of the election in a pamphlet entitled *In the Kingdom of the Blind* (2002). The second part of Baudrillard's title is the well-known phrase, "the one-eyed man is King." The essay was a companion piece to an essay he wrote in 1997, *Exorcism in Politics or the Conjuries of Imbeciles*, in response to Bruno Latour, who had argued that for better or worse Le Pen was the only one with ideas in contemporary French politics. In his 1997 essay, Baudrillard argued that if Le Pen did not exist, French politicians would have had to invent him so that his rants would give the French political class something to coalesce around and to argue against. In his post-election essay, Baudrillard began by calling French politics an *opera buffa* or "comedy of political manners." He argued that the French public was indifferent to politics or rather the "spectacle" of politics that was continually being offered up to them. The "blindness" of the left and right in France, Baudrillard warned, is that they think that they can eliminate Le Pen from the political arena by simply excluding and ignoring him.

Baudrillard argued: "Anti-democratic ideologues can be easily combated and disqualified, but it is not a question of that: it is a question of ever present malaise in representation, in both the democratic and anti-fascist camp. By excluding the National Front, we make them the beneficiary of the full potential for this malaise, they become the focal point for all this latent indifference and end up personifying the violent political counter-transference of an entire society facing off against itself" (p. 32). According to Baudrillard, the tactic of exclusion, rather than eliminating Le Pen and his ideas, actually strengthens him and allows him to spread as a "virus" through French society unseen but ever present. He points to the irony of the fact that to exclude Le Pen, leftists who would never have voted right ended up having to vote for Chirac whom they

---

[50] Editorial, "La fin d'une illusion." *Le Monde* (Paris) June 12, 2002.

6.11 *"The cup is empty." June 2002*

otherwise disliked intensely. So in short, Le Pen was manipulating the
political process in France. According to Baudrillard, the solution was for
the French political class to come up with new political ideas.

Chirac's campaign slogan "Yes to the Republic" contrasted starkly to
Le Pen's nationalist depiction of the Front as the party of France. In the end,
the Republic – assimilationist, democratic and French – *not European* – was
the core of the *narrative* that won the election for Chirac. But this was
not the end of the story. Even though Le Pen lost, on some level he also
won. The 2002 election and the horror of Le Pen continued to reverberate
on a subliminal, and sometimes not so subliminal, level throughout French
politics.

The 2002 election marked another turning point in the story of Le Pen
and his relation to the political culture of contemporary France. It also
signaled a shift in France's reengagement with itself as a nation-state as
well as its position in an expanding Europe. On June 12, 2002, *Libération*
ran a cover with a picture of Zinédine Zidane with his face in the dirt on the
soccer field. The caption reads, "The cup is empty" (Fig. 6.11). The
nostalgia and sadness in the headline spoke not only to soccer but to
France itself. The French nation-state seemed to have its head, if not in

the dirt, at least buried in the sand. The conversation that Le Pen opened between April 1997 and April 2002 on Europeanization and globalization had another installment in May 2005 when French citizens overwhelmingly refused to ratify the European constitution. It is to the path from the election to the constitution – from April 21, 2002 to May 29, 2005 that we shall turn.

7

The "new" April 21: from the presidential elections to the referendum on the European constitution

Dédiabolisation: "people like me"

In the aftermath of the 2002 election, Jean-Marie Le Pen appointed his daughter, Marine, to a position of prominence in the National Front. Le Pen's plan aimed to moderate the party's image and to capitalize on the publicity that the election provided. From 2002 through the 2007 presidential campaign, the National Front emphasized that it spoke to the hopes and dreams of ordinary French people such as the inhabitants of Amélie's Montmartre. In an interview given to the *New York Times* a year after the election, Marine Le Pen pointed to the salience of ordinary people for the ongoing success of the National Front. She told the reporter, "My emergence is a signal that, 'There are people like you in the National Front ... 70-year old men and traditional Catholics, and young female divorcees like me.'"[1]

In the two years between the 2002 presidential elections and the 2004 regional elections, national, European and global events turned in directions that moved Le Pen's positions closer to mainstream public opinion and official politics. Marine Le Pen described this movement as *dédiabolisation* – literally in English "de-demonization" – and it was her core campaign strategy in the 2007 presidential elections. In the post-2002 election period, Chirac continued his focus on the traditional National Front issue of security. He appointed his protégé Nicolas Sarkozy, now President of France, to the post of Minister of the Interior. Soon after the 2002 election, the French press began to draw comparisons between Sarkozy and Le Pen. *Le Monde* proclaimed on its front page,

---

[1] Elaine Sciolino, "The New Face of France's Far Right." *New York Times* April 27, 2003, p. 16.

"The 'Sarkozy effect' jostles the right."[2] To the chagrin of the National Front, Sarkozy promptly designed a law on security which, while stopping short of reinstating the death penalty, was as tough as any that they could have designed. The Sarkozy law, as it is colloquially labeled, went into effect in March 2003.[3] The law greatly expanded the powers of the police and limited the rights of suspects in crimes large and small. The passage of the law met with public protests in the streets of Paris. Large parts of the French public, particularly residents of the *banlieues*, viewed it as an infringement upon human rights.

In the summer of 2003 the government convened the Stasi Commission to address the issue of *laïcité*. The headscarf affair first occurred in 1989. At that point, despite intense debate in the public sphere, it was left unresolved and up to the discretion of local schools whether they would allow young Muslim women to wear their veils to class. In December 2003, the Stasi Commission consisting of academics and legislators recommended that individuals should not conspicuously display religious symbols in government spaces – such as public schools (*Commission de réflexion sur l'application du principe de laïcité dans la République* 2003).[4] Practically, this meant that French schoolgirls could not wear their headscarves to school. The argument that the commission made was that the wearing of religious symbols violated the principle of *laïcité*, the absolute separation of sacred from secular – that was a bedrock principle of French Republicanism. Seen as a blow to multiculturalism, the Stasi Commission recommendations were also a way to shield Muslim girls from the potential abuse of fathers and male relatives and to undercut Islamic fundamentalism.

National laws on the display of religious symbols and the wearing of the headscarf vary across Europe. In March 2004, the French National Assembly voted by a large majority (494 yes; 36 no; 31 abstentions) to pass into law the recommendations of the Stasi Commission. The banning of the headscarf in schools in France is an instance of the reassertion of a distinctively French and national principle. The National Front was not opposed to either the Stasi Commission's upholding of the principle of *laïcité* or the law that limited the wearing of the headscarf. The defense of

---

[2] Varié, "L'effet Sarkozy bouscule la droite." *Le Monde* (Paris) December 11, 2002, front page, pp. 8–9.

[3] Security remained Le Pen's issue. On May 20, 2006, he gave a speech to the National Assembly and argued for the reinstatement of the death penalty.

[4] Bowen (2007) and Scott (2007) provide cogent analyses of *laïcité* and its relation to the wearing of the headscarf in contemporary France. Weil (2004a) and Baubérot (2004), members of the Stasi Commission, provide their version of how the commission arrived at its recommendations.

laïcité was a cousin of Chirac's decision not to support the European Charter for Regional or Minority Languages. The two actions are rarely tied together – yet they should be. Both are harbingers of the reassertion of nation-ness that was becoming part of mainstream French political discourse.

In spring 2003, the United States invaded Iraq. The French led the European opposition to the United States in the United Nations. Opposition to the war and to the United States as head of the New World Order did not put Le Pen in opposition to the mainstream of France. On June 6, 2004, Chirac stood on the sands of Normandy at Colleville-sur-Mer and gave an address to commemorate the sixtieth anniversary of the Allied invasion and liberation of France from the Nazis. Aiming his remarks at George W. Bush who was present, Chirac proclaimed: "The moment of remembrance is also a moment for words of peace ... In a dangerous world, where violence and hatred too often stir up men and peoples, the message of these heroes of 'The Longest Day,' the flame our fathers bore so proudly and have now passed on to us, are our common heritage which implies a corresponding duty for us. It implies a duty of remembrance, a duty to recall this still recent past when fanaticism, the rejection of those who are different from us, the rejection of others, cast men, women and children into the night and fog of the death camps. Let us never forget that without a compass, without fidelity to the lessons of history, there can be no future."[5] Chirac was chiding the United States. He could as easily have been warning the French against Le Pen and its own worst national tendencies while emphasizing past virtues.

In contrast to 1998, the socialists claimed victory in the March 2004 regional elections where they managed to outflank the right. The 2004 elections generated widespread relief that Le Pen and the National Front were gone and fueled socialists' hopes for the 2007 presidential elections. In an interview given to *L'Express*, political scientist Dominique Reynié warned that the National Front would not disappear. He made the argument that the steady trajectory of the National Front represented a new form of political attraction. The National Front voters were no longer the hard-core right, but rather people who were insecure in what he described as the "new situation" of European and global markets. Reynié continued, "If the Front vote is older and stronger in France than elsewhere, it is not because the French are more racist than other Europeans, but because it is

---

[5] Speech by Jacques Chirac, President of the Republic at the binational Franco-American Ceremony, Available Embassy of France in the United States www.info-france-usa.org (accessed June 14, 2004).

in France that the state is more powerful. It is a demand for protection rather than a demand of nationality that fuels the Front vote."[6]

In June 2004, the National Front regained ground in the European parliamentary elections. A stunning malaise and disaffection for Europe distinguished the election. Abstention rates were high in the fifteen member states.[7] Among the eight new states admitted from the former Eastern Europe, abstention rates were consistently over 50% and reached a high of 80% in Slovakia and 79% in Poland. Euroskeptic parties gained ground. The *Financial Times* observed that the election results did not augur well for the European project: "Europe was swept by a wave of protest last night, as voters in the European elections delivered a damning verdict on their national leaders and against the European Union itself ... The rebellious mood was also reflected in growing disquiet about the EU, with a record number of Eurosceptic candidates returned to the 732-seat European parliament ... The results came days before Europe's leaders meet in Brussels to try to agree to the next phase of EU integration by endorsing the draft constitutional treaty. Their ability to sell the constitution to hostile voters, many of whom will be asked to ratify the treaty in national referendums, was called into doubt by the results."[8] More Europeans watched the European soccer games on June 13, 2004 than turned out to vote.

The campaign for the constitution

In spring 2003, American Secretary of Defense Donald Rumsfeld famously scorned France and Germany as being "old Europe" because of their opposition to the war in Iraq. Rumsfeld had it wrong as France and Germany were architects of the new Europe which was increasingly becoming a problem not just to the United States but to Europe itself. The lack of enthusiasm for the European elections among European citizens was emblematic. The European constitution was a final challenge. The campaign for the European constitution and its defeat in France was an arena where nation-ness and anti-globalization came together. When the votes were in, it was clear that National Front voters were not the only French citizens who were fearful for their social and political security. It

---

[6] Interview with Dominique Reynié, "La France au fond des urnes." *L'Express* (Paris) March 22, 2004, pp. 52–53.
[7] Muxel (2005, p. 51) charts the declining rate of participation from 1979 to 2004.
[8] Raphael Minder and George Parker, "Voters Snub Europe's Leaders: Center-right Wins most Seats in New Parliament as the Heads of Britain, France and Germany Suffer Protest Backlash." *Financial Times* (London) June 14, 2004, p. 1.

was also the first time that politicians turned to the fear of the National Front as embodied in the date, April 21, to mobilize for an issue that was not intrinsic to the National Front.

On May 29, 2005, 70% of the French population turned out to vote on the following question: "Do you approve the bill [*le projet de loi*] that authorizes the ratification of a treaty establishing a Constitution for Europe?" The French voted to reject the European constitution by a decisive 55.6%. Three days later, 62% of the Dutch voted to reject the constitution. One month later, British Prime Minister Tony Blair who was considering a referendum in 2006 drew back to his original position that Britain did not need to sign on to the constitution. Within less than a month, the core members of "old" Europe had placed the key symbolic document of "new" Europe on indefinite hold.

Sanguine beginnings

It was not lack of effort on the part of the government that doomed the French vote on the European constitution. In fall 2004, the French government had reason to be sanguine about the outcome of the referendum. A Eurobarometer poll (European Commission 2004b) reported that 70% of the French people supported a European constitution – although there was no specification as to whether it meant the constitution that was actually on the table. An Ipsos poll (2004), taken in late September 2004, obtained results that were similar to the Eurobarometer poll: 64% percent of the Ipsos respondents expressed support for the constitution. In this early poll, 66% of socialists polled supported a "yes" vote. In the referendum itself, only 41% of Socialist Party members voted "yes" – a shift that analysts considered decisive to the defeat of the referendum.

The European Commission and the leaders of its member states signed off on the draft of the constitution on June 18, 2004. A national popular referendum was a choice not a requirement. A parliamentary vote, such as the Italian and German governments held, would have sufficed to affirm the treaty.[9] French President Jacques Chirac instead decided to call a referendum and announced it on the national holiday of Bastille Day, July 14, 2004. The French Ministry of Foreign Affairs launched a far-reaching television and public information campaign that cost the government 10 million euros. The government created a website that

---

[9] Chirac was criticized for signing the Amsterdam Treaty in 1997 without submitting it to a popular referendum. The referendum on the constitution was a political ploy, an attempt to avoid the previous criticisms, that backfired.

published the constitution, and all sorts of positions and questions about it. A short twenty-eight-page pamphlet, *The Essential Europe, What it Brings us, What the Constitution Changes* (*L'essentiel sur l'Europe ce qu'elle nous a apporté, ce que la Constitution va changer*) captured the spirit of the official public discourse.[10] Pictures of green fields and young people engaged in cooperative activities punctuate the text written in PowerPoint style.

From Chirac's announcement to the actual vote, there were signs that a "yes" vote was not a given. It seemed unimaginable that France – an architect of European integration from its inception in the postwar period – would reject a document crafted under the guidance of their own former President Valéry Giscard d'Estaing. "Local knowledge" suggested that the treaty would narrowly pass as had Maastricht in 1992. The center right, Chirac's party, as well as the French Greens supported the constitution. The National Front, the Communist Party and the anti-globalization organization ATTAC actively campaigned against the constitution. In an article in *Le Monde Diplomatique*, publication venue of ATTAC, a journalist described the constitution as "the great leap backward," a "road map for privatization" and a shrine for the "free market principle."[11]

The argument that the constitution was a "neoliberal" text was redolent in the arguments of all the opposition parties even if they were in radically different political camps. The French Socialist Party was divided on the issue of support for the constitution. In September 2004, Laurent Fabius declared that he would lead the socialist opposition to the constitution. In December 2004, the Socialist Party held an internal referendum on the constitution and voted 58 percent to support the constitution. The Socialist Party referendum placed the party and its leader François Hollande officially in the camp of the "yes" vote – even if in the end the divided party sunk the constitution.

Hope and fear, market and culture dominated the political posters that were plastered on billboards and public walls all over France in the period leading up to the referendum. The socialists viewed the market as a source of progressive social change. A Socialist Party poster proclaimed "5 Reasons to Say Yes to the European Constitution." A hand holding a red carnation, the classic socialist symbol, lay inside the "O" of a "Oui" emblazoned in stark black script against a background of bold red. The

---

[10] www.constitution-europeenne.fr/fileadmin/allerplusloin/lessentiel_sur_leurope.pdf.
[11] Serge Halimi, "The Great Leap Backwards." *Le Monde Diplomatique* June (website, English edition, http://mondediplo.com/2004/06/08privatisationroadmap).

five reasons were rational and market driven. According to the poster, a "yes" vote would ensure that France and Europe would be "more social, democratic, protected, efficient and stronger." The emotional valence of the socialist poster was weak compared to the strident National Front posters. For example, a Front poster screamed out, "Turkey in Europe: I Vote NO! I Protect France!" Another Front poster proclaimed, "Outsourcing [*Délocalisations*] Layoffs. A Solution: The Nation."

French national politics did not account for all of the problems with the acceptance of the constitution. Every French household received a copy of the constitution in the mail. The act of deciphering the 448 articles of "indigestible text that seemed deliberately opaque" became, as one journalist described it, a "national sport."[12] Pierre Encrevé, linguist and director of a committee to simplify bureaucratic language, described the text as "unreadable." Encrevé claimed without irony: "I took six hours to read very attentively the 191 pages, and, truly, all the possible implications were not always clearly apparent to me. There are ambiguities and obscurities, but, for someone who has done secondary studies, it is less difficult to follow than Foucault or Bourdieu."[13]

The "oui": April 21, 2002 as iconic event and political metaphor

The polls conducted in mid-March 2005 began to indicate that the percentage of voters prepared to vote "non" was increasing.[14] During this period, Chirac asked the EU lawmakers to tone down a provision in the constitution known as the "Bolkestein directive." The "directive" contained in the draft constitution allowed "service workers" to offer their "services" in any European country based on the fees that would be charged in their "country of origin."[15] The EU Parliament passed a watered-down version of the controversial "directive" in February 2006. Opponents of the treaty used the "directive" to generate images of "Polish plumbers" flooding into France offering their services at below market rate.

The "no" began rising in March and continued through early May when the polls indicated that both sides of the issue were coming close together.

---

[12] Eric Aeschimann, "Les Français toqués d'analyse de texte." *Libération* (Paris) May 21, 2005.

[13] Eric Aeschimann, "L'impression d'opacité vient de l'absence de notice explicative." *Libération* (Paris) May 21, 2005.

[14] Perrineau (2005, p. 230) provides a detailed list of the polls that had appeared regularly in the French newspapers.

[15] The "directive" is found in the draft constitution, Part III, Title III, Chapter 1 (section 2, subsection 3 [articles 29–35]).

But the "no" took off in early May and the "yes" never regained momentum. As the numbers in favor of "no" climbed, French politicians substituted emotion for reason, and threat for argumentation, as they tried to scare the French into voting "yes." By spring 2005, April 21, 2002, the date that Jean-Marie Le Pen came in second to Jacques Chirac in the first round of the presidential elections, had become an iconic event that French politicians exploited.

In contrast to the fantasy of waves of "Polish plumbers" who would presumably flood into France and deprive stalwart French plumbers of their jobs, April 21, 2002 was a collectively experienced political event. An invasion of "Polish plumbers" – a metaphor for cheap service work – represented a possibility, not a lived national experience. As the previous chapter described, April 21, 2002 generated a collective emotional *choc* or shock among French citizens when they realized that Jean-Marie Le Pen could actually become their President. Supporters of the "yes" invoked April 21, 2002 as a political metaphor aimed at generating fear that would translate into support for the constitution. French politicians referred to April 21, 2002 in the months leading up to the referendum without ever mentioning Jean-Marie Le Pen by name in their hope to reignite the feeling of a collective threat to national honor.

By April 2005, political metaphors saturated the French public sphere. François Bayrou, leader of the center right UDF Party, resorted to biblical imagery to implore the French people to vote "yes." While addressing university students in Lille, a dissenting voice told Bayrou that he made it sound as if it would rain for forty days if the French voted "no." Bayrou responded, "I tell you from within every fiber of my being that it will rain for more than forty days."[16] The rain metaphor invokes Noah's Ark and the end of one world and the beginning of the new, but it also suggests Louis XV, "After the 'non,' the deluge!" Bayrou may have been unsuccessful with his biblical metaphors in 2005 but he did manage to run in the 2007 presidential elections and to come in third behind Ségolène Royal and ahead of Jean-Marie Le Pen. On April 11, German Foreign Affairs Minister Joschka Fischer came to Rennes with the French Foreign Affairs Minister to warn an audience that "The life of Europe was at stake."[17]

---

[16] Christiane Chombeau, "En cas de victoire du non, 'il pleuvra plus de 40 jours,' assure François Bayrou." *Le Monde* (Paris) April 4, 2005 (Le Monde.fr).
[17] Gaëlle Dupont and Jean-Baptiste de Montvalon, "La campagne a déchaîné les passions françaises." *Le Monde* (Paris) May 28, 2005 (Le Monde.fr).

On April 15, Jacques Chirac appeared on national television to promote the constitution before a live audience of French youth. Uncomprehending when confronted by the fear and pessimism of the youth, Chirac implored: "Do not be afraid, you do not have reason to have fear." The phrase "Do not be afraid" was identified with Pope John Paul II who first used it in 1979 on a visit to his native Poland which at that time was still behind the Iron Curtain. John Paul II made the phrase, "Do not be afraid!" a central theme of his papacy – using it on multiple occasions.[18] The popular and charismatic Pope died on April 2, 2005. Thirteen days later, Chirac borrowed his words in the hope that some of the Pontiff's charisma would transfer to the European cause. Chirac was not unique in his attempt to appropriate the Pope's charisma. As described in Chapter 4, Jean-Marie Le Pen had urged party loyalists to "not be afraid" in his speech that closed the 1997 congress in Strasbourg – the event whereby he began the process of "normalizing" the National Front in French politics.

By April 20, the French press and politicians sensing defeat became more strident in their warnings against a repeat of April 21, 2002. For example, some politicians argued that the French political classes had not reflected on the "lessons of April 21." A book, *France that Falls* (*La France qui tombe*) (2003), written by the economist and political commentator Nicolas Baverez, was worrying the French intellectual class. Baverez argued that April 21, 2002 "was not accidental" and that France had to begin to meet the challenges posed by globalization on the one hand and a disaffected middle class on the other if she were not to tumble into international irrelevance.

As the third anniversary of the 2002 first-round presidential election approached, politicians openly worried that a victory of the "no" would signal that politicians had never been able to overcome the challenges to France that April 21, 2002 had posed.[19] Pierre Nora, member of the French Academy and author of the multi-volume work on French identity and memory, *Les lieux de mémoire*, warned that "April 21 reveals a profound weakening, a diminishing of French influence, to which France has not adapted well." François Hollande, leader of the French socialists, argued as if the connection between the 2002 presidential elections and the referendum was self-evident. At the third anniversary of April 21,

---

[18] John Paul II used the phrase repeatedly as a way to argue that God could be called upon in strictly secular matters (John Paul II 1984).

[19] Philippe Ridet and Nicolas Weill, "Le choc du 21 avril 2002 aura-t-il répliqué le 29 mai 2005?" *Le Monde* (Paris) April 20, 2005 (Le Monde.fr).

Hollande announced a new strategy: "To save the 'yes,' we will explain [to the French public] that a victory of the 'no' will be a new April 21."

When it began to look as if the French socialist vote would be the tipping point in the referendum, and that it was tending toward "no," the secretary of the German Social Democratic Party, Franz Müntefering, came to Paris on May 2, 2005 and issued a joint declaration with François Hollande, his French counterpart, entitled, "One Europe solidaristic and social, strong for peace and justice in the world." The declaration began, "Europe is a magnificent and historic enterprise, for which we have struggled side by side, and for which we ought to continue in the future, to struggle together." The emissary from Germany was not auspicious as three weeks later the Social Democratic Chancellor Gerhard Schroeder called elections and then lost in October to the Christian Democrat Angela Merkel.

On the same day as the German secretary visited France, a group of German intellectuals that included Günther Grass, Jürgen Habermas, Alexander Kluge and Peter Schneider among others wrote an open letter to *Le Monde* (May 2, 2005) declaring that "Europe demands courage." Addressing themselves to the French citizens, or at least that portion of French citizens who regularly read *Le Monde*, they argued that France, "home of the enlightenment," should not "betray progress." They asked, "Do the French people really want to be holed up in a bunker with rightwing and leftwing nationalists?" The *coup de grâce* occurred on May 7, 2005 when German philosopher and enthusiastic supporter of Europe Jürgen Habermas published an essay in French in *Le Nouvel Observateur* warning the French left of the dangers of voting "no" on the European constitution in the referendum.[20] Habermas chided the members of the left who supported the "no" as irresponsible because they put Europe in danger of being a colony of American imperial ambitions.[21] Laurent Fabius, the unremitting voice of opposition to the constitution within the Socialist Party, did not help the socialist strategy when he pleaded in public on May 8 for the French to vote "no" on the constitution.

As May 29 was drawing near and the "no" remained decidedly ahead in the polls, the advocates of the "yes" intensified their advocacy. In the

---

[20] Jürgen Habermas ([1990] 1996, 1997, 2001), the distinguished German philosopher, has been in the forefront of the movement advocating for a constitution as a normative document in the project of Europe. He also led the intellectual resistance to the war in Iraq in the summer of 2003 (see Levy *et al.* 2005).

[21] Jürgen Habermas, "The Illusionary 'Leftist No': Adopting the Constitution to Strengthen Europe's Power to Act," appeared in English on www.signandsight.com/features/163.html.

beginning of May, Chirac addressed French artists and argued that culture was the core of the new constitution. To counter Fabius, Hollande argued, somewhat unconvincingly, that, "on May 29 there will not be a second round" – referring to Chirac's 82 percent result in the second round of the 2002 presidential elections, and again to April 21.[22] On May 26, Nicolas Sarkozy, Chirac's "take no prisoners" Minister of the Interior and current President of France, warned the French public to vote "yes" and "Don't take Europe hostage."[23]

On the evening of May 26, with the polls suggesting that the European constitution was veering toward defeat, Jacques Chirac made a final exhortation to the French public. He argued that the French were voting not on a sectarian political issue – that is that the referendum should not be on his presidency – but on an issue that would determine the future of themselves, their children, France and Europe. The referendum would show "the honor and vitality of democracy." Chirac solemnly intoned: "Above all we must not *mistake the question* [italics added]. The decision that is before us is far away from the traditional political cleavages. It is *neither right nor left* [italics added]. It is not a question of saying yes or no to the government. It is a question of your future, your children's future, the future of France and of Europe." The treaty would respond to "changes in the world," make Europe economically competitive "without abandoning our social model."[24]

Chirac characterized the choice before French citizens as "neither right nor left." His use of a phrase more commonly associated with Vichy displayed an uncharacteristic historical amnesia and suggests that Chirac and his party were grasping at straws in those final days. Tellingly, Chirac, for the second time in less than a month, invoked a historical metaphor that Jean-Marie Le Pen and the National Front had used. In 1997, the theme of the National Front party congress in Strasbourg was "Neither right nor left: French!" During that event, the media drew the connection to Vichy. "Do not be afraid!" "Neither right nor left" – the Pope the past; the cross the fasces. The confluence between Chirac's and Le Pen's choice of political metaphor is

---

[22] Renaud Dély and Paul Quinio, "Cette fois, il n'y aura pas de second tour." *Libération* (Paris) May 23, 2005 (Libération.fr).

[23] Reuters News Service, "Nicolas Sarkozy: 'Ne prenez pas l'Europe en otage.'" *Le Monde* (Paris) May 26, 2005 (Le Monde.fr).

[24] Claire Ane, "Jacques Chirac exhorte les Français à 'ne pas se tromper de question.'" *Le Monde* (Paris) May 26, 2005 (Le Monde.fr). See also, "Déclaration aux Français sur le référendum français sur le Traité constitutionnel pour l'Europe" www.elysee.fr/elysee/ elysee.fr/francais/interventions/interviews_articles_de_presse_et_interventions_televisees./ 2005/mai/declaration_aux_francais_sur_le_referendum_francais_sur_le_traite_constitution nel_pour_l_europe.29980.html.

suggestive of the rudderless state of current French political thinking as well as the plasticity of political images and metaphors.

Domesticating the "non"

The National Front's campaign against the constitution was deliberate and uncharacteristically restrained. Until the last few months, Jean-Marie Le Pen absented himself from center stage. From the beginning of the referendum campaign, election specialists assumed that National Front voters would determine the outcome of the vote. In an interview for *Libération* three days before the vote, the Front's election spokesperson Eric Iorio was confident that the National Front "will swing the vote toward the 'no.'"[25] Pascal Perrineau, director of the Centre for Political Research at Science-Po, corroborated Iorio's assertion, "Any majority for the 'no' is not possible without the FN."[26]

In contrast to the other members of the French political class, April 21, 2002 was a positive iconic event for the National Front. The conflict between market rationality and national culture that dominated the public debate over the constitution coincided with the National Front's standard repertoire of themes and narrative strategies. Along with a battery of posters that colorfully and vociferously supported the "No," the National Front also designed a subdued and sentimental poster that posited an alternative rationale (Fig. 7.1). The poster listed "14 good reasons to reject the constitution." It featured a blond princess walking down an aisle in a wedding gown, next to an ugly frog king with a crown of EU stars on his head. The logo on the poster was "Sometimes it is necessary to say NO!"

The flyer that accompanied the poster laid out the standard arguments for the constitution juxtaposed against a corresponding argument against the constitution. Many of the fourteen reasons focused on economic issues and linked them carefully to national and social issues. The flyer was in pastels – shades of pink, yellow and blue. It was childlike and playful. The fourteen reasons had little cartoon characters with the frog king trying to sneak in his points. Among these points was the widely held popular belief that the constitution could be amended if it proved unwieldy. Eight of the fourteen points had to do with various aspects of an "economic war" that would ensue if the treaty was ratified.

---

[25] Christophe Forcari, "Le FN s'attribue déjà la victoire du non 'social-national,'" *Libération* (Paris) May 26, 2005, p. 12.

[26] Christophe Forcari, "Une contribution décisive contre le traité." *Libération* (Paris) May 26, 2005, p. 12.

7.1 *Political poster, National Front, 2005*

During the spring of 2005, as part of her strategy of *dédiabolisation*, Marine Le Pen was polishing her image. She was preparing for the 2007 presidential campaign and writing her memoir, *À contre flots* (*Against the Tide*). The princess/frog poster captured Marine Le Pen's alternative vision of Europe and France as well as a softer, more domesticated and feminine National Front. Marine Le Pen has long blond hair as did the poster princess. Ironically, when the National Front came in fourth place in the first round of the 2007 presidential elections, party operatives blamed Marine Le Pen's strategy for the Front's poor showing.

Defending the national-social: unemployment, neoliberalism
and the boomerang of April 21, 2002

In a phrase eerily evocative of the 1930s, Carl Lang, then the third ranking member of the Directorate of the National Front, told *Libération* that the "national-social" would carry the "non."[27] Lang was not unique in this assessment. It was "local knowledge," as a *Le Monde* reporter argued, "Social Europe is the eternal weak point of the construction of the Union."[28] Lang attributed the weakness of the "social" within the constitution to the rupture in the Socialist Party between an "ingrown left bourgeoisie" and a "popular traditional strata." The National Front was not alone in its attack on the neoliberal or free market dimensions of the constitution. The campaign against the constitution created strange and unwilling bedfellows. The anti-globalization group, ATTAC, and the French Communist Party were opposed to the treaty on virtually the same grounds as the Front. The Socialist Party never overcame its internal split between those in favor of the market versus social Europe. Indeed the split, as Lang pointed out, represented the bifurcated nature of its constituency. Chirac and his party argued for both the national and neoliberal dimensions of the constitution. Their slogan was "The constitution would make France strong." In contrast to ATTAC and the French Communists, the Front was uniquely positioned to champion the "national" *and* to attack neoliberalism. ATTAC and the communists, no matter how much they opposed globalization, could hardly argue, as the Front did, "France first!"

In contrast to the French political class that warned against a repeat of April 21, 2002, Jean-Marie Le Pen and the National Front embraced the date as a positive iconic event. In the two months preceding May 29, Le Pen became more visible and the National Front began to graft the "no" vote onto a political strategy that looked ahead to the French presidential elections of 2007. Jean-Marie Le Pen gave three significant speeches in the period before May 29. Each of these speeches linked high unemployment rates to social and national issues. On April 9, 2005, Le Pen addressed National Front representatives at a party convention in Strasbourg where he blamed the European project for escalating unemployment and *délocalisation* – the movement of French industry abroad, or outsourcing in American parlance. Le Pen proclaimed that "Europe is not a model of virtue."[29] Le Pen emphasized the unemployment figures that later contributed to the rejection of the constitution. He argued that

---

[27] See footnote 25.
[28] Jean-Louis Andreani, "Le déficit social européen et la Constitution." *Le Monde* (Paris) April 1, 2005. While the protection of the French social model was at the core of much of the opposition to the constitution, the threat that the EU poses to traditional social policies is not unique to France. For elaborations, see Offe (2003), Smith (2004) and Rosanvallon ([1995] 2000).
[29] www.frontnational.com/doc_interventions_detail.php?id_inter=34.

the unemployment figure was closer to 20% and not to the 10% that the government typically reported. Le Pen elaborated a complicated mathematical analysis that showed that in 1970 hardly 5% of the population was unemployed. He blamed escalating unemployment on plant closings and *délocalisations* – in other words, structural unemployment due to globalization. Interviewed at the Strasbourg convention, Le Pen said he was convinced that, "The French, high and low [he is referring to social class here], will take its revenge silently and the result of the referendum will explode like a bomb on the night of May 29. May 29 will become the boomerang of April 21.[30]

The *tour de force* of the Front's campaign against the constitution was Le Pen's speech on May 1.[31] As described in earlier chapters, Le Pen's May 1 speech is always topical – linked to the issue of the year. Since 1997, he increasingly emphasized globalization and linked it to an anti-Europe rhetoric. Europeanization and globalization became virtually synonymous in Front parlance. Europe as an enemy of French labor has become a salient Front theme.

Le Pen began his May 1, 2005 speech by blaming the "social democracy of Chirac and Jospin" that treats the people as a "pack of lambs" by tolerating mass unemployment. Calling unemployment a "veritable cancer," he argues that the "impotent and corrupt political class" uses the "European fantasy" as "an escape hatch from their responsibilities." Displaying the French penchant for history as political metaphor, Le Pen points to the false promise of the Popular Front in 1936 to bring "peace, bread and liberty" to the French people. Instead, Le Pen argues the Popular Front brought "ration cards, prison camps and deportations." He reminds his audience that members of the Popular Front "threw the powers of the Republic into the hands of Marshal Pétain."

Le Pen evoked the memory of the Nazi occupation to deploy charges of antisemitism against his critics – charges they usually deploy against him.[32] Pointing out that in 2004 there were 280,000 legal and 150,000 illegal immigrants in France, Le Pen argues that no one who makes this point should be labeled a "racist, xenophobe or antisemite!" Le Pen continues: "Europe is not prosperity, full employment, social progress;

---

[30] Vie du Front, "Non, je garde la France." *FDA (Français d'Abord!: Le magazine de Jean-Marie Le Pen)* (May 2005, 402), p. 19. A month later on May 21, the National Front held a colloquy on "France Confronts *Délocalisations.*"

[31] www.frontnational.com/doc_interventions_detail.php?id_inter=36.

[32] Rousso (1991, p. 197) describes Le Pen as "obsessed with the 1940s." Rousso also points out that Le Pen has continually denied any personal association with the antisemitism of Vichy.

it is unemployment, the end of French enterprise! This is the reality that they ask us to applaud!" Echoing Émile Zola's *J'accuse*, Le Pen asks his audience "three questions": "Do you want to renounce the independence of your country? Do you accept no longer being master of your destiny? Do you accept a foreign constitution from which you will never be able to exit?" Le Pen's talks often run to fifteen typescript pages and as rhetoric they are remarkably well constructed even if long-winded.

The end of the May 1 speech displays a populist rhetoric that has a broader appeal than Le Pen's more typical nationalist rhetoric. The "people" is an inclusive concept. Arguing that the European constitution is "essentially materialist," Le Pen asks his audience whether they have ever heard anyone cry "Long live 'Europe' except in a bank." Le Pen concludes, France is not only "supermarkets and statistics," France has a soul that is "laughter and tears, our prayers and songs, our errors and hopes." He ends on a sentimental note with an appeal to the French people, "peasants, workers, artisans, small businessmen, soldiers and functionaries." Le Pen concludes on a strong populist note: "The poor more than the well-to-do need a Nation that is powerful with inviolable frontiers. The true internationals are the lords of the manor who have existed from time immemorial. The urban poor are also tightly bound to the pavement as peasants had been to the soil."

Appropriating the "non": events as political metaphor

The "choc" of May 29: a replica of April 21, 2002

On the evening of May 29, when it was clear that the referendum would fail to pass, French President Jacques Chirac addressed the nation and said that the French had "democratically" expressed themselves with a "sovereign decision." Chirac said that in the spirit of democracy he would respect the choice even though he did not agree with it. He also agreed to take heed to the "uncertainties" and "expectations" that the French expressed during the public discussion of the treaty.[33]

The day after the referendum, political scientist Pascal Perrineau, director of CEVIPOF (Centre d'Étude de la Vie Politique Française), described the referendum as a "replication of April 21, 2002." He assessed the vote as

---

[33] "Déclaration du Président de la République suite au référendum sur le Traité constitutionnel européen" www.elysee.fr/elysee/elysee.fr/francais/interventions/discours_et_decla rations/2005/mai/declaration_du_president_de_la_republique_suite_au_referendum_sur_ le_traite_constitutionnel_europeen.29995.html.

reflecting fissures in French political alignments as well as broader anxieties about the end of a French way of life. Perrineau described the vote as: "the vote of all of the contentious: extreme right, extreme left, Communist Party, the other half of the socialist electorate. It is a sign that the socialists are still part of a culture of government and a culture of rupture. But their vote responds also to a logic of opposition ... This referendum translates the French anxiety about identity; Europe is not as interesting as the prolonging of France. There is also post-enlargement malaise. This is the first time that France has said no to Europe since 1956. It is also the first divorce of the French–German couple."[34]

Serge July, founder and editorial commentator of *Libération*, provided a harsh and realistic assessment of the vote in terms of French political history. In his post-referendum editorial, entitled "Illusions in Distress," he argued that the referendum was another instance of a "revolt" that had been gaining momentum since the presidential elections of 1995 when Jean-Marie Le Pen came in third in the first round with 15% of the vote.[35] July marks the legislative elections of 1997 and April 21, 2002 as part of this not so silent "revolt." He argued that the French political class had failed to assess the impact of a constant 10% unemployment rate between 1986 and 2000. There is a generation of French youth who have lived their entire lives experiencing the debilitating and alienating results of structural unemployment. Given this fact, it is not surprising that Chirac confronted pessimism in his televised meetings with the French youth. What was surprising was that, as President of France, he did not grasp the generational effect that fourteen years of youth unemployment generated. Eurobarometer (European Commission 2005) data support July's analysis that the only age group that voted strongly in support of the treaty were persons aged fifty-five and over (54% yes.)

During the same time period 1986 to 2000, July reported, "the national debt passed 100 million euros, and external commerce plunged." According to July, three fatal illusions dominate French political thinking: first, that the state can do all, that is that the Thirty Glorious Years have not ended; second, that France still carries weight in global international relations; and third, that the French voted down the treaty because it was neoliberal. These are "illusions" that "fall hard." The implications of July's argument are that the rigidity of French

---

[34] Interview with Pascal Perrineau, "Ce référendum est un réplique du 21 avril 2002." *Le Monde* (Paris) May 30, 2005 (Le Monde.fr).

[35] Serge July, editorial, "Illusion en perdition." *Libération* (Paris) May 31, 2005 (Libération.fr).

assumptions about the world and the nation has placed France in danger of generalized stagnation.

The French political class had good reason to engage these illusions to mitigate the shock of the defeat of the constitution for which they had campaigned so hard and which the majority of French citizens rejected. With the exception of Paris and its suburbs, the "non" vote carried across France and even appeared in regions that had been supportive of Europe in the past. The demographer Hervé Le Bras argued that the spatial pattern of the vote suggested that the political geography of France had changed. France no longer had leftwing or rightwing regions but simply rich and "poor" regions – and the poorer the region on a number of standard indices the less likely were its residents to support the treaty. Le Bras concluded that it was time to take seriously the idea that there were "two Frances."[36]

Parties and politicians that had supported the constitution spoke in a restrained manner regarding its demise. François Hollande, General Secretary of the Socialist Party, observed that French citizens were consulted and participated in the referendum. Hollande argued that the French made a "major political decision" that will "engage us for a long time. It [the French vote] will be a danger for Europe but mostly ... the vote suggests above all the growth of a profound crisis all across our country."[37] Hollande argued that the current ruling group was unable to meet the challenges facing the country. Hollande feared that France would be held responsible for the "demise of Europe." With the 2007 presidential elections in mind, Hollande exhorted his fellow socialists whose "no" votes were widely perceived as defeating the treaty: "Europe must not be a victim of the interior disorder of the French and the profound malaise in our country. Europe must once more be rediscovered as a source of hope for its peoples and not a source of mistrust." According to Hollande, the solution is that "socialists, French socialists, European socialists – must meet this great challenge of the continent, [and for] French socialists to be there for their country to give it a perspective, a sense of direction, of hope and to move the left toward a project that will be credible, engaging and sincere."

It was disingenuous of Hollande to speak of the Socialist Party as the source of hope for a revitalized France in a new Europe. The raw numbers that became available after the referendum suggested that it was the

---

[36] Le Bras (1998) had previously tracked the relation between demographic change and the emergence of the extreme right.

[37] "Déclaration de François Hollande 29 mai 2005" www.ouisocialiste.net/article.php3?id_article=970.

division between the socialists on the issue that clearly cost the "oui."[38] Socialist Party adherents voted 59% "non" versus 41% "oui." In contrast in 1992 for the referendum on the Maastricht Treaty, socialists voted 76% "oui." In the 2005 referendum, the French communists and the National Front voted "oui" in roughly the same proportions – 5% and 4% respectively. In 1992, the communists voted 16% for Maastricht whereas the Front voted only 7% in favor of Maastricht.

The hope of May 29, 2005

The advocates of the "no" spoke out energetically in the post-referendum period. The French Communist Party, the anti-globalization group ATTAC and the National Front, as odd an ideological trio as one would wish to see, viewed the "no" as a wellspring of political possibility. On May 31, Marie-George Buffet, head of the French Communist Party, declared, "A great hope arose today." She argued that May 29, 2005 had "the dynamic of a popular coming together that evoked the great moments of the Popular Front or of May '68." The rejection of the constitution signaled that France demanded the "abandonment of the ultra-liberal projects of Brussels."[39]

On its website, the anti-globalization group ATTAC declared that the rejection of the constitution ushered in the "springtime of France" – an allusion to 1848 and the "springtime of peoples." ATTAC proclaimed, "The French people came to write a page of history. For the first time in fifty years, they expressed their refusal to see Europe constructed on the sole basis of market criteria and objectives. For the first time in thirty years, the people affirm their will to put an end to disastrous politics, neoliberal intrigues."[40] After the Dutch vote, ATTAC exuberantly referred to France and the Netherlands as the two black sheep of Europe. In a front-page article in *Le Monde Diplomatique*, Ignacio Ramonet, who seven years earlier had proclaimed, "let's disarm the markets," announced that the "no" signified "a rebel France who honored its tradition as a political nation par excellence. She saved the Old Continent, and aroused a new hope of peoples and the anxiety of established elites."[41]

---

[38] These divisions continued through the 2007 presidential elections and arguably into the post-election period as Royal and Hollande competed for control of the Socialist Party.

[39] Originally published in *Irish Political Review*, June 2005, www.atholbooks.org/europe/buffet.php.

[40] "La victoire d'un peuple debout et informé." *Grain de Sable* 516 (June 1, 2005) www.france.ATTAC.org/a5120.

[41] Ignacio Ramonet, "Espoirs." *Le Monde Diplomatique* 52 (June 2005), p. 1. For a discussion of the founding of ATTAC, see Ancelovici (2002); for a discussion of its influence in France, see the essays in Wieviorka (2003).

On the day after the referendum, the National Front called for the resignation of Chirac. The Front website displayed a poster that proclaimed, "The People Spoke: Chirac Resignation!" Le Pen's message on the night of May 29 was relatively sober: "The French people have clearly said NO to the Constitution of the European Union and also refused the feudalization of France to a supranational State. They rejected the construction of a Europe that was neither European, nor independent, nor protective ... They reaffirmed the political independence of France and its sacred right to provide for itself." Le Pen advanced his own cause as he criticized the government: "The President of the Republic and the Government, which was involved without reservation in the campaign in favor of the YES, have been clearly disavowed. The National Front appeals to the French people to unite to confront the grave difficulties which are the consequence of politics followed for thirty years, and to promote indispensable reforms for the defense of our fundamental national interests." Marine Le Pen accompanied her father on French television and joyously remarked, "This is the first time that I have gone on television to comment on a victory."[42]

While the French Communist Party and ATTAC were invoking the revolutions of 1848 and 1968, the National Front invoked its own revolution – April 21, 2002. In the spirit of revolutionary exuberance, Le Pen urged his supporters to attend the party *Fête des Bleu-Blanc-Rouge*: "United as a Front, we will be able to open the path of renewal that our people desired from April 21, 2002 to May 29, 2005."[43] In many respects, the National Front won even though Le Pen lost on April 21, 2002. For Le Pen, May 29, 2005 and April 21, 2002 signaled the beginning of a new political era. These dates also signaled that the governing classes had misread two political facts: first, that the "people" supported the idea of Europe – writ large; and second, that the National Front was an extreme and irrelevant political actor. The defeat of the constitution in France only intensified the fear of a repeat of April 21, 2002 among mainstream politicians as they looked ahead to the 2007 presidential elections. The riots in the *banlieues* in fall 2005 and the massive public protests against the *contrat première embauche* (CPE) in the spring of 2006 did little to abate this fear.

---

[42] Christiane Chombeau, "Le FN célèbre la victoire du non, mais s'interroge déjà sur 2007." *Le Monde* (Paris) May 31, 2005, p. 9. For Le Pen's speech see, www.frontnational.com/doc_interventions_detail.php?id_inter = 38.

[43] Jean-Marie Le Pen, "Chacun à son poste!" *FDA* (September 2005, 406), p. 3.

Fête des Bleu-Blanc-Rouge *2005: "Le Pen/Le Peuple"*

Riding the emotional wave of the twin victories of April 21, 2002 and May 29, 2005 the Front's annual *Fête des Bleu-Blanc-Rouge* unofficially began Le Pen's 2007 presidential campaign.[44] The Front traditionally held its *Fête* on the periphery of Paris in the pelouse de Reuilly, a park on the northern side of the bois de Vincennes. After its permit was denied in 2003, the Front moved the festival in 2005 to the exposition hall at Le Bourget, a suburb of Paris. Le Bourget is on the same RER commuter train line that tourists take to Charles de Gaulle airport – although tourists probably take the express that conveniently skips all the stops in the exurbs. The trip on the local train is grim. The architectural landscape deteriorates as the train leaves central Paris and travels toward the industrialized exurbs of Paris. The train to Le Bourget travels through the area that was in flames during the weeks beginning on October 27, 2005. As the train pulls into the local stations, French Communist Party posters recruiting new members dominate the platforms. Le Bourget, and areas similar to it, is fertile recruiting ground for left and right. Beset by both immigrants and urban poverty, Le Bourget was an odd location for the Front *Fête*.[45]

The National Front provided free buses that picked up *Fête* participants at the RER station in Le Bourget and transported them to the large exhibition hall on the outskirts of the town. The domesticated version of the Front, as represented by the frog and the princess poster, appeared in another incarnation at the exhibition hall where a large silkscreen rendition of the *Fête* poster adorned the building (Fig. 7.2). The festival poster features a blond child, a young boy of no more than three years, with the colors of the French flag painted on his face.[46] The theme of the *Fête*, "French pride," is superimposed above the face of the child. *Fête* literature, pamphlets and flyers have the phrase "Passionately French" on them. The Front describes the *Fête* as a meeting of "friendship" and displays itself as welcoming to everyone – from immigrants who assimilate to children in Iraq. Unemployment and outsourcing figure in the posters. However, the dominant images are of youth and the future – a requisite for a party headed by a seventy-eight-year-old man. Le Pen's wife, Jany,

---

[44] I attended the *Fête des Bleu-Blanc-Rouge* at Le Bourget on October 8 and 9, 2005.

[45] I witnessed two French police frisk two Arab-looking youths, hold them against a wall and then let them go during one of my two trips to Le Bourget, which suggests how prevalent the practice of police harassment may be.

[46] French friends and colleagues have told me that the child does not "look" French.

7.2 *Political poster*, Fête des Bleu-Blanc-Rouge, *October 2005*

founded an organization named SOS Enfants d'Irak. She visited Iraq to offer food and supplies to suffering children and photographs of her visit dominate several of the exhibition booths.

In contrast to the earlier *Fêtes*, the 2005 event had toned down its images of blatant racism and energized its constituency. The Front's security guards dressed in black still hand search the bags of everyone entering the *Fête*. The Front has added metal detectors to its security procedures. Post-9/11, metal detectors are not particularly remarkable. A cadre of party members who did not look either shabby or dangerous have joined the elderly Frontists and tough-looking youths who traditionally frequent the *Fête*. While one would not mistake the crowd at the *Fête* for the fashionable denizens of Saint-Germain des Prés, in contrast to the past the younger Frontists seem almost stylish. The appearance of the participants suggests that a more middle-aged and slightly more educated group is augmenting the Front's traditional lower-middle-class constituency.

In addition to the usual fare of *faux* history tracts that focused on Joan of Arc and Clovis, the bookstands also displayed more policy-oriented works, such as a book of interviews with Bruno Gollnisch, *La réaction c'est la vie!*; a book on the 2002 presidential elections, *Le tour infernal 21 avril– 5 mai 2002: analyse d'une fantasmagorie électorale*; and a book on plant closings, *Délocalisations: ce n'est pas une fatalité! Actes du colloque du mai 21, La France face aux délocalisations.* A new generation of party leaders that included Marine Le Pen, Bruno Gollnisch and Carl Lang participated in open forums on "French youth," "French entrepreneurship," "social ambition" and "French unity, the place of France in the world, our civilization." The sessions were packed and there was standing room only in the special tents in which they occurred.

Turkey, and the Front's opposition to its entry into the European Union, was the remaining object of general ill will displayed at the *Fête*. A booth and several posters arguing that Turkey is not part of Europe struck a discordant note. The front-page headline of the *National Hebdo*, the Front's party newspaper, for the week of October 6–12 was, "Viennese Waltz and Turkish March." The front page featured a cartoon of a red-faced Turk with a beard and an excessively hooked nose wearing a red hat and with a saber in his pocket. The Turk's teeth are sharp and protrude out as if to bite his visibly terrified lederhosen-clad companion with whom he is dancing. On the inside pages of the newspaper is an article entitled "Betrayal of Europe," referring to October 3, 2005 – the date that marked the opening of talks regarding Turkey's membership in the European Union.

Le Pen's speech on late Sunday afternoon is the traditional high point that closes the *Fête*. In 1998, Le Pen spoke in the open air to a group of mainly elderly people. With little technology to support his speech in 1998, he spoke to an audience that consisted principally of empty seats. He ended the 1998 speech by giving medals of distinction to Front members who had loyally served the party. The honorees were white haired and the general feeling in 1998 was one of old age and decay. Viewed against Le Pen's 1998 speech, his closing speech in 2005 was astonishing. At Le Bourget there was standing room only in the closed auditorium that accommodated about 5,000 people. The event was highly choreographed. The room was strobe lighted with red, white and blue – the colors of the French flag as well as the name of the *Fête*. A chorus of youths dressed in white tee shirts with the words *Le Pen Le Peuple* marched up and down on the stage and waved French flags. This was the first time that this event would be televised as the head of TELECOM 1 (TC1) said it was unfair to give air time to all the other declared presidential candidates and not to

Le Pen.[47] A Front functionary led a warm-up session. On both sides of the stage were large television screens that captured the images on the stage for those in the back of the auditorium. Party volunteers handed out small French flags to members of the audience.

Le Pen entered the auditorium to emotional chants of "President, President, President!" His speech continued the theme of the national and the social that he and his party had begun in the spring.[48] Le Pen's speech focused on unemployment and the failure of the present French government to ameliorate its effects. He attacked the socialists for "thirty years of disaster" – making ironic reference to the *Trente Glorieuses*, the thirty years of prosperity between 1945 and 1975. He pointed out that France was "paralyzed" and laid the blame for this paralysis on all French politicians. Le Pen labeled his main competitor on the right as the "duplicator" and asked Bruno Mégret and his constituency that had broken away from the Front in 1999 to return to the fold.

Le Pen saw France's only hope in a break with the past that would lead to a "French renaissance and the defense of workers and the French people." The audience responded with shouts of "President, President!" to his call for a "true revolution." He took up issues of immigration and attacked *droit du sol*, the right to become a citizen if you are born on the territory. He resurrected the old Front adage that French nationality must be "inherited or merited." He reiterated the Front's support of "national preference" for French citizens. His support of the 1905 law that separates Church and state places him with the governing class that on the recommendations of the Stasi Commission in December 2003 banned the wearing of conspicuous religious symbols in public schools that was signed into law in 2004.

Le Pen asserted that the presidential elections of 2007 would determine the future of the French people. The theme that the 2007 election would be a turning point for France became the universal theme of the election espoused by all the candidates. In this regard, Le Pen was merely articulating the *Zeitgeist*. Le Pen promised to run against all those who have "lied, misled and betrayed the French people for three decades." His conclusion was strong and emotional. In contrast to his more strident and intensely nationalistic appeals of the past, Le Pen's appeal focused on security and democracy as twin elements of a reconstituted people's France. He abandoned the microphone and the podium and moved to the

[47] Despite the presence of the television cameras, or perhaps because of it, the festival received sparse coverage in the press the next day.
[48] www.frontnational.com/doc_interventions_detail.php?id_inter=3.

edge of the stage to literally shout out his closing lines: "We launch a fraternal appeal to all those who have the sentiment of having been tricked, deceived, abandoned, to those who are discouraged and even desperate. You can take your revenge and win with us the battle of France." Wrapping himself in the language of Article 2 of the French constitution, Le Pen cried out: "The Republic is the government Of the People, By the People, For the People – French people, who have done many things and who can yet do so much more for the good of France, of Europe and the World. Arise and march to the fight for the Victory of France!"

"Le Pen/Le Peuple" flashed on the screens where Le Pen's image had been and he called his decidedly youthful team of party supporters up to the stage. The youth in white tee shirts and French flags served as a chorus in the background on the stage; white confetti and balloons of blue, white and red dropped from the ceiling. Le Pen and his circle broke into *La Marseillaise* and asked the audience to join in. The conclusion was focused and emotional. Amid the snowfall of confetti the flashing blue, red and white lights and the singing of the national anthem one felt a flow of emotional energy in the crowd – that was frighteningly real.

Summary: the multiple meanings of "non"

The triumph of the "grumpy populists"

In the immediate aftermath of the French vote, public discussion within France as well as in Europe and in the United States focused upon the impact that the French rejection would have on the European project. On June 6, 2005, *The Economist* graphically captured the spirit of this commentary. An image of Jacques-Louis David's painting of the assassinated Marat in his bath adorned its post-referendum cover. The cover headline proclaimed in bold letters, "The Europe that Died" followed in small letters by "and the one to save." The list that his assassin Charlotte Corday presented to gain entrée to his chamber lies in Marat's lifeless hand. The cover is a thinly veiled comment on the treachery embedded in the rejection of the constitution.

The headline of *Le Monde* on May 31, 2005 proclaimed, "Chirac Disavowed, Europe Destabilized." A cartoon image depicted the word "non" with an exclamation point floating on a sea. France is drawn as an island in the center of the "o" and the ship of Europe is in the background sailing away without the bickering French.[49] Richard Bernstein writing in

---

[49] *Le Monde* (Paris) May 31, 2005, front page.

the *International Herald Tribune* asserted "50 Years of Rationality Interrupted in France."[50] David Brooks, the *New York Times* opinion writer, asserted that "fear" rather than "hope" governs how Europeans view their future. Brooks claimed that "the [European] liberal project of the postwar era has bred a stultifying conservatism, a fear of dynamic flexibility, a greater concern for guarding what exists than for creating what doesn't."[51]

German historian and public intellectual Michael Stürmer argued in the *Wall Street Journal* that the "non" was a course correction reacting against bureaucratic hubris and the overconfidence of political elites. In Stürmer's view, the principal difficulty was that the French, and later Dutch, "no" slowed the momentum on talks scheduled to begin on October 3, 2005 on the staging of Turkey's entry to the EU. Stürmer emphasized the fact that the EU constitution merely consolidated a series of treaties that are still in effect and will continue to be in effect independently of the outcome of the referenda.[52] On a more emotional note, British historian and political commentator Timothy Garton Ash warned in an article in the *Guardian* that the rejection of the constitution suggested a "declining civilization" and sent him back to reading the work of Arnold Toynbee.[53]

In commentary appearing in the *Financial Times* among other venues, Andrew Moravcsik (author of the standard recent political history of the European project, *The Choice for Europe: Social Purpose and State Power from Messina to Maastricht* [1998]) argued that "Europe works well without the grand illusions."[54] Reasoning in the same vein as Stürmer, Moravcsik notes that the constitutional treaty summarized but did not supersede previous treaties so that in the long run the future of Europe as a project did not depend on a formal constitution. More importantly, he argued that the technical details of the constitution were not particularly engaging for the majority of European citizens. In short, the constitutional treaty was not a charismatic document. According to Moravcsik, submitting the constitution to a popular referendum made the idea of Europe fodder for the extreme ideologies of "grumpy populists" who mapped their

---

[50] *International Herald Tribune* (Paris) June 3, 2005, p. 2.
[51] David Brooks, "Fear and Rejection." *New York Times* (New York) June 2, 2005, p. A25.
[52] Michael Stürmer, "Non." *Wall Street Journal* (New York) May 31, 2005, p. A16.
[53] Timothy Garton Ash, "Comment and Analysis: Decadent Europe." *Guardian* (London) June 9, 2005, p. 25f.
[54] Andrew Moravcsik, "Europe Works Well Without the Grand Illusions." *Financial Times* June 14, 2005. Moravcsik (2006) covers the same territory in a more academic vein.

national discontent and fears onto the opaque and bureaucratic prose of the constitution.

Between Zollverein *and* patrie*: from the populist to the national moment*

The French "non" meant "no" to the draft treaty but it also had multiple other meanings. Every event has a front story and a back story. The front story is the simple and immediate explanation of outcomes. With regard to the "non," the front story, the one repeated over and over in the newspapers, was straightforward and confirmed by opinion polls in the immediate aftermath of the vote. Unemployment and fear of unemployment were the principal reasons for the "non" in France, followed by general discontent with the government.[55] OECD's (2005) annual economic survey of France released shortly after the referendum notes that the unemployment rate in France for 2004–2005 was 10.1 percent and that it had not been below 8 percent for twenty years.

Unemployment achieves a different interpretive valence depending on which political party or group was deploying it. In contrast to the front story that focuses on explanation, the back story focuses upon the context in which events take place and opens an interpretive space. A constitution is as much a symbolic as a legal document.[56] This duality inherent in all constitutions underscores a transparent but overlooked point that speaks to both the French and Dutch vote. When the governing strata submitted the issue of Europe writ large to the people, they ultimately did not approve. The "no" vote made clear to the governing classes just how remote and unpopular "Europe" was to ordinary citizens. Post-referendum

---

[55] For example, the day after the referendum, *Le Monde* (May 30, 2005) reported, "La crainte pour l'emploi est la raison principale du rejet de la Constitution par les Français" (Fear over jobs is the main reason for the rejection of the constitution by the French). Eurobarometer (European Commission 2005) reported the following economic reasons for the "no" vote: outsourcing (31%); fear of unemployment (26%); dislike of the "liberal text" (19%); weakens "social Europe" (16%).

[56] On this point, see Norton (1993, pp. 123–138). In the fall of 2004 when it began to be clear that the French referendum might be problematic, Thomas Ferenczi, editorial writer for *Le Monde*, argued that the European constitution was largely a symbolic document and that the popular acceptance of the symbols would be crucial to the success or failure of the referendum. He listed three symbolic dimensions, first, naming the treaty a "Constitution" meant that the European "people" were an entity; second, the document created a European Minister of Foreign Affairs – suggesting that there could be a European diplomacy and military policy; and third, that there could be a "social economy of markets" – that is that Europe could be both "social democratic" and "neoliberal" at the same time (Thomas Ferenczi, "Constitution: l'Europe des symboles." *Le Monde* [Paris] October 6, 2004, pp. 1, 21).

Eurobarometer (European Commission 2005) data in France revealed that 61 percent of those who voted "yes" and 60 percent of those who voted "no" had decided on how they would vote at the beginning of the referendum campaign. For this reason, what was claimed about the "no" after the vote was as politically important as the failed strategies that led to the referendum's defeat.[57]

The French vote on the European constitution brings this analysis back to the broader issues of Europeanization that the first and second chapters laid out. French politicians of all stripes represented the referendum as a choice between rationality and culture, market and nation – *Zollverein* and *patrie*.[58] The public discussion of the European constitution in France, before and after the referendum, underscored the peculiarities and contradictions constitutive of the expanding process of European integration. For example, when the European Commission ran a competition to determine who would design the euro bills, they listed as a prerequisite for consideration that artists submit designs that featured buildings and landscapes that looked European but were not recognizable as to place (Berezin 2006c). Unlike the placeless spaces on the euro bills, Europe *is* a place of nation-states (Entrikin 1991). Citizenship in a member nation-state is a prerequisite for European citizenship. Citizens of Europe are, first, citizens of established nation-states.[59]

A central tension of the European project lies in its attempt to reconceptualize political space (Ansell and Di Palma 2004; Katzenstein 2005; Agnew 2005; Sassen 2006) within the territorial boundaries of existing nation-states. In contrast to nineteenth-century nation-state projects which aggregated smaller territorial units, the expanded project of Europeanization disaggregates and reaggregates established national political space. Disaggregation and reaggregation have political and social consequences (Berezin 2003). On the macro level, European integration disequilibrates the existing mix of national cultural practice and legal norms that govern European nation-states – what Chapter 2 described as a *consolidation regime*. For example, the National Assembly voted on February 28, 2005 to amend the French constitution in order to legally

---

[57] For a compressed political analysis, see Hainsworth (2006) and Ivaldi (2006); the essays in Perrineau (2005) provide useful statistical data.
[58] Berezin and Díez Medrano (2008) outline this discussion in the literature.
[59] The literature on post-nationalism (for example, Soysal 1994; Deflem and Pampel 1996) and the viability of the nation-state (essays in Joppke 1998; Paul *et al.* 2003) debates the substantive significance of this fact.

call the referendum on the EU constitution.[60] On the micro level, European integration violates longstanding habits of collective national attachment, or *national experience*.

The French "non" underscored the reassertion of national identities and nation-ness across the political spectrum as an unintended consequence of the accelerated process of European integration. In short, European integration by threatening to make the national space "unfamiliar" to many citizens opens the door to contestation of all sorts. At the practical and emotional level, the combination of macro and micro disequilibration made the constitution project vulnerable to the appeals to economic uncertainty and national identity that proponents of the "non" skillfully deployed.

National experience, the collective experience of living on a territory with a distinct set of cultural and legal norms (written in national constitutions) over time produces thick attachment based on national security, individual enfranchisement and shared culture (language, religion, practices) that does not easily dissolve – even in the face of what appears to be a new political and economic order – that is, European integration. The National Front exploited this insight early on, but the "non" vote on the constitution suggests that the passion for the nation was not an isolated emotion held by political extremists – but a widely shared French feeling.

---

[60] The constitutional amendment is Title XV "On the European Communities and the European Union" (art. 88–1 to 88–5). English version available at www.assemblee-nationale.fr/english/8ab.asp#TITLE%20XV.

PART III

Theorizing Europe and rightwing populism

8

Reasserting the national against Europe: politics and perception

Shocking events as templates of possibility

In an early essay on American Progressivism, Walter Lippmann ([1914] 1985) quipped that "Nations make their histories to fit their illusions" (p. 101). Lippmann had the correct words – but in the incorrect order. National histories make national illusions – as well as hopes, dreams and capacities to imagine new political possibilities. The past conditions the present, but not in any purely path-dependent or evolutionary way. National histories speak to the legacies of *consolidation regimes* – the relation between people and polity – that shaped particular territorially bound nation-states. The thick description of events from the 1997 National Front party congress in Strasbourg to the French "non" in 2005 – from an explicitly National Front event to a national event – underscores the persistence of *national experience* and its resistance to rapid and exogenous forces of social and political change.

Yet, events also serve as templates of possibilities and sites of collective evaluation. Events, such as the ones discussed in the previous chapters, may alter collective national perceptions as well as generate powerful emotions – such as hope and fear, euphoria and shock, pride and shame. For this reason, events are powerful analytic tools. A study of events provides analytic leverage on the problem of rightwing populism in general and the National Front in particular that eludes a more restricted mode of analysis. Shifting the unit of analysis from political attitudes, voting behavior and strategy to events locates the National Front on a broad canvas of European, as well as French, politics, culture and society. The French rejection of the European Constitutional Treaty makes salient the ambivalence, if not outright resistance, of French political culture to the increasing incursions of Europeanization. This chapter situates the career of the National Front as outlined in the last five chapters within the context of French politics and Europeanization. This chapter analyzes how the increasing pace of European integration placed the National Front, the French state and French civil society on parallel paths. It returns to the question posed in the Introduction: would there be a *right-wing populist moment*, would Le Pen have become a political force, if it were not for the accelerated pace of European integration?

From April 21, 2002 to May 29, 2005 through a glass darkly

French citizens, or at least those groups of citizens who supported the constitution, were in shock when it went down in defeat. The distress that was visible on the faces of French politicians and citizens was a replay of the shock of April 21, 2002. The French media represented both events – Le Pen's second place in the first round of the 2002 presidential race and the defeat of the constitution – as political earthquakes.

Analysts of French politics and defenders of French moral culture never tire of pointing out that nothing of material consequence happened on either April 21, 2002 or May 29, 2005.[1] Electors catapulted Chirac back to the presidency. The political surprise of April 21, 2002 transformed what had been a boring and tight electoral competition into an emotionally intense national event. Le Pen's second-place showing handed the election to his opponent. Applying a similar line of reasoning to the referendum on the European constitution, May 29, 2005 was a symbolic defeat with no tangible consequences as the European Union treaties remained in place.[2]

If "happened" meant that Jean-Marie Le Pen would have become President of France on May 5, 2002, or that the European Union would have fallen apart after May 29, 2005, then indeed nothing happened on those dates. In their immediate outcomes, the first round of the 2002 presidential elections and the referendum on the European constitution had limited consequences. But the collective perception that something had happened, rather than what actually happened, endowed both events

---

[1] See, for example, Guiraudon and Schain (2002) on www.europanet.org/pub/Guiraudon-Schain_sep02.html (accessed February 2, 2007) on the 2002 French elections.

[2] See Moravcsik (2006) for an articulation of this position. When Germany assumed the presidency of the European Union on January 1, 2007, Angela Merkel immediately began an effort to revive a redrafted version of the treaty. Her efforts culminated in the Treaty of Lisbon, which representatives of the member states signed on December 13, 2007. National parliaments were planning to ratify the Lisbon Treaty without submitting it to a popular referendum. Ireland was the only EU member that required a referendum. Irish citizens rejected the Lisbon Treaty on June 12, 2008 – once more putting the European project in jeopardy.

with significance. As argued in Chapter 5, 1999, the year of its presumed demise, was a positive, not a negative, turning point for the National Front. Similarly, April 21, 2002 and May 29, 2005 were turning points in France's collective perception of itself as a political community. In April 2002 and May 2005, political language and perceptions imploded. As points of political reference, left, right and center seemed to collapse among themselves. People and groups who would normally be on radically different sides of issues ended up employing the same political vocabulary.

April 21, 2002 and May 29, 2005 rendered two social and political facts salient. First, French citizens affirmed with their votes that Le Pen's issues, no matter how distasteful the messenger, were French, as well as National Front, issues. The 2002 presidential elections and the 2005 constitutional referendum were a collective iteration of Laurent Fabius's oft-quoted remark that Le Pen raised good questions for which he provided bad answers. Second, both dates produced a feeling of collective shock and national embarrassment. In April 2002, public figures of diverse political persuasions continually asked how the nation-state that created and designed The Declaration of the Rights of Man and of the Citizen (August 1789) could have allowed a xenophobic racist, such as Jean-Marie Le Pen, to come in second place for the highest public office in the nation. On May 29, 2005, political voices asked how a nation-state that was a founding member of Europe could reject a constitution that its own former President, Valéry Giscard d'Estaing, had helped to design. Commentators conveniently omitted in the public hand wringing after the referendum's defeat that France may have been a founding member of Europe but it was also an ambivalent founding member of Europe. Charles de Gaulle found it difficult to reconcile his "certain idea of France [*certaine idée de la France*]" and his visions of French *grandeur* with the requirements of an international body that would govern Europe.[3]

The defeat of the referendum on the European constitution, analyzed in conjunction with the intractable electoral presence and continuing public influence of Jean-Marie Le Pen, suggests that the rightwing populist moment is more than simply a racist and xenophobic response to strangers but represents a response to deep issues of societal and political change. In April 2007, Le Pen made his fourth run for the presidency of France. Marine Le Pen's campaign strategy of *dédiabolisation* represented a fundamental understanding of the logic of *thin* commitments. Her strategy

---

[3] On de Gaulle's vision of Europe, see Gordon (1993 in general, Chapter 1 in particular); on his foreign policy in general, see Hoffmann (1974, pp. 283–331); on France and the early European treaties, see Moravcsik (1998, pp. 103–122).

arguably made mainstream politicians nervous as they looked ahead to the presidential elections of 2007. By fall of 2005, it was becoming increasingly clear that the National Front would not have had the "successes" of 2002 and 2005 if immigration and racism had been its only issues.

Conventional wisdom in public and academic discourse routinely links the National Front and immigration. Conventional wisdom is not myth but it is not absolute fact either; rather its grounding lies in a reality that reveals only a partial truth. The history of French immigration and immigration policy suggests a more complex picture.[4] The French state from the Mitterrand era to the present has addressed the issue of immigration and with brief exceptions has continued to tighten entry requirements and restrict access to citizenship (for summaries, see Weil 2001b; Guiraudon 2005; Hollifield 2004; Hargreaves 2007). Immigrants are a problem because they are poor, unemployed and, most importantly, Muslim and resisting assimilation, not because they are immigrants *per se*. France is a republic. Assimilation and its articulation in Republicanism is a core national value.[5]

However, not all immigrants to France, many of them second generation, are poor and unemployed. Children of immigrants schooled in France often do assimilate and become French. On the other hand, illegal immigrants and asylum seekers of various stripes make up the largest percentage of immigrants to contemporary Europe. These groups pose an immigration challenge that is not unique to France. Illegal immigration is a European issue not a national issue. The French and subsequently the Dutch rejection of the European constitution made it clear that Europe and neoliberalism, the dismantling of social Europe, was also a trans-European issue.

Mapping thin *commitments: the career of the National Front*

The description of May 29, 2005 as the "new" April 21 was more than just a political metaphor that politicians grasping for rhetorical straws, as well as votes, strategically deployed. Both dates shared a common collective emotional valence and bore a substantive political connection to the career of the National Front. Jean-Marie Le Pen never lost the patina of ill-repute nor the intellectual antipathy of the professional classes toward

---

[4] Weil (2001b, particularly pp. 216–226) provides the best short analysis of that complexity.
[5] For a philosophical discussion of the concept of Republicanism, see Ferry and Renaut (1992, pp. 117–128); Nord (1995) places the concept in its historical context. Lamont (2000) makes this point with force.

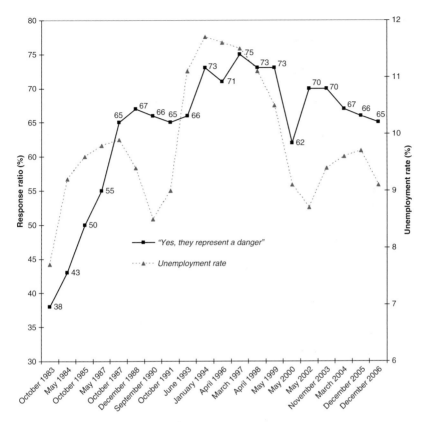

8.1 *Trends in public perception of the National Front as "threat" and unemployment rate in France*

his lower-middle-class constituency (Mayer [1999] 2002). The National Front and its supporters remained virtually synonymous with racism and xenophobia in most segments of the French public sphere. But this was a view that was more descriptive of the National Front in 1995 than it was of the National Front as it approached the 2007 presidential elections.

Longitudinal polling data from TNS-Sofres provide a visual image of the trajectory of *thin* commitments. A December 2006 TNS-Sofres poll taken in the wake of the spring 2007 presidential elections revealed that the public's perception of the National Front as a "danger" to French democracy had lessened consistently over time (Fig. 8.1). TNS-Sofres began this poll in 1983 after the National Front's breakthrough election in Dreux. The graph in Figure 8.1 suggests an increasing recognition among the

French public that the National Front posed a threat to democracy that continues until 1999 when the party split and did poorly in the European parliamentary elections. The public and academic perception in 1999, as discussed in Chapter 5, was that Le Pen was gone. The TNS-Sofres data support that assessment. Not surprisingly, the fear of the National Front climbed again in the wake of the 2002 presidential elections and began to decline steadily beginning in 2003.

The public perception of Le Pen as a threat maps closely onto the national unemployment rate, which is not surprising given that unemployment was the principal reason that citizens gave when asked what determined their electoral preferences. The years between 1987 and 1990 stand out on the graph because there is an inverse relation between the unemployment rate and fear of the National Front suggesting a collective moral evaluation of Le Pen that was independent of economic considerations.

TNS-Sofres began another poll in 1997 that tracked public perception of Le Pen's position on issues. People polled were asked whether they found Le Pen's position on issues to be correct (*juste*), excessive or unacceptable. The percentage of respondents who found Le Pen's ideas "unacceptable" peaked in April 1998 at 48%. The relation between those who found his ideas "unacceptable" and "excessive" has varied inversely since 1997. Since 2005, the number of respondents who found his ideas "excessive" has increased sharply from a low of 36% in March 1997 to a high of 47% in December 2006. The number of respondents who found Le Pen's ideas "correct" has remained relatively constant since reaching a high of 16% in May 2002. Figure 8.2 provides a graph of these percentages.

The inverse relation between the percentage of those who found Le Pen's ideas merely "excessive" and those who found his ideas "unacceptable" suggested the progression of *thin* commitments among certain members of the French citizenry. Taken in conjunction with the narrative presented in this book, these figures suggest that Le Pen and his ideas, or the National Front and its positions, were becoming if not more and more a part of French political culture – at least moving on parallel tracks. The percentage of people who found Le Pen's ideas "unacceptable" was always surprisingly low. But the difference between "excessive" and "correct" is more nuanced and politically important. If the public thinks that Le Pen is extreme in his formulations but substantively on the mark, they are more likely to either cast a vote for him directly, or cast a vote for a politician who adopts his positions without the stigma of the National Front attached to it. Arguably, Nicolas Sarkozy was shrewd enough to capitalize on these perceptions during his successful bid for the French presidency.

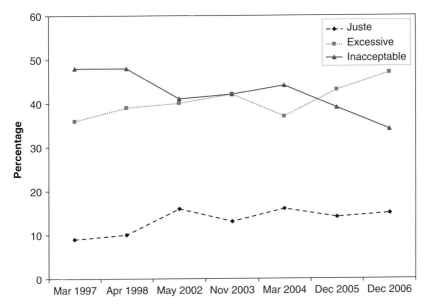

8.2 *Judgments regarding the positions of Jean-Marie Le Pen*

The book's analysis of events, coupled with the polling data, suggests that the public perception of Le Pen has shifted since he emerged in the early 1980s. The National Front continues to have elements of racism and xenophobia. For example, some view its opposition to Turkey's entry to the European Union as a racist position. But opposition to Turkey's membership is not unique to Le Pen and the National Front. For example, in January 2007 when Nicolas Sarkozy, then Minister of the Interior and now President of France, accepted the UMP's nomination as 2007 presidential candidate, he made the following strong Front-esque comment: "Europe, I imagine as a multiplier of power not as a factor of impotence, as a protection, not as a Trojan horse of all dumpings [*tous les dumpings*], for action and not for submission. I believe in Europe as the founding fathers wanted it, as a common will, not as a collective renunciation. I have lived all my life as a convinced European. But I want to have the liberty to say that Europe must determine its frontiers, [so] that all the countries of the world do not have the vocation to integrate in Europe – beginning with Turkey. To enlarge without limit takes the risk of destroying European political union; I will not accept it."[6] Sarkozy's adapting of the term

[6] "Le discours d'investiture de Nicolas Sarkozy." Le Monde.fr, January 15, 2007 (accessed January 16, 2007).

"dumpings" is hardly suggestive of the universalistic humanitarianism that France and French politicians (not the same thing) claim as their own.

Le Pen still occasionally makes politically outrageous and morally questionable remarks. In a January 2005 newspaper interview, Le Pen commented that the "German occupation [of France] was not particularly inhumane" and that the German Gestapo merely protected the French people.[7] In February 2005, Le Pen said that in the future France would have 25 million Muslims and not 5 million and that Muslims would rule France. For this remark, the Paris Court of Appeals upheld a ruling fining him 10,000 euros for inciting racial hatred. Being fined is a way of political life for Le Pen. His daughter Marine Le Pen had zero tolerance for these remarks that she deemed inappropriate for the "new" National Front. Marine Le Pen viewed her father's comments as undermining her disciplined plan to *dédiaboliser* the National Front in form and substance.

Le Pen's sporadic outbursts underscore how much has changed since the National Front began in 1972 in response to the events of May '68. As the narrative in the preceding chapters suggests, the evolving trajectory of the National Front reveals that immigration as a defining issue has receded before issues of Europeanization and globalization. By 2006, the National Front was no longer reducible to racism and xenophobia. The French state and public opinion, as well as the National Front, were moving in similar directions. This is not to suggest that France and the French were becoming increasingly more racist, intolerant and xenophobic, rather it suggests that Le Pen's issues were increasingly French issues.

Riding the wave of events

Beginning in 1997, with its party convention in Strasbourg, the National Front has engaged in refashioning itself as a potential coalition partner. The Front's hope to normalize itself (*se banaliser*) in the minds of the French electorate was a recurrent fear of the center left and center right. Until its setback in the 2007 presidential elections, the National Front rode the crest of the wave of political events from accelerated European integration to Islamic terrorism to riots in the *banlieues* that attracted thinly committed voters who shared its positions on issues rather than its ideological package. In 1998, the National Front made a strong showing in the regional elections that shocked the French public and mobilized other political parties into action against Le Pen (Perrineau and Reynié 1999).

---

[7] Christiane Chombeau, "Pour M. Le Pen, 'l'occupation allemande n'a pas été particulièrement inhumain.'" *Le Monde* (Paris) January 13, 2005 (Le Monde.fr).

In January 1999, the National Front suffered an internal split. In June 1999, Le Pen and Mégret divided the extreme right vote in the European parliamentary elections. The split in the National Front between Le Pen and Mégret, combined with the subsequent weak showing in the European elections, led political analysts to conclude that, if the Front was not entirely gone from the French political scene, its days of political influence were over.

But as Chapter 5 argued, the break in the National Front and the party's defeat in the 1999 European elections were a turning point not an end. Contrary to expectation, the National Front began to grow rather than contract in influence as the new millennium began. The year 1999 was the end of the beginning, rather than the beginning of the end, for the National Front. Without giving him credit (a source of endless irritation to Le Pen), leftwing populist and rightwing centrist politicians began to articulate the National Front's less extreme positions. Voices outside of, as well as within, the political establishment began to attack globalization and the neoliberal market as well as launch a defense of French culture and identity.

In 1999, the idea that Europeanization and globalization were iterations of the same economic processes began to become part of a broad public discourse in France and throughout Europe as evidenced by the founding of the anti-globalization group ATTAC in Paris in 1998 (Ancelovici 2002). In 1999, Jacques Chirac refused to allow France to sign the European Charter for Regional or Minority Languages – an EU initiative to promote the preservation of regional languages. According to Chirac, signing the Charter would require a revision of the French constitution that made French the language of France and threaten one of the "grand principles of the Republic." In short, the legal affirmation of regional languages threatened French identity and political cultural practices.

Events in the national and international arena turned in directions that served to benefit the National Front politically. In 2001, Jean-Marie Le Pen had the good sense to remain silent after 9/11 and to extend condolences to the United States. Le Pen and the Front were on the same side of the Iraq War issue as the French government. Le Pen's wife went to help the children of Iraq. In foreign affairs, Le Pen and the French political mainstream were on the same side of many issues. In December 2002, Chirac's Minister of the Interior, and now French President, Nicolas Sarkozy instituted a tough law on crime with a view toward containing illegal immigrants. Jean-Marie Le Pen viewed this as a usurpation of his position of zero tolerance for crime. In December 2003, the government-appointed Stasi Commission recommended that the 1905 law that legislated the separation of Church and state, *laïcité*, be upheld. This decision banned the wearing of conspicuous religious symbols in public places – which in practice meant that young Muslim women could not wear headscarves if they attended public schools.

The French state has displayed a peculiar ambivalence to various dimensions of European integration and has repeatedly pulled back from Europeanization in ways that support national identity over European identity. The headscarf debate is the most publicized example, but the regional language issue was a more telling if less prominent instance of retreat. On the surface, the decision to interpret *laïcité* in a way that banned the wearing of religious symbols seemed to fly in the face of two European directives. First, in 2000, the European Commission against Racism and Intolerance (ECRI), an organ of the Council of Europe, asked France to revise its "egalitarian Republican model" as it exposed children of immigrants to possible acts of discrimination. Second, in 2003, the European Council issued a directive that called for the harmonization of immigration and asylum policies in all of the European Union. Patrick Weil (2004b), a member of the Stasi Commission, explained that it was difficult to affirm a law which seemed to take away the freedom of young Muslim women to wear a religious symbol. Yet, as Weil argues, in the larger picture the law supported freedom in general: "The historical success of the French model of secularization, *laïcité*, rests on its guarantee to individuals of state protection against pressure from any religious group. But its future success requires a flexible capacity to respect cultural and religious diversity – and to consider this diversity not a burden, but a challenge and an opportunity."

The multiple contexts of the shocks of April 21, 2002 and May 29, 2005

The French "non" underscored the reassertion of national identities and nation-ness across the political spectrum as an unintended consequence of the accelerated process of European integration. The "shocks" of April 21, 2002 and May 29, 2005 are less shocking when situated within the context of a broader stream of events in France and in Europe. The point is not that these events stand in causal relation to each other but that they function more as a *pas de deux* in ballet where the stability of one dancer, usually the male, makes the actions of the other dancer possible.

Systematic scrutiny of the years between 1983 and the present in France using the career of the National Front as the basis of analytic periodization reveals a striking pattern. The political career of the National Front can be reconstructed in five time periods: first, the *Ascendance* (1983–1994); second, the *Mobilization* (1995–1997); third, *Banalisation* (1998–1999); fourth, *Climbing Back* (2000–2002); and fifth, *Dédiabolisation* (2002 to the present). Viewed within the context of events in French civil society, the French state and the European Union, the National Front is less eccentric than suggested by either its self-representation or the claims of its critics. The trajectory of events within civil society, the state and the European Union maps more or less well at different points in time onto the career of the National Front. (Table 8.1 charts these tendencies.)

The *Ascendance* of the National Front coincides with the presidency of socialist François Mitterrand. The Front's move to normalization from the *Mobilization* to the present day corresponds with the center right presidency of Jacques Chirac. Exogenous to the trajectory of the Front and France is the consolidation of the European Union as well as its expansion to include nation-states from the former Eastern Europe. In the international arena, the period begins with a Europe in which East versus West meant communist versus democratic.

In the period from the elections in Dreux in 1983 to the 1995 presidential elections, Le Pen established himself as a colorful extremist. In these years, he developed his "France First" arguments. His crude antisemitic remarks, particularly his oft-quoted comment on the gas chambers as a "detail" of World War II, came during a period when France as a whole was beginning to rethink its relation to its Vichy past. During the 1980s, small groups such as SOS Racisme organized events against the National Front and against racism in general.[8] In 1985, *Libération* fanned the flames of public opinion against Le Pen when it published an article that featured five witnesses who testified that Le Pen had engaged in acts of torture when he was in the army in Algeria.

Activists also used the French courts to file suits against Le Pen for "crimes against humanity," as hate speech falls under that rubric in French law. The response in French civil society to Le Pen in the 1980s was limited. A small number of French intellectual groups, several of which were based at the Academy, worked against Le Pen. This is not to say that there was no social protest in France during this period. Hundreds of thousands of French citizens took to the streets in the defense of public education. In 1990, hundreds of thousands marched against the desecration of the Jewish cemetery in Carpentras (see Chapter 6, Table 6.2; Mayer 1992).

---

[8] Mayer (1995a) provides a detailed account of extra-parliamentary mobilization against the National Front in the 1980s and early 1990s.

Table 8.1. *Events and the trajectory of the National Front, 1983 to present*

Endogenous events				Exogenous events
NATIONAL FRONT	FRENCH CIVIL SOCIETY	FRENCH STATE	*PERIOD*	EUROPEAN UNION
Ascendance	**Intellectuals' protest**	**Mitterand era**	1983	
Electoral breakthrough (1980s)	SOS Racisme begins (1985)	Reform of Immigration and Nationality Law		• Single European Act (1986)
"France First"	Riots in the banlieues (early 1990s)	"Good Questions, Bad Answers"	1994	• Schengen Accords (1990) • Maastricht Treaty (1992)
Mobilization	**Youth mobilization**	**Neoliberalism**	1995	
Strasbourg (1997)	"Political Horror that Menaces Us!"	"Wave of Privatizations"	1996	• European Stability Pact
"Neither Right Nor Left: French"		Debré law, political cohabitation	1997	• Amsterdam Treaty
Banalisation	**Transnational mobilization**	**Multi- culturalism**	1998	• European Central Bank in Frankfurt
Turning point – success, rupture, defeat	ATTAC and Bové	World Cup win "No" to Regional Languages Charter	1999	
Climbing back	**Global and national**	**New Republican moment**	2000	• Nice Treaty • Charter of Fundamental Rights • Eurozone established
Le Pen 17%, proceeds to 2nd round of presidential elections (2002)	ATTAC protests "Le Choc" – Le Pen enters 2nd round	"Yes to the Republic" Chirac re- elected (2002)	2001 2002	
Dédiabolisation	**Protest broadens**	**Reasserting the national**	2003	
Marine Le Pen: "People Like Me"	Riots in banlieues (2005) Riots against CPE (2006)	Sarkozy security law (2003) Law affirming laïcité (2004) "No" to EU constitution (2005)	2004 2005 2006	• Expansion to 25 members • European Constitutional Treaty • Discussion to admit Turkey to EU
National and anti- globalization	Anti- globalization	National and ambivalent globalization	*Present moment*	Globalization

EU CONSOLIDATION

EU EXPANSION

During the twelve-year period from the election in Dreux in 1983 to the presidential elections of 1995 when Le Pen had his breakthrough moment, he targeted immigration as a social and political problem. Le Pen was not alone in these concerns. The French state was moving in the direction of revamping its immigration laws. The history of immigration law in France in the past twenty-five years is tortuous. It moves back and forth between being more or less restrictive. In general, official immigration policy took as its guiding principle that it was not immigration *per se* but the integration of immigrants into French society that was at issue (Weil 2005; Kastoryano 2002). In 1985, Mitterrand established the High Council on Population and the Family to deal with declining birth rates among the French native-born. By the early 1990s, demographers began to identify low birth rates as a problem throughout Europe. The lack of replacement population undermined the social base of the European pension system even before neoliberal economic policies attenuated its strength.[9] In 1986, Mitterrand appointed Jacques Chirac the head of a committee to reform the 1945 nationality law.

By 1990, immigration in terms of numbers had stabilized not only in France but throughout Europe (Withol de Wenden 2004). The object of immigration control shifted to undocumented immigrants, family reunification and to tightening the restrictions on entry and exit. In 1990 and 1991, there was the first stream of riots in the *banlieues* outside of Paris. In response to these riots as well as to the first headscarf affair in 1989, integration superseded immigration as a policy concern.[10] By 1993, the French state had passed laws which at least on paper had solved many of these conflicts (Feldblum 1999, pp. 129–145; Hollifield 2004). In March 1993, the French penal code was revised to include strict censures against discrimination based upon race and other ascribed criteria.

In June 1993, the Code of Nationality (law of 1945) was revised emphasizing the importance of engaging in French cultural practices and requiring that the French-born children of immigrants had to request French citizenship instead of having it granted automatically (Schor 1985; Weil 2002). The National Front used the phrase, "Inherit it or merit it" to describe this process and it focused upon the acquisition of French culture and identity. In sum, between 1983 and 1995, the French state was very

---

[9] The literature on immigration, particularly immigration in France, is voluminous. This book makes no attempt to be comprehensive or to expertise other than what the logic of its argument requires. Feldblum (1999) and Brubaker (1992) provide analyses of the reform of French citizenship law in the period of the 1980s.

[10] Wacquant (1995) describes these riots; Beriss (1990), Feldblum (1999, pp. 136–146) and Kaltenbach and Tribalat (2002, pp. 188–233) discuss the "headscarf affair."

much involved in the reform of immigration law. No matter how it suited late twentieth-century realities, tightening immigration policy and restricting the acquisition of French nationality went against the self-image of the French as guardians of universalism (Weil 2001a). Paradoxically, the consistent ideological position was to let the National Front give voice to immigration issues while the state legislated.

French scholars and citizens did not expect the rise of the National Front and the tightening of immigration policy to characterize the years between 1983 and 1995 in future national history texts. The notable event during this period was the presidency of François Mitterrand – a presidency that had such salience that it was referred to as the "Mitterrand Experiment" (Ross *et al.* 1987). Contrary to expectation, Mitterrand and his socialist–communist governing coalition did not remain committed to the leftwing agenda which had swept it into office (Daley 1996). Within three years of assuming the presidency, pragmatism trumped ideology. Mitterrand appointed Laurent Fabius as his Prime Minister in 1984, replaced him with Jacques Chirac in 1986, and neoliberalism (although they did not call it that at the time) replaced socialism. The state passed the first privatization law in 1986. Extensive privatizations of French industry continued through the 1990s. In 1993, French banks were privatized and the Bank of France became independent.[11]

During the same period, European integration was taking on a new form. The accelerating pace of European economic integration necessitated many of the economic reforms that the Mitterrand presidency initiated. Jacques Delors became president of the European Commission in 1985 and he began to press forward with a vision of an expanded Europe (Ross 1995). In the same year that Mitterrand was turning his attention to the issue of immigration in France, Delors was promoting a single market to be achieved by 1992 and the signing of the first Schengen Agreement that eliminated border controls between Belgium, France, Germany, Luxembourg and the Netherlands. In 1986, France signed the Single European Act that entered into force in 1987.

In November 1989, the Berlin Wall fell and Germany was reunited in October 1990. The landscape of Europe was changing as rapidly as were its central players. In 1992, France marginally passed the Maastricht Treaty

---

[11] Hall (1986), Prasad (2006) and Schmidt (1996) contain extended discussions of French economic policy and take up the issue of privatization. Gordon and Meunier (2001, pp. 18–26) and Hall (1986, pp. 192–226; 2001) contain the best concise accounts of this process.

with a vote of 51 percent.[12] The project to increase the pace of European integration began in France with Delors, yet it could not be described as a popular project among the French. The referendum only squeaked through due to the support of the Socialist Party. Signing on to a larger European project also meant signing on to a great deal of regulation of the economy. In December 1993, the European Union issued a White Paper on growth and competitiveness. This was arguably the beginning of an accelerated process of neoliberalism throughout Europe as the territory had to become more market oriented and more competitive in global arenas.

Mitterrand began his presidency with a high level of personal and institutional charisma that offered a terrain of hope for an invigorated France. Chirac began his presidency in 1995 with France in a state of malaise.[13] By 1995, the year that Mitterrand ended his presidency and Chirac began his, the National Front buoyed by Jean-Marie Le Pen's coming in fourth place with 15 percent of the vote in the first round of the presidential elections began a period of concentrated *Mobilization*. Events in Brussels and beyond were transforming the France that Mitterrand encountered as he began his term in office. The consolidation of Europe as a political and economic project as well as international events such as the end of the Cold War drove political and social transformation. The French state began to tighten immigration procedures and to emphasize competitiveness in European and global markets as evidenced in the move to privatize French industry.

Given this expansive landscape of events, immigrants were necessary but not sufficient for the forward march of the National Front. Chirac began his presidency with an unemployment rate of 11.3 percent and an economy in decline (Keeler and Schain 1996). The year 1995 was marked by waves of social protest against social legislation, more waves of privatization and a plan in Madrid to institute a single currency – the euro. By the time that Le Pen received his 15 percent of votes in the 1995 presidential elections, France was overrun with social unrest and unemployment and the encroaching reality of Europeanization. Globalization, neoliberalism, unemployment and Europe provided Le Pen with a respectable set of collective social and political problems that lacked the patina of racism. As a Le Pen calling card, racism was never far away – as his remark in 1996

---

[12] Cameron (1996, pp. 325–382) documents French citizens' increasing withdrawal of support from European integration that the Maastricht vote confirmed.

[13] Toinet (1996, pp. 279–298) discusses the peculiar political trope, "malaise," which is a cousin concept to the French trope of "choc."

at the National Front summer university that he believed in the "inequality of races" indicated.

Neoliberal economic policy dominated the years between 1995 and 1997 – the period that culminated with the National Front congress in Strasbourg and Chirac's dissolving of the National Assembly. Chirac continued with the privatization of French state-owned industry that he had begun under Mitterrand and opened France to foreign capital (Gordon and Meunier 2001, p. 25). France ended 1996 with 12.3 percent unemployment and the burden of the European Union's Stability Pact that required all member nations to get their financial houses in order in preparation for the single currency.

When Lionel Jospin became Prime Minister in 1997 in Chirac's cohabitation government, France appeared ready for a change. The Socialist Party introduced the thirty-five-hour bill to make French industry more flexible and workers more productive.[14] The Weil report on integration and immigration proposed policy changes that softened the harsher aspects of the Debré law and the Pasqua law on immigration control. The signing of the Amsterdam Treaty in October exerted further pressure on the French government to increase economic productivity. The Amsterdam Treaty became a frequent target of National Front attack because it made clear that external forces were demonstrating that typical French solutions to economic problems were not working.

By 1998, the period of *Banalisation*, French economic issues were beginning to appear more pressing and it was also clear that the cohabiting government was having no greater success than previous governments in solving these problems. In the March regional elections, Le Pen appeared less threatening and, as Chapter 5 detailed, he was able to strike political bargains with the center right in several regions. This is not to suggest that he was not seen as a recidivist racist and his remarks such as a repeat of his gas chambers comment did not help to alleviate this perspective, but as Chapters 4 and 5 show as the 1990s were advancing, Le Pen's speeches were becoming more and more Europe and globalization oriented. Le Pen gave his first dramatic speech against the tyranny of globalization at his 1998 May Day speech.

During the period that Le Pen was focusing upon inserting himself and his party into the French political structure as a legitimate force, the character of social protest in France was changing to include issues that were not unique to France (Imig and Tarrow 2001). In 1997 and 1998,

---

[14] On the successes and failures of the thirty-five-hour policy, see Hayden (2006) and Smith (2004, pp. 212–219).

groups such as SOS Racisme expanded beyond their base of intellectual members and involved French youth in public mobilization against Le Pen. In 1998, the founding of ATTAC in Paris signaled a change in the character of protest in France and elsewhere. ATTAC France staged its first significant mobilization in Nice in December 2000. The target of this mobilization was the meeting of the European Council that signed the Charter of Fundamental Rights. According to the protesters, the Charter, which did not protect the "right to work," challenged traditional notions of European solidarity. Social protest in France and elsewhere was becoming more diffuse, less focused on national issues and more aimed at globalization and neoliberalism (Tarrow 2005, pp. 30–36).

As argued in Chapter 5, 1999 was a turning point for the National Front – the end of the beginning not the beginning of the end. Although actors in French civil society, such as the leaders of ATTAC and the farmer activist José Bové, did not draw attention to the similarities between their positions on national and European issues and the positions of the National Front, the parallels were unmistakable. Beginning in 1999 through the summer of 2001 when the riots in Gothenburg, Sweden and Genoa, Italy effectively shut down ATTAC, the location of social protest and civil society turned toward anti-globalization activists. The violence that ensued in 2001 halted the momentum of ATTAC not only in France but throughout Europe and gave rise to another form of movement that was genuinely transnational. The first meeting of the World Social Forum in Porto Alegre, Brazil (a parallel summit to the World Economic Forum in Davos, Switzerland) made the critique of globalization a transnational venue (Tarrow 2005, pp. 130–136).

In the years between 2000 and the presidential elections of 2002, the National Front did not disappear completely from public view. For the most part during this period, the National Front worked assiduously behind the scenes while more and more national and international events were moving in directions that favored its policy ideas. In 2000, the European Council issued a mandate for flexibility in the European economy that called for a harder look at national labor and social welfare systems that provided job and pension security for workers but which made it difficult for various member states to meet the norms of the Stability Pact (Smith 2004).

During the same year, the European Commission intervened in French national politics by asking France to consider whether Republicanism as a philosophy of integration was not inherently discriminatory against some groups. The year 2000 ended with the reaffirmation of the "double jeopardy" which meant that immigrants could be punished for their behavior and sent to jail and deported after they served their sentence. Fear of unemployment (the numbers had increased considerably since 1997), increasing anti-globalization activity in the public sphere and increasing pressure from the European Union to achieve economic stability coupled with a tightening of internal security characterized the period leading up to September 2001.

The attacks on the World Trade Center in New York on September 11, 2001 permanently changed the meaning of internal and external security throughout the world. France was no exception. The attacks in the United States made clear that immigrants could be a real as well as imagined security threat. What changed in France and in Europe after September 11 was that it was now legitimate to question immigrants and Islam. It was on this landscape of heightened and legitimized suspicion that Le Pen came in second place to Chirac on April 21, 2002. Following this "choc," protesters from all walks of life spontaneously joined the crowds in the streets of Paris and beyond to say "no" to Le Pen. Within the context of external and internal pressure coming from Europe and international terrorism, the 2002 presidential elections put additional pressures on the social and political fissures that lay just below the surface of French society. Le Pen's second place revealed those fissures as fully articulated political and social fault lines – an earthquake.

After Le Pen lost to Chirac in the second round of the presidential, he temporarily retreated and charged his daughter Marine Le Pen with the task of developing a softer public face and political strategy, *Dédiabolisation*. Chirac's government took on the task of being tough on crime, defending *laïcité* and dealing with the question of Europe and a newly salient immigrant problem focused on asylum and illegal entries, not to mention integration of second- and third-generation immigrant groups. By the time that the European constitution was on Chirac's agenda in the spring of 2004, the French state was looking at a Europe that had expanded to twenty-five members and an increasingly interventionist European Council that had given a directive to harmonize asylum and immigration policy throughout Europe. May 29, 2005 should not have been a "choc." By the date of the vote, it was increasingly clear that on all levels France was experiencing a reaffirmation of nation-ness that was no longer unique to the National Front.

Thinning borders and thickening identities

Collective ambivalence and national insecurity

Extraordinary events marked the period that followed the rejection of the European constitution. Other members of the European Union viewed

France, and the Netherlands, as having leveled a serious blow to the European project. French citizens and politicians of all ideological persuasions made it clear that the rejection of the constitution was a rejection of neoliberalism, market culture and an expanded European project. Two days after the defeat of the constitutional referendum, Chirac replaced his Prime Minister Jean-Pierre Raffarin with Dominique de Villepin. Raffarin had been given the task in 2002 of addressing France's economic problems and his removal was a part-symbolic and part-substantive attempt to confront these issues yet again. The new Prime Minister was yet another attempt on Chirac's part to respond to the economic insecurities at the core of the "no" vote.

In October and November of 2005, riots swept the *banlieues* on the outskirts of Paris and beyond. These riots replicated the riots that had occurred in the early 1990s, primarily in the summers of 1990 and 1991, and suggested that fifteen years of attention had not solved the problems of the urban poor who were mostly second- and third-generation immigrants. Integration and opportunity were still on the horizon rather than an accomplished fact. As the riots were widely viewed as responses to poverty and unemployment rather than racist conflict *per se*, Villepin put his efforts into providing opportunities for youth employment. His plan, the CPE (*contrat première embauche*), permitted French firms to hire workers less than twenty-six years of age with a two-year probationary contract.

Aimed at enhancing French firms' flexibility in hiring and firing and decreasing youth unemployment, the plan met with widespread protest throughout France in March and April 2006 when French youth took to the streets of Paris and beyond. The month of public protest and unrest, coming less than six months after the fall riots, forced Villepin to back off from the plan. This defeat also put an end to Villepin's presidential hopes. Along with backing down on the CPE, Villepin had come up with a series of protectionist schemes under the rubric of "economic patriotism" that aimed to protect French industries from merging with European firms. The two leading candidates in the 2007 presidential elections, the socialist Ségolène Royal and the center right Nicolas Sarkozy, both espoused versions of Villepin's protectionist approach to the French economy.

The French rejection of the European constitution represented the culmination of several tendencies in French politics and society that had been operative since the early 1980s. These tendencies were not the exclusive province of Jean-Marie Le Pen and the National Front. Le Pen gave early articulation to issues from fear of unassimilated and unassimilable immigrants to ambivalence toward a Europe in which France would not and could not be the dominant political actor. Since both the position on

Europe and the position on immigrants contradicted France's established national self-conception or identity, it took an outsider to give voice to the tendencies. Table 8.1 lays out diagrammatically the contours of the argument that the preceding chapters have advanced. Read across within each time period, it appears that the National Front, French civil society, the state and the European Union are all running on different and sometimes conflict-ridden tracks. Reading downwards to the present, convergence across spheres emerges.

European events from Maastricht to the constitution expand the European Union's institutional as well as geographic reach and challenge national articulations and practices of social solidarity and political sovereignty. In the international arena, world markets and the economy are increasingly global and transnational. Remaining competitive in a global marketplace requires different approaches to organizing capital and by definition forces a rewriting of the standard European social contract. The effects of economic insecurity are further compounded by a world that the threat of international terrorism and religious conflict is making *de facto* physically less secure. The combination of religious conflict, world poverty and the disintegration of East and West Europe created asylum problems parallel to those in the post-World War II period but not so easily solvable.

In the face of globalization, Europeanization and neoliberal solutions, Le Pen and the National Front have reasserted their commitment to the national. This is not surprising as the National Front was always the party of "France First"; what is more surprising is the increasing reassertion of the nation among segments of the French public that consider themselves cosmopolitan. French public protest has targeted Europe and globalization as threats to the nation. Whether French citizens were marching against Europe, against the constitution, against the American war in Iraq, or against the CPE, the effects of globalization were its targets. Yet, while the discussion has focused on public protest, France is also a society where *Le Monde* journalist Viviane Forrester's book on globalization, *The Economic Horror* (*L'horreur économique*), first published in 1996, sold over 350,000 copies in France, and won a major French literary prize (Smith 2004, p. 57).

Politically problematic contradictions occurred within France itself. On the one hand, France was becoming increasingly national in orientation if such a thing could be possible in a nation-state with a *hegemonic consolidation regime* predicated on the tightest of fit between culture and institutions. The reassertion of nation-ness that the previous chapter on the European constitution described captures the increasing ambivalence among French citizens and their representatives toward the neoliberalism and market-oriented reforms that full participation in European and global markets requires of the state. It is axiomatic that the European project in its present iteration is a neoliberal project aimed at transforming Europe from a solidaristic and collectivist political culture to a market-oriented and individualistic culture. Europe forces French citizens to find the social and economic security to which they have long been accustomed in market competition – not in the state. The exigencies of globalization have set the stage for an Americanization of Europe that extends beyond the importation of popular culture and McDonald's.[15] Nicolas Sarkozy has played both sides of this dilemma. He supported the European constitution in 2005 and has, since his election, taken a leading role in drafting a more limited version of the document. He has also supported policies that defend French industry.

Events, process and trajectory: detaching the message from the messenger

The career of the National Front juxtaposed against the trajectory of events in French civil society and the state is revelatory (Table 8.1). The National Front is national and against Europe, neoliberalism and globalization; actors in civil society are primarily, even if for different reasons, local and anti-liberal; the French state is national and – despite the central role that it played in the process of European integration – a victim of contradictory impulses as manifested in its ambivalence toward neoliberalism and Europe. Europe the exogenous force is by definition looking outwards and drawing in the various nation-states of Europe and beyond to its project. In short, the expanding process of Europe is dragging French political actors of different ideological persuasions and albeit with different motivations along remarkably similar paths.

Analyzing the French National Front through the lens of events permits this convergence of collective actors to emerge. Historical context, sensitivity to temporal and spatial ordering, suggests a complex causality. The analysis of events from the Front's congress in Strasbourg in 1997 to the French vote on the constitution makes salient factors that other methodological approaches to the study of the rightwing populist moment miss.

First, the narrative of these pages reverses the often espoused argument that the populist right favors the market over a collectivist social

---

[15] De Grazia (2005) makes the argument that Americanization in Europe is particularly pernicious because it effects the very conception of the meaning of production and forces an emphasis upon consumer capitalism.

democratic Europe (Kitschelt 1995). Le Pen began his public critique of globalization and Europeanization ahead of even anti-globalization activists. The story told in these pages makes a strong case to support the claim that being anti-market, anti-neoliberal and anti-individualist is a stance that exists independently of political position. The constitutional failure in France clearly revealed that being anti-market is potentially a leftwing, rightwing and center issue.

Second, the National Front employed provocative language around the issue of immigration while the French state focused on revising the immigration laws and the Code of Nationality. Immigration was a French, not exclusively a National Front, issue even if it was politically expedient to attribute it solely to the National Front. Restrictive immigration legislation was a product of immigration and immigrants, legal and illegal, asylum seekers and European Union directives.

Third, all members of the French public sphere from politicians to protesters to ordinary citizens independently of their political leanings could and did deploy the language of the Rights of Man. Issues of the market, immigrants and the national identity of France, and issues of security and incorporation, challenged how citizens worked and belonged in the polity. Europeanization required readjustments of national cultural incorporation policies and made multiple features of French cultural and political life seem insecure. Europe was not simply the perceived threat but the actual threat as its policies forced nation-states to rewrite the rules of the political cultural game from shared currency to shared immigration policy to shared economic policy. The *hegemonic consolidation regime*, the very tight fit between state and culture in France, virtually guaranteed that the nation-state would retreat into itself in the face of Europe which could only be a collective threat.

In the French case, Europe has had a paradoxical effect upon the rightwing populist moment. By driving all political groups back to the nation, it helped to *dédiabolise* the National Front in a manner that the National Front could never do on its own. Events and the collective French response to events did not improve the political possibilities of the National Front. As the National Front's messages became increasingly detached from the messenger, it made it possible for institutionally legitimate political actors to appropriate that message without the taint of Jean-Marie Le Pen. The National Front's ideological "success" led to its political failure.

9

Discovering the national in Europe

Italy in the shadow of France

The trajectory of the Italian rightwing coalition, particularly the career of Gianfranco Fini and the political role of the Italian fascist past, brings us back to the broader analytic issues which began this study of the rightwing populist moment. The juxtaposition of the shadow case of Italy against the fully developed case of France allows for the development of a more nuanced account of rightwing populism that incorporates Europeanization as well as the relations between culture, identity and the state.

Discussions of the rightwing populist moment invariably contrast Italy and the Casa delle Libertà (House of Liberties) with France and Le Pen as instances of a similar class of political phenomena. Following the line of argument advanced in this book, Italy provides a sharp contrast to France, and other iterations of European populism more generally, because it represents a diametrically opposite political process and phenomenon. Jean-Marie Le Pen and the National Front represented the intensification of a set of characteristically conservative French ideals that French politicians of the left, right and center reappropriated. In contrast, Gianfranco Fini and the National Alliance signaled a break, not with Italian democracy, but with the political meaning of the fascist past and the postwar era.

As Chapter 1 described, the Italian elections of March 1994 were a pivotal moment in Italian political development as well as in the trans-European legitimation of the populist right. Yet, as the Introduction noted, the term rightwing populist is a label of convenience and not analytic precision. Populist and rightwing imperfectly captures the Italian phenomenon. The Casa delle Libertà coalition was only rightwing by virtue of Fini's fascist past and populist by virtue of the Northern League. Umberto Bossi was the closest in spirit to an exclusionary, xenophobic populist, but the Northern League was always a marginal coalition member (Agnew 1995; Agnew and Brusa 1999).

The March 1994 Berlusconi government did not last a year. Events in Italy between 1994 and 2001 when the second Berlusconi government came into office were uneventful with respect to casting the Italian right in the same mold as its trans-European counterparts. The reasons for this were contextual. Had it not been for a series of political corruption scandals popularly known as *Tangentopoli* which involved a wide swath of what had been the Italian governing classes, there would have been no space for a coalition of the type that Berlusconi formed to emerge. The corruption scandals of the early 1990s eliminated from power the Christian Democrats who had dominated Italian politics from 1948. The elimination of the traditional center right left a space for a new right to form. But "right" in this instance simply meant not communist or socialist – in short everything that was not left.[1]

In contrast to France, the end of the Cold War had a significant effect upon Italian domestic politics. Historically, the Italian left had been emotionally if not programmatically identified with the communist bloc. Its dissolution was a final blow to a party and a political culture that had already atrophied if not disappeared. As the opening narrative of this book suggests, the emptiness of May Day in Turin in 1984 was a sign of the weakening of that political culture. The end of the Italian Communist Party quickly followed the fall of the Berlin Wall. Its replacement, the Democratic Party of the Left, was simply not strong enough in March 1994 to mount a challenge to Berlusconi, although it quickly got its opportunity a year and a half later on May 17, 1996 when Romano Prodi became Prime Minister with his first Olive Tree coalition.

While Italy was not immune to the party instability that characterized France as well as other European countries, many other factors that were operative in France and elsewhere simply had different valence in Italy. First, immigration is a relatively new political issue in Italy, as the country has traditionally been a place of emigration rather than immigration. While immigration to Italy is relatively understudied in contrast to France, scholars tend to agree that as an issue it is not particularly attached to left or right – playing to all sides of the political spectrum at various points in time (Perlmutter 1996; Zincone 2006; Colombo and Sciortino 2004; Andall 2007). Further, in a country of family fortunes, many of which are still intact, and a culture of artisanship, entrepreneurship and tax

---

[1] See Ginsborg (2003, pp. 137–213) for a discussion of the political scandals that led to the end of the First Republic.

evasion, neoliberalism has a particularly Italian iteration. The market has always played a peculiar role in Italian politics and society. On the one hand, the secondary and underground economy was a way of life. Yet, Italy has always been workerist (Tarrow 1977; Hellman 1988). It had the strongest postwar Communist Party and trade union organizations, but its goal was fairness to workers not social redistribution, as evidenced by Italy's weak welfare state relative to other European countries.

If postwar Italy was never Sweden, it was also never France. The right that emerged in 1994 and returned in 2001 was a center right with a firm commitment to the market and, in sharp contrast to France, to Europe (Pasquino 2001). Berlusconi's 2001 campaign rhetoric deployed market metaphors. He offered his fellow citizens a "Contract with the Italians" that promised fiscal solvency in five years if elected Prime Minister. Forza Italia's party statement, the *Charter of Values* (*Carta dei valori*), exalted the culture of individualism deployed in the service of the nation. Its first chapter described the party as an "about face in the history of Italy." Other chapters espoused "progress as individual and common good," "the centrality of the person," "reciprocal respect" and "no peace without freedom." The document simultaneously rejected what it saw as the vices of the left and supported a neoliberal ideology of "free choice" – with globalization and Europe replacing the social solidarity of the international working classes and Catholic doctrines of religious solidarity.

In France, Europe is perceived as a threat or a source of ambivalence. In Italy, Europe is an opportunity, even if that opportunity is simply a chance to regularize a recalcitrant economic and political culture (Padoa-Schioppa 2001; Ferrera and Gualmini 2004; Hine 2004; Golden 2004). Paradoxically, through Europe, Italy can knit together the fragments of a national identity that never quite congealed despite 130 years of Italian unification and a fascist regime that made fascist and Italian identity one of its mandates. The fascist period is a glaring omission in Forza Italia's *Charter of Values*' discussion of the "sources of our identity." According to the *Charter*, the heroes of the "Christian and lay humanism" that form the core of Italian identity and culture are Dante, Alessandro Manzoni the nineteenth-century novelist, Alcide De Gasperi the founder of the postwar Christian Democratic Party and Luigi Einaudi the first President of the postwar Italian Republic.

In contrast to France, Italian politicians of all political persuasions have embraced Europe – even if for different reasons. Only the extra-parliamentary extremes of Italian political culture have expressed strident, and sometimes violent, critiques of neoliberalism. Academic economists who have worked on government austerity policies or policies aimed at increasing the flexibility of firms to hire and to fire have been assassinated in the streets twice in less than twenty years. In 1985, Enzo Tarantelli, an American-trained economics professor, who was working with the Bettino Craxi government on the *scala mobile*, a plan to index wages to inflation, was assassinated as he got into his car in Rome. In 2002, Marco Biagi, also an economist, was shot in the streets of Bologna when he was working with the Berlusconi government on Article 18. Romano Prodi, the center left politician who has twice been Prime Minister, is a former economics professor from the University of Bologna.

Revisiting the Italian case, particularly the career of Gianfranco Fini and the National Alliance, establishes the type of contrasts that permit sharper generalization about the rightwing populist moment to emerge. The remainder of this chapter shifts the focus to Fini and the place of historical fascism in his career and Italian politics more generally. Silvio Berlusconi has received the international media attention not only because of his flamboyant personality, his media monopoly and his allegedly criminal behavior, but also because he did succeed in becoming Prime Minister. His 2001 to 2006 government gave him the opportunity to assert his pro-Americanism by committing Italian troops to Iraq, which was not a popular move and met with widespread public protest.

As noted in Chapter 1, Berlusconi is probably corrupt in his business dealings, a source of embarrassment to Italian professionals and intellectuals and an object of admiration among a substantial part of non-elite Italian citizens. The press frequently points out that, with the exception of Benito Mussolini, no Italian Prime Minister has remained in office as long as Berlusconi. He left office in May 2006 when Romano Prodi's center left coalition took over the reigns of government and returned in April 2008 when the coalition fell apart. Despite the labels attached to him, Berlusconi was and is neither a fascist nor a populist.[2] The Italian tradition that captures Berlusconi's public persona is the nineteenth-century theatrical figure of the *mattatore* – the combination of business impresario and leading actor who dominated the stage and played fast and loose with the written script.[3]

The 1994 Berlusconi governing coalition was rightwing because the National Alliance, previously the Movimento Sociale Italiano (MSI),

---

[2] For the latest iteration of this, see Paul Ginsborg, "Review of Alexander Stille, *The Sack of Rome*." *New York Review of Books* 54 (2007, no. 1): 50–52. Shin and Agnew (2008) provide an alternative account.

[3] On the role of the *mattatore*, see Berezin (1994).

had originated in the Salò Fascist Party of 1943 to 1945.[4] From the pivotal election in 1994, through the second and now third Berlusconi governments, Gianfranco Fini, head of the National Alliance, remains a viable and important political force. Fini's career is indistinguishable from the trajectory of the National Alliance. In 1994, Fini labeled himself as a "post-fascist," but the days in which he identifies himself as any sort of a fascist are long behind him.[5] Some members of the Italian and the international press choose to resurrect the "post-fascist" label. For example, Fini publicly endorsed the Italian translation of Nicolas Sarkozy's (2007) political biography *Testimony* (*Témoignage*) and called Sarkozy a "creative pragmatist." The French communist newspaper *L'Humanité*, in a move to discredit Sarkozy's presidential bid, noted that Fini was a "post-fascist" and that this "fascist" connection could be an embarrassment.[6] This was more about French politics than Fini's current political attitudes. Fini has traveled a long way since the day in 1994 that he gave an interview to the Turin newspaper *La Stampa* and said that Mussolini was the greatest statesman of the twentieth century. In 2002, he publicly repudiated that statement as he was about to assume his position as Italy's representative to the committee that would draft the European constitution. In the years between 1994 and 2002, Fini was not only distancing himself from that remark but from other European rightwing politicians such as Haider and Le Pen.[7]

In the past few years, Fini has found himself in the awkward position of learning that the traditional members of the National Alliance are finding him too liberal. From 2001 to 2008, Fini has held national office from Minister of Foreign Affairs to president of the Chamber of Deputies. Fini and the National Alliance are hardly on the fringes of Italian politics. In contrast, Le Pen and the National Front have never attained a position in national-level French government. After the 2007 French presidential elections, Le Pen's chance of entering a national government has almost vanished.

Fini was born in 1952, whereas Berlusconi, despite his recent cosmetic surgery, was born in 1936. Time is on Fini's side, although his advantages

---

[4] The MSI did not officially change its name to the National Alliance until its party congress in Fiuggi in January 1995 (Alleanza Nazionale 1995). Tarchi (2003b) provides a short history of programmatic changes.

[5] Fella (2006) provides a brief history of Fini's trajectory.

[6] Alessandro Mantovani, "Gianfranco Fini, l'ami italien de Sarkozy." *L'Humanité* (Paris) January 26, 2007, p. 4.

[7] A link between Fini and Le Pen did exist in the distant past. In 1988, after Le Pen made his first dramatic showing in a French presidential ballot, Fini invited him to speak at an MSI meeting in Rome on the "future of Europe" (Tassani 1990, p. 137).

extend beyond his age. The trajectory of Fini and the National Alliance intersects with Forza Italia and the Northern League – the other major parties in the Casa delle Libertà (House of Freedoms) coalition – but it is a mistake to not make distinctions among the party leaders. Silvio Berlusconi has the bravado of the media magnate and self-made man. Finesse is not his strong suit. In July 2003, when he began his six-month term as rotating president of the European Union Council of Ministers, Berlusconi immediately entered into a dispute with a German member of parliament and "inadvertently" suggested that he was a Nazi. Umberto Bossi, head of the Northern League, has always been a destabilizing actor (Agnew 2002, pp. 167–187; Bossi 1996). He founded the nation of Padania within northern Italy and called for it to secede from Italy. Among the three, Fini has always been the most disciplined as he pursued his personal agenda to become an Italian Charles de Gaulle.

The past in the present: resisting fascism and affirming democracy

In November 2004, Gianfranco Fini became the Italian Minister of Foreign Affairs in Italy. This was a new stage in his career that thrust him into the international arena. Between 1994 when he joined the first Berlusconi coalition and 2004, Fini went from being the head of a disreputable minority, even fringe, party to being the public face of Italy in diplomatic relations abroad. In November 2003, Gianfranco Fini visited Israel, and publicly atoned for his party's participation in fascism – calling it "absolute harm." He described the Republic of Salò as a "shame" and the 1938 racial laws as "infamous."[8] Alessandra Mussolini, granddaughter of Benito Mussolini and a National Alliance member of the Italian Parliament, broke with Fini over this statement and founded an offshoot branch of the National Alliance, the party of Social Action that remained true to its fascist past.

In Italian popular perception or at least in some segments of the populace, Fini and the National Alliance always had a fascist past. But the trip to Israel in November 2003 was a part of Fini's long journey toward rewriting that past – what one newspaper commentator labeled as "the long march of the Italian right."[9] Before leaving for Israel, Fini had a

---

[8] "Fini: fascismo male assoluto." *La Repubblica* (Rome) November 25, 2003, headline. Recent research (Brustein 2003) suggests that until the passage of the 1938 racial laws a rather high degree of toleration for Jews existed in Italy in contrast to other European nation-states in the interwar period.

[9] Ezio Mauro, "La lunga marcia della destra italiana." *La Repubblica* (Rome) November 5, 2003, front page.

public dialogue sponsored by *La Repubblica* with Amos Luzzatto, president of the Union of the Italian Jewish Communities (Unione delle Comunità Ebraiche Italiane). Fini declared his commitment and the commitment of his party to democracy. He acknowledged April 25, the day that the Republic of Salò fell and that the Allies "liberated" Italy from the Nazi occupation, as the founding date for the Republic and said that it should be celebrated as the birth of democracy. He declared the first part of the Italian constitution inviolable.[10]

April 25 signaled the birth of the Italian postwar republic. The interpretation of April 25 is intimately connected to the politics of memory in the First Republic as well as to the political normalization of Gianfranco Fini and the National Alliance. When Fini said that he believed in the values of April 25, he was affirming his belief in Italian democracy and arguing that the date belonged to all Italian citizens – no matter what their political past had been. April 25 is the public holiday that celebrates Liberation Day in Italy and it goes largely unrecognized until it is politically expedient to do so (Cenci 1999). The story of April 25 is intimately connected to the normalization of Fini.

The electoral reforms of 1993 and the election of March 1994 marked the end of the First Republic – the nexus of political institutions and cultural arrangements that had been in place since the 1948 constitution (Diamanti and Mannheimer 1994). The legitimated presence of the National Alliance in the Italian government produced a wave of scholarship focused on trying to revise Italy's relationship to its fascist past, which had presumably slumbered in the years between April 1945 and April 1994. Nanni Balestrini's *Una mattina ci siam svegliati* (*One Morning We Were Awakened* [1995]), Ernesto Galli della Loggia's *La morte della patria* (*The Death of the Nation* [1996]) and Renzo De Felice's *Rosso e nero* (*Red and Black* [1995]) suggest the tenor of these works. Contrary to what this literary outpouring would suggest, fascism had never disappeared from the Italian political landscape.

Fascism was the unmentioned and ever present "other" of postwar political culture that played itself out in a series of competing public narratives that centered around the Resistance, as well as in the continuing electoral presence of the Movimento Sociale Italiana. The MSI, a legal political party since the end of the war, had never played any role in the government, yet it maintained a steady 6 to 8 percent of the national vote (Ignazi 1989; 2003). The political legitimacy of Berlusconi's first coalition,

---

[10] I Dialoghi, "La destra, gli ebrei e i conti con il fascismo." *La Repubblica* (Rome) November 4, 2003, front page.

particularly the inclusion of the National Alliance, was highly dependent upon the public understanding of the meaning of the Italian fascist past.

From this standpoint, fascism was a constantly mutating virus that infected Italian political culture between 1945 and 1994. We can detect the fault lines that emerged at the time of the 1994 election in those mutations. The Italian Resistance, the popular mobilization against the Nazi invaders, was the linchpin of the various narratives of fascism in postwar politics (Focardi 2005; Cossu 2006; Gundle 2000; Cooke 2000). The "myth" of the Resistance was the ideological underpinning of the First Republic (Zapponi 1994; Serneri 1995; Legnami 1995; Gobbi 1992). The trope of good and evil which served as the leitmotif of the resistance story was a particularly compelling political narrative in a political system based upon personalized and clientilistic politics (La Palombara 1964; Putnam 1993). As a founding myth of the recon- structed government, the resistance myth was flawed from its inception. The fact that the Resistance as "myth" has entered the popular Italian vocabulary suggests how far it had gone toward crumbling – even before the cataclysmic events of March 1994.

The elements of the resistance narrative were simple. The Resistance "saved" Italy (from whom is left ambiguous) and prepared the way for democratic reconstruction. Italian resistance fighters, consisting of mem- bers of the Communist Party, old elements of the Popolari Party, monar- chists and politically unaffiliated civilians, engaged in armed underground activity to aid the Allies in fighting the German Nazi enemy. The fiction of unity among the diverse groups was essential for the postwar reconstruc- tion. The resistance story narrated a solid Italian front against a German enemy, and from its inception failed to incorporate Italian complicity in the war. Roberto Rossellini's popular film, *Rome: Open City* (1945), dramatizes these contradictions. Shot in Rome with amateur as well as professional actors while the bombs were still falling, the film is striking that among its cast of characters it includes no Italian fascists. In the film, the enemy is German. The Italians are virtuous resistance fighters. In actuality, Italians and Germans had fought side by side against the Allies until Mussolini's government fell in 1943. Resistance fighters represented a small proportion of the Italian population (not more than 300,000 mem- bers) and were an ideologically diverse group with widely divergent inter- ests – that is, the uneasy wedding of what would later become Christian Democrats and Italian communists (Ellwood 1985). The communists provided necessary man and woman power to the Resistance, but they were more than a slight inconvenience when the new post-liberation gov- ernment was in formation.

The multiple narratives of Resistance from the beginning had a political purpose. These narratives took the following forms. The Resistance was a united front against the Nazi enemy. In effect, the Resistance was a form of civil war in which personal scores were settled in the name of political commitment. If the Resistance was a united front, a war of liberation, then all participants in the Resistance had an equal stake in the new postwar republic. This was a useful position for a while but it became totally useless as the Christian Democrats sought to keep the communists out of national office.

On the other hand, if the Resistance was part of a civil war then no one had a particular stake in the new republic. Keeping the war of liberation alive was always a benefit to the left, sometimes a benefit to the Christian Democrats. The civil war story could sometimes benefit the Christian Democrats, but it always benefited the secular right because in this version blame could not be assigned for the twenty years of the fascist regime and everyone could become part of the new republic – including former fascists. The civil war narrative was always a favorite of the right until the left began to appropriate it in the mid-1980s.

Ending World War II in 1994: to whom does April 25 belong?

In the immediate aftermath of the March 1994 election, segments of the Italian media and scholars began to narrate the election as an anomalous political event. A "how did this happen" narrative emerged on the pages of the left center press, *La Repubblica*, *La Stampa*, *Il Corriere della Sera*. The right (*Il Secolo*) and the left (*L'Unità* and *Il Manifesto*) were far more certain of the genesis of the election. The "how did this happen" narrative attenuated the significance of the fissures that had characterized postwar Italian political culture. The competing narratives that entered the Italian public sphere through popular culture and public demonstrations in the month following the March election provided a more trenchant vision of the changes that had ensued.

On April 8, the editors of *Il Manifesto*, with the support of the reconstructed Communist Party's Achille Occhetto, responded to Mussolini and Fini with a call to all Italians to take to the public piazzas on April 25, the national Liberation Day holiday, to protest the election as an assault on democracy. On "Liberation Day" 1994, post-fascists and reconstructed communists appropriated public space to debate the meaning of fascism – old and new. On April 25, 300,000 people led by a coalition of parties that had lost the March election marched in the pouring rain to Piazza del Duomo in Milan. They labeled the march a non-partisan effort to dramatize commitment to "pride in democracy," and their marching slogan was "Don't you dare [*Non ci provate*]." The RAI's broadcast of the demonstration showed throngs of protesters under a sea of umbrellas. Reporters interviewed ordinary citizens who explained that they were marching to say "no to fascism." People carried signs saying, "Not a civil war; a war of liberation." The participants, mostly in their sixties, touted the values of the constitution and asserted that they were doing this for their children. In addition to the demonstrators in the rain, the RAI flashed to scenes of commemoration ceremonies throughout Italy. In Marzabotto, there was a ceremony to honor the resistance victims of the Nazi massacre. In other cities, people carried placards with the names of children who had been placed in jail during the war. In the same broadcast, Claudio Pavone, the Italian historian whose book *Una guerra civile* (*A Civil War* [1991]) reopened the intellectual debate on the Resistance and cast a long look back on the twenty years of the regime, said that he was hoping that the annual celebration of Liberation Day in Italy would come to mimic Bastille Day in France with Italian citizens dancing in the streets!

In the period of less than a month between the elections and the Liberation Day mobilization, three narratives, each with clear constituencies, had emerged that may be broadly characterized as follows: first, "let's save democracy" (the losers' narrative [the left]); second, "let's forget the past" (the winners' narrative [the right]); and third, "how did this happen?" (the proponents of ideological neutrality and a rejection of the past). How do we reconcile these multiple narratives and what relation do they bear to postwar Italian politics and culture?

While proponents of "Let's save democracy" were marching in Milan and elsewhere, Gianfranco Fini was in Rome, where he attended a Mass in the Basilica of Santa Maria degli Angeli e dei Martiri to celebrate a "feast of reconciliation" and "national pacification." Standing on the steps of the Basilica, Fini proclaimed, "We think of the future, enough of the fences and hatreds of the past." He added, "I would hope that before long April 25 can be considered the date on which historically the Second World War ended and on which Italians found motive to reconcile among themselves and to look to the future, not to continue to maintain the barriers and hatreds of the past."[11] When Fini stood on the steps of the Basilica in Rome and spoke to the "hatreds of the past," he was saying that the war was not only literally over as it had been for almost fifty years but that it

---

[11] Paolo Boccacci, "Fini, una messa per dimenticare." *La Repubblica* (Rome) April 26, 1994, p. 5.

should also end as a political metaphor and anchor of divisive national politics. It took Fini ten more years, from 1994 to 2004, the year that he assumed his position as Minister of Foreign Affairs, to put his personal past to public rest.

Italian spring 2002: looking inward to the piazza and outward to France and Europe

The spring of 2002 was one of those peculiar moments in Italian political history where national and international events came together, played off each other and forced Italian politicians of all political stripes to re-articulate and recalibrate longstanding political values and positions. The French were in the streets in April and in early May 2002 to protest Le Pen. In contrast, the hundreds of thousands of protesting Italians populated the central piazzas of Rome, Milan and Bologna in numbers and with an intensity that had not been seen since the early 1980s. The impetus behind the demonstrations was the reform of Article 18 of the Italian Workers' Statute.

In 2001, the Italian employers' organization the Confindustria requested the abolition of Article 18 in the name of greater flexibility to enable the Italian economy to meet the requirements of the EU Stability and Growth Pact. Article 18 made it virtually impossible to fire workers for any reason since if a worker was let go they had the right to appeal their dismissal to a judge who virtually always reinstated the worker. Berlusconi's plan was to reform rather than completely eliminate Article 18. The three major Italian labor unions were opposed to the reform and had different degrees of resistance to the reform of Article 18. Sergio Cofferati, leader of the CGIL, the largest Italian trade union with former ties to the parties of the left, emerged as the spokesperson for the opposition. Cofferati's position was that labor must be protected at all costs against neoliberal economic reforms. On March 2, 2002, millions demonstrated in Rome under the banner of the "Olive Tree," the leftwing coalition against Berlusconi and his reforms.

In the first two weeks of March, Berlusconi was engaged in continual verbal conflict with the unions. Berlusconi returned from the EU meeting in Barcelona in mid-March declaring that the "EU wants flexibility." The trade unions threatened a general strike, to which Berlusconi replied, "I do not fear the *piazza*."[12] While the government and the unions were trading

---

[12] Antonio Polito, "Berlusconi: non temo la piazza." *La Repubblica* (Rome) March 17, 2002, front page, p. 16.

threats, Marco Biagi, an academic economist consulting with the government on these industrial relations reforms, was assassinated on March 19 by resurrected Red Brigade terrorists on the streets of Bologna while bicycling home from work.

The assassination met with demonstrations throughout Italy. Eighty thousand people showed up in the central piazza in Bologna to demonstrate against the return of terrorism. The unions declared a general strike. Biagi's widow refused a state funeral for him as she claimed that the government had failed to protect him. Four days after the assassination, 3 million according to the unions, 700,000 according to the police, descended on the center of Rome to protest the assassination and the government. On March 24, 2002, the headline of *La Repubblica* read: "A piazza as we have never seen it before [*Una piazza mai vista*]." Fini, who was sympathetic to the social contract implied in Article 18, accused the left of "conservativism" with the government being the true "reformers." On April 16, 2002, Italy had its first general strike in over twenty years. Headlines of Italian newspapers read, "Italy is closed"; "A strike for Justice."

While the Italian press and public were discussing the return of the left as a political force in Italy, the "earthquake" of Le Pen hit six days later in France. In the wake of the French elections, Italian politicians and public turned their attention across the Alps. The combination of the "earthquake" of Le Pen and the strikes in Italy occurring in proximity to the April 25 Liberation Day holiday provided a public venue for politicians and intellectuals of all political persuasions to situate themselves vis-à-vis the Italian and French events. On April 23, 2002, political scientist Ilvo Diamanti wrote on the front page of *La Repubblica* that France and Italy represented a "common anomaly." This was followed the next day, April 24, 2002, by a lead editorial by Eugenio Scalfari, editor in chief of *La Repubblica*, that began, "The European Left after the Massacre."

In an interview with *La Repubblica*, Gianfranco Fini took the opportunity of Le Pen's second place to distinguish his party and positions from the National Front which he described as a "crude right." In the late 1980s, Fini had made political overtures to Le Pen, but by 1993 Fini was beginning to view Le Pen as a liability and not an asset. In 1998, as reported in Chapter 5, Fini gave an interview to *Le Monde* where he broke absolutely with Le Pen. In the 2002 *La Repubblica* interview, Fini declared that, "I seek to analyze complex problems and I do not make an appeal to the instincts, the profound emotions, to the gut of the electorate." Fini described Le Pen as an "alien," whereas he himself represented the "reformist right." Fini praised Carlo Azeglio Ciampi, the President of

Italy, for teaching Italians to value a non-chauvinistic identity that could accommodate being Italian and being part of Europe.[13] In January 2002, Fini assumed the role of Italian representative to the committee that would draft the constitution that the French would reject on May 29, 2005. As early as April 2002, Fini warned of the danger that France might reject the treaty.

Earlier in April 2002, the National Alliance had had its second party congress in Bologna. During that congress, Fini presented himself as a leader who could be Prime Minister – if the moment arrived. He expressed regret at the assassination of Marco Biagi and affirmed his commitment to the European social contract, at least the trade unionist version that was distinctively Italian. He spoke of a need to balance the demands of Europe and the demands of Italian worker culture. He firmly told those members of the Alliance who did not want to forget their fascist roots that this position was unacceptable. The past was "over." Fini argued that the task of the National Alliance in 2002 was "governing for the future." He defined the mission of the National Alliance as "moderate and social."[14]

April 25, 2002 was a day for which every trope in Italian political culture was deployed for radically different reasons. Celebrations were held in all the major cities. Carlo Ciampi, the President of Italy, led the celebration in the Piazza Venezia in Rome where he celebrated "the heroism of common people," and said that it is necessary to "construct Europe from memory, not forgetfulness." Cofferati, fresh from the victory of the general strike, led the celebration in the Piazza del Duomo in Milan. Striking a direct blow to Fini and Berlusconi, who were absent from public celebration, Cofferati said that all Italians must say "no to facile revisions of the Resistance." Fini once more repudiated fascism – this time from Rome he wrote to Luzzatto again, "April 25 celebrates the values of liberty and democracy. They are values which the Italian right fully recognizes without reserve, with a constructive spirit in the name of national conciliation and true history – as President Ciampi has remembered and has said no to a certain revisionism, and wants to guarantee to the young a future that will never again know hateful religious, ethnic or racial discrimination. In Italy and in every part of Europe."[15]

---

[13] Goffredo de Marchis, "Fini: 'Le Pen è un alieno, noi una destra riformista.'" *La Repubblica* (Rome) April 23, 2002, p. 13.

[14] Danielle Rouard, "Italie: le congrès de l'Alliance nationale consacre la stratégie de 'recentrage' de Gianfranco Fini." *Le Monde* (Paris) April 9, 2002. See also Tarchi (2003b).

[15] "Ciampi: no al revisionismo. Centinaia di migliaia in piazza. Fini: credo nel 25 aprile," *La Repubblica* (Rome) April 26, 2002, front page, headlines.

The article ends with a reference to Fini's 1994 speech on the steps of Santa Maria degli Angeli e dei Martiri where he asked to move on from the past. In the Piazza del Duomo in Milan, Cofferati was also invoking April 25, 1994 – the day that the piazza was filled with marchers against the first Berlusconi government. Two hundred thousand people filled the piazza in 2002 as they had done in 1994. Cofferati's speech, as reported in the former Communist Party newspaper *L'Unità*, united the dignity of labor to the values of freedom. Cofferati's speech seemed dated. The end of the article inadvertently told the tale. Describing the event in 1994, the reporter noted, "It rained then, torrential rain without end. Yesterday, it was sunny and the air was almost summerlike. It was difficult then and so it is today: in one case and in the other an immense crowd in the street to defend democracy." The irony here is that the crowd spoke to the past and the Italian political habit to occupy the piazza in times of stress. But contemporary events, from the Italian engagement in the Iraq War to Italy's support of the European project, suggest that for most Italians World War II is finally over – the future had arrived.

The strength of weak Italian identities

As argued in Chapter 2, identities have two dimensions that analysts often conflate, to the detriment of analytic clarity. *First*, identities are categorical and epistemological; and *second*, they are ontological and emotional. The categorical is embedded in institutional arrangements – state, market, family, religion. Law is constitutive of the categorical – citizenship law, labor law, laws regulating private life, laws separating Church and state. The ontological speaks to the degree of emotional identification with a category. In practice, the epistemological and the ontological are intertwined in various ways. The separation is an analytic not an empirical distinction. It is important to keep them separate analytically because while the categorical is collective and always present, the emotional is highly contingent – an individual or a group can go for a long time without ever asserting their identities. The articulation of identity is *contingent*. Identities, collective or otherwise, tend to be asserted when they are threatened in some way – which is why war is a mechanism of identity building. In times when threat is absent, rituals of affirmation are central to identity formation and maintenance.

As discussed in Chapter 2, the conflation of the categorical and the emotional dimensions of identity have a kinship relation to the concept of the modern nation-state. Discussions of nationalism have focused on extreme articulations of national chauvinism. Discussions of the state meld the structural or bureaucratic and the cultural – a melding that has been particularly detrimental in discussions of Italy and Italian civic solidarity. Italy is a modern state. It has had even through the fascist period a continuous state – a continuous civil administration. The Italian state may not always be efficient, it may be plagued by clientelism and corruption, but it is a state. With the exception of the period of fascism, it has been a more or less democratic state.[16]

Where Italy has been weak is in the development of ordinary civic nationalism – nation-ness of the sort that characterizes many of the other European nation-states. Using the terminology developed in Chapter 2, Italy had a *flexible consolidation regime* in contrast to the French *hegemonic consolidation regime*. This is not to say that Italy did not and does not have an intellectual class that has theorized what the contours of an Italian nation would be (Patriarca 1996; 2001). What Italy lacked in the early periods of unification was a practical intellectual class to develop the institutions of civic solidarity. To use Philip Nord's (1995) concept, Italy did not experience a "Republican Moment" in the French sense. Unlike France, Italy did not have a Third Republic that unleashed an army of school teachers to make peasants into Italians whether they liked it or not (Weber 1976). In Italy, the fascist regime took up the campaign of political socialization and institution building in the 1930s. When the regime fell, the institutions that it had put in place were marked by the taint of fascism. What Italy lacked or left underdeveloped were certain core institutions of civic solidarity, which made national identity formation problematic. For example, language standardization came late and literacy rates were low until the postwar period; the educational system was chaotic from the nineteenth century into the twentieth. Marzio Barbagli (1982) has famously described the system as "educating for unemployment."

Italian historians and political philosophers have begun to identify and reflect upon the political and social implications of the lack of a cohesive national identity. Bodei (1998) elegantly formulates this as "we, the divided"; Schiavone (1998) describes "Italians without Italy." The deficits of Italian political socialization are well known at the expense of its

---

[16] Berezin (1997a) develops this argument. In 1945, after the collapse of the fascist regime, Italians retreated to the familiar identities attached to Church and family – which also had strong institutional supports. The institutional order of the Catholic Church assured that its effect on the lives of ordinary Italians was not merely at the level of emotion. In the postwar period, the Catholic Church had much institutional clout and it struggled to maintain its institutional power through the entire period. La Palombara (1964) and Warner (2000) engage this point.

positive features that have been underemphasized. In contrast to what it lacked, Italy had and has a tradition of strong *sub-national or extra-national* identities buttressed by institutional arrangements that militated against the formation of a strong national identity. The state had a central administration and there were rules of belonging, that is, citizenship rights, but no secular center to make one feel Italian. In addition, the out-migration of the late nineteenth century and early twentieth did not leave Italians, those who left as well as those who stayed behind, with the feeling that citizens were cherished members of the national community.

Sub-national or extra-national identities and institutions – the Church, the political party – provided a cogent source of identity to Italians. Family identities manifested themselves in benign forms such as conservative politics and the tradition of small and large family firms, and in less benign forms as the Mafia. Regional identities – North versus South, and ever finer gradations – formed the core of Italian place identity. All of these identities and institutions played off each other in various ways, and had various strengths and perhaps would have gone on to perpetuity if it were not for a series of exogenous and contingent events.

The corruption scandals known as *Tangentopoli* led to the collapse of the postwar Christian Democratic Party. This opened up a political space that Berlusconi, Fini and Bossi could fill. But the collapse of the First Republic came in temporal proximity to international events that when combined with the Italian event produced a synergy that transformed Italian liabilities into assets. The first such international event was the end of interwar Eastern European communism in 1989. This had an effect throughout Europe but was particularly salient for the Italian Communist Party, which had defined itself at least in its earlier days in relation to the Eastern Bloc. The new Italian Communist Party, the Democratic Party of the Left, never had the cohesiveness of the old party, as evidenced by the fact that it went through two name changes and splintered within a few years into more traditionally leftwing parties. The second significant event was the 1992 Maastricht Treaty. European integration was long in the works and Italians were always positive to Europe. Maastricht was sig-nificant because it signaled the beginning of an accelerated pace of European integration. Less easy to tie to a specific date was the fact that Italy, which had been historically a country of out-migration until the mid-1980s, began to become a country of in-migration (Colombo and Sciortino 2004, pp. 52, 54).

These international events rearranged but did not eliminate what Bodei (1998) labeled as the "divisions" among Italians. In addition, they created possibilities for new divisions. "Europe" writ large, the presence of "others" from Africa, Eastern Europe and Albania, and even new political parties, had to be incorporated into an Italian public grappling with new political parties and ideas.

The fall of the Berlin Wall and attendant events made communism in general seem less viable, although by 1989 European and Italian communism were significantly weaker than they had been at any previous time during the postwar period. The beginning of long-term secular trends that Maastricht initiated resulted in new economic and productive arrangements throughout Europe. In this context, the sub-national identities and regional economies that had plagued Italy in the past began to appear as a potentially positive and not a divisive force (Bagnasco 1977). In addition, the presence of immigrants forced Italians to consider differences that were less parochial than the historical antagonism between the North and South. The Northern League was born out of the fear of these "new" differences, while it simultaneously enforced "old" differences in its rhetorical attacks on the South (Agnew 1995; Sciortino 1999).

These international events – the collapse of communism, the Maastricht Treaty, the inflow of immigrants coupled with the internal politics of corruption and *Tangentopoli* – opened a political space that made the outcomes of the 1994 election possible. March 1994 was a pivotal date for Italian political history that was long in the making. March 1994 was a turning point for Italian political development because it made it no longer possible to evade the issue of the fascist past. Gianfranco Fini's position in the governing coalition as a "post-fascist" marked the election as an extraordinary and anomalous political event. Before 1994 it seemed unimaginable that a party with links to the old Fascist Party could be part of the government. In 2006, it is easy to forget the process of normalization that occurred between the first and second Berlusconi governments vis-à-vis the presence of Fini – who by 2004 was the Italian Minister of Foreign Affairs.

In contrast to Jean-Marie Le Pen and other European rightwing politicians, Fini was part of an Italian and not a trans-European populist process. Fini and fascism's rehabilitation was the end point of a cultural shift that began in the mid-1980s in the commercial sphere. In the mid-1980s, a series of films and made-for-television movies emerged that viewed fascism as just another part of the Italian past. Alberto Negrin's 1985 film, *Mussolini and I*, depicted Mussolini as, if not a hero, a harassed family man. The Taviani brothers' 1984 film, *The Night of the Shooting Stars*, emphasized the civil war dimension of the 1943 to 1945 period. In November 1984, a large exhibition mounted in the Roman Coliseum entitled "The Economy between the Two Wars" left out fascism entirely and concentrated on "Italian achievement," although fascism *was* the economy between the two wars.

The election of 1994 re-created the fascist past – which side one was on and what one did – as one of Bodei's "divisions": contiguous identity points that sometimes matter and sometimes do not. A group of high-school students was invited to the RAI television studio to view *Combat Film*, a documentary on the Resistance, aired after the 1994 election. They were interviewed after the broadcast. These high-school students would now, fourteen years later, be in their early thirties. One young woman when asked about the film, replied in exasperation, "Mussolini did good things and bad things, like all people. This is not my Italy!"

The young woman's comment was in many ways an emblematic statement of a paradoxical "end of ideology" affirmation that made Fini possible. Her comment also signaled the opening of a marketplace of identities, a neoliberal approach to identity and commitment, manifest in low voter participation and volatile political alignments and results. While Fini was an Italian iteration, political volatility that began in the mid-1980s was not unique to Italy but was a trans-European phenomenon.

Differences, divisions, are only collective liabilities if one's model of the polity is the nineteenth- and twentieth-century nation/state where the collective national culture provides the emotional support for the bureaucratic state. But for the reasons elaborated, Italy and Italians never made the leap that married culture to a national state. Italy's *flexible consolidation regime* positions it well for the twenty-first century, an age of recalibrated nation-states – particularly in the European context. Just because Italians have a weak national identity, it does not mean they lack identity. Following Bodei (1998), Italian identity is "division." In the Italian instance, division or weak national identity is a virtue not a vice, because it allows Italy and Italians the emotional, political and economic flexibility to operate in a transnational European political space.

And Europe – European integration and expansion – is the dominant issue on the European continent, particularly in light of globalization, terrorism, Islamic fundamentalism and of course the Iraq War. As Eurobarometer data reveal (Fig. 9.1), Italians have been consistently favorable to the European community. Level of support among Italian respondents is consistently higher than among French respondents and even higher than the European Union average. Perhaps not surprisingly, Italians place more trust in European institutions than their own. The level of trust in the European Parliament is considerably higher among Italians than among the French and it exceeds the European Union average (Fig. 9.2).

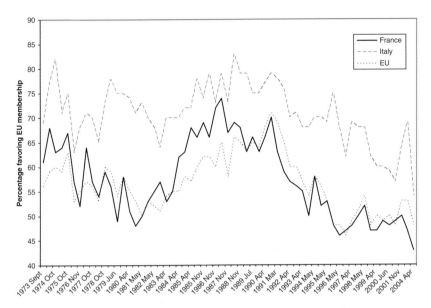

9.1 *Comparison of public attitudes toward EU membership in France and Italy, 1973–2004. Note: Percentage of respondents who replied "a good thing" to the question, "Generally speaking, do you think that (your country's) membership of the European Community (Common Market) is . . . ?"*

When it comes to the issue of Europe, the comparison between Italy and France is instructive. France and its political culture of Republicanism is, to borrow from Benedict Anderson ([1983] 1991), the quintessential modern "imagined community." The differences between Article 1 of the Italian constitution that proclaims a "democratic republic based on labor" – as flexible a principle as one could imagine – and Article 2 of the French constitution that specifies French as the national language, the national anthem, the flag and motto, "Liberty, Equality Fraternity" as well as popular government are as striking as they are conceptually worlds apart. The Italian constitution does not mention the flag until Article 12, and Article 6 protects linguistic minorities. But then who in 1947 Italy would write into a constitution that Italian was the national language?

In France, the expanding process of European integration has triggered a reassertion of the national in ways large and small. The rejection of the European constitution in May 2005 was one in a series of events from the trivial (as when Jacques Chirac walked out of an international economic

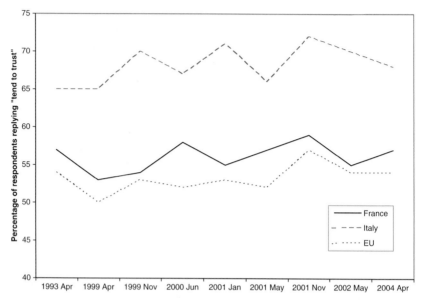

9.2 *Comparison of public attitudes toward European Parliament in France and Italy, 1993–2004. Note: Percentage of respondents who replied "tend to trust" to the question, "For European Parliament, please tell me if you tend to trust it or tend not to trust it?"*

meeting because a French businessman chose to speak in English to the assembled group) to the more serious failure to come to terms with a viable employment policy, the riots of fall 2005 in the suburbs and the demonstrations of spring 2006 against the first employment contract.

Italy is paradoxically finding its national voice in Europe – that is, Europe as an object of identification is helping to produce an Italian national identity that looks outward as well as inward. In one of those perpetual Italian paradoxes, Gianfranco Fini, the conservative nationalist leader, has been one of the most outspoken advocates of Italy's European and international project. In contrast to many European politicians, Fini has sat down for extended conversations with journalists that have appeared in book format. In *Un'Italia civile* (*Civil Italy*) (Fini and Staglieno 1999), one such conversation, Fini cited Ernest Renan and Ernest Gellner. He spoke to the issues of Europe and globalization. He espoused a commitment to a "Europe of *Patrie*" in the mode of Charles de Gaulle.

In 2003, before his appointment as the Italian representative to the European Constitutional Committee, Fini articulated his support of

Europe in *L'Europa che verrà: il destino del continente e il ruolo dell'Italia* (*The Europe that Will Come: The Destiny of the Continent and the Role of Italy* [Fini and Fusi 2003]). Again invoking Charles de Gaulle as his model, Fini argued that a national and a European identity are complementary and do not exclude each other: "European culture *is* European identity. Can one think of a Europe that is not profoundly steeped in single national cultures – and of Italian culture in particular?" (p. 21) Fini argues that a European *demos* is "forming." Youth are at the core of the new *demos* as well as the Internet, which breaks down barriers. Paradoxically, Fini supports the idea that since English is the language of technology it will also be the language of Europe – even if one must continue to learn and use one's national language. When asked if he is committed to a human or a national identity, Fini replies, "We cannot neglect the fact that the concept of identity is always married to the concept of community, the smallest is the family, the largest is already Europe today. Although according to others, it is not Europe but the West" (p. 27).

In a wide-ranging interview with *Le Point* in March 2005, Fini discussed the upcoming constitutional referendum in France.[17] Fini argues that while he would not interfere with French sovereignty, he had doubts about the French submitting the constitution to a popular referendum and called the vote a "great responsibility." When the interviewer reminds Fini that he had originally opposed Maastricht, Fini replies that he had come to believe that a "strong Europe" would unite the values of Europe and America and attenuate the possibility of American domination. At the end of the interview, Fini declared that he could align himself with a variety of European politicians from Joschka Fischer to Nicolas Sarkozy, as he made his decisions on principles, not ideology.

When the French rejected the European constitution, Fini declared publicly that France was placing the European project in danger. On June 7, 2005, less than a week after the Dutch "no" vote on the constitution, Fini gave the keynote address at the Fiftieth Anniversary Commemoration of the Messina Conference. Less than a week after the Dutch "no" vote on the constitution, Fini reminded his audience of the ritual significance of Messina. The French National Assembly had rejected the European Defense Community Project and it appeared that the project of Europe had stalled. Fini argued that Italy had a responsibility to preserve the "legacy of the constitution." He argued that:

---

[17] Dominique Dunglas, "Interview with Gianfranco Fini." *Le Point* (Paris) March 10, 2005 (accessed January 26, 2007).

The result of the referendums in France and the Netherlands should not, therefore, lead to resignation and paralysis. On the contrary: fifty years ago in Messina the Europe of the Founding Fathers found the impetus – by overcoming the divisions of the past – to move beyond apparently insurmountable obstacles that in reality were no less tall then than they are now. By saying "yes" to Europe these leaders breathed life into a complex and ambitious but nonetheless successful undertaking. They knew how to set aside rivalries and self-interest by sharing the most sought after and treasured symbol of them all: sovereignty. They were not afraid to test the conviction, which later events would prove to have been well-founded, that cooperation, mutual trust, shared values, interests and objectives would harm no one and benefit all.[18]

In Italy, weak national identities are strong because they provide flexibility and possibility. They permit Italians to embrace Europe whether they understand it or not, as the euro and the currency debacle shows, but they also provide a chance to retreat – as the in vitro referendum suggests. While the answer is not in yet, the "democratic republic of labor" underscores the flexible sense of nation-ness that portends well for Italy's European future.

---

[18] "Speech by Minister Fini at the Fiftieth Anniversary of the Messina Conference, 7 June 2005. Italy: Ministry of Foreign Affairs" www.esteri.it/eng (accessed January 26, 2007).

Conclusion
The future of illiberal politics: democracy and security

Reprise: a comparative historical sociology of the present

The politics of fear: comparing France and Italy

This book has argued that the rightwing populist moment is an instance of illiberal politics that requires reformulation in historical and cultural terms, rather than as commonly explained in exclusively political or demographic terms. Without the phenomenon of expanding European integration which requires that nation-states rewrite cultural and social contracts to the advantage of some citizens and the disadvantage of others, the occurrence of a rightwing populist moment would be less likely. The other side of the argument is that immigration, the standard explanatory variable, is not sufficient to explain the cross-European nature of rightwing populism or its electoral salience. By focusing upon events as its unit of analysis – events that were often experienced as shocks or anomalies in the nation-states in which they occurred – this book takes a *comparative historical approach to the present*. Events and their collective evaluations yield a more process driven and contextual account of the rightwing populist moment.

The claim that the neoliberal project of Europe and the illiberal politics of rightwing populism are inextricably linked restates telegraphically the central argument that this book theorizes. In the period between 1994 and the present, France and Italy, albeit in different ways and with different valences, were the pivotal sites of rightwing populism in Europe. In both instances, as Chapters 8 and 9 demonstrate, the right has been absorbed into national politics in ways that underscore the national *consolidation regime* – the legacy of the political cultural relation between a people and polity – theorized in Chapter 2. Both cases permit us to think more generally about the issue of rightwing populism as an instance of illiberalism that has appeared in the emerging neoliberal polity.

Italy and France typically figure in comparative discussions of the European right. France appears because of the presence of Jean-Marie Le Pen and the National Front; Italy because of the trio of Gianfranco Fini, Umberto Bossi and Silvio Berlusconi. On any number of points of culture and political development, Italy and France share similarities. For example, they had new postwar constitutions; they were founding members of the European Union and signatories to the Treaty of Rome; they had active Communist parties until the 1980s; they had student revolts in the 1960s; they were culturally Catholic although the institutional relation between Church and state differed in both countries. Each experienced postwar development and affluence.

Italy and France differ in two respects that are germane to the analysis developed in this book. First, their experience of the World War II period was different. Italian fascism was a homegrown product whereas Vichy was an outcome of occupation as well as of collaboration. Second, France and Italy had a different legacy of the formation of the national state – different *consolidation regimes*. France's *hegemonic consolidation regime* and Italy's *flexible consolidation regime* yielded radically different types of *national experience* and *national habits* of being and belonging.

In the instance of the National Front, three dates with concomitant events speak to its trajectory and meaning for French politics and culture. The first is January 1999 when the Mégret faction split off from the National Front. This split led to the Front's poor showing in the European elections of June 1999 and the perception among academics and others that the National Front was gone from the French political scene. As discussed in Chapter 5, the year 1999 marked a turning point in the meaning and influence of the National Front. The "defeat" of the National Front was fraught with paradox. Its issues were becoming increasingly French issues as the party and Le Pen appeared to be on a downward trajectory. Europeanization as an iteration of globalization, which Le Pen labeled as the "new slavery of today," became a particularly salient French issue during this period.

The other two dates, April 21, 2002 and May 29, 2005, are more than symbols. Le Pen's advance to the second round of the presidential elections on April 21, 2002 signaled the disarray of French political culture to its citizens – as well as to the international community. As discussed in Chapter 6, the national shame of April 21, 2002 was emotional but there was also a pragmatic dimension.[1] April 21, 2002 displayed that Le Pen's

---

[1] As evidence of the symbolic valence of April 21, 2002, a LexisNexis search of the French-language press revealed that in the five years between April 2002 and April 2007, "April 21" as a political metaphor appeared in 908 headlines.

ideas and problems were French issues, not National Front issues – so that ordinary citizens, and not only cadres of party militants, voted for him in the first round.

French fears and anxieties around the issues of Europeanization and globalization that Le Pen had articulated reached their climactic moment when French citizens rejected the European constitution on May 29, 2005. The vote on the European constitution, the subject of Chapter 7, detached Le Pen's issues from Le Pen, the message from the messenger, as the majority of the French asserted their nation-ness. The year 1999 was significant for the National Front; whereas April 21, 2002 and May 29, 2005 marked crucial transitions in the French perception of itself as a nation and polity. April 21 signified political possibilities rather than political realities; May 29 signified that France was no longer the leader of Europe, the cosmopolitan center that it had always imagined itself to be (Kramer 2006; Berezin 2006a). Although unseen at the time, both events – arguably – contributed to the overwhelming victory of Nicolas Sarkozy in the 2007 presidential elections.

Events on April 21, 2002 and May 29, 2005 solidified a politics of fear and insecurity in the face of European political realities. The fear of a repeat of April 21 dominated the first round of the French presidential campaign of 2007. It contributed to the articulation of contradictory political positions and the reassertion of nation-ness on the part of the two leading candidates. The socialist candidate Ségolène Royal found herself in the improbable position of arguing that the French should all own a French flag and display it on national holidays as well as singing the *Marseillaise*. But it was Nicolas Sarkozy, the center right candidate, running on the slogan "Together, everything becomes possible," who most successfully and plausibly appropriated Le Pen's language of national identity, toughness on crime and opposition to Turkey's entry to the European Union.

On the morning of April 23, 2007, French intellectuals, media and politicians proclaimed that the first round of the 2007 presidential elections redeemed the shame of April 21, 2002. On April 22, 2007, Jean-Marie Le Pen received only 11 percent of the vote in the first round of the presidential elections. This was the lowest score that he had received since he first ran for President in 1974. As in 1999, Le Pen's political efficacy seems to have evaporated. Le Pen's issues, globalization, Europe and the need to develop viable policies that integrate second- and sometimes third-generation immigrants into French society, have not disappeared. When political candidates, most flagrantly Sarkozy, lifted Le Pen's political narrative from his person, *thinly* committed voters moved their votes to less controversial candidates.

Le Pen's relatively weak showing in the first round of the 2007 presidential elections presumably represented *thick* commitment to the National Front and its positions. As Le Pen proclaimed on the evening of his defeat, "We have won the battle of ideas: nation and patriotism, immigration and insecurity were put at the heart of the campaign of my adversaries who spread these ideas with a wry pout." Appropriation is not a particularly new political strategy in France or elsewhere. Chapter 5 described the state's appropriation of the 1998 World Cup victory when Chirac and Jospin stood together and sang the national anthem on Bastille Day.

In contrast to France, Italy had its anomalous rightwing event in 1994 when post-fascists became part of the first Berlusconi governing coalition. The peculiarities of Italian political culture in the end vitiated the right's significance. The day in April that figures in Italian politics is April 25 – the anniversary of the liberation of Italy from the Nazis. In contrast to April 21, 2002, the event that April 25 marks occurred in 1945 – the relatively distant past. As discussed in earlier chapters, Umberto Bossi is a regional separatist who while politically useful at times to the right does not articulate any far-reaching positions. Silvio Berlusconi is a political and economic entrepreneur who plays fast and loose with the law. He is also aging and has not nurtured a political heir. Gianfranco Fini, who identifies himself with Nicolas Sarkozy, can no longer be classified as any kind of fascist – no matter what his past.

Italy as *shadow comparison* places the Europe issue in bold relief. Europeanization, as a code for globalization, was and is a threat to the French; whereas it is an opportunity for the Italians. Threat and opportunities are matters of degree not absolutes, yet the differences are salient. In France, for example, an editorial in *Libération* written three days after the first round of the presidential elections accused Sarkozy of being a liberal. The editorial intoned: "Your project is liberal," and if "globalization" is "chosen" there will be consequences, "The market left to its own regulation as the world knows brings efficacy, but also injustice."[2]

In June 2007, as newly elected President of France, Nicolas Sarkozy went to Brussels to renegotiate the European constitution which his party had supported in 2005. Upon his return to France after the meeting, Sarkozy proclaimed that he had succeeded in eliminating a clause in the new treaty that supported "free and undistorted competition" and that this

---

[2] Laurent Joffrin, "Editorial: Quelle haine?" *Libération* (Paris) April 25, 2007. Libération.fr (accessed April 25, 2007).

signaled "the end of competition as an ideology and dogma."[3] Sarkozy's comments uttered from either political expediency or conviction reflected the ambivalence toward Europe and globalization that characterized all segments of French society. The French right tends to support the entrepreneurship of small businesses, which it views as fundamental to a strong nation – but small-scale business enterprises and unbridled global capitalism should never be confused for each other. Sternhell (1994) made this point with respect to the 1920s and 1930s in Europe. In short, the economic policy of a nation-state is deeply connected to its collective and normative understanding of how a just society should operate.

Harsh words aside, neoliberalism remains an issue that the new President of France must manage. In the French case, the ramifications of European integration have moved the right's issues into the mainstream of French politics and diminished the political capacity of the extreme right. In the Italian case, Europe as an issue has tamed the populist right, such as Bossi, and underscored the nationalist rather than the anti-democratic tendencies of Fini's conservative right. On the morning after the first round of the 2007 French presidential elections, Fini, referring to Sarkozy, told the *Corriere della Sera* that "A right that speaks to all has won."[4]

Why do the French and Italian experiences matter?

From the mid-eighteenth century to the present, some articulation of the sovereign nation-state has embodied modern political territoriality (Poggi 1978). We need not reify the nation-state to invoke it as an analytic frame. It makes sense to theorize the nation-state as a political form with historical and experiential significance when trying to understand the challenges to *national experience* that European integration poses. As discussed in Chapter 2, "nation-state" projects relate peoples to polities. The term "project" denotes any set of ongoing actions where collective actors attempt to institutionalize new sets of norms, values or procedures. Project is a felicitous formulation because it links culture to organization.[5]

Consolidation regime is the term that this book develops to capture the dynamic and historically contingent character of the process of the union

---

[3] "The Sarko Show." *The Economist* (London) June 30, 2007, p. 59.

[4] Paola Di Caro, "Fini: 'Ha vinto la destra che parla a tutti.'" *Corriere della Sera* (Milan) April 23, 2007. Corriere.it (accessed January 25, 2008).

[5] I use the term "project" (Berezin 1997a) to speak about the Italian fascist state; Fligstein and Mara-Drita (1996) use a variation of the term to discuss the formation of the Single Market Policy in Europe.

of culture and organization that is at the core of the nation-state project and productive of national identity. Institutions regulated by law created the categories that situated individuals within the European nation-state. Competition as well as necessity united individual identities to institutions. The success or strength of a national identity project depends, first, upon the other identities with which it must compete; and second, the strength of the competing institutions that buttress those identities.

In France, the *hegemonic consolidation regime* yielded a tight fit between nation and state – culture and institutions. The consequences of the French iteration of a *hegemonic consolidation regime* were that strong national identities became a liability in the face of difference and paradoxically promoted a defense of tradition and national culture that the extreme right was the first, but not the only party or group, to articulate. Sarkozy capitalized on this legacy in his 2007 presidential campaign. In the last speech of his campaign delivered before the May 5 vote, Sarkozy proclaimed that he wanted to be "national without being nationalist," "of the people without being populist."[6] The cultural salience of Le Pen's positions was a reason why when Sarkozy came along, who was willing to detach the message from the messenger, he was able to garner broad support.

Italy never had a strong national culture in the same sense as the French. Its *flexible consolidation regime* was multicultural in the broadest sense – a federation of cultures under the umbrella of Italy – making its identities malleable and ready for cultural and political contingencies. Paradoxically, while this flexibility contributed to internal conflict, it made Italy and Italians receptive to Europe – if not to the full economic package. Europe became a venue against which Italians could frame themselves as a nation. Europe fostered an Italian national identity whereas it seemed to fragment French national identity. In Europe, Italians found an entity that transcended their regional differences around which they could unite. Thus in the Italian case a weak national identity was a virtue, not a vice.

In the logic of the argument advanced here, Italy and France mirror each other. In France, strong national identities are challenged in the face of an exogenous factor such as Europeanization and promote a general reassertion of nation-ness on the cultural and institutional level; whereas in Italy an opposite process occurs: weak national identities become strong in the face of an exogenous force such as Europeanization. In both instances, the populist right becomes weakened and absorbed into the nation-state.

[6] "Discours de Nicolas Sarkozy, Réunion publique de Montpellier, Jeudi May 3, 2007" (www.sarkozy.fr).

In both France and Italy, the *consolidation regime*, the legacy of the relation between the state and the nation, the people and the polity, patterned the populist response to Europe and the form of the absorption of the populist response into nation-ness.

What more generalizeable points can be drawn from the Italian and French instances? Do the Italian and French cases suggest that the right is never a political threat to democracy and that the legacies of the relation between people and polity institutionalized in *consolidation regimes* will attenuate the non-democratic tendencies of anti-liberal parties? A provisional answer is that it will depend on the nature of the threat, the exogenous element, and the nature of the relation between the people and the polity – the national culture and the national state and the strength of the institutions that mediate that relation.

The egregious threat of terrorism, as evidenced in Europe and the United States, pushes nation-states toward a revamping of national attitudes toward privacy and the restriction of civil liberties that many argue compromises democratic principles of toleration and fairness. In contrast to terrorist activity, Europeanization is a less lethal, yet more complicated, threat that finds expression in cultural terms, that is, national identity terms, but in practice compromises national iterations of economic well-being. The French debates on the European constitution illustrated the cultural dimension of economic ideas. Europe threatens the social as well as the national, and arguably it is the social that might have greater salience for ordinary citizens than dreams of Euro flags and anthems.

This brings us back to the practical importance of *consolidation regimes*. Italy may have a sometimes inefficient state and has had corruption in its institutions, but it has had a modern state that has been in place since 1860. The same holds true for France. In both France and Italy, albeit for different reasons and with different attendant processes, the legacy of institutional arrangements tempered extremism. *Consolidation regimes* hinge on the legacy of the relation between people and polity, between citizens and political and cultural institutions. But, they are more than simply institutional arrangements. *Consolidation regimes* are sites of national experience that produce habits – ways of interpreting and acting the national space – that become particularly salient in times of threat broadly conceived.

Although every nation-state would require a detailed analysis of its own, there are expectations and generalizations that one can sketch from the arguments advanced in this book. Nation-states from northern Europe, England and Sweden for example, have been less vulnerable to the parliamentary salience of rightwing populism. It bears reminding that this is not a claim about the presence of fringe groups such as neo-Nazis and skin-heads, rather it is a claim about political salience.[7] This is not because England and Sweden are more or less democratic than southern and central Europe, rather, their *hegemonic consolidation regimes* were based on geographic location and relatively monolingual cultures. Longstanding monarchies have helped to deflect extreme nationalist energies. In addition, Sweden and Britain have kept their distance from full engagement in the European Union as neither entered the eurozone and both bypassed the vote on the constitution. In contrast, the Netherlands and Belgium, where rightwing parties have emerged, are consociations. They have built duality into their national cultures and this makes them vulnerable to rightwing parties. Unlike France and Italy, the coexistence of two recognized national cultures makes it difficult to decide where to retreat in the face of exogenous threats.[8]

Polities where the sub-national culture is ethnic and that lack a legacy of a modern liberal state tend to produce *brittle consolidation regimes*. These types of polities with weak national culture and a weak state are vulnerable to extremist and populist demands when they need to build or rebuild political institutions. According to the logic of this argument, nation-states in the former Eastern Europe would be particularly vulnerable to populist appeals. When communist regimes fell, states in the former Eastern Europe that were bureaucratic expressions, such as the former Yugloslavia, gave way to ethnic conflict. Arguably, Europe plays both ways in this situation. In some instances it can serve as an opportunity to shake free from the past; and in others it can be viewed as a threat to the dominant ethnic sub-national culture. But it is no accident that, as discussed in Chapter 7, the turnout for the European elections in 2004, the first elections after accession, was lower in the East than anywhere else, even though turnout for European elections in general tends to be low.

Experience and political perception

Europe: a new consolidation regime?

What does the European Union mean today and how does it bear on the past and future of illiberal politics?[9] Europeanization is a political reality that is not disappearing. Europe is not aiming to create a new polity

---

[7] See, for example, Pred (2000) on Sweden; Holmes (2000, pp. 106–161) on Britain.

[8] Lijphart (1975; 1977) provides the standard work on consociation. The Netherlands is his first case.

[9] For full-length scholarly studies, see Moravcsik (1998), Ross (1995) and Milward (2000).

modeled on the nation-state. However, its transnational institutions that call for the harmonization of various social and fiscal policies across the continent invariably chip away at some of the modern nation-state's prerogatives.

The identification in Chapter 2 of different types of *consolidation regimes* suggests that the territorially defined nation-state project was not a seamless effort. Its development was contingent, conflicted and contested and its emergence varied as to time and space – history and culture. The European Union is arguably another variation on the nation-state theme with important differences.[10] The European Union consolidated in the Maastricht Treaty in 1992 is a supra-national political project that transforms Europe today into a geographical space where territory, membership and identity are once again sites of contestation and renegotiation.

National elites involved in the project of Europe from its inception never intended for integration to involve a new nation-state project. Yet, in the past decade, collective actors of various types, from intellectuals such as Jürgen Habermas ([1990] 1996; 1997; 2001) to European Union bureaucrats, have given voice to a Europe that seems to threaten to rewrite the rules of the relation between peoples and polity and move in the direction of a new *consolidation regime*. A trans-European public discourse has emerged that focuses on European citizenship and the issue of a European constitution and has, if not replaced, at least provided public distraction from the economic mission of the Union.[11]

But what can citizenship mean in a supra-national body whose members have no direct voice in governance? European integration challenges the prerogatives of territoriality and by extension disequilibrates the existing mix of national culture and legal norms. Post-national imaginings not withstanding, much empirical evidence (for example, Diez Medrano 2003; Berezin and Díez Medrano 2008) and historical analysis (Calhoun 2007) suggests that the national has not retreated. By threatening to make the national space "unfamiliar" to many citizens, Europe, as this book has illustrated, opens a space for contestation and reaction as well as positive change.

---

[10] Goldstein (2001) takes up the issue of "federal sovereignty" in comparative perspective. Morgan (2005) is one of the few scholarly works that argues for a European "superstate." Security in the more narrowly militaristic sense of the term is an important component of Morgan's argument.

[11] Bruneteau (2000) argues that European Union, or the idea of it, was a linchpin of instrumental and contingent national political goals and not a normative vision of European solidarity.

The raw material for a *consolidation regime*, a European political community in the Weberian sense, is flawed on two counts. First, Europe as a political space is territorially ambiguous.[12] Regulatory decrees are trans-European. Membership is nation-state based. Only individual member states, not the European community, may bestow citizenship. The ability to work across national borders – one of the attractions of the EU for the educated and upwardly mobile middle classes – frequently bogs down in a mass of red tape that defies the rational language of the Schengen Accords (Romero 1990; Favell 2008; Fligstein 2008).[13] Second, Europe as a cultural space lacks "affectivity" – that is, emotional attachment (Weiler 1999, p. 329). Old European nation-states, as Weber argues, crafted a fiction of shared culture and history from a widely diffused community of popular memory. "Europe" shares little common civic space or cultural past from which to forge an identity except for memories of war – and that was usually between member states (Mann 1998).

As Darnton (2002) reminds us, European identity *per se* is not new. A shared high culture among the university educated – usually European men – who spoke and read in various national languages – usually English, German and French in addition to their own – was the Procrustean bed of the "old" European identity. Exclusive social and professional networks forged one part of the old European identity. Nineteenth-century innovations such as mass schooling and conscription helped to foster bonds of national solidarity among workers and members of the lower middle classes (Hobsbawm 1983; Weber 1976). Post-Maastricht European identity claims to be popular and inclusive. In contrast to old European identity, new European identity is a product of political, and not cultural, demand.

The "unbundling" of nation-state sovereignty and the logistical problems that it brings to ordinary citizens is as likely to strengthen existing national identities as it is to generate a feeling of common Europeanness (Wallace 1999; Berezin 1999a; 2003). Bureaucrats in Brussels who seek to turn ordinary Germans, French and Italians into Europeans face the twin obstacles of a contradictory legal framework and thin cultural demand (Deflem and Pampel 1996). The tangle of interpretation and administration that besets the European Union in the fullest meaning of that term – juridical, social and cultural – suggests that a transnational polity with a

---

[12] For concise technical discussions of the legal issues involved, see Wouters (2000) on national constitutions and Davis (2002) on citizenship law.
[13] Suzanne Daley, "Despite European Unity Efforts, to Most Workers There's No Country Like Home." *New York Times* (New York) May 12, 2001, p. A6.

loyal and attached citizenry – a citizenry that identifies itself as European – is in the distant future. It also points to an unpleasant underside of union. Political aggregation upwards yields social disaggregation downwards, and downward disaggregation has the potential to create political and cultural disruption and conflict. In short, the legacy of the relation between a people and a polity embedded in diverse types of *consolidation regimes* is not subject to easy or immediate modification.

Experiencing the nation-state

As argued in the Introduction and Chapter 2, experience, particularly *national experience*, is the social and cognitive entity that unites the macro-level and micro-level dimensions of this argument. Habits of being and belonging coupled with structural and emotional security comprise the experiential dimension of the nation-state. When the European nation-state begins to mutate if not dissolve due to the push of European integration and the attendant processes of Europeanization, then the evolving political space reconfigures both the social and cultural relations and the institutional relations upon which the old nation-state had been built.

To the extent that the nation-state contained threat and minimized risk for its members – Poggi's argument as discussed in Chapter 2 – it provided experiential and legal security. Nation-states were arenas that adjudicated risk among people who were more or less like each other – they were not "naturally" like each other, nor were their "likenesses" only imagined or constructed. Propinquity in physical space and duration in time, shared history, played as much a role in creating a feeling of national belonging as any constructed narratives of nationhood. Institutional arrangements coupled with propinquity and duration managed to create groups of people who more or less thought of themselves as French or Italian or German or whatever.

Modern political community, the nation-state, is durable in time and rooted in bounded physical space. As a consequence, its inhabitants experience national membership as a familiar habit and the national landscape as a comfortable place. Roberto Michels (1949) in a 1929 essay on "Patriotism," noted that "Variety is strange to most persons. This factor necessitates that the national state, which is interested in the cohesion of its parts, smooth over extreme differences" (p. 157). William James (1956) in a classic essay, "The Sentiment of Rationality," gives a rational explanation for the emotional appeal of comfort. He argues that the "feeling of rationality and the feeling of familiarity are one and the same thing" (p. 78).

Novelty according to James is a "mental irritant," whereas custom is a mental sedative. James argues that the core of rationality is that it defines expectation. The expectation of continuity is rational because it is emotionally satisfying.[14] Viewed from the perspective of comfort, emotional attachment to place, what the Germans call *Heimat*, is not an irrational particularism but a rational response to environmental factors.[15]

No small part of the nation-state's legitimacy derived and derives from its emotional appeal to comfort. Security, economic and political, is the practical component of comfort (Rothschild 1995; Lipset 1959).[16] The nation-state made its citizens feel safe by assuaging fear and guaranteeing public and private security – what Loader and Walker (2007) refer to as "civilizing security." Public national security institutionalized in the military and the police protected the property of the nation and the property of the individual (Deflem 2002). Social security located in the fiscal institutions of the state protected the life of the individual and the family. These institutions of security did not mean that there was no war, crime or poverty, but rather provided mechanisms for making people feel secure in their familiar places – or at home in the nation-state.

Security, familiarity and comfort in the public sphere – what I am labeling *national experience* – are not without contradictions. As Norton (2004, p. 116) argues, experience "confers only limited understanding." Norton's insight suggests the underside of experience in general and *national experience* in particular. Because experience interrogates reality through the lens of what one already knows, it may tend toward conservativism and reluctance to change. On the other hand, the repeated experience of national security in the broadest meaning of that term could tend toward a cosmopolitan democracy and a welcoming of others. Secure people are democratic people because individual and collective security fosters the spirit of largesse and generosity that a thick democracy requires. Insecure people are fearful and risk averse. Insecure people expand the community of potential enemies and threats; secure people expand the community of friends.

Experiencing the new Europe: the interplay of security and insecurity

Security and comfort have a pragmatic as well as cognitive and emotional dimension. The institutions of the nation-state use the legal system to

---

[14] For a fuller articulation of this position and its relation to politics, see Berezin (2002).
[15] For a critique of the uncritical acceptance of this view, see Calhoun (1999).
[16] Beck (1992) in a now classic account identified "risk" as a hallmark of modernity.

situate its members within it. These institutions cut both ways. Members of the nation-state also rely on national institutions to situate themselves within the polity. Members of secure nation-states develop forms of social and cultural capital as well as monetary capital that are tied to the national state. These forms of capital, from something as simple as speaking a single common language (we have only to remember Chirac's refusal to sign the Regional Languages Charter) to state-supported religion to social welfare policies, make citizens more or less equal as they participate in the community of the nation-state.

European integration not only recalibrates the nation-state. It poses a challenge to citizens of nation-states because on an individual level it alters the parameters of social and cultural capital and by extension monetary capital. Putnam's now classic *Making Democracy Work* (1993) generated a large literature within social science around the relation between social capital and democracy. In capsule form, Putnam argued that civic associations where citizens learned to engage in cooperative activities spawned relations of trust that contributed to collective commitment to democracy. Social capital was the label that Putnam assigned to the process that he theorized. While Putnam was primarily interested in politics, the social scientists extended the concept to account for a whole range of social and economic processes (Portes 1998).[17]

Putnam borrowed the concept of social capital from James Coleman (1990). Among more culturally oriented social scientists, the term is inextricably linked to Pierre Bourdieu, who in early essays (1983; 1985; 1989) identified cultural and social capital as a non-monetary asset that was a vital dimension of social position. No matter the etiology of the term, scholars (most likely influenced by the monetary metaphor) tend to speak of social and cultural capital as something that one has more or less of. Fungibility is another dimension of capital – monetary, social and cultural – that is frequently ignored in discussions of democracy and social capital. Yet, fungibility is crucial to social inclusion as well as exclusion and to individual as well as collective affinity for democracy.

Security defined stability in the old Europe; mobility defines security *and* insecurity in the new Europe. The "new" Europe is shifting the site of security from the collectivity to the individual. Although not expressed in precisely these terms, the French debate over the European Constitutional Treaty echoed these ideas. New Europe establishes virtual markets as well

---

[17] Somers (2005) provides a trenchant critique.

as capital markets – that is, it advantages those who have cultural and social capital that is *not tied* to a nation-state. Practically, this points to language markets and credential markets. People who speak multiple languages and who have technical university credentials can participate in multiple social, cultural and material (i.e., money and goods) markets. The new European professionally educated middle classes are oriented toward Europe as well as the nation. Paradoxically, mobility markets also advantage workers at the low end of the labor market: immigrants who come into nation-states and take the low-end work that the middle of the labor market – those whose virtual capital is tied to the nation-state – look down upon.

A central puzzle in discussions of rightwing populism is how to account for the diverse groups that it attracts. According to the logic of the argument advanced in this book, the answer to the phenomenology of attraction does not lie in the characteristics of individuals but in the fungibility of capital which individuals possess. People who cannot participate in new markets, whose social and cultural capital is tied to old European nation-states – the elderly, the poorly educated, as well as small merchants and public sector bureaucrats – lack fungibility and have limited capacities to move.

Rightwing sensibilities begin on the ground – in the home, the neighborhood, the local community. All individuals are tied to the particular places they are in – in one way or the other. They feel attachment to their territory on the local, regional and national level. Citizens of modern democracies have exit and voice capacities. Voice generates loyalties. But they tend to exercise their exit capacities only under the duress of market or political forces.

Most residents of modern nation-states are not migrants, which is why the negotiability of virtual capital is central to a strong democracy. Individuals or groups may have much virtual, that is social and cultural, capital in terms of strong and weak ties – dense communal bonds – but frequently that capital is not negotiable in multiple spaces. The less negotiable a group or individual's virtual capital is across borders, the more the group or individual will identify with the place that they are in. So that it is not immigration or the presence of strangers on the territory that makes for modern xenophobic reactions, rather it is the lack of exit capacity available to those whose social and cultural capital is negotiable only in restrictive spaces. The neoliberal dilemma at the core of the "new" Europe is that it demands the capacity, if not the actuality, of mobility and fungible forms of virtual capital. Those who possess capital – social, cultural, financial – that is only *national*, experience Europe as a threat.

Secure states are democratic states

A thick democracy – that is, a democracy that merges sentiments and institutions – is difficult. It is difficult because it requires not only wealth, a material foundation, but also a generalized public sense of largesse and empathy. But these are aristocratic as opposed to populist virtues – not because the mass public is intrinsically intolerant, unjust and unfair but because it is frequently not in the ordinary person's interest to voluntarily share scarce cultural and material resources.

From the vantage point of history, it is fairly accurate to argue that while democracy in theory and practice goes back to Aristotle, democracy was only widely institutionalized with the modern European nation-state, or to put it another way, the political organization that was formed in Europe between 1789 and 1989. Modern nation-states made democracy possible by providing citizens with an expanded notion of security – domestic and international. Security is an emotional and practical concept – much like honor in non-modern societies. Security was institutionalized in the major institutions of membership of the modern nation-state – the army, the schools and social welfare – as well as in targeting enemies and identifying friends.

Zolberg (2002) in his discussion of the United States' response to 9/11 argues that movement not immigration is the core of global society. (However, the immigrant is sometimes a convenient image upon which to project insecurity and fear.) Free movement across borders (i.e., refugees and immigrant groups who move out of necessity do not fit this category) requires capital – monetary, social and cultural – that travels. But here also lies the hard fact. Only certain groups of people, that is, the educated, multilingual, technical or professional class, can take full advantage of freedom of movement. The majority of ordinary Europeans have economic, social and cultural capital that is firmly tied to their nation-state of origin.

To adapt Hirschman's (1970) classic formulation to the case in point, when a group's exit capacity is low – as it is for the unemployed youth, elderly and small businesspeople who find populist nationalist parties appealing – investment in place becomes more intense. Groups who lack the forms of capital to participate in new social, cultural and economic markets reassert the national. They over-identify with place, in this case the nation-state, and look to organizations which promise to guard the gates against security threats – real and imagined.

The democratic deficit that the new Europe must resolve does not lie in whether ordinary citizens have a voice in Brussels. The challenges to contemporary European democracy lie in the new relation between security and insecurity in all its forms – material, cultural and emotional – that Europeanization and globalization demands. Until Europe – all of its twenty-seven member nation-states – manages to create a new twenty-first-century "World of Security" that is global, tolerant, fair and inclusive, populism will continue to lurk in the interstices of even procedurally democratic nation-states.

Bibliography

Abbott, Andrew. 1997. "On the Concept of Turning Point." *Comparative Social Research* 16: 85–105.

2001. *Time Matters: On Theory and Method.* University of Chicago Press.

Abdelal, Rawi, Yoshiko M. Herrera, Alastair Iain Johnston and Rose McDermott. 2006. "Identity as a Variable." *Perspectives on Politics* 4 (4): 695–711.

Accornero, Aris and Eliana Como. 2003. "The (Failed) Reform of Article 18." Pp. 199–220 in *Italian Politics: A Review, the Second Berlusconi Government*, vol. XVIII, ed. Jean Blondel and Paolo Segatti. New York and Oxford: Berghahn.

Adams, Julia, Elisabeth S. Clemens and Ann Shola Orloff, eds. 2005. *Remaking Modernity: Politics, History, and Sociology.* Durham, NC: Duke University Press.

Agnew, John A. 1995. "The Rhetoric of Regionalism: The Northern League in Italian Politics." *Transactions of the Institute of British Geographers* 20: 156–172.

2002. *Place and Politics in Modern Italy.* University of Chicago Press.

2005. *Hegemony: The New Shape of Global Power.* Philadelphia: Temple University Press.

Agnew, John and Carlo Brusa. 1999. "New Rules for National Identity? The Northern League and Political Identity in Contemporary Northern Italy." *National Identities* 1: 117–133.

Agulhon, Maurice. 2000. *De Gaulle: histoire, symbole, mythe.* [Paris]: Plon.

Alba, Richard D. and Victor Nee. 2003. *Remaking the American Mainstream: Assimilation and Contemporary Immigration.* Cambridge, MA: Harvard University Press.

Alesina, Alberto and Francesco Giavazzi. 2006. *The Future of Europe: Reform or Decline.* Cambridge, MA: MIT Press.

Alexander, Jeffrey C. 1987. *Twenty Lectures: Sociological Theory since World War II*. New York: Columbia University Press.

2004. "Cultural Pragmatics: Social Performance between Ritual and Strategy." *Sociological Theory* 22 (4): 527–573.

2006. *The Civil Sphere*. Oxford University Press.

Alleanza Nazionale. 1995. *Pensiamo l'Italia: il domani c'è già: valori, idee e progetti per l'Alleanza Nazionale*. Rome: Tesi Politiche Approvate dal Congresso di Fiuggi.

Ancelovici, Marcos. 2002. "Organizing Against Globalization: The Case of ATTAC in France." *Politics and Society* 30 (3): 427–463.

Andall, Jacqueline. 2007. "Immigration and the Italian Left Democrats in Government (1996–2001)." *Patterns of Prejudice* 41 (2): 131–153.

Anderson, Benedict. [1983] 1991. *Imagined Communities: Reflections on the Origin and Spread of Nationalism*. London: Verso.

Anderson, Christopher J. and Jonas Pontusson. 2007. "Workers, Worries, and Welfare States: Social Protection and Job Insecurity in 15 OECD Countries." *European Journal of Political Research* 46: 211–235.

L'année politique: économique et sociale en France. Vols. 1983–2004. Paris: Moniteur.

Ansell, Christopher K. and Giuseppe Di Palma, eds. 2004. *Restructuring Territoriality: Europe and the United States Compared*. Cambridge University Press.

Antonio, Robert J. 2000. "After Postmodernism: Reactionary Tribalism." *American Journal of Sociology* 106 (1): 40–87.

Apter, Emily S. 1999. *Continental Drift: From National Characters to Virtual Subjects*. University of Chicago Press.

Ardagh, John. 1999. *France in the New Century*. London: Penguin Books.

Aristotle. 1979. *The Politics*, trans. T. A. Sinclair. New York: Penguin.

Art, David. 2006. *The Politics of the Nazi Past in Germany and Austria*. Cambridge University Press.

2008. "The Organizational Origins of the Contemporary Radical Right: The Case of Belgium." *Comparative Politics* 40 (4): 421–440.

Baeckeroot, Christian. 1992. *Famille: pour une politique familiale*. Paris: Éditions Nationales.

Bagnasco, Arnaldo. 1977. *Tre Italie: la problematica territoriale dello sviluppo italiano*. Bologna: Il Mulino.

1986. *Torino: un profilo sociologico*. Turin: Einaudi.

Bail, Christopher A. 2008. "The Configuration of Symbolic Boundaries Toward Immigrants in Twenty-One European Countries." *American Sociological Review* 73 (1): 37–59.

Baldwin-Edwards, Martin and Martin Schain, eds. 1994. "The Politics of Immigration in Western Europe." *West European Politics*, special issue 17 (2).

Balestrini, Nanni. 1995. *Una mattina ci siam svegliati*. Milan: Baldini and Castoldi.

Ballinger, Pamela. 2007. "Borders of the Nation, Borders of Citizenship: Italian Repatriation and the Redefinition of National Identity after World War II." *Comparative Studies in Society and History* 49 (3): 713–741.

Barbagli, Marzio. 1982. *Sotto lo stesso tetto*. Bologna: Il Mulino.

Barkan, Joanne. 2000. "Tony Blair and Gerhard Schroeder: the Third Way/*die neue Mitte*: A Manifesto." *Dissent* 47 (2): 51–65.

Barraclough, Richard. 1998. "Umberto Bossi: Charisma, Personality and Leadership." *Modern Italy* 3: 263–269.

Bartolini, Stefano and Peter Mair. 1990. *Identity, Competition, and Electoral Availability: The Stabilization of European Electorates 1885–1985*. Cambridge University Press.

Bates, Robert H., Avner Greif, Margaret Levi, Jean-Laurent Rosenthal and Barry R. Weingast, eds. 1998. *Analytic Narratives*. Princeton University Press.

Baubérot, Jean. 2004. "La commission Stasi vue par l'un de ses membres." *French Politics, Culture and Society* 22 (3): 135–141.

Baudrillard, Jean. 2002. *Au royaume des aveugles, précédé par De l'exorcisme en politique, ou la conjuration des imbéciles*. Paris: Sens & Tonka.

Baverez, Nicolas. 2003. *La France qui tombe*. Paris: Perrin.

Beck, Ulrich. 1992. *Risk Society: Towards a New Modernity*. Newbury Park, CA: Sage Publications.

Beckert, Jens. 2008. *Inherited Wealth*. Princeton University Press.

Bell, Daniel. [1962] 2000. *The End of Ideology: On the Exhaustion of Political Ideas in the Fifties*. Cambridge, MA: Harvard University Press.

Bell, David A. 2001. *The Cult of the Nation in France: Inventing Nationalism, 1680–1800*. Cambridge, MA: Harvard University Press.

Berezin, Mabel. 1994. "Cultural Form and Political Meaning." *American Journal of Sociology* 99 (5): 1237–1286.

1996. "The Dead are Equal: History Making, Moral Relativism and the Rise of the New Italian Right." Comparative Study of Social Transformation (CSST), Working Paper 109, University of Michigan.

1997a. *Making the Fascist Self: The Political Culture of Interwar Italy*. Ithaca, NY: Cornell University Press.

1997b. "Politics and Culture: A Less Fissured Terrain." *Annual Review of Sociology* 23: 361–383.

1999a. "Emotions Unbound: Feeling Political Incorporation in the New Europe." Paper presented to the American Sociological Association Meeting, Chicago.

1999b. "Political Belonging: Emotion, Nation and Identity in Fascist Italy." Pp. 355–377 in *State/Culture*, ed. George Steinmetz. Ithaca, NY: Cornell University Press.

2000. "The Euro is More than Money: Converting Currency, Exchanging Identity, and Selling Citizenship in Post-Maastricht Europe." *Policy Newsletter* 1 (1), Center for Economy and Society, University of Michigan Business School (www.bus.umich.edu/cse/).

2001. "Emotion and Political Identity: Mobilizing Affection for the Polity." Pp. 83–98 in *Passionate Politics: Emotion and Social Movements*, ed. Jeff Goodwin, James M. Jasper and Francesca Polletta. University of Chicago Press.

2002. "Secure States: Towards a Political Sociology of Emotion." Pp. 33–52 in *Sociological Review Monograph*. London: Blackwell.

2003. "Territory, Emotion, and Identity: Spatial Recalibration in a New Europe." Pp. 1–30 in *Europe Without Borders: Remapping Territory, Citizenship and Identity in a Transnational Age*, ed. Mabel Berezin and Martin Schain. Baltimore: Johns Hopkins University Press.

2006a "Appropriating the 'No': The French National Front, the Vote on the Constitution, and the 'New' April 21." *PS: Political Science and Politics* 39 (April): 269–272.

2006b. "The Festival State: Celebration and Commemoration in Fascist Italy." *Journal of Modern European History* 3 (1): S. 60–74.

2006c "Great Expectations: Reflections on Identity and the European Monetary Union." Pp. 97–107 in *The Year of the Euro: The Cultural, Social and Political Import of Europe's Single Currency*, ed. Robert Fishman and Anthony Messina. South Bend, IN: University of Notre Dame Press.

2006d. "Xenophobia and the New Nationalisms." Pp. 273–284 in *Handbook of Nations and Nationalism*, ed. Gerard Delanty and Krishan Kumar. London: Sage Publications.

2007a. "Fascism." Pp 1644–1647 in *The Blackwell Encyclopedia of Sociology*, ed. George Ritzer. Oxford: Blackwell.

2007b. "Revisiting the French Front National: The Ontology of a Political Mood." (*Special Issue: Racist and Far Right Groups*) *Journal of Contemporary Ethnography* 36 (2) (April): 129–146.

Berezin, Mabel and Juan Díez Medrano. 2008. "Distance Matters: Place, Political Legitimacy and Popular Support for European Integration." *Comparative European Politics* 6: 1–32.

Berezin, Mabel and Martin Schain, eds. 2003. *Europe Without Borders: Re-mapping Territory, Citizenship and Identity in a Transnational Age.* Baltimore: Johns Hopkins University Press.

Berger, Suzanne. 1972. *Peasants Against Politics: Rural Organization in Brittany, 1911–1967.* Cambridge, MA: Harvard University Press.

Beriss, David. 1990. "Scarves, Schools and Segregation: The Foulard Affair." *French Politics and Society* 8: 1–15.

Berman, Sheri. 2006. *The Primacy of Politics: Social Democracy and the Making of Europe's Twentieth Century.* Cambridge University Press.

Bermeo, Nancy. 2003. *Ordinary People in Extraordinary Times: The Citizenry and the Breakdown of Democracy.* Princeton University Press.

Betz, Hans-Georg. 1993. "The New Politics of Resentment: Radical Right-wing Populist Parties in Western Europe." *Comparative Politics* 25 (4) (July): 413–426.

1994. *Radical Right Populism in Western Europe.* New York: St. Martin's Press.

Birnbaum, Pierre. [1998] 2001. *The Idea of France.* New York: Hill and Wang.

Bizeul, Daniel. 2003. *Avec ceux du FN: un sociologue au Front national.* Paris: Éditions la Découverte.

Blair, Tony. 1998. *The Third Way: New Politics for the New Century.* Fabian Pamphlet 588. London: The Fabian Society.

Bleich, Erik. 2003. *Race Politics in Britain and France.* Cambridge University Press.

Blyth, Mark. 2002. *Great Transformations: Economic Ideas and Institutional Change in the Twentieth Century.* Cambridge University Press.

Bobbio, Luigi. 1979. *Lotta continua: storia di una organizzazione.* Rome: Savelli.

Bobbio, Norberto. 1994. *Destra e sinistra.* Rome: Donzelli.

Bodei, Remo. 1998. *Il noi diviso: ethos e idee dell'Italia repubblicana.* Turin: Einaudi.

Boldini, Sergio. 1998. "Il corteo del Primo Maggio come autorappresentazione delle classi lavoratrici." Pp. 57–67 in *La piazza del popolo,* ed. Nicolo Pasero and Alessandro Tinterri. Rome: Meltemi.

Boltanski, Luc and Laurent Thévenot. [1991] 2006. *On Justification: Economies of Worth,* trans. Catherine Porter. Princeton University Press.

Borneman, John and Nick Fowler. 1997. "Europeanization." *Annual Review of Anthropology* 26: 487–514.

Bossi, Umberto. 1996. *Il mio progetto: discorsi su federalismo e Padania*. Milan: Sperling & Kupfer.

Boswell, Laird. 2005. "Right-Wing Extremism in Frontier Regions: The French National Front and the Crisis of Alsatian Identity." Working Paper. Center for 21st Century Studies, University of Wisconsin-Milwaukee.

Bourdieu, Pierre. 1983. "The Forms of Capital." Pp. 241–258 in *Handbook of Theory and Research for the Sociology of Education*, ed. John G. Richardson. New York: Greenwood.

1985. "The Social Space and the Genesis of Groups." *Theory and Society* 14: 723–744.

1989. "Social Space and Symbolic Power." *Sociological Theory* 7: 14–25.

Bové, José. 2001. *The World is Not for Sale: Farmers Against Junk Food*. London: Verso.

Bowen, John R. 2007. *Why the French Don't Like Headscarves: Islam, the State, and Public Space*. Princeton University Press.

Brubaker, Rogers. 1992. *Citizenship and Nationhood in France and Germany*. Cambridge, MA: Harvard University Press.

2006. *Nationalist Politics and Everyday Ethnicity in a Transylvanian Town*. Princeton University Press.

Brubaker, Rogers and Fred Cooper. 2000. "Beyond 'Identity.'" *Theory and Society* 29: 1–47.

Bruff, Ian. 2003. "The Netherlands, the Challenge of Lijst Pim Fortuyn, and the Third Way." *Politics* 23 (3): 156–162.

Bruneteau, Bernard. 2000. "The Construction of Europe and the Concept of the Nation State." *Contemporary European History* 9 (2): 245–260.

Brustein, William I. 2003. *Roots of Hate: Anti-Semitism in Europe Before the Holocaust*. Cambridge University Press.

Burawoy, Michael. 2003. "Revisits: Toward a Theory of Reflexive Ethnography." *American Sociological Review* 68: 645–679.

Büthe, Tim. 2002. "Taking Temporality Seriously: Modeling History and the Use of Narratives as Evidence." *American Political Science Review* 96 (3): 481–493.

Caciagli, Mario. 1988. "The Movimento Sociale Italiano-Destra Nazionale and Neo-Fascism in Italy." *West European Politics* 11 (2): 19–33.

Calhoun, Craig. 1997. *Nationalism*. Minneapolis: University of Minnesota Press.

1999. "Nationalism, Political Community and the Representation of Society: Or, Why Feeling at Home is not a Substitute for Public Space." *European Journal of Social Theory* 2 (2): 217–231.

2007. *Nations Matter*. London and New York: Routledge.

Cameron, David R. 1996. "National Interest, the Dilemmas of European Integration, and Malaise." Pp. 325–382 in *Chirac's Challenge: Liberalization, Europeanization, and Malaise in France*, ed. John T. S. Keeler and Martin A. Schain. New York: St. Martin's Press.

Campi, Alessandro. 2006. *La destra di Fini: i dieci anni di Alleanza nazionale, 1995–2005*. Lungro di Cosenza, Italy: Marco.

Camus, Jean-Yves. 1996. *Le Front national: histoire et analyses*. Paris: Éditions Olivier Laurens.

Canovan, Margaret. 1996. *Nationhood and Political Theory*. Cheltenham: Edward Elgar.

1999. "Trust the People! Populism and the Two Faces of Democracy." *Political Studies* 47: 2–16.

Capoccia, Giovanni. 2004. "Defending Democracy Against the Extreme Right in Inter-War Europe: A Past still Present?" Pp. 83–107 in *Western Democracies and the New Extreme Right Challenge*, ed. Roger Eatwell and Cas Mudde. London: Routledge.

2005. *Defending Democracy: Reactions to Extremism in Interwar Europe*. Baltimore: Johns Hopkins University Press.

Caramani, Daniele. 2004. *The Nationalization of Politics: The Formation of National Electorates and Party Systems in Western Europe*. Cambridge University Press.

Carlucci, Kristin, Saul Garlick and Beth Hanley. 2007. "Foreword: Special Issue on Populism." *SAIS Review* 37 (1): 1–2.

Carrier, Peter. 2000. "'National Reconciliation?' Mitterrand, Chirac, and the Commemorations of Vichy 1992–95." *National Identities* 2: 127–143.

2005. *Holocaust Monuments and National Memory Cultures in France and Germany since 1989: The Origins and Political Function of the Vél' d'Hiv in Paris and the Holocaust Monument in Berlin*. New York: Berghahn Books.

Cassen, Bernard, Liêm Hoang-Ngoc and Pierre-André Imbert. 1999. *Attac %%: contre la dictature des marchés*. Paris: Vo Éditions.

Castel, Robert. 2003. *L'insécurité sociale: qu'est-ce qu'être protégé?* Éditions du Seuil et la République des Idées.

Cautrès, Bruce and Nonna Mayer, eds. 2004. *Le nouveau désordre électoral: les leçons du 21 avril 2002*. Paris: Presses de Sciences Po.

Cenci, Cristina. 1999. "Rituale e memoria: la celebrazioni del 25 aprile." Pp. 325–378 in *Le memorie della Repubblica*, ed. Leonardo Paggi. Scandicci, Florence: La Nuova Italia.

Centeno, Miguel Angel. 2002. *Blood and Debt: War and the Nation-state in Latin America*. University Park: Pennsylvania State University Press.

Cerquiglini, Bernard. 1999. *Les langues de la France.* Rapport au Ministre de l'Éducation Nationale, de la Recherche et de la Technologie et à la Ministre de la Culture et de la Communication. April (www.culture. gouv.fr, accessed October 7, 2006).

Cerulo, Karen A. 1997. "Identity Construction: New Issues, New Directions." *Annual Review of Sociology* 23: 385–409.

Charter of Fundamental Rights of the European Union. 2000. *Official Journal of the European Communities* 2000/C 364/01 (December 18).

Clemens, Elisabeth S. 2007. "Toward a Historicized Sociology: Theorizing Events, Processes, and Emergence." *Annual Review of Sociology* 33: 527–549.

Clemens, Elisabeth S. and James M. Cook. 1999. "Politics and Institutionalism: Explaining Durability and Change." *Annual Review of Sociology* 25: 441–466.

Cohen, Jean L. 1985. "Strategy or Identity: New Theoretical Paradigms and Contemporary Social Movements." *Social Research* 52: 663–716.

Cohen, Patrick and Jean-Marc Salmon. 2003. *21 avril 2002: Contre-enquête sur le choc Le Pen.* Paris: Éditions Denoël.

Coleman, James S. 1990. *Foundations of Social Theory.* Cambridge, MA: Harvard University Press.

Colombo, Asher and Giuseppe Sciortino. 2004. "Italian Immigration: The Origins, Nature and Evolution of Italy's Migratory Systems." *Journal of Modern Italian Studies* 9 (1): 49–70.

Conan, Eric and Henry Rousso. 1998. *Vichy: An Ever-Present Past.* Hanover, NH: University Press of New England.

Connolly, William E. 1991. *Identity/Difference: Democratic Negotiations of Political Paradox.* Ithaca, NY: Cornell University Press.

Cooke, Philip. 2000. "The Resistance Continues: A Social Movement in the 1970s." *Modern Italy* 5 (2): 161–173.

Cordellier, Serge and Sarah Netter, eds. 2003. *L'état des régions françaises: un panorama unique et complet – 2003.* Paris: Éditions La Découverte.

Cornelius, Wayne A. and Marc R. Rosenblum. 2005. "Immigration and Politics." *Annual Review of Political Science* 8: 99–119.

Cossu, Andrea. 2006. "The Commemoration of Traumatic Events: Expiation, Elevation and Reconciliation in the Remaking of the Italian Resistance." Quaderno 33, Facoltà di Sociologia, Università degli Studi Di Trento, Trento, Italy.

Council of Europe (EC). 1997. Council Regulation No. 1035/97 of 2 June 1997 establishing a European Monitoring Center on Racism and Xenophobia.

Curtis, Sarah A. 2000. *Educating the Faithful: Religion, Schooling and Society in Nineteenth-century France*. DeKalb, IL: Northern Illinois University Press.

Daley, Anthony, ed. 1996. *The Mitterrand Era: Policy Alternatives and Political Mobilization in France*. New York University Press.

Darnton, Robert. 2002. "A Euro State of Mind." *New York Review of Books* 49 (3): 30–32.

Dauncey, Hugh and Geoff Hare. 1999. "'33 Jours de fête': A Diary of France 98." Pp. 184–204 in *France and the 1998 World Cup: The National Impact of a World Sporting Event*, ed. Hugh Dauncey and Geoff Hare. London: Frank Cass.

Davis, Roy. 2002. "Citizenship of the Union ... Rights for All? *European Law Review* 27: 121–137.

DeClair, Edward G. 1999. *Politics on the Fringe: The People, Policies, and Organization of the French National Front*. Durham, NC: Duke University Press.

Declert, Vincent, Christophe Prochasson and Perrine Simon-Nahum, eds. 2003. *Il s'est passé quelque chose ... le 21 avril 2002*. Paris: Éditions Denoël.

De Felice, Renzo. 1995. *Rosso e nero*. Milan: Baldini and Castoldi.

Deflem, Mathieu. 2002. *Policing World Society: Historical Foundations of International Police Cooperation*. Oxford University Press.

Deflem, Mathieu and Fred C. Pampel. 1996. "The Myth of Postnational Identity: Popular Support for European Unification." *Social Forces* 75 (1): 119–143.

De Grazia, Victoria. 2005. *Irresistible Empire: America's Advance through Twentieth-Century Europe*. Cambridge, MA: Belknap Press of Harvard University Press.

DeJean, Joan E. 2005. *The Essence of Style: How the French Invented High Fashion, Fine Food, Chic Cafés, Style, Sophistication and Glamour*. New York: Free Press.

Della Porta, Donatella. 1995. *Social Movements, Political Violence, and the State: A Comparative Analysis of Italy and Germany*. Cambridge University Press.

Della Porta, Donatella and Sidney Tarrow, eds. 2005. *Transnational Protest and Global Activism*. Lanham, MD: Rowman & Littlefield.

De Master, Sara and Michael K. Le Ro. 2000. "Xenophobia and the European Union." *Comparative Politics* 32 (4): 419–436.

Deutsch, Karl W. 1953. *Nationalism and Social Communication*. Cambridge University Press.

Dézé, Alexandre. 2004. "Le populisme ou l'introuvable Cendrillon." *Revue Française de Science Politique* 54: 179–190.

Diamanti, Ilvo and Renato Mannheimer, eds. 1994. *Milano a Roma: guida all'Italia elettorale del 1994*. Rome: Donzelli.

Díez Medrano, Juan. 2003. *Framing Europe*. Princeton University Press.

Duplan, Christian. 2003. *Mon village à l'heure Le Pen*. Éditions du Seuil.

Dupoirier, Elisabeth, ed. 1998. *Régions: la croisée des chemins: perspectives françaises et enjeux européens*. Paris: Presses de Sciences Po.

Durand, Géraud. 1996. *Enquête au coeur du Front national*. Paris: Jacques Grancher.

Durkheim, Émile. [1895] 1966. *The Rules of Sociological Method*. New York: The Free Press.

Earl, Jennifer, Andrew Martin, John D. McCarthy and Sarah A. Soule. 2004. "The Use of Newspaper Data in the Study of Collective Action." *Annual Review of Sociology* 30: 65–80.

Eatwell, Roger. 1994. "Why Are Fascism and Racism Reviving in Western Europe?" *Political Quarterly* 65 (3) (July–September): 313–325.

2000. "The Rebirth of the 'Extreme Right' in Western Europe?" *Far-Right in Europe: In or Out of the Cold? Parliamentary Affairs*, special issue 53 (3): 407–531.

2002. "The Rebirth of Right-Wing Charisma? The Cases of Jean-Marie Le Pen and Vladimir Zhirinovsky." *Totalitarian Movements and Political Religions* 3 (3): 1–23.

2003. "Ten Theories of the Extreme Right." Pp. 47–73 in *Right-Wing Extremism in the Twenty-First Century*, ed. Peter H. Merkl and Leonard Weinberg. London: Frank Cass.

Eatwell, Roger and Cas Mudde. 2004. *Western Democracies and the New Extreme Right Challenge*. London and New York: Routledge.

Eichengreen, Barry J. 2006. *The European Economy since 1945: Coordinated Capitalism and Beyond*. Princeton University Press.

Eichengreen, Barry, James Tobin and Charles Wyplosz. 1995. "Two Cases for Sand in the Wheels of International Finance." *Economic Journal* 105 (428): 162–172.

Eley, Geoff. 2002. *Forging Democracy: The History of the Left in Europe 1850–2000*. Oxford University Press.

Eliasoph, Nina. 1998. *Avoiding Politics: How Americans Produce Apathy in Everyday Life*. Cambridge University Press.

Ellwood, David W. 1985. *Italy, 1943–1945*. New York: Holmes & Meier.

Entrikin, J. Nicholas. 1991. *The Betweenness of Place: Towards a Geography of Modernity*. Baltimore: Johns Hopkins University Press.

Entzinger, Han, Marco Martiniello and Catherine Wihtol de Wenden, eds. 2004. *Migration between States and Markets*. Aldershot: Ashgate Publishing.

Erb, Rainer and Hermann Kurthen. 1997. "Selected Chronology of Antisemitic and Extreme Right-Wing Events in Germany during and after Unification, 1989–1994." Pp. 263–285 in *Antisemitism and Xenophobia in Germany after Unification*, ed. Hermann Kurthen, Werner Bergmann and Rainer Erb. Oxford University Press.

Esping-Andersen, Gosta. 1997. "Welfare States at the End of the Century: The Impact of Labour Market, Family and Demographic Change." Pp. 63–80 in *Family, Market and Community: Equity and Efficiency in Social Policy*, Social Policy Studies, no. 21. Paris: OECD.

European Commission. 1999. *Affirming Fundamental Rights in the European Union: A Time to Act*. Brussels: European Commission.

2004a. *Citizenship and Sense of Belonging*. Special Eurobarometer Wave 60.1. European Research Group. http://ec.europa.eu/public_opinion/archives/ebs/ebs_199.pdf.

2004b. "Public Opinion on the European Union," Eurobarometer 62: National Report Executive Summary, France. http://ec.europa.eu/public_opinion/archives/eb/eb62/eb62_fr_exec.pdf.

2005. "The European Constitution: Post-referendum Survey in France." Brussels: Eurobarometer.

Evans, Peter B. 1997. "The Eclipse of the State? Reflections on Stateness in an Era of Globalization." *World Politics* 50 (1): 62–87.

Evans, Peter B., Dietrich Rueschemeyer and Theda Skocpol, eds. 1985. *Bringing the State Back In*. Cambridge University Press.

Favell, Adrian. 2008. *Eurostars and Eurocities*. Oxford: Blackwell.

Feldblum, Miriam. 1999. *Reconstructing Citizenship: The Politics of Nationality Reform and Immigration in Contemporary France*. Albany, NY: State University of New York Press.

Fella, Stefano. 2006. "From Fiuggi to the Farnesina: Gianfranco Fini's Remarkable Journey." *Journal of Contemporary European Studies* 14 (1): 11–23.

Fererra, Maurizio and Elisabetta Gualmini. 2004. *Rescued by Europe?: Social and Labour Market Reforms in Italy from Maastricht to Berlusconi*. University of Amsterdam Press.

Ferraresi, Franco. 1996. *Threats to Democracy: The Radical Right in Italy after the War*. Princeton University Press.

Ferry, Luc and Alain Renaut. 1992. *From the Rights of Man to the Republican Idea*, trans. Franklin Philip. University of Chicago Press.

Fhima, Catherine. 2000. *Chronologie de la France au XXe siècle.* Paris: Éditions Découverte.

Finer, Samuel E. 1975. "State and Nation-Building in Europe: The Role of the Military." Pp. 84–163 in *The Formation of National States in Western Europe,* ed. Charles Tilly. Princeton University Press.

Fini, Gianfranco and Carlo Fusi. 2003. *L'Europa che verrà: il destino del continente e il ruolo dell'Italia.* Roma: Fazi.

Fini, Gianfranco and Marcello Staglieno. 1999. *Un'Italia civile.* Milan: Ponte alle Grazie.

Fiss, Peer C. and Paul M. Hirsch. 2005. "The Discourse of Globalization: Framing and Sensemaking of an Emerging Concept." *American Sociological Review* 70: 29–52.

Fligstein, Neil. 2008. *Euroclash: The EU, European Identity, and the Future of Europe.* Oxford University Press.

Fligstein, Neil and Iona Mara-Drita. 1996. "How to Make a Market: Reflections on the Attempt to Create a Single Market in the European Union." *American Journal of Sociology* 102 (1): 1–33.

Fligstein, Neil and Alec Stone Sweet. 2002. "Constructing Politics and Markets: An Institutionalist Account of European Integration." *American Journal of Sociology* 107 (5): 1206–1243.

Focardi, Filippo. 2005. *La guerra della memoria: la Resistenza nel dibattito politico italiano dal 1945 a oggi.* Rome: Laterza.

Føllesdal, A. (1998) "Survey Article: Subsidiarity." *Journal of Political Philosophy* 6: 190–218.

Fort, Susanna. 1994. "Naziskin: fenomenologia dello spiritato." *Ponte* 50 (6) (June): 60–69.

Fourcade-Gourinchas, Marion and Sarah L. Babb. 2002. "The Rebirth of the Liberal Creed: Paths to Neoliberalism in Four Countries." *American Journal of Sociology* 108: 533–579.

Fourest, Caroline and Fiammetta Venner. 1998. *Le guide des sponsors du Front national et de ses amis.* Paris: R. Castells.

Friedland, Roger and Robert R. Alford. 1991. "Bringing Society Back In: Symbols, Practices and Institutional Contradictions." Pp. 232–263 in *The New Institutionalism in Organizational Analysis,* ed. Walter W. Powell and Paul J. DiMaggio. University of Chicago Press.

Fritzsche, Peter. 2001. "The Case of Modern Memory." *Journal of Modern History* 73: 87–117.

Gal, Susan and Gail Kligman. 2000. *The Politics of Gender after Socialism: A Comparative Historical Essay.* Princeton University Press.

Galli della Loggia, Ernesto. 1996. *La morte della patria.* Rome: Laterza.

Gaspard, Françoise. 1995. *A Small City in France*, trans. Arthur Goldhammer. Cambridge, MA: Harvard University Press.

Gaulle, Charles de. 1971. *Memoirs of Hope: Renewal and Endeavor*. Translated. New York: Simon and Schuster.

Geertz, Clifford. 1980. *Negara: The Theatre State in Nineteenth-Century Bali*. Princeton University Press.

Gerber, François. 1998. *Et la presse créa Le Pen* ... Paris: Raymond Castells Éditions.

Gerson, Stéphane. 2003. *The Pride of Place: Local Memories and Political Culture in Nineteenth-Century France*. Ithaca, NY: Cornell University Press.

Giddens, Anthony. 1994. *Beyond Left and Right: The Future of Radical Politics*. Cambridge: Polity.

   1998. *The Third Way: The Renewal of Social Democracy*. Cambridge: Polity Press.

Gieryn, Thomas F. 2000. "A Space for Place in Sociology." *Annual Review of Sociology* 26: 463–496.

Ginsborg, Paul. 2003. *Italy and Its Discontents*. New York: Palgrave Macmillan.

   2004. *Silvio Berlusconi: Television, Power and Patrimony*. London: Verso.

Givens, Terri E. 2005. *Voting Radical Right in Western Europe*. Cambridge University Press.

Gobbi, Romolo. 1992. *Il mito della Resistenza*. Milan: Rizzoli.

Gobetti, Piero. 2000. *On Liberal Revolution*, ed. Nadia Urbinati. New Haven: Yale University Press.

Golden, Miriam A. 1997. *Heroic Defeats: The Politics of Job Loss*. Cambridge University Press.

   2004. "International Economic Sources of Regime Change: How European Integration Undermined Italy's Postwar Party System." *Comparative Political Studies* 37 (10): 1238–1274.

Goldhagen, Daniel Jonah. 1996. *Hitler's Willing Executioners: Ordinary Germans and the Holocaust*. New York: Knopf.

Goldstein, Leslie Friedman. 2001. *Constituting Federal Sovereignty: The European Union in Comparative Context*. Baltimore: Johns Hopkins University Press.

Gordon, Philip H. 1993. *A Certain Idea of France: French Security Policy and the Gaullist Legacy*. Princeton University Press.

Gordon, Philip H. and Sophie Meunier. 2001. *The French Challenge: Adapting to Globalization*. Washington, DC: Brookings Institution Press.

Gorski, Philip S. 2003. *The Disciplinary Revolution: Calvinism and the Rise of the State in Early Modern Europe*. University of Chicago Press.

Gotman, Anne. 2001. *Le sens de l'hospitalité*. Paris: Presses Universitaires de France.

Gould, Roger V. 1995. *Insurgent Identities: Class, Community, and Protest in Paris from 1848 to the Commune*. University of Chicago Press.

Gras, Solange. 1982. "Regionalism and Autonomy in Alsace since 1918." Pp. 309–354 in *The Politics of Territorial Identity*, ed. Stine Rokkan and Derek W. Urwin. London: Sage.

Greenfeld, Liah. 1992. *Nationalism: Five Roads to Modernity*. Cambridge, MA: Harvard University Press.

Griffin, Larry J. 1993. "Narrative, Event-Structure Analysis, and Causal Interpretation in Historical Sociology." *American Journal of Sociology* 98: 1094–1133.

Grimm, Dieter. 1997. "Does Europe Need a Constitution?" Pp. 239–258 in *The Question of Europe*, ed. Peter Gowan and Perry Anderson. London: Verso.

Guillen, Mauro F. 2001. "Is Globalization Civilizing, Destructive, or Feeble? A Critique of Five Key Debates in the Social Science." *Annual Review of Sociology* 27: 235–260.

Guiraudon, Virginie. 2005. "Immigration Politics and Policies." Pp. 154–169 in *Developments in French Politics*, vol. III, ed. Alistair Cole, Patrick Le Galès and Jonah Levy. Basingstoke: Palgrave.

Guiraudon, Virginie and Gallya Lahav. 2006. *Immigration Policy in Europe: The Politics of Control. West European Politics*, special issue 29 (2).

Gundle, Stephen. 2000. "The 'Civic Religion' of the Resistance in Post-war Italy." *Modern Italy* 5 (2): 113–132.

Habermas, Jürgen. [1990] 1996. "Citizenship and National Identity." Pp. 491–515 in *Between Facts and Norms: Contributions to a Discourse Theory of Law and Democracy*. Cambridge, MA: MIT Press.

1997. "Reply to Grimm." Pp. 259–264 in *The Question of Europe*, ed. Peter Gowan and Perry Anderson. London: Verso.

2001. "Why Europe Needs a Constitution." *New Left Review* 11 (September–October): 1–12.

Hagan, John, Hans Merkens and Klaus Boehnke. 1995. "Delinquency and Disdain: Social Capital and the Control of Right-Wing Extremism among East and West Berlin Youth." *American Journal of Sociology* 100 (4): 1028–1052.

Hainsworth, Paul. 2000. "From Joan of Arc to Bardot: Immigration, Nationalism, Rights and the Front National." Pp. 53–67 in *Rewriting Rights in Europe*, ed. Linda Hancock and Carolyn O'Brien. Aldershot: Ashgate.

2006. "France Says No: The 29 May 2005 Referendum on the European Constitution." *Parliamentary Affairs* 59 (1): 98–117.

Hainsworth, Paul and Paul Mitchell. 2000. "France: The Front National from Crossroads to Crossroads?" *Parliamentary Affairs* 53: 443–456.

Hall, Peter A. 1986. *Governing the Economy: The Politics of State Intervention*. Oxford University Press.

2001. "The Evolution of Economic Policy." Pp. 172–190 in *Developments in French Politics*, vol. II, ed. Alain Guyomarch, Howard Machin, Peter A. Hall and Jack Hayward. Basingstoke: Palgrave.

2003. "Aligning Ontology and Methodology in Comparative Politics." Pp. 373–404 in *Comparative Historical Analysis in the Social Sciences*, ed. James Mahoney and Dietrich Rueschemeyer. Cambridge University Press.

Hall, Peter A. and Rosemary C. R. Taylor. 1996. "Political Science and the Three New Institutionalisms." *Political Studies* 44: 936–957.

Hansen, Randall and Patrick Weil. 2001. "Citizenship, Immigration and Nationality: Towards a Convergence in Europe?" Pp. 1–23 in *Towards a European Nationality*, ed. Randall Hansen and Patrick Weil. New York: Palgrave.

2002. *Dual Nationality, Social Rights and Federal Citizenship in the US and Europe: The Reinvention of Citizenship*. New York: Berghahn Books.

Hargreaves, Alec G. 2007. *Multi-Ethnic France: Immigration, Politics, Culture and Society*. New York and London: Routledge.

Harris, David and John Darcy. 2001. *The European Social Charter*, 2nd edn. Vol. XXV The Procedural Aspects of International Law Monograph Series. Ardsley, NY: Transnational Publishers, Inc.

Harris, Sue. 2000. "Festivals and *Fêtes Populaires*." Pp. 220–228 in *Contemporary French Cultural Studies*, ed. William Kidd and Siân Reynolds. London: Arnold.

Harvey, David. 2005. *A Brief History of Neoliberalism*. Oxford University Press.

Hayden, Anders. 2006. "France's 35-Hour Week: Attack on Business? Win-Win Reform? Or Betrayal of Disadvantaged Workers? *Politics and Society* 34 (2): 503–542.

Hazareesingh, Sudhir. 1998. *From Subject to Citizen: The Second Empire and the Emergence of Modern French Democracy*. Princeton University Press.

Hellman, Judith Adler. 1987. *Journeys Among Women: Feminism in Five Italian Cities.* Oxford University Press.

Hellman, Stephen. 1988. *Italian Communism in Transition: The Rise and Fall of the Historic Compromise in Turin, 1975–1980.* Oxford University Press.

Hermet, Guy. 1998. *La trahison démocratique: populistes, républicains et démocrates.* Paris: Flammarion.

2001. *Les populismes dans le monde.* Paris: Fayard.

Hine, David. 2004. "Explaining Italian Preferences at the Constitutional Convention." *Comparative European Politics* 2: 302–319.

Hirsch, Francine. 2005. *Empire of Nations: Ethnographic Knowledge and the Making of the Soviet Union.* Ithaca, NY: Cornell University Press.

Hirschman, Albert O. 1970. *Exit, Voice, and Loyalty; Responses to Decline in Firms, Organizations, and States.* Cambridge, MA: Harvard: University Press.

Hobsbawm, Eric. 1983. "Mass-Producing Traditions: Europe, 1870–1914." Pp. 263–307 in *The Invention of Tradition,* ed. Eric Hobsbawm and Terence Ranger. Cambridge University Press.

Hoffmann, Stanley. 1956. *Le mouvement Poujade.* Paris: A. Colin.

1974. *Decline or Renewal? France since the 1930s.* New York: Viking Press.

Hollifield, James F. 1991. "Immigration and Modernization." Pp. 113–150 in *Searching for the New France,* ed. James F. Hollifield and George Ross. London: Routledge.

1992. *Immigrants, Markets, and States: The Political Economy of Postwar Europe.* Cambridge, MA: Harvard University Press.

2004. "France: Republicanism and the Limits of Immigration Control." Pp. 183–214 in *Controlling Immigration: A Global Perspective,* ed. Wayne A. Cornelius, Takeyuki Tsuda, Philip L. Martin and James F. Hollifield. Stanford University Press.

Holmes, Douglas R. 2000. *Integral Europe: Fast-capitalism, Multiculturalism, Neofascism.* Princeton University Press.

Holmes, Stephen. 1993. *The Anatomy of Antiliberalism.* Cambridge, MA: Harvard University Press.

Hossay, Patrick. 2002. "Country Profiles." Pp. 317–345 in *Shadows over Europe: The Development and Impact of the Extreme Right in Europe,* ed. Martin Schain, Aristide Zolberg and Patrick Hossay. New York: Palgrave Macmillan.

Ignazi, Piero. 1989. *Il Polo escluso-profilo del Movimento Sociale Italiano.* Bologna: Il Mulino.

1994a. *L'estrema destra in Europa.* Bologna: Il Mulino.

1994b. *Postfascisti? Dal Movimento sociale italiano ad Alleanza nazionale*. Bologna: Mulino.

2003. *Extreme Right Parties in Western Europe*. Oxford University Press.

Ihl, Oliver, Janine Chêne, Éric Vial and Ghislain Waterlot, eds. 2003. *La tentation populiste au coeur de l'Europe*. Paris: La Découverte.

Ikegami, Eiko. 2005. *Bonds of Civility: Aesthetic Networks and the Political Origins of Japanese Culture*. Cambridge University Press.

Imig, Don and Sidney Tarrow. 2001. *Contentious Europeans: Protest and Politics in an Emerging Polity*. Lanham, MD: Rowman & Littlefield.

Immergut, Ellen M. 1998. "The Theoretical Core of the New Institutionalism." *Politics & Society* 26: 5–34.

Informations Syndicales Antifascistes. 2003. *Le Front national au travail*. Paris: Éditions Syllepse.

Inglehart, Ronald. 1977. *The Silent Revolution*. Princeton University Press.

Ionescu, Ghita and Ernest Gellner, eds. 1969. *Populism: Its Meaning and National Characteristics*. New York: Macmillan.

Ipsos. 2004. "Les Français et le référendum sur la Constitution européenne." Banque des Sondages, 9/28/2004. Ipsos.fr.

Italian Politics: A Review. 1986–2003. Vols. I–XVIII. Bologna: Istituto Carlo Cattaneo.

Ivaldi, Gilles. 2006. "Beyond France's 2005 Referendum on the European Constitutional Treaty: Second-Order Model, Anti-Establishment Attitudes and the End of the Alternative European Utopia." *West European Politics* 29 (1): 47–69.

Ivarsflaten, Elisabeth. 2005. "The Vulnerable Populist Right Parties: No Economic Realignment Fuelling Their Electoral Success." *European Journal of Political Research* 44: 465–492.

Jackman, Robert W. and Karin Volpert. 1996. "Conditions Favouring Parties of the Extreme Right in Western Europe." *British Journal of Political Science* 26: 501–521.

James, William. 1956. "The Sentiment of Rationality." Pp. 63–110 in *The Will to Believe and Other Essays in Popular Philosophy*. New York: Dover Publications, Inc.

Jay, Martin. 2005. *Songs of Experience: Modern American and European Variations on a Universal Theme*. Berkeley: University of California Press.

Jennings, Eric. 1994. "'Reinventing Jeanne': The Iconology of Joan of Arc in Vichy Schoolbooks, 1940–44." *Journal of Contemporary History* 29: 711–734.

John Paul II, Pope. 1984. *"Be Not Afraid!": John Paul II Speaks Out on His Life, His Beliefs, and His Inspiring Vision for Humanity.* New York: St. Martin's Press.

Joppke, Christian, ed. 1998. *Challenge to the Nation-State: Immigration in Western Europe and the United States.* Oxford University Press.

Jospin, Lionel. 2001. *The Flame, Not the Ashes.* Nottingham: Spokeman Books for Socialist Renewal, new series, no. 9.

   [2001] 2002. *My Vision of Europe and Globalization.* Cambridge: Polity.

   2002. *Le temps de répondre: Lionel Jospin: entretiens avec Alain Duhamel.* Paris: Stock.

Judt, Tony. 1992. *Past Imperfect: French Intellectuals, 1944–1956.* Berkeley: University of California Press.

   2000. "Tale from the Vienna Woods." *New York Review of Books,* March 23: 8–9.

   2005. *Postwar: A History of Europe since 1945.* New York: Penguin Press.

Judt, Tony and Denis Lacorne, eds. 2005. *With Us or Against Us: Studies in Global Anti-Americanism.* New York: Palgrave Macmillan.

Kaltenbach, Jeanne-Hélène and Michèle Tribalat. 2002. *La République et l'Islam: entre crainte et aveuglement.* Paris: Éditions Gallimard.

Karapin, Roger. 2002. "Far Right Parties and the Construction of Immigration Issues in Germany." Pp. 187–219 in *Shadows over Europe: The Development and Impact of the Extreme Right in Europe,* ed. Martin Schain, Aristide Zolberg and Patrick Hossay. New York: Palgrave Macmillan.

Kastoryano, Riva. 2002. *Negotiating Identities: States and Immigrants in France and Germany.* Princeton University Press.

Katzenstein, Peter J. 2005. *A World of Regions: Asia and Europe in the American Imperium.* Ithaca, NY: Cornell University Press.

Katzenstein, Peter J. and Robert O. Keohane, eds. 2007. *Anti-Americanisms in World Politics.* Ithaca, NY: Cornell University Press.

Keck, Margaret E. and Kathryn Sikkink. 1998. *Activists beyond Borders: Advocacy Networks in International Politics.* Ithaca, NY: Cornell University Press.

Keeler, John T. S. and Martin A. Schain, eds. 1996. *Chirac's Challenge: Liberalization, Europeanization, and Malaise in France.* New York: St. Martin's Press.

Kertzer, David I. 1980. *Comrades and Christians: Religion and Political Struggle in Communist Italy.* Cambridge University Press.

   1996. *Politics and Symbols: The Italian Communist Party and the Fall of Communism.* New Haven: Yale University Press.

Kitschelt, Herbert. 1995. *The Radical Right in Western Europe*. Ann Arbor, MI: University of Michigan Press.

Klandermans, Burt and Nonna Mayer. 2006. *Extreme Right Activists in Europe: Through the Magnifying Glass*. London: Routledge.

Klausen, Jytte. 1999. "The Declining Significance of Male Workers: Trade-Union Responses to Changing Labor Markets." Pp. 261–290 in *Continuity and Change in Contemporary Capitalism*, ed. Herbert Kitschelt, Peter Lange, Gary Marks and John D. Stephens. Cambridge University Press.

2005. *The Islamic Challenge: Politics and Religion in Western Europe*. Oxford University Press.

Knapp, Andrew. 2004. *Parties and the Party System in France: A Disconnected Democracy?* Basingstoke: Palgrave Macmillan.

Koenig-Archibugi, Mathias. 2003. "National and European Citizenship: The Italian Case in Historical Perspective." *Citizenship Studies* 7 (1): 85–109.

Kohn, Margaret. 2003. *Radical Space: Building the House of the People*. Ithaca, NY: Cornell University Press.

Koopmans, Ruud and Susan Olzak. 2004. "Discursive Opportunities and the Evolution of Right-Wing Violence in Germany." *American Journal of Sociology* 110 (1): 198–230.

Koopmans, Ruud and Paul Statham. 1999. "Challenging the Liberal Nation-state? Postnationalism, Multiculturalism, and the Collective Claims Making of Migrants and Ethnic Minorities in Britain and Germany." *American Journal of Sociology* 105 (3): 652–696.

Koopmans, Ruud, Paul Statham, Marco Giugni and Florence Passy. 2005. *Contested Citizenship: Immigration and Cultural Diversity in Europe*. Minneapolis: University of Minnesota Press.

Kramer, Jane. 1996. *The Politics of Memory: Looking for Germany in the New Germany*. New York: Random House.

Kramer, Steven Philip. 2006. "The End of French Europe?" *Foreign Affairs* (July/August) (foreignaffairs.org).

Krasner, Stephen. 1999. *Sovereignty*. Princeton University Press.

Kraus, Peter. 2000. "Political Unity and Linguistic Diversity in Europe." *European Journal of Sociology* 41 (1): 138–163.

Kriesi, Hanspeter. 1999. "Movements of the Left, Movements of the Right: Putting the Mobilization of Two New Types of Social Movements into Political Context." Pp. 398–423 in *Continuity and Change in Contemporary Capitalism*, ed. Herbert Kitschelt, Peter Lange, Gary Marks and John D. Stephens. Cambridge University Press.

Kumar, Krishan. 2005. *The Making of English National Identity.* Cambridge University Press.

Kymlicka, William. 1995. *Multicultural Citizenship: A Liberal Theory of Minority Rights.* Oxford: Clarendon Press.

Laborde, Cécile. 2001. "The Culture(s) of the Republic: Nationalism and Multiculturalism in French Republican Thought." *Political Theory* 26 (5): 716–735.

LaCapra, Dominick. 2004. *History in Transit: Experience, Identity, Critical Theory.* Ithaca, NY: Cornell University Press.

Lafont, Valerie. 2001. "Lutter contre l'immigration et s'engager au Front National." Pp. 163–184 in *Les croisés de la société fermée: l'Europe des extrêmes droites,* ed. Pascal Perrineau. Paris: Aube.

Lahav, Gallya. 2004. *Immigration and Politics in the New Europe: Reinventing Borders.* Cambridge University Press.

Laitin, David D. 1998. *Identity in Formation.* Ithaca, NY: Cornell University Press.

Lamont, Michèle. 2000. *The Dignity of Working Men: Morality and the Boundaries of Race, Class and Immigration.* Cambridge, MA: Harvard University Press; New York: Russell Sage Foundation.

Lamont, Michèle and Virag Molnar. 2002. "The Study of Boundaries in the Social Sciences." *Annual Review of Sociology* 28: 167–195.

Lamont, Michèle and Laurent Thévenot, eds. 2000. *Rethinking Comparative Cultural Sociology: Repertoires of Evaluation in France and the United States.* Cambridge University Press.

La Palombara, Joseph. 1964. *Interest Groups in Italian Politics.* Princeton University Press.

Le Bohec, Jacques. 2004. *L'implication des journalistes dans le phénomène Le Pen; interactions entre les journalistes et J.-M. Le Pen.* Paris: L'Harmattan.

Le Bon, Gustave. 1982. *The Crowd: A Study of the Popular Mind.* Marietta, GA: Larlin Corporation.

Lebovics, Herman. 1992. *True France: The Wars over Cultural Identity, 1900–1945.* Ithaca, NY: Cornell University Press.

2004. *Bringing the Empire Back Home: France in the Global Age.* Durham, NC: Duke University Press.

Le Bras, Hervé. 1991. *Marianne et les lapins: l'obsession démographique.* [Paris]: O. Orban.

1998. *Le démon des origines: démographie et extrême droite.* Paris: Éditions de l'Aube.

Le Galès, Patrick. 1998. "Government and Governance of Regions: Structural Weaknesses and New Mobilizations." In *Regions in Europe*, ed. Patrick Le Galès and C. Lequesne. London: Routledge.

2002. *European Cities: Social Conflicts and Governance*. Oxford University Press.

Legnami, Massimo. 1995. "Resistenza e democrazia: cinquant'anni di storia d'Italia." *Italia Contemporanea* 198: 5–17.

Le Pen, Jean-Marie. 1984. *Les Français d'abord*. Paris: Éditions Carrere-Michel Lafon.

1985. *Pour la France: programme du Front national*. Paris: Albatros.

1989. *L'espoir, entretien avec J. P. Gabriel et P. Gannat*. Paris: Albatros.

1991. *Le Pen 90: analyses et propositions*. Paris: Maule Éditions de Présent.

1999. *Lettres françaises ouvertes*. Paris: Objectif France SARL.

Le Roy Ladurie, Emmanuel. 2001. *Histoire de France des régions: la périphérie française des origines à nos jours*. Paris: Éditions du Seuil.

Leruth, Michael F. 2001. "French Intellectuals Come to Terms with Globalization." *Contemporary French Civilization* 25 (1): 43–83.

Lesselier, Claudie and Fiammetta Venner, eds. 1997. *L'extrême droite et les femmes: enjeux et actualité*. Brussels: Éditions Golias.

Levi, Margaret. 1998. "Conscription: The Price of Citizenship." Pp. 108–147 in *Analytic Narratives*, ed. Robert H. Bates, Avner Greif, Margaret Levi, Jean-Laurent Rosenthal and Barry R. Weingast. Princeton University Press.

Levreau, Jean-Louis. 2002. *Le syndrome Tapie*. Paris: Ramsay.

Levy, Carl. 2005. "The European Union after 9/11: The Demise of a Liberal Democratic Asylum Regime?" *Government and Opposition* 40: 26–59.

Levy, Daniel, Max Pensky and John Torpey, eds. 2005. *Old Europe, New Europe, Core Europe: Transatlantic Relations after the Iraq War*. London and New York: Verso.

Levy, Jonah D. 1999. *Tocqueville's Revenge: State, Society and Economy in Contemporary France*. Cambridge, MA: Harvard University Press.

Lewis-Beck, Michael S., ed. 2004. *The French Voter: Before and after the 2002 Elections*. Basingstoke: Palgrave Macmillan.

Lie, John. 2004. *Modern Peoplehood*. Cambridge, MA: Harvard University Press.

Lijphart, Arend. 1975. *The Politics of Accommodation: Pluralism and Democracy in the Netherlands*. Berkeley: University of California Press.

1977. *Democracy in Plural Societies: A Comparative Exploration*. New Haven: Yale University Press.

Lippmann, Walter. [1914] 1985. *Drift and Mastery: An Attempt to Diagnose the Current Unrest*, with a revised introduction and notes by William E. Leuchtenburg. Madison: University of Wisconsin Press.

Lipset, Seymour Martin. 1959. "Some Social Requisites of Democracy: Economic Development and Political Legitimacy." *American Political Science Review* 53: 69–105.

Lipset, Seymour Martin and Stein Rokkan, eds. 1967. *Party Systems and Voter Alignments: Cross-National Perspectives*. New York: The Free Press.

Livi-Bacci, Massimo. 2000. *The Population of Europe: A History*. Malden, MA: Blackwell.

Loader, Ian and Neil Walker. 2007. *Civilizing Security*. Cambridge University Press.

Lumley, Robert. 1990. *States of Emergency: Cultures of Revolt in Italy from 1968 to 1978*. New York: Verso.

McKeever, Lucy. 1999. "Reporting the World Cup: Old and New Media." Pp. 161–183 in *France and the 1998 World Cup: The National Impact of a World Sporting Event*, ed. Hugh Dauncey and Geoff Hare. London: Frank Cass.

Mahoney, James. 2000. "Path Dependence in Historical Sociology." *Theory and Society* 29: 507–548.

2003. "Long Run Development and the Legacy of Colonialism in Spanish America." *American Journal of Sociology* 109 (July): 50–106.

Maier, Charles S. 2000. "Consigning the Twentieth Century to History: Alternative Narratives for the Modern Era." *American Historical Review* 105 (3): 807–831.

Mann, Michael. 1993. *The Sources of Social Power*, vol. II: *The Rise of Classes and Nation-states, 1760–1914*. Cambridge University Press.

1997. "Has Globalization Ended the Rise and Rise of the Nation-state?" *Review of International Political Economy* 4 (Autumn): 472–496.

1998. "Is There a Society Called Euro?" Pp. 184–207 in *Globalization and Europe*, ed. Roland Axtmann. London: Pinter.

2004. *Fascists*. Cambridge University Press.

Mannheimer, Renato. 1991. *La lega lombarda*. Milan: Feltrinelli.

Manza, Jeff and Clem Brooks. 1999. *Social Cleavages and Political Change: Voter Alignments and US Party Coalitions*. Oxford University Press.

March, James G. and Johan P. Olsen. 1989. *Rediscovering Institutions: The Organizational Basis of Politics*. New York: Free Press.

Marcus, Jonathan. 1995. *The National Front and French Politics: The Resistible Rise of Jean-Marie Le Pen*. London: Macmillan.

Mares, Isabela. 2003. *The Politics of Social Risk: Business and Welfare State Development*. Cambridge University Press.

Markovits, Andrei S. 1998. "Reflections on the World Cup '98." *French Politics and Society* 16: 1–29.

Marks, John. 1999. "The French National Team and National Identity: 'Cette France d'un "bleu métis.""" Pp. 41–57 in *France and the 1998 World Cup: The National Impact of a World Sporting Event*, ed. Hugh Dauncey and Geoff Hare. London: Frank Cass.

Marshall, T. H. 1964. "Citizenship and Social Class." Pp. 71–134 in *Class, Citizenship and Social Development: Essays by T. H. Marshall*. University of Chicago Press.

Martin, Pierre. 1996. *Le vote Le Pen: l'électorat du Front national*. Paris: Notes de la Fondation Saint-Simon.

Martin, Roger. 1998. *Main basse sur Orange: une ville à l'heure lepéniste*. Paris: Calmann-Lévy.

1999. "Les élections du 15 mars 1998 dans la région Rhône-Alpes." Pp. 219–237 in *Le vote incertain: les élections régionales de 1998*, ed. Pascal Perrineau and Dominique Reynié. Paris: Presses de Sciences Po.

Martin, Virginie. 2002. *Toulon sous le Front national: entretiens non-directifs*. Paris: L'Harmattan.

Martinez, Jean-Claude. 1994. *Cent discours pour la France: le Front national à Strasbourg*. Paris: Éditions Lettres du Monde.

Massey, Douglas S., Joaquín Arango, Graeme Hugo *et al.* 1998. *Worlds in Motion: Understanding International Migration at the End of the Millennium*. Oxford: Clarendon Press.

Mayer, Nonna. 1992. "Carpentras and the Media." *Patterns of Prejudice* 26 (1 and 2): 48–63.

ed. 1995a. *Les collectifs anti-Front national*. Paris: FNSP – CNRS.

1995b. "The Dynamics of the Anti-Front National Countermovement." *French Politics and Society* 13 (4): 13–32.

[1999] 2002. *Ces Français qui votent FN*. Paris: Flammarion.

2003. "Le Pen's Comeback: The 2002 French Presidential Election." *International Journal of Urban and Regional Research* 27 (2): 455–459.

Mayer, Nonna and Pascal Perrineau. 1992. "Why Do They Vote for Le Pen?" *European Journal of Political Research* 22: 123–141.

eds. 1996. *Le Front national à découvert*. Paris: Presses de Sciences Po.

Mayer, Nonna and Vincent Tiberj. 2004. "Do Issues Matter? Law and Order in the 2002 French Presidential Election." Pp. 33–46 in *The French Voter: Before and after the 2002 Elections*, ed. Michael S. Lewis-Beck. Basingstoke: Palgrave Macmillan.

Mayeur, Jean-Marie. 2006. "A Frontier Memory: Alsace." Pp. 409–442 in *Rethinking France* [*Les lieux de mémoire*], ed. Pierre Nora, trans. Mary Trouille. University of Chicago Press.

Mégret, Bruno. 1998. *La Nouvelle Europe*. Saint-Cloud: Éditions Nationales.

Meguid, Bonnie M. 2005. "Competition between Unequals: The Role of Mainstream Party Strategy in Niche Party Success." *American Political Science Review* 99 (3): 347–359.

Mény, Yves and Yves Surel, eds. 2002. *Democracies and the Populist Challenge*. New York: Palgrave Macmillan.

Messina, Anthony M. 2007. *The Logics and Politics of Post-WWII Migration to Western Europe*. Cambridge University Press.

Meunier, Sophie. 2007. "The Distinctiveness of French Anti-Americanism." Pp. 104–145 in *Anti-Americanisms in World Politics*, ed. Peter J. Katzenstein and Robert O. Keohane. Ithaca, NY: Cornell University Press.

Michels, Roberto. 1949. "Patriotism." Pp. 156–166 in *First Lectures in Political Sociology*, trans. Alfred De Grazia. New York: Harper Torchbooks.

Miglio, Gianfranco. 1991. *Una costituzione per i prossimi trent'anni*. Rome: Laterza.

Miguet, Arnauld. 2002. "The French Elections of 2002: After the Earthquake, the Deluge." *West European Politics* 25 (4): 207–220.

Miller, David. 1995. *On Nationality*. Oxford: Clarendon Press.

Millet, Catherine. 2001. *La vie sexuelle de Catherine M.: récit*. Paris: Seuil.

Milward, Alan S. 1984. *The Reconstruction of Western Europe, 1945–51*. Berkeley: University of California Press.

2000. *The European Rescue of the Nation-State*, 2nd edn. London and New York: Routledge.

Mitra, Subrata. 1988. "The National Front in France – a Single Issue Movement." *West European Politics* 11 (2): 47–64.

Moch, Leslie Page. [1992] 2003. *Moving Europeans: Migration in Western Europe since 1650*. Bloomington, IN: Indiana University Press.

Moravcsik, Andrew. 1998. *The Choice for Europe: Social Purpose and State Power from Messina to Maastricht*. Ithaca, NY: Cornell University Press.

2000a. "De Gaulle between Grain and Grandeur: The Political Economy of French EC Policy, 1958–1970 (Part I)." *Journal of Cold War Studies* 2 (2): 3–43.

2000b. "De Gaulle between Grain and Grandeur: The Political Economy of French EC Policy, 1958–1970 (Part II)." *Journal of Cold War Studies* 2 (3): 4–68.

2000c. "The Origins of Human Rights Regimes: Democratic Delegation in Postwar Europe." *International Organization* 54: 217–52.

2005. "Europe Works Well Without the Grand Illusions." *Financial Times* (June 13) FT.com.

2006. "What Can We Learn from the Collapse of the European Constitutional Project?" *Politische Vierteljahresschrift* 47 (2): 219–241.

Moravcsik, Andrew and Kalypso Nicolaidis. 1999. "Explaining the Treaty of Amsterdam: Interests, Influence, Institutions." *Journal of Common Market Studies* 37 (1): 59–85.

Morgan, Glyn. 2005. *The Idea of a European Superstate: Public Justification and European Integration.* Princeton University Press.

Morgan, Kimberly J. 2006. *Working Mothers and the Welfare State: Religion and the Politics of Work–Family Policies in Western Europe and the United States.* Stanford University Press.

Moss, Bernard H. 1998. "Economic and Monetary Union and the Social Divide in France." *Contemporary European History* 7: 227–247.

Mudde, Cas. 2000. *The Ideology of the Extreme Right.* Manchester University Press.

2004. "The Populist Zeitgeist." *Government and Opposition* 39 (3): 542–563.

2007. *Populist Radical Right Parties in Europe.* Cambridge University Press.

Muxel, Anne. 2005. "Les abstentionnistes: le premier parti européen." Pp. 45–76 in *Le vote européen*, ed. Pascal Perrineau. Paris: Presses de Sciences.

National Front (FN). 1993. *300 mesures pour la renaissance de la France.* Paris: Éditions Nationals.

2001. *Pour un avenir français: le programme de gouvernement du Front national.* Paris: Godefroy de Bouillon.

2002. *The National Front at 30 Years.* (Video)

Newell, James, ed. 2002. *The Italian General Election of 2001: Berlusconi's Victory.* Manchester University Press.

Newell, James L. and Martin Bull. 1997. "Party Organisations and Alliances in Italy in the 1990s: A Revolution of Sorts." *Western European Politics* 20 (June): 81–109.

Noiriel, Gérard. 1996. *The French Melting Pot: Immigration, Citizenship and National Identity*, trans. Geoffrey de Laforcade. Minneapolis: University of Minnesota Press.

Nora, Pierre. 1989. "Between Memory and History: *Les Lieux de Mémoire.*" *Representations* 26: 7–25.

Nord, Philip. 1995. *The Republican Moment*. Cambridge, MA: Harvard University Press.

Norris, Pippa. 2005. *Radical Right: Voters and Parties in the Electoral Market*. Cambridge University Press.

Norton, Anne. 1993. *Republic of Signs*. University of Chicago Press.

  2004. *95 Theses on Politics, Culture, and Method*. New Haven: Yale University Press.

Oakes, Leigh. 2001. *Language and National Identity: Comparing France and Sweden*. Amsterdam: J. Benjamins Publishing Co.

Offe, Claus. 1996. "Modern 'Barbarity': A Micro-State of Nature?" *Constellations* 2 (3): 355–377.

  2000. "Civil Society and Social Order: Demarcating and Combining Market, State and Community." *European Journal of Sociology* 41 (1): 71–94.

  2003. "The European Model of 'Social' Capitalism: Can it Survive European Integration?" *Journal of Political Philosophy* 11: 437–469.

Olick, Jeffrey K. and Joyce Robbins. 1998. "Social Memory Studies: From 'Collective Memory' to the Historical Sociology of Mnemonic Practices." *Annual Review of Sociology* 24: 105–140.

Ozouf, Mona. 1963. *L'école, l'église et la République, 1871–1914*. Paris: A. Colin.

Padoa-Schioppa, Tommaso. 2001. "Italy and Europe: A Fruitful Interaction." *Daedalus* 130 (Spring): 13–44.

Pasquino, Gianfranco. 2001. "The Italian National Elections of 13 May 2001." *Journal of Modern Italian Studies* 6 (3): 371–387.

  2002. "The Political Context 1996–2001." Pp. 29–36 in *The Italian General Election of 2001*, ed. James Newell. Manchester University Press.

Passerini, Luisa. 1984. *Torino operaia e fascismo*. Rome: Laterza.

Patriarca, Silvana. 1996. *Numbers and Nationhood*. Cambridge University Press.

  2001. "Italian Neopatriotism: Debating National Identity in the 1990s." *Modern Italy* 6 (1): 21–34.

Patterson, Orlando. 2007. "Review of William H. Sewell, Jr., *Logics of History*." *American Journal of Sociology* 112 (4): 1287–1290.

Patterson, Thomas E. 2002. *The Vanishing Voter: Public Involvement in an Age of Uncertainty*. New York: Vintage Books.

Paul, T. V., G. J. Ikenberry and John A. Hall, eds. 2003. *The Nation-state in Question*. Princeton University Press.

Pavone, Claudio. 1991. *Una guerra civile*. Turin: Bollati Boringhieri.

Paxton, Robert O. 1972. *Vichy France: Old Guard and New Order, 1940–1944*. New York: Knopf.

2004. *The Anatomy of Fascism.* New York: Knopf.

Pedersen, Susan. 1993. *Family, Dependence, and the Origins of the Welfare State: Britain and France, 1914–1945.* Cambridge University Press.

Pérez-Díaz, Víctor M. 1993. *The Return of Civil Society: The Emergence of Democratic Spain.* Cambridge, MA: Harvard University Press.

Perlmutter, Ted. 1996. "Immigration Politics Italian Style: The Paradoxical Behaviour of Mainstream and Populist Parties." *Southern European Society and Politics* 1 (2): 229–252.

Perrineau, Pascal. 1997. *Le symptôme Le Pen.* Paris: Librairie Arthème Fayard.

ed. 2001. *Les croisés de la société fermée: l'Europe des extrêmes droites.* La Tour d'Aigues: Éditions de l'Aube.

2003. *Le désenchantement démocratique.* La Tour d'Aigues: Éditions de l'Aube.

ed. 2005. *Le vote européen 2004–2005.* Paris: Presses de Sciences Po.

Perrineau, Pascal and Dominique Reynié, eds. 1999. *Le vote incertain: les élections régionales de 1998.* Paris: Presses de Sciences Po.

Perrineau, Pascal and Colette Ysmal, eds. 2003. *Le vote de tous les refus: les élections présidentielle et législatives de 2002.* Paris: Presses de Sciences Po.

Petersen, Roger D. 2002. *Understanding Ethnic Violence: Fear, Hatred, and Resentment in Twentieth-Century Eastern Europe.* Cambridge University Press.

Pettigrew, Thomas F. 1998. "Reactions Towards the New Minorities of Western Europe." *Annual Review of Sociology* 24: 77–103.

Pierson, Paul. 2004. *Politics in Time: History, Institutions, and Social Analysis.* Princeton University Press.

Pinder, John. 2001. *The European Union: A Very Short Introduction.* Oxford University Press.

Piore, Michael J. and Charles F. Sabel. 1984. *The Second Industrial Divide: Possibilities for Prosperity.* New York: Basic Books.

Platone, François and Henri Rey. 1996. "Le FN en terre communiste." Pp. 268–283 in *Le Front national à découvert*, ed. Nonna Mayer and Pascal Perrineau. Paris: Presses de Sciences Po.

Poggi, Gianfranco. 1978. *The Development of the Modern State: A Sociological Introduction.* Stanford University Press.

Polletta, Francesca. 2006. *It was Like a Fever: Storytelling in Protest and Politics.* University of Chicago Press.

Polletta, Francesca and James M. Jasper. 2001. "Collective Identity and Social Movements." *Annual Review of Sociology* 27: 283–305.

Pontusson, Jonas. 2005. *Inequality and Prosperity: Social Europe Vs. Liberal America*. Ithaca, NY: Cornell University Press.

Portes, Alejandro. 1998. "Social Capital: Its Origins and Applications in Modern Sociology." *Annual Review of Sociology* 24: 1–24.

Prasad, Monica. 2005. "Why is France so French? Culture, Institutions, and Neoliberalism, 1974–1981." *American Journal of Sociology* 111: 357–407.

    2006. *The Politics of Free Markets: The Rise of Neoliberal Economic Policies in Britain, France, Germany, and the United States*. University of Chicago Press.

Pred, Allan. 2000. *Even in Sweden: Racisms, Racialized Spaces, and the Popular Geographical Imagination*. Berkeley: University of California Press.

Prowe, Diethelm. 1994. "'Classic' Fascism and the New Radical Right in Western Europe: Comparisons and Contrasts." *Contemporary European History* 3 (3): 289–313.

Putnam, Robert D. with Robert Leonardi and Raffaella Y. Nanetti. 1993. *Making Democracy Work: Civic Traditions in Modern Italy*. Princeton University Press.

Quazza, Guido. 1976. *Resistenza e storia d'Italia: problemi e ipotesi di ricerca*. Milan: Feltrinelli.

Quillian, Lincoln. 1995. "Prejudice as a Response to Perceived Group Threat: Population Composition and Anti-immigrant and Racial Prejudice in Europe." *American Sociological Review* 60: 586–611.

Rainer, Erb and Hermann Kurthen. 1997. "Selected Chronology of Antisemitic and Extreme Right-Wing Events in Germany during and after Unification, 1989–1994." Pp. 263–285 in *Antisemitism and Xenophobia in Germany after Unification*, ed. Hermann Kurthen, Werner Bergmann and Rainer Erb. Oxford University Press.

Rajsfus, Maurice. 1998. *En gros et en détail: Le Pen au quotidien, 1987–1997*. Paris: Éditions Paris Méditerranée.

Reinhard, Philippe. 1991. *Bernard Tapie, ou, la politique au culot: Bernard Tapie*. Paris: France-Empire.

Rémond, René. 1969. *The Right Wing in France from 1815 to De Gaulle*. Philadelphia: University of Pennsylvania Press.

    2005. *Les droites aujourd'hui*. Paris: Éditions Louis Audibert.

Renan, Ernest. [1882] 1996. "What is a Nation?" Pp. 42–55 in *Becoming National*, ed. Geoff Eley and Ronald Grigor Suny. Oxford University Press.

Reumaux, Bernard and Philippe Breton. 1997. *L'appel de Strasbourg: le réveil des démocrates*. Strasbourg: La Nuée Bleue.

Revel, Jean-François. 2002. *L'obsession anti-américaine: son fonctionnement, ses causes, ses inconséquences.* Paris: Plon.

Reynié, Dominique. 1999. "Mobilisation électorale et mobilisation d'opinion." Pp. 71–111 in *Le vote incertain: les élections régionales de 1998,* ed. Pascal Perrineau and Dominique Reynié. Paris: Presses de Sciences Po.

"Right-Wing Extremism in Western Europe." 1988. *West European Politics,* special issue 11 (2).

Ringmar, Erik. 1996. *Identity, Interest, and Action: A Cultural Explanation of Sweden's Intervention in the Thirty Years War.* Cambridge University Press.

Robert, Michel. 2003. *Petit manuel anti-FN: pour un Réveil citoyen.* Villeurbanne: Éditions Golias.

Robert, Philippe. 2002. *L'insécurité en France.* Paris: Éditions la Découverte.

Robin, Corey. 2004. *Fear: The History of a Political Idea.* Oxford University Press.

Roché, Sébastian. 1998. "Expliquer le sentiment d'insécurité: pression, exposition, vulnérabilité et acceptabilité." *Revue Française de Science Politique* 48 (2): 274–305.

Rogers, Susan Carol. 2002. "Which Heritage? Nature, Culture, and Identity in French Rural Tourism." *French Historical Studies* 25: 475–503.

Rokkan, Stein. 1975. "Dimensions of State Formation and Nation-Building: A Possible Paradigm for Research on Variations within Europe." Pp. 562–600 in *The Formation of National States in Western Europe,* ed. Charles Tilly. Princeton University Press.

Romero, Federico. 1990. "Cross-border Population Movements." Pp. 171–191 in *The Dynamics of European Integration,* ed. William Wallace. London and New York: Pinter.

Rosanvallon, Pierre. [1995] 2000. *The New Social Question: Rethinking the Welfare State,* trans. Barbara Harshaw. Princeton University Press.

2000. *La démocratie inachevée: histoire de la souveraineté du peuple en France.* Paris: Éditions Gallimard.

2004. *Le modèle politique français: la société civile contre le jacobinisme de 1789 à nos jours.* Paris: Éditions de Seuil.

Ross, George. 1995. *Jacques Delors and European Integration.* Cambridge: Polity Press.

1999. "Europe Becomes French Domestic Politics." Pp. 87–114 in *How France Votes,* ed. Michael S. Lewis-Beck. New York and London: Chatham House Publishers.

Ross, George, Stanley Hoffmann, Sylvia Malzacher, eds. 1987. *The Mitterrand Experiment: Continuity and Change in Modern France.* Oxford University Press.

Rothschild, Emma. 1995. "What is Security?" *Daedalus* 142 (Summer): 53–98.

Rousso, Henry. 1991. *The Vichy Syndrome: History and Memory in France since 1944.* Cambridge, MA: Harvard University Press.

Roversi, Antonio. 1995. "I naziskin italiani: studio di un caso." *Polis* 9 (3) (December): 425–446.

Rydgren, Jens. 2007. "The Sociology of the Radical Right." *Annual Review of Sociology* 33: 241–362.

Sa'adah, Anne. 2003. *Contemporary France: A Democratic Education.* Lanham, MD: Rowman & Littlefield.

Saguy, Abigail C. 2003. *What is Sexual Harassment?: From Capitol Hill to the Sorbonne.* Berkeley: University of California Press.

Sahlins, Marshall. 1991. "The Return of the Event, Again: With Reflections on the Beginnings of the Great Fijian War of 1843 to 1855 between the Kingdoms of Bau and Rewa." Pp. 37–99 in *Clio in Oceania: Toward a Historical Anthropology*, ed. Aletta Biersack. Washington, DC: Smithsonian Institution Press.

Sahlins, Peter. 1989. *Boundaries: The Making of France and Spain in the Pyrenees.* Berkeley: University of California Press.

Salvati, Michele. 1995. "The Crisis of Government in Italy." *New Left Review* (September/October): 76–95.

Samson, Michel. 1997. *Le Front national aux affaires: deux ans d'enquête sur la vie municipale à Toulon.* Paris: Calmann-Lévy.

Sarkozy, Nicolas. 2007. *Testimony: France in the Twenty-First Century.* New York: Pantheon Books.

Sassen, Saskia. 2006. *Territory, Authority, Rights: From Medieval to Global Assemblages.* Princeton University Press.

Savidan, Patrick. 2004. *La république ou l'Europe?* Paris: Librairie Générale Française.

Scarry, Elaine. 1999. "The Difficulty of Imagining Other Persons." Pp. 277–309 in *Human Rights in Political Transitions*, ed. Carla Hesse and Robert Post. New York: Zone Books.

Schain, Martin A. 1987. "The National Front and the Construction of Political Legitimacy." *West European Politics* 10 (2): 229–252.

1996. "The Immigration Debate and the National Front." Pp. 169–197 in *Chirac's Challenge: Liberalization, Europeanization and Malaise in France*, ed. Martin A. Schain and John T. S. Keeler. New York: St. Martin's Press.

1997. "Review Essay: Herbert Kitschelt, *The Radical Right in Western Europe.*" *Comparative Political Studies* 30: 375–380.

1999. "The National Front and the Legislative Elections of 1997." Pp. 69–86 in *How France Votes*, ed. Michael S. Lewis-Beck. New York and London: Chatham House Publishers.

Schain, Martin, Aristide Zolberg and Patrick Hossay, eds. 2002. *Shadows over Europe: The Development and Impact of the Extreme Right in Europe.* New York: Palgrave Macmillan.

Scheler, Max. [1915] 1992. *On Feeling, Knowing, and Valuing: Selected Writings.* University of Chicago Press.

Schiavone, Aldo. 1998. *Italiani senza Italia: storia e identita.* Turin: Einaudi.

Schmidt, Vivien Ann. 1996. *From State to Market?: The Transformation of French Business and Government.* Cambridge University Press.

Schmitter, Philippe C. 2001. "Parties Are Not What They Once Were." Pp. 67–89 in *Political Parties and Democracy*, ed. Larry Diamond and Richard Gunther. Baltimore: Johns Hopkins University Press.

Schnapper, Dominique. 1995. "Penser la 'préférence nationale.'" Pp. 199–210 in *Combattre le Front national*, ed. David Martin-Castelnac. Paris: Vinci.

2002. "Citizenship and National Identity in Europe." *Nations and Nationalism* 8 (1): 1–14.

Schor, Ralph. 1985. *L'opinion française et les étrangers en France, 1919–1939.* Paris: Publications de la Sorbonne.

Sciortino, Giuseppe. 1999. "'Just before the Fall': The Northern League and the Cultural Construction of a Secessionist Claim." *International Sociology: Journal of the International Sociological Association* 14: 233–260.

Scott, Joan W. 1996. "The Evidence of Experience." Pp. 379–406 in *The Historic Turn in the Human Sciences*, ed. Terence J. McDonald. Ann Arbor: University of Michigan Press.

2005. *Parité!: Sexual Equality and the Crisis of French Universalism.* University of Chicago Press.

2007. *The Politics of the Veil.* Princeton University Press.

Serneri, Simone Neri. 1995. "Italian Resistance." *Contemporary European History* 4: 367–81.

Sewell, William H. 1996a. "Historical Events as Transformations of Structures: Inventing Revolution at the Bastille." *Theory and Society* 25: 841–881.

1996b. "Three Temporalities: Toward an Eventful Sociology." Pp. 245–280 in *The Historic Turn in the Human Sciences*, ed. Terence McDonald. Ann Arbor: University of Michigan Press.

2001. "Space in Contentious Politics." Pp. 89–125 in *Silence and Voice in the Study of Contentious Politics*, ed. Ronald R. Aminzade, Jack A. Goldstone, Doug McAdam *et al.* Cambridge University Press.

2005. *Logics of History: Social Theory and Social Transformation.* University of Chicago Press.

Shields, James. 2006. "Political Representation in France: A Crisis of Democracy?" *Parliamentary Affairs* 59 (1): 118–137.

2007. *The Extreme Right in France: From Pétain to Le Pen.* London: Routledge.

Shin, Michael E. and John Agnew. 2008. *Berlusconi's Italy: Mapping Contemporary Italian Politics.* Philadelphia: Temple University Press.

Silverstein, Paul A. 2004. *Algeria in France.* Bloomington, IN: Indiana University Press.

Simmel. Georg. [1908] 1971. "Sociability." Pp. 127–140 in *On Individuality and Social Forms*, ed. Donald N. Levine. University of Chicago Press.

Skach, Cindy. 2005. *Borrowing Constitutional Designs: Constitutional Law in Weimar Germany and the French Fifth Republic.* Princeton University Press.

Slaughter, Anne-Marie. 2004. *A New World Order.* Princeton University Press.

Smelser, Neil J. 1998. "The Rational and the Ambivalent in the Social Sciences." *American Sociological Review* 63: 1–15.

Smith, Philip. 2005. *Why War?: The Cultural Logic of Iraq, the Gulf War, and Suez.* University of Chicago Press.

Smith, Rogers M. 2003. *Stories of Peoplehood: The Politics and Morals of Political Membership.* Cambridge University Press.

Smith, Timothy B. 2004. *France in Crisis: Welfare, Inequality and Globalization since 1980.* Cambridge University Press.

Sniderman, Paul M., Pierangelo Peri, Rui J.P. de Figueiredo, Jr. and Thomas Piazza. 2000. *The Outsider: Prejudice and Politics in Italy.* Princeton University Press.

Sofres. 2005. *L'image du Front national dans l'opinion*, December 7–8, 2005. Paris: Sofres. http://2007.tns-sofres.com/etude.php?id=209.

Somers, Margaret R. 1993. "Citizenship and the Place of the Public Sphere: Law, Community, and Political Culture in the Transition to Democracy." *American Sociological Review* 58 (October): 587–620.

1994. "The Narrative Constitution of Identity: A Relational and Network Approach." *Theory and Society* 23: 605–649.

1995. "What's Political or Cultural about Political Culture and the Public Sphere? Towards an Historical Sociology of Concept Formation." *Sociological Theory* 13 (2): 113–144.

1996. "Where is Sociology after the Historic Turn? Knowledge Cultures, Narrativity and Historical Epistemologies." Pp. 53–90 in *The Historic Turn in the Human Sciences*, ed. Terrence J. McDonald. Ann Arbor: University of Michigan Press.

2005. "Beware Trojan Horses Bearing Social Capital: How Ideational Power Turned Gdansk into a Bowling Alley." Pp. 233–274 in *The Politics of Method in the Human Sciences: Positivism and its Epistemological Others*, ed. George Steinmetz. Durham, NC: Duke University Press.

Somers, Margaret R. and Gloria D. Gibson. 1994. "Reclaiming the Epistemological 'Other': Narrative and the Social Constitution of Identity." Pp. 37–99 in *Social Theory and the Politics of Identity*, ed. Craig Calhoun. London: Blackwell.

Souchard, Maryse, Stéphane Wahnich, Isabelle Cuminal and Virginie Wathier. 1997. *Le Pen – les mots: analyse d'un discours d'extrême-droite*. Paris: Le Monde Éditions.

Soudais, Michel. 1996. *Le Front national en face*. Paris: Flammarion.

Soysal, Yasemin N. 1994. *Limits of Citizenship: Migrants and Postnational Membership in Europe*. University of Chicago Press.

1997. "Changing Parameters of Citizenship and Claims-Making: Organized Islam in European Public Spheres." *Theory and Society* 26 (4): 509–527.

Spillman, Lyn and Russell Faeges. 2005. "Nations." Pp. 409–437 in *Remaking Modernity: Politics, History, and Sociology*, ed. Julia Adams, Elisabeth S. Clemens and Ann Shola Orloff. Durham, NC: Duke University Press.

Stasi, Bernard. 1984. *L'immigration: une chance pour la France*. Paris: R. Laffont.

Steinmetz, George, ed. 2005. *The Politics of Method in the Human Sciences: Positivism and its Epistemological Others*. Durham, NC: Duke University Press.

2008. "Sewell's *Logics of History* as a Framework for an Integrated Social Science." *Social Science History* 32 (4).

Sternhell, Zeev. 1986. *Neither Right nor Left: Fascist Ideology in France*. Berkeley: University of California Press.

1994. *The Birth of Fascist Ideology*. Princeton University Press.

Stille, Alexander. 2006. *The Sack of Rome: How a Beautiful European Country with a Fabled History and a Storied Culture Was Taken Over by a Man Named Silvio Berlusconi*. New York: Penguin Press.

Storia d'Italia, cronologia 1815–1990. 1991. Novara: Istituto Geografico De Agostini.

Stoss, Richard. 1988. "The Problem of Right-Wing Extremism in West Germany." *West European Politics* 11 (2): 34–46.

Suny, Ronald Grigor. 2001. "Constructing Primordialism: Old Histories for New Nations." *Journal of Modern History* 73 (4): 862–896.

Sweet, Alec Stone, Neil Fligstein and Wayne Sandholtz. 2001. "The Institutionalization of European Space." Pp. 1–28 in *The Institutionalization of Europe*, ed. Alec Stone Sweet, Neil Fligstein and Wayne Sandholtz. Oxford University Press.

Swyngedouw, Marc. 2000. "Mesure de la volatilité Électorale en France (1993–1997)." *Revue Française de Science Politique* 50: 489–514.

Sznader, Mario. 1995. "Italy's Right-wing Government: Legitimacy and Criticism." *International Affairs* 71 (1): 83–102.

Taggart, Paul. 2002. "Populism and the Pathology of Representative Politics." Pp. 62–80 in *Democracies and the Populist Challenge*, ed. Yves Mény and Yves Surel. New York: Palgrave Macmillan.

Taguieff, Pierre-André. 2001. *The Force of Prejudice*, trans. and ed. Hassan Melehy. Minnesota: University of Minnesota Press.

2002. *L'illusion populiste: de l'archaïque au médiatique*. Paris: Berg International Éditeurs.

2004. *Le retour du populisme: un défi pour les démocraties européennes*. Paris: Encyclopaedia Universalis France.

Taguieff, Pierre-André and Michèle Tribalat. 1998. *Face au Front national: arguments pour une contre-offensive*. Paris: Éditions la Découverte.

Tajfel, Henri. 1981. *Human Groups and Social Categories: Studies in Social Psychology*. Cambridge University Press.

Tarchi, Marco. 1995. *Cinquant'anni di nostalgia*. Milan: Rizzoli.

1997. *Dal MSI ad AN: organizzazione e strategie*. Bologna: Il Mulino.

2003a. *L'Italia populista: dal qualunquismo ai girotondi*. Bologna: Il Mulino.

2003b. "The Political Culture of the Alleanza Nazionale: An Analysis of the Party's Programmatic Documents (1995–2002)." *Journal of Modern Italian Studies* 8 (2): 135–181.

Tarrow, Sidney. 1977. *Between Center and Periphery: Grassroots Politicians in Italy and France*. New Haven: Yale University Press.

1989. *Democracy and Disorder: Protest and Politics in Italy 1965–1975*. Oxford: Clarendon Press.

2005. *The New Transnational Activism*. Cambridge University Press.

2006. "President's Letter: Space and Comparative Politics." *APSA-CP* 17 (1) (Winter): 1–4.

Tassani, Giovanni. 1990. "The Italian Social Movement: From Almirante to Fini." Pp. 124–145 in *Italian Politics*, vol. IV, ed. Raffaella Y. Nanetti and Raimondo Catanzaro. London: Pinter.

Teitelbaum, Michael S. and Jay Winter. 1998. *A Question of Numbers: High Migration, Low Fertility and the Politics of National Identity.* New York: Hill and Wang.

Terrio, Susan J. 1999. "Crucible of the Millennium?: The Clovis Affair in Contemporary France." *Comparative Studies in Society and History* 41: 438–457.

Thelen, Kathleen. 1999. "Historical Institutionalism in Comparative Politics." *Annual Review of Political Science* 2: 369–404.

Thogmartin, Clyde. 1998. *The National Daily Press of France.* Birmingham, AL: Summa Publications.

Throop, Jason. 2003. "Articulating Experience." *Anthropological Theory* 3(2): 219–241.

Tiersky, Ronald, ed. 2001. *Euro-Skepticism: A Reader.* Lanham, MD: Rowman & Littlefield.

Tilly, Charles. 1985. "War Making and State Making as Organized Crime." Pp. 169–191 in *Bringing the State Back In*, ed. Peter B. Evans, Dietrich Rueschemeyer and Theda Skocpol. Cambridge University Press.

1986. *The Contentious French.* Cambridge, MA: Belknap Press of Harvard University Press.

2002. *Stories, Identities, and Political Change.* Lanham, MD: Rowman & Littlefield.

Toinet, Marie-France. 1996. "The Limits of Malaise in France." Pp. 279–300 in *Chirac's Challenge: Liberalization, Europeanization, and Malaise in France*, ed. John T. S. Keeler and Martin A. Schain. New York: St. Martin's Press.

Tranfaglia, Nicola. 1996. *Un passato scomodo: fascismo e postfascismo.* Rome: Laterza.

Tribalat, Michèle. 1999. *Dreux: voyage au coeur du malaise française.* Paris: Syros.

Tribalat, Michèle, Jean-Pierre Garson, Yann Moulier-Boutang and Roxane Silberman. 1991. *Cent ans d'immigration, étrangers d'hier français d'aujord'hui: apport démographique, dynamique familiale et économique de l'immigration étrangère.* Presses Universitaires de France – Institut National d'Études Démographiques.

Tumblety, Joan. 1999. "Contested Histories: Jeanne d'Arc and the Front National." *The European Legacy* 4 (1): 8–25.

Turner, Bryan S. 2001. "The Erosion of Citizenship." *British Journal of Sociology* 52 (2): 189–209.

United Nations. 2000. *Replacement Migration: Is it a Solution to Declining and Aging Population?* Population Division, Department of Economic and Social Affairs. New York: United Nations Press.

Urbinati, Nadia. 1998. "Democracy and Populism." *Constellations* 5 (1): 111–124.

Van de Steeg, Marianne. 2006. "Does a Public Sphere Exist in the European Union? An Analysis of the Content of the Debate on the Haider Case." *European Journal of Political Research* 45: 609–634.

Van Holsteyn, Joop J. M. and Galen A. Irwin. 2003. "Never a Dull Moment: Pim Fortuyn and the Dutch Parliamentary Election of 2002." *West European Politics* 26 (2): 41–66.

Veugelers, John. 1997. "Social Cleavage and the Revival of Far Right Parties: The Case of France's National Front." *Acta Sociologica* 40: 31–50.

Veugelers, Jack and Michèle Lamont. 1991. "France: Alternative Locations for Public Debate." Pp. 125–156 in *Between States and Markets: The Voluntary Sector in Comparative Perspective*, ed. Robert Wuthnow. Princeton University Press.

Viard, Jean. 1996. *Aux sources du populisme nationaliste: l'urgence de comprendre Toulon, Orange, Marignane*. La Tour d'Aigues: Éditions l'Aube.

1997. *Pourquoi des travailleurs votent FN et comment les reconquérir*. Paris: Éditions du Seuil.

Viaut, Alain. 2004. "The Charter for Regional or Minority Languages: Sociolinguistic Particularities and the French Configuration." Working Paper 15, CIEME, Barcelona, Spain (www.ciemen.org/mercator).

Von Beyme, Klaus. 1988. "Right-Wing Extremism in Post-War Europe." *West European Politics* 11 (2): 1–18.

Wacquant, Loïc. 1995. "Pour comprendre la 'crise' des banlieues." *French Politics and Society* 13 (4): 68–81.

Wallace, William. 1999. "The Sharing of Sovereignty: The European Paradox." *Political Studies* 57: 503–521.

Warner, Carolyn M. 2000. *Confessions of an Interest Group: The Catholic Church and Political Parties in Europe*. Princeton University Press.

Warner, Carolyn M. and Manfred W. Wenner. 2006. "Religion and the Political Organization of Muslims in Europe." *Perspectives on Politics* 4 (3): 457–479.

Waters, Sarah. 1998. "New Social Movements in France: The Rise of Civic Forms of Mobilization." *West European Politics* 21: 170–186.

2003. *Social Movements in France: Towards a New Citizenship*. Basingstoke: Palgrave Macmillan.

Watkins, Susan Cott. 1991. *From Provinces into Nations*. Princeton University Press.

Weber, Eugen. 1976. *Peasants into Frenchmen*. Stanford University Press.

Weber, Max. [1922] 1978. *Economy and Society: An Outline of Interpretive Sociology*, ed. Gunther Roth and Claus Wittich. Berkeley: University of California Press.

[1927] 1981. *General Economic History*. New Brunswick, NJ: Transaction Books.

[1949] 1968. *The Methodology of the Social Sciences*. New York: Free Press.

Weil, Patrick. 1991. *La France et ses Étrangers*. Éditions Calmann-Lévy.

2001a. "The History of French Nationality: A Lesson for Europe." Pp. 52–68 in *Towards a European Nationality: Citizenship, Immigration and Nationality Law in the European Union*, ed. Randal Hansen and Patrick Weil. New York: St. Martin's Press.

2001b. "The Politics of Immigration." Pp. 211–226 in *Developments in French Politics*, vol. II, ed. Alain Guyomarch, Howard Machin, Peter A. Hall and Jack Hayward. Basingstoke: Palgrave.

2002. *Qu'est-ce qu'un Français? Histoire de la nationalité française depuis la Révolution*. Paris: Grasset.

2004a. "Lifting the Veil." *French Politics, Culture and Society* 22 (3): 142–149.

2004b. "A Nation in Diversity: France, Muslims and the Headscarf." March 25. Open Democracy www.opendemocracy.com.

2005. *La République et sa diversité: immigration, intégration, discrimination*. Paris: Seuil.

Weiler, Joseph H. 1999. "To Be a European Citizen: Eros and Civilization." Pp. 324–357 in *The Constitution of Europe: "Do the New Clothes Have an Emperor?" and Other Essays on European Integration*. Cambridge University Press.

Weiss, Linda. 1998. *The Myth of the Powerless State*. Ithaca, NY: Cornell University Press.

Who Were the Fascists: Social Roots of European Fascism? (1980). ed. Stein Ugelvik Larsen, Bernt Hagtvet and Jan Petter Myklebust. Bergen: Universitetsforlaget.

Wieviorka, Michel, ed. 1992. *La France raciste*. Paris: Seuil.

ed. 1994. *Racisme et xénophobie en Europe*. Paris: La Découverte.

ed. 2003. *Un autre monde: contestations, dérives et surprises dans l'anti-mondialisation*. Paris: Balland.

William, Jean-Claude. 1991. "Le Conseil d'État et la laïcité: propos sur l'avis du 27 novembre 1989." *Revue Française de Science Politique* 41: 28–58.

Withol de Wenden, Catherine. 2004. "Admissions Policies in Europe." Pp. 285–294 in *International Migration*, ed. Douglas S. Massey and J. Edward Taylor. Oxford University Press.

Wouters, Jan. 2000. "National Constitutions and the European Union." *Legal Issues of Economic Integration* 27 (1): 25–92.

Ysmal, Colette. 1999. "Domination des droites et crépuscule de la droite modérée." Pp. 163–182 in *Le vote incertain: les élections régionales de 1998*, ed. Pascal Perrineau and Dominique Reynié. Paris: Presses de Sciences Po.

———. 2003. "France." *European Journal of Political Research* 42: 943–956.

Zakaria, Fareed. 2003. *The Future of Freedom: Illiberal Democracy at Home and Abroad*. New York: W.W. Norton.

Zapponi, Niccolò. 1994. "Fascism in Italian Historiography, 1986–93: A Fading National Identity." *Journal of Contemporary History* 29: 547–568.

Ziblatt, Daniel. 2006. *Structuring the State: The Formation of Italy and Germany and the Puzzle of Federalism*. Princeton University Press.

Zincone, Giovanna. 2006. "The Making of Policies: Immigration and Immigrants in Italy." *Journal of Ethnic and Migration Studies* 32 (3): 347–375.

Zolberg, Aristede. 2002. "Guarding the Gates." Pp. 285–301 in *Understanding September 11*, ed. Craig Calhoun, Paul Price and Ashley Timmer. New York: The New Press.

Zweig, Stefan. 1943. *The World of Yesterday, an Autobiography*. New York: The Viking Press.

Index